Cargo Cult as Theater

Cargo Cult as Theater

Political Performance in the Pacific

Dorothy K. Billings

LEXINGTON BOOKS
Lanham • Boulder • New York • Toronto • Oxford

LEXINGTON BOOKS

Published in the United States of America
by Lexington Books
An imprint of The Rowman & Littlefield Publishing Group, Inc.
4501 Forbes Boulevard, Suite 200, Lanham, Maryland 20706

PO Box 317
Oxford
OX2 9RU, UK

Copyright © 2002 by Lexington Books
First paperback edition 2005

All rights reserved. No part of this publication may be reproduced, stored in a retrieval system, or transmitted in any form or by any means, electronic, mechanical, photocopying, recording, or otherwise, without the prior permission of the publisher.

British Library Cataloguing in Publication Information Available

Library of Congress Cataloging-in-Publication Data

Billings, Dorothy K., 1933–
   Cargo cult as theater : political performance in the Pacific / Dorothy K. Billings.
     p. cm.
   Includes bibliographical references and index.
   ISBN 0-7391-0238-9 (alk. paper) — ISBN 0-7391-1070-5 (pbk.: alk. paper)
     1. Cargo cults—Papua New Guinea—Kavieng. 2. Rites and ceremonies—Papua New Guinea—Kavieng. 3. Kavieng (Papua New Guinea)—Politics and government. 4. Kavieng (Papua New Guinea)—Social life and customs. I. Title.
GN472.75 . B56 2002
306'.09958'3—dc21   2001029684

Printed in the United States of America

♾™ The paper used in this publication meets the minimum requirements of American National Standard for Information Sciences—Permanence of Paper for Printed Library Materials, ANSI/NISO Z39.48–1992.

Contents

Preface		vii
I Introduction		
1	The Research So Far	3
2	Field Work	27
II Interviews and Documents		
3	The Johnson Cult	85
III Analysis, Interpretation, and Conclusion		
4	Analysis and Interpretation	163
5	Theories: Cults, Movements, Ceremonies, and Culture	215
6	Cargo Cult as Political Theater	237
Bibliography		245
Index		261

Preface

Many people have helped me in many ways in the preparation of this book. I wish to thank them all. Here I will mention only a few by name.

In the early days many people in the government of the Territory of Papua and New Guinea made my work possible. I wish to thank District Commissioners in Kavieng M. Healy and W. Seale as well as District Officer K. Williamson for assistance in overcoming the initial difficulties of field work. For practical assistance and information, I want to thank Mr. B. Benhem, Mr. M. Brightwell, Mr. B. Cristaldi, Mr. M. Gray, Mr. I. MacDonald, and Mr. L. Menjies of the Department of District Administration; Mr. M. Chilcat and Miss A. Leysen of the Department of Welfare; Mr. B. Campbell, Mr. R. Perry, Mrs. Perry, and Mr. R. Sheridan of Malaria Control; Mr. C. Reason of the Copra Marketing Board; and Mr. David Brown, Department of Agriculture, gave me time and information. Captain W. Busch of the government launch rescued me on more than one occasion. Miss M. Jacobs and Mr. J. Specht, also students of the Territory, gave me hospitality when I was in Rabaul. Dr. T. Schwartz very kindly allowed me to see a report he had written on New Hanover, which helped me in the beginning to see what questions I needed to try to answer. He also visited me in Lavongai village and offered interesting perspectives from his long experience in Manus and the Sepik.

I often thought of a line from a Tennessee Williams play: "I find myself dependent on the kindness of strangers." Without the help of the European expatriate residents of the Kavieng District, who regularly provided me transportation and other services, my work would have been much more difficult, expensive, and tedious. I want to thank especially Mr. and Mrs. J. Grose, Mr. J. Hancock, Mr. and Mrs. R. Herman, Mr. H. Lattimur, Mr. A. Midgeley, Mr. and Mrs. P. Parks, Mr. and Mrs. J. Stanfield, Mr. and Mrs. S. and Mr. T. Thomas, and Mr. P. Williams.

Some of the residents of the Kavieng District gave me support far beyond the call of duty and became valued friends. For offering me the benefit of their experience, the pleasure of their company, and the comforts of their hospitality, I am especially grateful to planters Mr. J. Betheras, Mr. J. Birch, Mr. S. Doll, Mr. W. Lussick, Mr. and Mrs. P. R. K. Murray, Mr. J. White, and Mr. J. Walker; teachers at Medina Ms. Margaret Evers (now Mrs. Peter Thoday) and Ms. R. Wheeler; at Utu, Mr. and Mrs. D. Stewart; and later at Manggai High School, Ms. Barbara Neasmith; Kavieng residents Mr. and Mrs. T. Francis and Mr. L. Pearson; Cooperative Societies officer Mrs. K. Fischer; and visitors to the Territory Mrs. J. Gannon and Mr. and Mrs. R. Hill.

I could not have done my work without the help of the missions. I want to thank Sr. M. Mildred, Sr. M. Clematsia, and Fr. P. Kelly at Lemakot Catholic Mission station in New Ireland. Bishop A. Stemper gave me the opportunity to work in New Hanover by allowing me the use of the facilities and transportation of the mission. The sisters at Analaua, led by Sister M. Columbine, gave me hospitality at what the priests sometimes gratefully called the "Analaua Hilton." Fr. B. Jakubco and Fr. H. Fischer of Analaua gave me help and information. Mr. and Mrs. Pitts, of the mission plantation at Metakavil, took the time to inform me and give me their views.

My friends at the Lavongai Catholic Mission station are very nearly collaborators in this work: Fr. B. Miller, Sister M. Liboria, and Sr. M. Regine, all of the order M.S.C. They gave me warm welcome and aid in every way in 1967. When I returned in 1972 and 1974, Sr. M. Gertrude and Sr. M. Veronica, along with Fr. Miller, gave me cheerful hospitality. On later return visits Fr. D. DeLuca and Br. Tony Freitas kindly helped to keep me informed and get me around, on land and sea.

The Methodist missionaries also gave me crucial help and friendship. Rev. O. Dale gave me initial permission to use mission facilities, and Miss N. Anderson, Miss V. Beckett, and Rev. A. Taylor gave me hospitality at Ranmelek in New Hanover. They allowed me to accompany them in the mission boat, the *Daula*, on their rounds which gave me the opportunity to travel around the entire island of New Hanover.

Mr. Carroll Gannon of the Public Health Department and Mr. Keith Hill of the Department of Agriculture and Fisheries gave me hospitality, encouragement, transportation, and the substantial benefit of their views and knowledge. Without their assistance, the information I have on New Hanover would be greatly diminished in quality and quantity.

Over the past thirty-five years, I have benefitted from the help and support of many friends, colleagues, students, and family members. I cannot pass on without naming some of these: Anneke S. Allen and family, Susan Allen, Ward J. Barrett, Bob and Mary Ann Beattie, D. G. L. and Carol S. Bobb, Pawel Boski and family, Ernest Bubienic, Joan M. Campbell, Yvonne Zacharias DeMonte, Deema and Dharma DeSilva, Judith Eisenberg-Dullea, Mary Jean Bates Evans, Eleanor Finlayson, Kathryn Fulton, Gary Greenberg, Patricia Grinager, Martha Welday Grutchfield, Mary McDonough Harren, Evelyn Payne Hatcher, Nancy Lawrie Hoffman, Tamara James, Susan Johnson, Erin Kenny, Esther G. Kilkelly, Gretchen Chesley Lang, Patricia C. Langridge, Jay Mandt, Richard C. Mitchell, Susan Hascall McKinney, Fr. Stephen Muth, Harry Oxley, Tom and Leslie Page and family, Peter Petzling, James S. Phillips Jr., Dana Raphael, Steven R. Roberts,

Tomasa Rosales, David Ryniker, Vyatcheslav Roudnev, Nescha Teckle, Susan Thiemann Sommer, Janet Twomey, Ben Urish, Christie Barnes Watkins, and Mashitah Yusoff.

I want to thank those who sponsored my work. My original research in 1965-67 was funded by the University of Sydney. My return in 1972 was funded by the National Institute of Mental Health, and subsequent returns were partially or totally funded by Wichita State University. I wish to thank especially Liberal Arts and Sciences Dean Paul Magelli, Graduate Dean Lloyd Benningfield, and Vice-President and Dean of Students James J. Rhatigan for their continuing support and encouragement.

For help in preparation of the manuscript at various stages along the way I want to thank Mrs. G. Ellis, Mrs. F. Majors, and Mrs. B. Johnson. Their cheerfulness in the face of ongoing impending disaster is as much appreciated as their competence. Fran Majors, who also prepared the manuscripts of several other faculty members at Wichita State University, coined the phrase "the loneliness of the long-distance researcher"; a condition which she did a great deal to alleviate through her interest in the work. Mrs. Brenda Johnson, Academic Support Programmer for the University Computing Center, brought me and my manuscript into the age of computers without ever losing her composure. Her powers over the recalcitrant machine are greatly to be admired. These are the people who work on the front lines, and nothing would get done without their skill and experience.

I had the rare privilege of having some friends and colleagues go with me to the field. In 1974, Marc Isaacson of the Graphic Design department at Wichita State University accompanied me with all his cameras to make the visual records I knew we needed. He contributed not only his photographic talents and high energy, but also his observations and company. His cooking skills were a great hit in Mangai. In 1983, Kate Golson, who had spent time with her father, Jack Golson, in the New Guinea Highlands, spent three weeks with me and gave me the insights of youth that I had overlooked. She made a return visit in 1986, and met my friend Jerry Martin, later to become Director of the Museum of Anthropology at Wichita State University, on a collecting tour which took him to Mangai. I counted myself extremely lucky to have the company of my cousin, Lt. Col. Dona Harbison Hildebrand, USAF (ret.), who had spent years in Asia in the Air Force, with me in 1994. And my friend Mary Jean Bates Evans came with me in 1998: she helped get me into anthropology when we were undergraduates at the University of Wisconsin, where C. W. M. Hart was my first teacher. Later he was my valued colleague at Wichita State University. It is great to have company, but it is also enlightening to have the insights of other visitors. We made a lot of extra work for my village friends, but they were always gracious and unstinting in their hospitality.

The first time I went to New Ireland, I went with my colleague Nicolas Peterson. He gave me every assistance, practical and professional. I learned a great deal from him and very much appreciate having had the opportunity to work with him. The only disadvantage that came from it was that the people of Mangai never quite forgave me for coming back without him.

To my teachers I owe a special debt. Prof. Ralph Piddington, Prof. Peter Lawrence and Prof. W. R. Geddes all, at various times, continued to take full responsibility for giving me the assistance I needed when, because of our various institutional affiliations, I was not officially their student. Prof. Lawrence offered me the great benefit of his experience in the Territory of Papua and New Guinea and gave me the advice I continually sought from him. Prof. Geddes brought me to the University of Sydney to teach and gave me the opportunity to complete my Ph.D. there under his supervision. It was a great privilege to work with an anthropologist who, long before others advocated it, wrote and filmed his field reports in what are now called "experimental" styles. He brought back with him to the Universities of Auckland and Sydney students from the villages of Fiji, Borneo, and Thailand so that he could prepare indigenous students to join in the work of anthropology. My good friends Mrs. Fancy Lawrence and Mrs. Ngaere Geddes continue to give me every assistance, in Sydney and in general.

My parents, the late Dr. Neal and the late Mrs. Gladys Lockard Billings, gave me financial assistance, moral support, intellectual insights, and continuing aid whenever I needed it. I very much appreciate their unfailing help. My brother, Thomas N. Billings, and his family continue to support me in many different ways. Someday I hope that my niece, Bridget Billings Bilinski, and my nephew, Bruce Billings, and their families can come together with my Papua New Guinea families, here or there or somewhere.

Finally, I thank the people about whom this book is written. Some of their names appear throughout in the text, and more of them will appear in subsequent publications. Over all the years of my research, so far, Apelis Kasino, "Kas," and his wife Milika, and her daughter, Rakasou, and her son, Makalo, welcomed me into their home. Kas was the Mangai village school teacher when Nic and I arrived in 1965, and he applied his skills to tutoring us in his language and culture. In New Hanover, the Local Government Councilor Silakau welcomed me and his family always made me feel at home: his wife, Ngurvarilam, and their children, Anton, Rosalie, Josephine, and Antonia. Silakau died in 1986, and Kas died in 1994, but their families still welcome me. So many people have helped me along the way, I cannot pretend to name them all; though I remember them with gratitude. It takes a village to raise an anthropologist, and I thank especially the people of the villages of Mangai, Livitua, Lauen, and Lavongai.

Many who peopled the Kavieng District in 1965-67 have died while I have labored to produce this tribute to them, and to the cultures they have built. I offer it, then, to their descendants in hopes that they will find it in some small way worthy of their heritage. I am very grateful for the opportunity they gave me to learn from and to share their lives.

I

Introduction

1

The Research So Far

The "Johnson cult" of New Hanover island, at the time of writing in 2001, continues in some form; so I cannot say how, or that, it ended. It began in 1964 when half the Lavongai people of New Hanover voted for President Johnson of America to represent them in their House of Assembly, a newly formed parliament which led the people of Papua New Guinea to independent nationhood in 1975. The cult has gone through various permutations over the years, creating its most substantial legacy in an economic development organization called Tutukuvul Isukal Association (T.I.A.), which may, or may not, endure.

Why would people on a remote island north of New Guinea want Lyndon B. Johnson for their leader? What, and how, did they know of him? The image of the bewildered savage was strong in the accounts of the election that reached the international press. The Lavongai vote made a great story, one which inspired curiosity but also incredulity among anthropologists. I happened to be searching for a place to do field work in New Guinea at the time, and I turned my attention to the folks who had caught the public eye. I thought that they must be interesting people, and I was not disappointed.

This book attempts to tell the story of the cult from the points of view of the many different persons whom I met and interviewed, and of the persons reported in documents from various sources that I examined. There is no doubt that it is the point of view of the "cultists," I hope, that guides this account. It was their story that I went to New Hanover to hear, and it was they who wanted their story told. However, had they had no antagonists there would have been no cult; so the perspective of "the enemy" is at least surveyed, if not plumbed in depth.

This book also attempts to make an anthropological interpretation of the cult. My analysis does not, I believe, diminish or contradict the interpretation of cultists but, rather, builds on it. Cultists and other local actors with whom I have discussed my interpretation have usually found it to be either obvious or, sometimes, clarifying; and they have been, perhaps, pleased that they have been understood. But many puzzles remain, and only time will tell in what direction the people of New Hanover choose to take their lives.

Field Research

General Description

In the Beginning
Accompanied by anthropologist Nic Peterson, I first went to the Territory of Papua and New Guinea in pursuit of the "Johnson cult" in January and February 1965. We had gotten permission from authorities in the territory to go to New Hanover, but when we arrived at the local government center in Kavieng, New Ireland, we were not allowed to proceed. Local administrators thought that our presence would be "disruptive." However, they offered us the use of their quarters (the Tikana Local Government Council house) in Mangai village, and, as we had only two months free to pursue our study, we followed the course of least resistance.[1]

The priorities of our research in New Ireland were affected by our continuing attempts to go to New Hanover, and this situation persisted when I returned to the Territory in 1966.[2] It was not until February 1967, however, that I was finally permitted to go to New Hanover. As it turned out, this unplanned sojourn was most fortuitous, as I learned much about each culture by studying the other. Contrast provided essential clarity.

Nic Peterson and I agreed after our first two months in New Ireland that we did not really have a clear impression of what the people and culture were really like. Everyone was extremely kind to us, but why? In 1966 and 1967 I felt that I had learned what to say and do, but I was not really sure why, or why the two places seemed so different in so many ways, large and small. As I sorted through my notes and cards over the months and years that followed, I became much more certain that I had finally understood what these two cultures were all about; but it was not until I returned in 1972 and found that I could carry on discussions with informants about the nature of their societies and could, at last, ad lib in these cultures that I really felt quite sure that I had found their lodestars.

Over the Years: Continuing Research
I returned to the Kavieng area during the summer breaks in 1972,[3] 1974, 1988, 1990, and 1994. I spent some of my sabbatical months there in 1983 and 1998. I have remained in correspondence with the people in the village as well as with some of those who, in 1965, had already received a formal Australian education and were working outside the village or outside Papua New Guinea. In 1999, I received my first e-mail from New Ireland: it was from Mesulam Aisoli, brother of Konda, who was among the first to help Nic and me in 1965. I also remained in contact with some of the missionaries of the area, especially with Fr. Bernard J. Miller, M.S.C. Some of the people in New Hanover regularly sent me handwritten

or typed reports or other documents. I was fortunate to meet both Powdermaker and Lewis, whose work in Lesu was closely related to mine in Mangai (Powdermaker, 1933; Lewis, 1969); and also to meet two New Ireland men who knew W. R. Groves well and mourned his death when it was announced on the radio in 1967.[4]

Over the years I have presented papers at professional meetings published some of my interpretations, and sent copies of this research to various people and institutions in the Kavieng District and in Papua New Guinea. I had difficulty getting a visa to return in 1983 (Billings, 1992b), but my problem, like that of most other anthropologists, was related to general government policies and not, with one exception, to the will of the local people. The people in the villages where I lived and worked always welcomed me and helped me. Now, I believe, we are friends. I hope I have done them no harm, and perhaps even a bit of good. They have certainly done me a lot of good. I am always trying to find a way to give back even a fraction of what they have given me. Our friendship and enhanced mutual understanding are the most important outcomes of all this for me, and perhaps for them, too.

Field Sites

While I traveled a lot both in New Ireland and New Hanover, I had a home base on each island. So many people helped me and made it all possible that I am reluctant to mention anyone by name. However, all would agree that the families of Apelis Kasino "Kas," in Mangai, and Silakau, in Lavongai, were my daily protectors and providers, and continue (after the deaths of these men) to be my valued friends.

Mangai

Mangai village is about thirty miles down the road from Kavieng. The road was crushed coral in 1965, considered one of the best in the Territory at that time. It was built by local people under orders from Franz Boluminski, administrator of the area (1910-1913) under German rule—a man remembered for riding his horse down the reef before there was a road. Paved in the late 1990s, it is now called "Boluminski Highway." Nic and I lived in the concrete building constructed for the local government council, under the care and tutelage of the local teacher, Kas, and his family: his wife, Milika, and her children, daughter Rakasou (who now, with her husband Bill Klink, has six children of her own) and son Makalo. They have continued to look after me, in the concrete brick house that Kas built, on all my return visits.[5]

Lavongai

Lavongai village is across the river from the Lavongai Catholic Mission. In 1966-67, this meant a short walk across a felled coconut tree plus a pull on a bamboo raft; or, at low tide, a wade across the sand bar. I lived in the thatch government rest house, which all villages were required to build in those days, with drinking water brought from the mission tanks, and with the help and care of Counselor Silakau and his family: his wife, Ngurvarilam, his son, Anton, and daughters Rosalie, Josephine, and Antonia. During one of my later returns, a younger son, Bernard Miller, steered the motor boat which brought me to his village.[6]

Presentation of the Data

My purpose here is to describe and interpret what came to be called the "Johnson cult," which began and continues in New Hanover; but which never spread, as many people thought it would, to neighboring New Ireland. I believe that this distribution differential is not an accident of history, but an expressive consequence of structurally different cultures.

Here I present a summary and selection of data from both New Ireland and New Hanover, in order to convey my idea of what happened and of the information on which I base my comparison of the cultures of two groups of people. I offer a translation of some of what people said, a brief description of what they did, a report of some of their written documents, and a brief analysis of what I think these all meant.

Interviews and Documents

In 2001 I have fewer misgivings than I did in 1968 about presenting a great deal of verbatim material and about relentlessly making known my own place in the collection of the data and my own process of discovering patterns. In the l960s, these practices were more forbidden than they are now, when some scholars require them.[7] I think now, as I did then, that taboos against the appropriate inclusion of the personal situation of the researcher derive from academic biases that support privacy, modesty, and anonymity as well as sometimes irresponsibility behind the false fronts of "objectivity," confidentiality, and "professionalism." The anthropologist must always be at least present, and often active, in any situation in which information is gathered; and to omit one's own role is, thus, to omit a fundamental aspect of every situation reported; and is, therefore, unscientific.

Within a scientific frame of reference, there is no intellectual justification for presenting generalizations masquerading as "abstract analyses" without also presenting the procedures, operations, and events from which, for better or for worse, these generalizations derive.[8] Humanists also must have data with which to work. It is in trying to understand what people mean, in all their various forms of expression, that anthropologists are ultimately dependent upon the interpretive approaches of the humanities. Here again, data that reproduce as closely as possible that which they represent must be demanded by any honest scholar.

Ethical considerations alone must lead us to demand the opportunity to hear the people whose culture is reported speak for themselves. The ethical implications of misinterpretation, which must in some degree be present in all science and art, have been much discussed in the latter half of the twentieth century, as colonialism has changed into neocolonialism and various other global structures. There is no way to eliminate scientific, ethical, and artistic "error" when all frames of reference, now called "paradigms," are constructed from fundamentally human and cultural perspectives. And no way to change judgment into "fact." It is awareness, however dim, of this inevitability which may help us to avoid elevating our findings to truths, and the quantification of our worst mistakes of superficiality.

People deserve to be viewed through at least some of their own words. I believe that it is better to give some details of our records rather than to hide behind abstractions that touch no one, for good or evil. The anthropologist who reports historical events, personal encounters, and translations of interviews and speeches increases his or her own ethical liability, especially with regard to invasion of privacy; but such reports also give the people about whom they are written, and their descendants, the chance to interpret to others the comedies and tragedies, beauty and ugliness, successes and failures of their individual and collective lives; and to expand, protest, reverse, or deny the account. I have decided in the end, without asking any of my informants for help or approval in most cases, what of our lives together to make public. I have decided, after much thought, to take this particular kind of ethical risk not just out of respect for art and science, which are best served by truth, but out of the deepest respect for the people about whom I write, their lives and their cultures. They are important people, and others have much to learn from them.

I offer this justification for the presentation of unusually large amounts of raw data. My original manuscript is five times longer than this one, and much more sorted data sits waiting for its place in another vehicle. In this abbreviated account of the "Johnson cult," I have tried to sacrifice neither precision nor significance.

Comparative Method

When I arrived in Lavongai village on 10 February 1967 to set up my new household, I learned within a few hours that many of the responses and routines I had learned during the preceding year in New Ireland were wrong. I was surprised, because the peoples of New Ireland and of New Hanover live on adjacent islands, mix in the port town (Kavieng), marry each other, and consider that they share the same general culture. Gradually, I realized that they did not have much opportunity to see each other in groups and did not know in what ways they were like or different from each other.

First impressions often yield primary insights, and first impressions are gained during the early days of field work, when most interactions concern the problems of the anthropologist's daily living conditions: food, shelter, water, hygiene, working equipment, communication, transportation. Thus, it was in relation to me and my attempts to settle into residence and achieve a daily living routine that I first noticed the differences between New Hanoverians and New Irelanders; and it was in trying to cope with the different situations, both at the level of maintaining my own water supply and at the level of obtaining esoteric information, that I felt that I finally came to some kind of understanding of the two cultures.

From my first day in New Hanover, life was easier for me in many ways, both personally and professionally. New Hanoverians recognized my wish for intervals of privacy because (I found out) they shared it. In New Ireland, people wanted to be sure that I always felt included, and they did not think people liked to be left alone. I found this very difficult at first, although I also valued their help and concern. I was trusted and accepted, and I returned gratefully to Mangai to be taken care of when I got the mumps in March 1967. By the end of my field work, I felt deeply obligated to many people in New Ireland, personally involved and committed to them as friends. When I return now to stay with them, with my most intensive work behind me, I no longer feel that I have to be on "company manners" all the time; and I am very pleased to live in the house with all the rest of the family.

New Hanoverians left me alone in many ways. With the exception of one family, no one ever gave me anything to eat in Lavongai in 1967; and I did not find it possible to eat regularly with the people as I had in New Ireland, even though I brought tinned food (as I had in New Ireland) to contribute to the meals when I was invited. Getting the help I needed in carrying water and supplies was a constant struggle. Some people thought that Lavongais were more able to share food in earlier days, but there was enough evidence to convince me that they were very different from New Irelanders in their food sharing customs.

However, the help I wanted most, of course, was help with my research, and in New Hanover that poured forth. I filled up tape after tape with interviews and conversations, whereas in New Ireland I only used my tape recorder for ceremonies. New Hanover lacked the elaborate plastic arts for which New Ireland is famous, and which called for many more photographs than I took in New Hanover; but they were never at a loss for words, which called for many more audiotapes than I used in New Ireland. They wanted me to tell their story to America and the world, and I said that I would try to do so, including all their wit and wisdom. I enjoyed their company, and they mine; and when I left we were sad, but we owed each other a less permanent personal relationship than I had in New Ireland.[9]

The successive periods of research in New Ireland and New Hanover enabled me to understand the cultures of each far more fully than I could have understood either had I spent my entire time in one place or the other. There are two major reasons for this:

1) I was able to subtract myself as the white observer in both places by contrasting my roles in them. I had thought that New Irelanders were restrained and

careful in my presence perhaps because I was a European and that they had learned to be careful with the people they called "master." However, after my experience in New Hanover, where I was treated without any special deference, I was able to go back to New Ireland and to see that the reserve in people's behavior characterized their relationships with each other, as well as with me.

2) The behavior of each people stood out for me when it contrasted with that of the other. For instance, I had written in my notes that New Ireland babies did not seem to cry very much, but I was not sure about this because I did not know how much babies cry. I found out in New Hanover how much more babies can cry, in any case, when I observed their perpetual howling.

Finding this comparative measure helped me to see that any standard I used, whether from my own culture or from the conclusion of some systematic anthropological study, was ultimately comparative. I could then see that I had been using my own culture as a standard in some cases, and other cultures studied by other anthropologists as standards in other cases, and that no amount of quantification, which I felt obligated but unable to achieve, could sort out the significant categories I needed to make a systematic description and analysis.

What I wanted to know was not easily categorized: I wanted to know what was valued, what made life worth living, what the people were really like. To know what they were really like, it helped me to see what they were not like. For instance, I had paid insufficient attention to New Ireland food sharing customs, assuming that all Pacific islanders share food with visitors, until I went to New Hanover and observed the absence of this pattern. I gradually began to accept the use of each culture as a whole, patterned standard against which to describe the other, each culture providing within itself a model that was not (not yet, anyway) rendered lifeless by the manipulations of some simplistic anthropological theory. The comparative method is, as I had forgotten at the time, the classical method of anthropology.

The Setting

Description: The Kavieng District, 1965-67

Kavieng is the port of entry and administrative headquarters for the Kavieng District, which includes New Hanover, northern New Ireland, and several other smaller islands. In 1965-68, it contained a few administration buildings along the waterfront; hospital facilities (separate for "Natives" and "Europeans"); two European stores of one large room each (Burns Philp and the New Guinea Company, formerly Carpenter's); about fifteen Chinese shops; and perhaps fifty European houses. An air strip which accommodated DC-3s nearly every day in 1965 was extended to receive Fokker Friendships less frequently in 1966. These same planes continued to provide service to Kavieng in 1998.[10]

The town population of some 600 was partly indigenous but included about 150 others: mostly Australians, but also Dutch, Germans, French Algerian, English, Malaysian, and American. Half again as many Chinese, as well as a few of mixed parentage, owned and managed shops. Visitors, who were and are largely business or government workers, were lodged at a small (eight rooms) hotel (bath and toilet at the end of the hall) or at the private, exclusively European Kavieng Club (four old, scarcely divided rooms, and some new rooms with private bath away from the main building).[11] In the 1970s and 80s, the Kavieng Hotel added a block with two dozen air-conditioned rooms, and the Malanggan Lodge began to serve, or hope for, tourists. In the 1990s, the town and its amenities appeared in a well-researched travel guide,[12] but even by 1998 it remained undiscovered by tourists in any substantial number.

Two primary schools (one under the auspices of the Roman Catholic mission) which conformed to a syllabus based on that of Australia, but altered to include local history and conditions, were and are located in the town. There was also an Australian-curriculum primary school, chiefly designed for expatriate usage but also attended by a number of students of indigenous and mixed parentage. There were and are five high schools throughout the district under government and mission supervision.

Mission headquarters in Kavieng still includes the large Roman Catholic Mission complex, comprising a church, offices, and convent; the Methodist Overseas Mission (now the United Church) church and residence; and a Seventh-Day Adventist church. The Catholic mission still maintains merchandise, engineering, educational, and medical departments in addition to its religious services.

Kavieng has a small, modern courthouse, new in 1965, containing three rows of benches for the public, for use by magistrates of the district court. It is also used by judges when the supreme court reaches, as it does only infrequently, Kavieng on circuit.

The town has a deep-water wharf for ships, drawing up to thirty-six feet in a good all-weather harbor protected by small islands. In 1967, approximately 12,000 tons of copra, the chief export, were shipped through Kavieng each year, with an additional 13,000 tons exported from New Ireland through the nearby large port of Rabaul in neighboring New Britain. Goods arrived in Kavieng on a large Burns Philp ship approximately every six weeks or on one of the ships owned by two Chinese trading firms serving this area. The European population was usually acutely aware that a ship was due as shortages of routine foods and other items developed and the store shelves became empty.

The area was governed in 1965-67 by the Department of District Administration (D.D.A.), which was headed by the district commissioner (D.C.), who supervised men of varying ranks. Patrol officers of this department were, in the past, the adventurers and explorers who changed the map of New Guinea from "uncontrolled" into "controlled" areas.[13] Their duties in 1965-67 consisted largely of administrative and police activities. Other departments of government were

Public Health, Law, Lands, Surveys and Mines, Agriculture, Stock and Fisheries, Forests, Customs and Immigration, Posts and Telegraphs, Welfare, and Business Development. In addition, the following Government Instrumentalities operated on a semi-commercial basis: Copra Marketing Board, Plant and Transport Authority, and the National Broadcasting Service. Most of these departments of government continued to operate in 1998 with local personnel.

History

Prehistory

As a result of extensive work on the Lapita Homeland Project, archaeologists in the Bismarck Archipelago have shown settlement in the area over 30,000 years ago, before the earliest date yet documented in the Papua New Guinea mainland (Allen, 1984; Allen et al, 1984; Allen and White, 1989; Kirch, 1997; Spriggs, 1989; White et al, 1978; White et al, 1988; White and Harris, 1997). The earliest date, 33,300 plus or minus 550 years B.P., is still (in 1998: J. Peter White, personal communication) attributed to Matenkupkum, a site in southern New Ireland (Gosden and Robertson, 1991; Allen et al, 1989). Panakiwuk, a cave inland from Mangai village where the people from Mangai and nearby villages lived and took refuge during the bombing raids of World War II, has been dated back 15,000 years to its earliest occupation.[14]

This team effort in the prehistory of the area (Bellwood, 1979; Terrell 1986; White et al, 1982), which began with an attempt to follow the distribution of Lapita pottery (Golson 1971; Green, 1979), has shown long-established trading systems, and has permitted the development of contrasting theoretical interpretations: one group of scholars sees the 3,000-year-old Lapita complex in the Pacific as a Melanesian construct, while others see it as an earlier development in Asia and the mark of a major population move (Swaddling, 1998).

While work on the archaeology of New Hanover has just begun,[15] the island is visible from the small islands between New Ireland and New Hanover; and there is evidence from preliminary archaeological investigations as well as other sources that it was not isolated from the long history now well-documented for its neighbors.[16]

History of Contact

As "cargo cults" are often explained partly as a response to European contact, it is important to begin with a review of European history in the area. Although Europeans sighted New Ireland from time to time during and after the seventeenth century, it was not until 1865 that Lt. Phillip Carteret R.N., commanding HMS Sloop *Swallow*, landed at English Cove on the south coast and established that it was a separate island.

Both German and English trading posts were set up in New Ireland in the 1870s. In 1884, the Imperial German government annexed and named the island

Neu Mecklenburg, just ten days after the proclamation of the British Protectorate over the south coast of New Guinea. Under the German administrator, Boluminski (1910-13), 210 miles of road were built, primarily down the east coast of New Ireland. His name and activities are well-remembered by the people, especially those of New Ireland, but also in New Hanover. George Brown established the first Methodist mission just south of New Ireland in the Duke of Yorks in 1875; and Vunapope, the Catholic mission headquarters in New Britain near Rabaul, was founded in 1852 (O'Neill 1961, 16).

But there were in 1965-67, among the living in New Ireland and New Hanover, those who remember "when the missions had not come yet." The Lemakot Catholic Mission station near Mangai village was established in the early 1900s, and rebuilt after it was completely destroyed during World War II (O'Neill 1961, 15), while the Lavongai Catholic Mission station near Lavongai village in New Hanover was not established until the 1920s. The Catholic Mission of the Sacred Heart entered the district in 1901 and was well-established in central and north Neu Mecklenburg (New Ireland), as was the Methodist Missionary Society over the whole district, when the Australians occupied Kavieng on 17 October 1914. An Australian military administration remained in control until 1921, when a civil administration took over under a "C" class mandate from the League of Nations.

The German administration everywhere is known for the economic development it sponsored. It began the first government coconut plantation on the island of Nusa, between New Ireland and New Hanover, in 1900. The Australians continued this development; in 1940 there were 164 plantations in the New Ireland District which produced 20,625 tons of copra.

Many men who were old in Mangai in 1965 had worked in the gold fields in New Guinea when they were young, in the 1920s and '30s, usually for three-year terms. Few had worked on plantations elsewhere; nor did they work on New Ireland plantations managed by Europeans, preferring to develop their own. Some middle-aged men had been away to school or in the army, or at least to the west coast of New Ireland to work on the road.

A few old men in New Hanover had been away to work when they were young, but many middle-aged men had been away from New Hanover only for brief visits, and some had never worked for wages on a plantation, as a boat's crew, or in any other regular job. Most who had worked for wages had done so only briefly and infrequently, or, if for longer periods, only on local plantations. One reason New Hanover men did not go away to work is that for a while, in the 1930s, there was restricted movement to and from the island because of the reported prevalence of leprosy. According to native informants, the doctors tried to prevent people from leaving New Hanover and tried to return men from there back to their homes. Whatever else this "quarantine" meant, it surely kept European recruiters from looking for labor in New Hanover. In the late 1960s, the leper hospital at Analaua island, just east of New Hanover, was closing down, as new medical knowledge reduced the fear of contagion, and new medicines allowed most patients to be sent home to recover. The reputation for leprosy in the 1930s has no doubt had a significant influence on the history of contact here, but it does not fully account for the inexperience of the people with the outside world.

World War II

Everyone in the area around Kavieng at the time will always remember the early morning hours of 21 January 1942, when the Japanese bombed Kavieng and, two days later, landed 5,000 troops in forty ships. Australian women and children had been evacuated, but many men remained and were taken prisoner. Some were shot in New Ireland and New Britain. Others died in June 1942, when the *Montevideo Maru*, carrying 900 prisoners of war to Japan, was torpedoed by an American submarine near the Philippines. A few made narrow escapes.[17]

During the war, the people of Mangai and other coastal villages in New Ireland went into the bush to live. They remember it as a hard time, especially so because they developed tropical ulcers, which they could not easily cure without European medicines and from which some of them died. They made friends with some of the Japanese and even married them. One Japanese man in particular was remembered fondly in Mangai, a man who had lived with them and brought them medicines for their sores. One of the characteristics people often mentioned when they told me about their days with the Japanese was that they did not have Sundays: they worked every day.

The Japanese never landed in New Hanover, perhaps, as is widely believed, because Sister Clematsia marched her leprosy patients down to the beach at Analaua to wave their poor sick limbs at a ship as it approached, which then turned and sped away. But people saw ships out at sea, and sometimes there were shots about which people later made up songs. Evidence that they did not also make up the shots presented itself in the bullet holes that marked the old German-built church and convent at the Lavongai mission.

Some men told me stories of trying to help their former European masters and friends who were incarcerated in Kavieng, but everyone had to appear to follow Japanese orders. Those who did not, it was said, had their throats cut or were hanged.

After the Japanese surrendered in August 1945, Australia again assumed authority for the Kavieng District, which then became part of the Trust Territory of Papua and New Guinea under the United Nations. Large grants were made to the colony by Australia to help overcome the destruction of the war and to develop resources and services. Redevelopment progressed rapidly in the 1950s. Aided by government grants, veterans came back to the plantations to restore and increase production of copra to the 25,000 tons exported in 1965-67, nearly 20 percent of Papua and New Guinea's total output. By 1970, there was a total population of 51,000 in the New Ireland District, 900 of whom were not indigenous: half were European and half Chinese or mixed race. A large majority of this total, 41,000, lived in New Ireland, while the second largest group, 7,000, lived in New Hanover.

Urged or pressured by the United Nations, Australia began to prepare the

Territory of Papua and New Guinea for self-government and independence. Progressively greater representation was allowed to indigenous persons until, in 1962, they constituted an unofficial majority in the legislative council.[18] The vote for Johnson of America in New Hanover in 1964 was part of the process of moving toward self-government, which was granted in 1973, and full independence, achieved in 1975.

Background: New Ireland and New Hanover

Related Anthropological Work

When I lived in these two islands, I did not know what styles I would find, or even consider the concept of "style." Though there was a great deal of research on New Ireland, and a substantial literature on cargo cults and millenarian movements, there was little on New Hanover. And "style" was not a recognized concept of contemporary anthropological research.[19]

There was already substantial anthropological literature on New Ireland, and on the central organizing importance of *malanggan* ceremony and art (Kramer, 1925; Chinnery, 1929; Groves, 1933, 1935, 1936; Powdermaker, 1933, 1961; Lewis, 1961). Chinnery thought it was "doomed to certain and early extinction" (1933: 251), but in 1965 we found it still flourishing as the final ceremony for the dead. (Billings and Peterson, 1967). It continued on in the 1990s.

I rather expected New Hanover to be like New Ireland, as most people in New Ireland did, and in some ways they were similar. In some ways, they were not. Over the years of my research, they came more into contact with each other, and we all became more aware of the differences, as well as of the similarities. I felt sure from early on in my field research, however, that if New Hanover did not have *malanggan*, there could be substantial structural differences in these cultures.[20] This turned out to be the case. Some of the people on both islands shared my anthropological interests while some did not, beyond their great willingness to help me.

Similarities and Differences of Culture and Structure

Structures of Cultures: Tikana and Lavongai

In order to facilitate a comparison of these two cultures, I will refer to the culture and people of New Hanover as Lavongai, a term which they use for themselves; and to the culture and people of northern New Ireland as Tikana. The people of northern New Ireland used this term not to designate themselves as a cultural group, as I am using it, but to name their local government council.

Fundamental similarities characterize environments, basic subsistence patterns, village size and subdivision, achieved rather than ascribed political status, and general patterns of colonial history. Compared to, for example, the peoples of the Amazon, the populations of both islands are settled. Compared to, for example, the Polynesians, both groups have simple material cultures and lack political stratification. Compared to, for example, Balinese and Javanese, both groups have relatively uncomplicated social relationships, undirected by specific etiquettes or requirements related to social status or group membership. Compared to practically anywhere else outside Melanesia in the world of slash and burn agriculture, e.g., the African Congo, political organization is minimal on both islands.

Despite these similarities, Tikana and Lavongai are guided by quite different cultures. There are fundamental differences in social structure and organization, preferred and practiced residence patterns, the importance and extent of reciprocal and ceremonial exchange, and the role of the Melanesian Big Man in the two societies. I believe these structural differences generate the respective styles of these two cultures.

In order to see the whole foundation for the differences I found in the Tikana and Lavongai styles of cultures, it is necessary to start with some basic facts about the history, languages, and structures of the two societies. The differences in the structure of corporate groups underlies, I argue, all other structural and stylistic differences between the two cultures. I will use the "ethnographic present" in the following description, which also describes the situation generally today. There have been no major structural changes. Where something has changed in any relevant way, I will note the change over time.

Language and Political Divisions

In all villages, people understand some words, at least, of several languages, and in 1966, most people (men, women, and children) spoke pidgin English, or Neo-Melanesian. This lingua franca is used throughout northern Papua New Guinea, not only between native peoples and Europeans, but among local peoples themselves who share no other common language.[21]

Tikana: The people of northern New Ireland, here called Tikana, speak several different languages.[22] The three most northern of these from the east coast across to the west are Tigak, Kara, and Nalik. These form a colonial subgroup in that they are administratively part of the Kavieng District, while their fellows further south are administratively part of the Namatanai District. The first syllables of the names of these three languages were used to give the name to the Tikana Local Government Council, begun in this area in 1957. Some important indigenous cultural characteristics, however, also distinguish these three groups from those further south; and I am using this name, as the local people do not, to designate an ethnic group in northern New Ireland. People of the three language groups regularly interact in marriage and *malanggan*.

The use by the administration of language groupings as a base from which to determine political divisions has perhaps led to some false identifications of language type where there has been population movement. The people of Mangai village, where I have lived and worked, say that they speak Kara, and they are in the Kara government subdivision. However, they also say that their language is "mixed." The reclassification by Lithgow and Claassen in 1968 puts Mangai in the Tigak language area, a view which fits the terms used for major kin categories.[23]

Lavongai: The Tigak and Tsoi Islands divide New Hanover and New Ireland. The culture of the Tigak islands is in some ways more like that of New Ireland than like that of New Hanover, although the absence of *malanggan* in these islands is important. The islands share the Tigak language with northern New Ireland. The Tsoi islands, like New Hanover, speak Tungak.[24] New Hanover is also called "Lavongai," a term which I will use, as local people do, for themselves, and to name both the entire island of New Hanover and also to name a large coastal village, where I lived. The name is also used to refer to the Lavongai Catholic Mission adjacent to the village.[25]

Subsistence

The people of New Ireland and of New Hanover share many characteristics with other Melanesians. They practice shifting agriculture and subsist mainly on root crops, sago, fish, chickens, and pigs. Some in both places work for wages or produce cash crops and add rice and tinned foods to their diet.

The organization of work contrasted in 1967 in that Lavongais tended to work alone or in nuclear families, while Tikana worked in larger groups of extended family and others.

Settlement Pattern

In both islands, people live primarily in coastal villages of 100-300, mainly in response to the orders of earlier colonial governments which wanted easy access. There are still a few villages "in the bush" in New Hanover. Villages in both islands are subdivided into hamlets wherein reside groups of kin and affines.

In both places, people identify with a hamlet. However, for Tikana ownership was clearly an attribute of those who lived there with their kin of other places; whereas Lavongai were often living in their fathers' hamlets, which they did not clearly own.

Social Organization

In both northern New Ireland and New Hanover, there are about a dozen exogamous matrilineal clans, each dispersed among several or many villages. Though they function very differently, in both places they are of fundamental importance in ascribing kinship status.

Tikana: The people of the Tigak, Kara, and Nalik language groups all have several, and the same, exogamous matrilineal clans. Clan names vary somewhat throughout northern New Ireland (east and west coast) and in different language and dialect areas, but the associated birds remain constant and confirm the unity of the clan. In villages further south, including Lesu, there are matrilineal moieties, which structure the organization of marriage and exchange.[26] While there is intermarriage and exchange between the north and the south, ad hoc rules have to be negotiated in these situations.

Matrilocal extended families form the Tikana corporate unit of ownership, production, and consumption. Usually referred to metaphorically by the name of the hamlet where they live, these matrilocal extended families generally function together with lineages or subclans of their own and of other clans in the exchanges of pigs, food, and currency which mark marriages and *malanggan*. Sometimes they also own a hamlet together with a matrilocal family of another clan. The history of these joint ownerships, which include ground in the bush for gardens and sago, is not fully known: it is merely said that people married and moved around. Women inherit their mother's land, which their brothers may use but cannot pass on to their children.

Lavongai: The people of New Hanover belong to twelve matrilineal clans distributed, as in New Ireland, unevenly around the island. The rules of land ownership are similar to those of New Ireland: a person owns only his mother's land. He may use his father's land if he gives a pig or a *mias* (red shell bead currency) on the death of his father, but he cannot, in theory, pass the land on to his children.

This law may have functioned more strictly in the past. In 1967, many people did not use their mother's land, and some had never visited it. This resulted from the strong New Hanover preference for viripatrilocal residence. All informants said that it was correct, both in 1967 and traditionally, to live on the husband's father's land; and many were so residing. The unit of residence, production, and consumption in New Hanover is the nuclear family. The combination of virilocal residence with matrilineal clans means that coresident children are likely to be of different clans, using land that belongs to their father's clan, not their own. Children of mothers from some distance away may not have visited their mother's, and, thus, their own, land.

The only group into which an individual may claim land, other than as an immediate descendant of a user, is the local clan cluster; a weakly recognized collection of the people in a single village who belong to the same clan. A person coming from another village could use some of the unused tracts within large areas said to be owned by his or his father's clansmen. A comparatively low sense of ownership seemed to derive from the absence of a strong continuing ownership group in New Hanover which jointly defended, as they did in New Ireland, the claims of individuals. In New Hanover, an individual instead tried to defend his own ownership claims in the name of his clan.

Economic Organization

Most Melanesians have some form of economic exchange built on reciprocal relationships and the exchange of pigs, shell valuables, and other goods.

In both Tikana and Lavongai societies, exchange involved the use of a standardized currency made of red shell, and in both societies its continued use with regard to marriage and death observances when it has given way to, or been supplemented by, first Australian and then Papua New Guinea currencies in some other situations, gives evidence that it has a ceremonial as well as an economic status

Tikana: New Irelanders had and have exchange occasions which structured and reinforced long term relationships in abundance. Tikana marriages are accomplished by generally equal exchanges between the families of the bride and groom. Similarly, *malanggan* exchanges create opportunities to equalize past offerings through delayed reciprocity.

Lavongai: Exchanges in New Hanover were largely impersonal, meant to acquire land or goods or a spouse, not an ongoing relationship. Marriage is accomplished in New Hanover by a one-way payment between two individuals: from the groom to some man of the bride's family, her father if he is alive and if she is living in his house.

Ceremonial Occasions

Tikana: Tikana had substantial ceremony and exchange of more or less equal wealth between families at the time of marriage, and ongoing exchanges throughout the marriage and beyond the death of one of the spouses; most notably as part of the famous ceremonial occasions called *malanggan*, in which the dead are remembered; and then, as they say, "finished." *Malanggan* ceremonies for the dead structure economic, political, and social relationships. *Malanggan* gatherings have been described and viewed as fundamental to the structure of New Ireland society by Kramer (1925), Groves (1933, 1935), Chinnery (1929), Powdermaker (1933), and Lewis (1969), among others. They are typical Melanesian gatherings in that they feature singing, dancing, and exchanges of pigs and shell currency: to these Tikana add the famous New Ireland *malanggan* carvings. *Malanggan* is a powerful institution that has not broken under outside pressures. It disappeared, along with Sundays as a day of rest, during the Japanese occupation of New Ireland; but after World War II *malanggan* (and Sundays) reappeared and, by 1965, again flourished.[27]

Lavongai: New Hanover used to have the institution of *maras*, known in at least two or three (but no more) villages. Big Men secluded young boys, in order to "make boys into men," and to make men and boys into warriors in the old days. There was no precise clan or village structuring to these secluded events, but there was strict sex structuring: women brought food to the secluded spot and left it for initiated men to collect and carry inside the enclosure. Some men now grumble that this institution fell to the criticism of the mission, but it was not widespread, and it could not have been strong.

Lavongai ate together at funerals, but had no further occasions for the dead. In 1967, communal feasts were prepared in New Hanover for mission and government events, but not in any traditional context. Within the memory of some old men, boys had been secluded for initiation into manhood, an institution called *maras*; and food was given by their families for the boys and the older men in whose charge they were. One young Lavongai who had lived in Mangai during a *malanggan* ceremony told me, "We are like you. When they're dead, they're dead."

Political Organization

In neither society is there any centralized authority, or any traditional authority at all other than that granted to Big Men, whose status was and is achieved in particular situations: clearly and widely in New Ireland, rarely and vaguely in New Hanover. In neither society was there any institutionalized leadership of the people in relationship to supernatural forces before the missions came.

Tikana: *Memai*, or "speakers," are Big Men, installed formally in that status, who organize *malanggan*. They have no bounded constituency, either of kin or locality; but their influence is defined mainly in local terms. Women sometimes lead *malanggan,* although only men are speakers (*memai*) for them.

Lavongai: In New Hanover, the men who organized an initiation of young men became Big Men and acquired the status *vaitas*: only three men in New Hanover in 1967 had earned that status, and they did not function in any leadership roles. Unlike Tikana *memai*, they had no special respect, but they were said to have "bossed" *maras*; and they had apparently some special powers which some people feared.

Religion

Tikana: Ceremony was pursued for its power to organize the living, not the dead in New Ireland. Despite some scholarly assumptions and assertions to the contrary, *malanggan* art represents not spirits but family and exchange history.[28] Until recently, evangelical attempts to "fire up" Christian confession met with polite but undogmatic, low key acquiescence. Church, like everything else in Tikana life, was an institution which organized group participation, not individual testimony.

Lavongai: Lavongai used "magic" to secure love and good luck, and to help in overcoming enemies from their traditional culture. Nowadays they seem to believe in a general way that there must be something, perhaps the white man's god, beyond what they see; but they were not given to passionate displays of religious faith, nor were they interested in the divisions between white groups about their Christian beliefs.

Styles of Culture: New Ireland and New Hanover

I have interpreted the cultures of New Ireland and New Hanover as contrasting in their fundamental structures, functions, and *styles*. The style of New Ireland culture is group-oriented, institutionalized, and egalitarian; while the style of New Hanover culture is individualistic, noninstitutionalized, and peck-ordered. These designations are relative, and were developed relative to each other. However, since I made my original interpretation (Billings, 1972), much work has been done theoretically and empirically in contrasting these two styles, as "Individualistic/ Collectivistic;" and my analysis fits well with what has been done by many others now, mostly in cross-cultural psychology.[29]

My subsequent research, including my nine periods of field research and the benefit of subsequent theoretical and empirical research by others, has, in my view, amply supported my early interpretations. I have defended this theoretical research in earlier publications, and I review it here only briefly.[30] It is the difference in *cultural style* which, I argue, allowed the Johnson cult to develop in New Hanover, but not in New Ireland. What follows is a brief summary of the general patterns, of structure and of style, of these two cultures, presented in terms which I first used for them in 1972.

Style of Tikana Culture: Group-Oriented, Institutionalized, Egalitarian

The matrilocal extended family is not just a "corporate group" in a social, economic, and political sense; it is central to Tikana identity. It is created and supported by adherence to explicit, institutionalized rules and alternatives which bring people together with land which they all feel is clearly theirs and to which they attach their labors and their sentiments without fear of dispossession. The hamlet where the family resides is not just a "resource": it is where they live, where they gain their identity; it is, always, Home. It is to these hamlets that women bring their husbands and where they bear their children; and, wherever they may lead their lives, it is to the cemeteries of these hamlets that people return when they die.

The matrilocal extended family is the rock on which New Ireland's group-oriented cultural style is built. In this basic family, children learn to trust, work with, give to, and enjoy other people in groups. Over time, even from day to day, the faces in the group change; but some people in it will grow old together where they were young together, welcoming new members who keep the group strong, grieving together over their lost dead, knowing they will finally bury each other.

New Ireland culture "follows the known path." Cultural patterns are formalized, institutionalized, ritualized; and individuals follow easy, known precepts (give, help) that maintain and expand the group by including outsiders without losing insiders. There is a place for everyone, and everyone is helped to take his or her place.

Extended families are open on every occasion to join up with another person or another group: for a day's sago processing project, a garden that will last several months, a house that will last several years, or a marriage that will last past the death of the spouses.

The style of integration between individuals within groups and between groups is egalitarian. The weak are made strong, and the strong have their strengths used up laterally rather than vertically, so that they do not rise above the group. They are its servants, not its masters, and so gain their authority.

Affinal bonds are of fundamental importance and are created and recreated, as are wider bonds, through egalitarian exchanges of wealth: pigs and shell currency. No individual is allowed to become too strong, just as none (children, the sick, the old, the visitor) are allowed to become too weak. Children, who all begin as outsiders everywhere, are honored and brought into the culture: they go first in everything, and they rarely cry. Individuals are group-oriented, and seek not to get ahead of others but to contribute to keeping the group together.

Disputes are not allowed to split the group, which nurtures public healing where division threatens. People worry not about receiving in exchanges, but about giving enough: help and food and being together, the giving of oneself, of one's presence, to an undertaking. Togetherness is the stuff of life for Tikana, who have made a success of it. The direction of interactions is ever outward and inclusive: when you want to give, you must "go outside," and you must "lose, lose, lose."

Emotional relationships between kin are channeled by institutionalized structure in explicit detail, in terms of taboos on overt acts (e.g., talking, touching, verbalizing personal names) and clear obligations (e.g., contributions of pigs, shell currency, and food on specific occasions). Strong, spontaneous emotional responses are not often seen, but neither is there evidence of strong emotional suppression or tension. People are told that they must tell out their views, and everyone listens to someone who is angry or upset. New Ireland culture provides formal institutionalized occasions for the expression of some emotions: wailing, to help the bereaved cry at funerals, and *malanggan*, to help them finally terminate their grief, years later; and to finish their obligations of the dead.

Physical and personal responsiveness is manifest in daily doings, conversations, and activities. The responsive style of body movement, or kinesic style,[31] typical of Tikana may be described as careful, controlled, slow, detailed, and responsive. These terms also describe the production and form of the famous *malanggan* carvings of New Ireland, as well as of their less famous decorations, and the style of their singing and dancing.

At the individual level, social and emotional interactions are structured by explicit cultural institutions; at the population level, the distribution of subsistence resources is structured by explicit cultural institutions. The institutionalized modes and media of interaction in this culture create and reinforce tendencies toward egalitarian integration of groups, wherein each individual securely belongs. The whole pattern is expressed in the arts, and in a thousand ways in daily life: explicitly and inexplicitly, it is communicated to succeeding generations and to other outsiders. Frequently repeated patterns—restraint, reserve, detail; interest in process and repetitive process rather than in goals, interest in giving and receiving, in helping and being together; incurious about the whole, unquestioning about the rituals—these are the redundancies in New Ireland that describe the *style* of the culture.

Style of Lavongai Culture: Individualistic, Noninstitutionalized, Peck-ordered

Many Lavongai do not have a place which they unambiguously call "home." Each generally uses land which he claims individually, but his land is often said to belong to his father or the clan of his predecessor there, usually his own or his father's; and sometimes other persons of these same clan have claims there too. But so do persons of other clans. Land use is basically individualistic, in that each individual generally claims a plot and hangs onto it, and the claim that land belongs to a particular clan does not reflect any strong political or social reality.

Since marriage is essentially an impersonal financial transaction, whoever received payment for a woman must refund the shell currency (*mias*) if she leaves her husband. Her next husband need pay only five *mias,* half price. Divorce is much more common than among the Tikana, where it is rare. No strong groups are involved in Lavongai marriages to work against their dissolution. Cross-cousin marriage was said to have been a preferred Lavongai marriage in the past, but these did not create strong groups. Men sometimes preferred to marry a cross-cousin, it was said, because he could trust her not to poison his water, since she was "one of the family."

Exchanges of goods, services, and monies were and are carried out in New Hanover between individuals, not organized by any group efforts. There was and is trade with some of the smaller islands, carried out impersonally for money, formerly with *mias*, today usually with the national currency. There were some gatherings where people ate communally, and where people ate food prepared by others, but no lasting ties came from such events. Similarly, male seclusion, *maras*, which brought some men together simultaneously excluded other men: a few men were made Big Men, *vaitas*, but *maras* created no reciprocal obligations and no enduring alliances.

New Hanover culture offers its individuals little in the way of formal institutions and requires little in return in the way of rituals or maintenance activities from its carriers. In the absence of known paths, each person may, or must, find his own. "We are like little streams coming off from a river," one man told me, "each one goes off in a different direction."

The style of integration among individuals in New Hanover is peck-ordered. There is some admiration for the man who does well for himself at the expense of others, even among those who paid a small part of the cost. Behavior, while not institutionalized, is stylized and conventionalized, of course; but in the absence of explicit structuring, New Hanoverians view themselves as self-made men, each possibly quite different from the others. As people work out their relationships, striving to gain or keep the upper hand, the weak (the physically handicapped, the visitor, the children) get weaker, and the strong are hard to find. Bullies rise and soon fall, having nothing with which to reach out beyond their personal sphere.

Interactions involving exchange of goods and services are atomizing rather than unifying and preclude any sort of group formation into which some are included and from which some are excluded.

The culture would not have survived if dependent children had not been fed, and they are fed and seem quite healthy. Children are fed, when father is full and finished, or perhaps after mother scolds them, and with admonitions, in any case. Food and other things do get distributed, in New Hanover as in New Ireland; but in New Hanover food is used to reject, rather than, as in New Ireland, to accept. Food must often be taken, as it is not easily given.

New Hanover tends to make each individual an outsider, after the age of two or three years. Children have a brief moment upon the stage until they are weaned. Then they are likely to be last in everything, last in the peck order, crying. A lonely little Lavongai displaced by a younger sibling is, e.g., killing a pet bird, while his New Ireland counterpart is swinging in a sling on his grandmother's back. Individuals in this culture need less to respond (as Tikana do) than to charm or plead. They want attention from their fellows, but it is the Self, not Togetherness, that is the stuff of life to them. They are at their best when they are sitting around together, laughing, talking, making fun of themselves and others, reenacting small scenes of triumph or despair, eloquently analyzing and interpreting the meaning of life (Stamm, 1958). Physically, they are assertive, playful, and somewhat destructive, in relation to people and things. Assertiveness, sometimes clumsiness, and a loose-limbed expressiveness characterizes the New Hanover kinesic style.

Disputing is a significant mode of integration in New Hanover, and a frequent one within the nuclear family. Strong, spontaneous emotional outbursts occur. Loud laughter, loud crying, or perhaps loud scolding may be heard, day or night.

There are no formal channels for the expression of emotion in New Hanover, although there used to be gatherings where people sang and danced and had fun. At funerals, the bereaved cry alone, and there is no further ceremony for the dead.

Emotional relationships between kin and affines are suggested but not standardized or institutionalized in behavior or ideology. People are interested in discussing the varying personalities of their kin and friends, a subject that Tikana are either unable or unwilling to approach. In New Hanover, in the absence of institutionalization of behavior, the personal habits and styles of one's companions become a matter of serious interest on which survival could depend. In New Ireland, anyone would give you food if you were hungry; but in New Hanover, people wonder who would, and how they would bring him or her to give it? Fear of going hungry (which they do, if they depend on others to feed them) is one important reason why Lavongais do not like to make journeys and do not like to go away to work.

At the individual level, social and emotional interactions are inexplicitly structured and isolating; at the population level, the distribution of subsistence resources is inexplicitly structured and isolating. Individualistic patterns, considered original, not traditional, are expressed in the arts of New Hanover: their songs are narrative, their stories tell of isolation, and their plastic arts are few, naturalistic, and roughly processed.

Frequently repeated patterns—assertiveness, provocativeness, impatience for results, and dislike of process; directness which defies ritual; interest in being given things, being helped, being protected; curiosity about the whys and wherefores, persistence in exploring alternatives to their own existence—these are the redundancies in New Hanover that describe the *style* of the culture.

Summary

The cultures of the Tikana of New Ireland and of the Lavongai of New Hanover differ from each other systematically, and in ways which channel behavior. Here I argue that the Lavongai generated, through their culture and in a colonial context, a resistance movement; presented in a typically Lavongai dramatic mode, and called by outsiders a "cargo cult." In 1972 (Billings, 1972) I argued that this behavior was seen very differently by Tikana of New Ireland, who found it wrong and rude to oppose authority, than it was by those noncultist Lavongai who did not join the movement; and that the "cult" would not "spread" to New Ireland because the Tikana culture could not accommodate or sustain such a movement.[32] For whatever reasons, the test of time has supported this prediction, so far.

Notes

1. Mangai residents Konda Aisoli (who died suddenly in 1984) and his wife, Suzanne Boas Aisoli (who died in 1996), and Tom Ritako and his wife, Ruby Aisoli Ritako, all willingly agreed to read whatever book I produced about New Ireland before it was published. I finally decided not to ask them to do this, however, lest they be partly blamed for whatever mistakes I make. They have all gone on to distinguished careers with the government of Papua New Guinea and in education. Nic Peterson and I deeply appreciated their help in getting us started in our work, and in helping us with language.

2. I expected to be in New Ireland only a short time, though this time I did bring with me copies of the work of Powdermaker (1933), Chinnery (1929), and Groves (1935, 1936). Konda Aisoli and his wife read the copy of Powdermaker that I brought with me and suggested many corrections, especially of spelling. I am sure they or their successors would do the same for my rendition of their words.

3. Thanks are due to the National Institute of Mental Health for a grant in support of this return. My subsequent periods of field research were partly funded by Wichita State University, as sabbatical leave and research grants. The University of Sydney funded my original research as a junior sabbatical leave. I am grateful to these institutions for their support.

4. Boski Tom in New Hanover told me about the death when I visited him in his village, Umbukul, in 1967. I knew Groves's son, Murray, also an anthropologist. In Tabar much later, in 1983, I met Aisoli Salin, who went with the Groves family to Australia when he was only a young boy. He is mentioned in one of Groves's articles (Groves, 1935). An old man when I met him in his village in Tabar, he spoke perfect English with what I thought was a Melbourne accent.

5. Rakasou and her family lived, in 1998, in neighboring Livitua village, in Tokanaka hamlet, in the house built by Milika's brother in their mother's hamlet. Kas had no immediate sister to whose son he was obliged to give his house in this matrilineal, matrilocal society.

6. On a later visit John, the son of Aini and Timui, major mission workers in Lavongai, provided transport and other help in his capacity as head of the Department of Agriculture and Fisheries.

7. Powdermaker (1966) was among those who led the way in publishing her experiences of fieldwork.

8. This kind of expansive presentation was more common in the first three decades of the twentieth century, when anthropologists presented their reports in museum publications and were not under pressure to sell affordable publications to the general public. The failure of anthropologists to demand as a minimal condition of our science the publication of data leaves us justifiably embarrassed among other scientists, as well as among humanists. Many of them, of course, share our problems.

9. I, of course, had contracted the profound and unpayable professional obligation to them that any anthropologist accepts anywhere.

10. The following account of Kavieng is based largely on the research and report provided to me by planter P. R. K. Murray of Baia Plantation, New Ireland. His work has been occasionally supplemented with information gathered from the Encyclopedia of Papua and New Guinea (Ryan, 1972).

11. By 1974, the Club had attained a smooth transition to a membership of largely mixed and indigenous clientele (some of whom were the long-time wives of European residents) while continuing to serve the local businessmen and area planters who founded it. In 1983 I watched television there with two young professional women, one from New Ireland and one from New Hanover, who had been my best "little girls" friends and informants in 1965-67. Their parents have never been to the Club.

12. Wheeler and Murray, 1983.

13. The story of how this was accomplished has been written by many of those who participated in it, among them J. K. McCarthy (1963).

14. The joint effort to map the prehistory of this area was begun in two test sites investigated by Nic Peterson (Peterson and Billings, 1965), and in major excavations by Jim Specht (Specht, 1968). Our work in New Ireland was begun in response to inquiry initiated by Apelis Kasino (Kas), teacher in Mangai village, and mentor and host to anthropologists. The teams of archaeologists stayed in Mangai with Kas and his family in the early days of their research as Nic and I had in 1965. Kas was the man who took Nic Peterson and me, and then Jim Allen and his team (Allen et al, 1988), to Panakiwuk cave. He and his family enjoyed the archaeologists very much, and Kas remained very interested in what they found. Apelis Kasino has made a major contribution to the understanding of his island's history and culture.

15. When I visited Australia in 1998 on my way to Kavieng I met archaeologists preparing to go to New Hanover. They were in touch with John Aini (see note 4, this chapter), who also mentioned to me that he was helping the archaeologists with transport and information.

16. Langiro of Mangai and Simberi, Tabar islands, told me a story about how the islands became separated when a dispute arose between two brothers.

17. A dramatic account of some of these escapes was given by the wife of a man who survived one, Mary Murray (1965). Some men remained (Feldt, 1967).

18. According to local informants, this was an ineffective advisory body which never gave weight to the native point of view.

19. Kroeber (1948) had used the concept in his interpretation of civilizations over time, and Benedict (1934) had used the similar category "pattern," to make comparative synchronic interpretations of cultures. However, these conceptualizations were treated as idiosyncratic rather than as systematic tools of analysis that others might usefully employ in anthropology. When Kroeber edited the disciplinary overview *Anthropology Today* (1953), he asked an art historian (Schapiro, 1953) to write the chapter on style.

20. I have published and presented many papers which expand, clarify, provide evidence for, and document by reference to independently developed, isomorphic theoretical frames of reference, the contrast I am summarizing briefly here. See especially Billings, 1987 and 1989b. See also Tonnies (1957) and Sorokin (1957).

21. Murphy (1962) and Mihalic (1957) have provided excellent introductions to pidgin English. Nic Peterson and I were fortunate in being able to use these and also audiotapes prepared at Australian National University by Donald Laycock.

22. See Lewis, 1969, pp. 26, 29; and Lithgow and Claassen, 1968. In the late 1960s Lithgow and Claassen were killed when their small missionary plane went down in the New Guinea highlands. They and their successors who are missionary students of language have made a very important contribution to our understanding in this area.

23. I did not do extensive work in language. However, the basic kinship terms in Mangai are Tigak, and the terms in Kara, spoken in Lauen village just down the road, are quite different.

24. Language names derive from the term for sibling of same sex in each language.

25. When I use the term "Lavongais," I am referring to the people of the entire island of New Hanover or Lavongai, not to the people of Lavongai village.

26. These are described by Powdermaker (1933).

27. Mangai's last big *malanggan* to date was in 1990, for Konda Aisoli, who died in 1983. Tom Ritako, his good friend and brother-in-law, led the proceedings. There is no reason to suppose that *malanggan* is in decline at this time, although it is different from what it was when transportation for people and supplies was by boat or on foot.

28. Their meaning and use is similar to that of the carvings of Native Americans of the Northwest Coast.

29. The early part of this research, which continues to grow, has been summarized by one of the major founders of it, Harry Triandis (1991).

30. Billings, 1969, 1972, 1987, 1989b, 1991a, 1991b, 1991d, 1992a, 1992c, 1992d, and 1994; Billings and Peterson, 1967.

31. Birdwhistell (1970) used this term. Later popular culture began to speak of "body language."

32. Some of the original anticultists, of Umbukul village, had a small resistance movement of their own in 1994 (Billings, 1994) trying to prevent Malaysian loggers from taking all their trees. The Tikana have not had any such confrontation with their government, so far. Noncultists were not reluctant to be confrontational with cultists during the cult, while Tikana remained in negotiation with those who disagreed with them.

2
Field Work

Finding the Problem and the Site

Getting Started

I begin my account of field work with the problems involved in getting to the field. The first problem is to decide where to go. Often it happens that anthropologists cannot go where they plan to go: which is how it happened for me, at least at first.

Beginnings: Election, 1964
   In February 1964, the Territory of Papua and New Guinea held elections to create a new governing structure: the House of Assembly. This election was undertaken by the Australian administration under pressure from the United Nations to prepare the people for self-government. Europeans in the territory in general, and administrators in particular, were surprised that the election was "successful": that is, people voted, and even those who had had very little contact with Europeans seemed to understand, at least partly, the purpose of the election. Often, people who were traditional leaders were elected, and, in general, everything had gone well.
   New Hanover was one of the few places where the election did not go well; and this, too, was surprising, because New Hanover had been "under control" for many years, and the people had long been in contact with European civilization. And yet half the people of New Hanover and of the adjacent Tigak Islands voted for President Johnson of America. This event and others which followed it came to be referred to by outsiders as "the Johnson cult." Many Europeans (administrators, missionaries, anthropologists) and some local people viewed these events as constituting a local version of the "cargo cults" well known in Melanesia.[1]

Public Knowledge about the Vote for Johnson in New Hanover

Anthropologists going into the field anywhere begin with public knowledge of the area. Little had been published about New Hanover before the 1964 election drew a great deal of publicity: front-page stories in Australian newspapers described the elections taking place in the Territory of Papua and New Guinea, which Australia governed, and mentioned or featured the New Hanover vote for Johnson. By the time the information reached *Newsweek* magazine (June 22, 1964) this is how it read:

SOUTH PACIFIC:
What Price LBJ?

Almost from the moment a U.S. Air Force geodetic survey team landed on tiny New Hanover island, to "position" this dot in the South Pacific, young Bos Malik became the Big Man on the atoll. If the Americans needed vegetables or other goods and services, Bos was right there with prompt delivery; and in return for service rendered, he received cigarettes, Hershey bars, and other delights of the American way of life.

But then one day a few months ago, the Americans told Bos that they were leaving. He was shattered. "Don't worry kid," said one of the Americans. "There's plenty more where this came from. The man to talk to is Lyndon Baines Johnson, President of the U.S.A."

This gave Bos an idea. Bring President Johnson to the island and back would come the American goods. It so happened that the island's Australian rulers were about to hold the first election in which everybody could vote. Campaigning vigorously on an All the Way with LBJ platform, Bos secured the support of the island's electorate.

What he lacked, as it turned out, was support of the Australians. On election day, Australian patrol officer I. T. Spencer, acting as registrar of voters, was confronted by a thousand Johnson supporters demanding the right to vote for their man. But as Mr. Johnson wasn't on the ballot, registrar Spencer refused their request. In that case, said Bos to his supporters, don't pay your taxes; instead, he suggested they give him the money to "buy" President Johnson, who would then rule the island—bringing with him, of course, cargoes of Hershey bars, cigarettes, and other luxuries. Before long, followers had given Bos $987 to make an early purchase of LBJ.

At this point, the Australians decided that things were getting out of hand. A district commissioner flew into the island and he was soon followed by 40 armed police. Bos and his followers reluctantly handed over the tax money, held in escrow for the Presidential purchase. But they still yearn for the rule of Lyndon. And they believe that their wish soon will be granted. For Bos has promised them that before the end of this month 600 U.S. troops will arrive aboard the queen Mary to take over New Hanover in the name of LBJ.

The whole election made a good story for the press. In a general article entitled, "Don't Eat the Candidate," *Newsweek* wrote (March 9, 1964:

In the coastal town of Port Moresby, burly Papuan tribesmen thrust hibiscus blossoms in their hair and danced to the polls in carnival spirit. In the snow-crested mountains of the interior, helicopters dropped teams among the murderous Kukukuku warriors and the wild Nembi people—who promised not to eat any candidates.

Time did not mention New Hanover specifically but did run an article on the elections entitled, "Stone Age Election" (February 28, 1964), which stated in part:

> Interest in the election has spurred the revival of native "cargo cults." Cultists believe that white men do not work, that they merely write secret symbols on scraps of paper, for which they receive planeloads of "cargo"—boats, tractors, houses, cars and canned goods. After the election, cultists believe that they will inherit the white man's magic to make goods materialize without doing any work. To show faith in their belief, some have killed their pigs in sacrificial offerings; others have hacked airstrips out of the bush for the planes that will bring in the cargo.

The elections in general, and the vote for Johnson in particular, made a good story not only for the press, but also for the conversations that filled the evening hours among European residents of the Territory of Papua and New Guinea. Planters worked cargo cult rumors for all they were worth over drinks in the pub, or in the club, or on the verandah. Government officials also pursued discussion of the subject, but their jokes fit mostly into a cops-and-robbers or western format, rather than the more cosmic, existential, theater-of-the-absurd, or indignant style that pleased the planters. One such rumor that found favor during my stay in Kavieng had to do with a Big Egg which was said to be believed to be hovering over New Britain about to hatch cargo.

Not everyone had the luxury of laughing. Planters whose business was threatened, or missionaries who were expected to bring the people back to their senses or back under control, were often not amused. Some felt perhaps more threatened than the evidence warranted, as is suggested by a letter to the editor of *Newsweek* (July 13, 1964) from a member of the Catholic Relief Services, New York City:

> "Cargo Cult"
> The account of Bos Malik's abortive attempt to "purchase" President Lyndon Johnson for New Hanover island (INTERNATIONAL, June 22) was incomplete.
> A deeper thrust by your correspondent into the activities of Bos would have uncovered a secret tribal society known in the Pacific as "cargo cult."
> The cargo cult, which blankets the Solomon Islands, is a compound of idolatry, witchcraft, and the crudest forms of immorality. It started during World War II when cult leaders told the natives that shiploads of cigarettes, chocolate, clothing, and other PX supplies were gifts from the gods and dead

relatives. With the end of the war, these "gifts" stopped. Meanwhile, cargo-cult leaders like Bos have convinced the natives that their gods and dead relatives continue to send them shiploads of gifts; but their enemies, the Australian authorities, have been intercepting them.

To Australian officials, the cult means prostitution, lawlessness, extortion, and black magic. Natives are told not to pay taxes but to give money to cult leaders to bribe the gods and dead relatives to continue the shipments.

Communists were quick to exploit this movement and have penetrated cult headquarters on the island of Buka off the western tip of Bougainville.

Catholic Relief Services is currently combining its efforts in education projects with those of the Australian Government to unshackle the natives from the influence of the cargo cult.

These accounts of public responses to cults represent the wide spectrum of views commonly offered by persons at some distance from events, where ethnocentric positions may be freely indulged without concern for the remote possibility that they might have consequences. There is information and impact in these views, however rumor-battered they may be; and the anthropologist, rather than ignoring them, must find out how to fit them together with all the rest that is discovered.

Preparing for Research

When I read these accounts of the Johnson cult by journalists, I was a senior tutor in the anthropology department at the University of Sydney, and looking for a site to do doctoral research in New Guinea. I applied for University funding for the Christmas holidays to make a preliminary plunge into New Hanover. My friend and like-minded anthropology graduate student and tutor Nic Peterson, recently arrived from Cambridge, thought with me that the situation cried out for anthropological attention, and we decided to make it a joint effort. We planned to take different sides of the island and find out what had happened. We hunted out documents and translations at the Australian School of Pacific Administration (A.S.O.P.A.), and Nic found an important informant in Sydney before we left: Rev. John Robbins.

The Reverend Mr. Robbins and New Ireland's West Coast

The Reverend Mr. Robbins of the Methodist Overseas Mission came to Sydney on leave in December 1964 just before we left for Kavieng for the first time. He had just come from tramping around the swamp area of New Ireland trying to round up people from west coast villages (Kaut, Kabin, Lokono) who had gone into the bush after a violent encounter with a tax collection group, an incident which was considered by many to be a part of the Johnson cult phenomenon. It was reported in an Australian newspaper (the *Sun-Herald*, September 27, 1964) under the headline, "RAID AT DAYBREAK: Blood May Flow Over Taxes." Forty native police, armed with tear gas, shotguns, and riot clubs, were ready to accompany four European police officers and six native affairs officers to Lokono "in an attempt to arrest fifty President Johnson cultists who attacked an Administration tax collection patrol the previous day." The newspaper account of the attack, as reported by District Officer (D.O.) K. R. Williamson is as follows:

> [Mr. Williamson] said Lokono village had been infiltrated by the "Vote for President Johnson" cult, and cult collectors from Lavongai had been there raising money to "buy" the United States' President.
> The clash began when an old Lokono villager refused to pay his £3 15s [$10 U.S. at that time] annual local government council tax.
> A court was held on the beach and the villager was convicted and sentenced to jail.
> As he was being escorted to a boat, fifty screaming natives broke from the jungle, attacked the patrol, and freed him.
> The natives were armed with spears, clubs, and large pieces of coral rock.
> Reports from Kavieng say the natives were aware that the patrol was coming and had buried piles of rocks under sand on the beach.
> They took care not to harm the European native affairs officers.
> The attack was so savage that the patrol was forced to withdraw to a boat.

Two years later, I talked to some of the people, both European and local, who had been part of the tax collection team, and their stories confirmed the newspaper account. One more important feature of this incident later became public: four policemen from the original patrol that had been attacked were subsequently dishonorably discharged from the constabulary for beating two prisoners taken into custody on this occasion.

The Reverend Mr. Robbins thought the administration had overreacted with police power. What was needed, he felt, was communication. Mr. Robbins and the administration service personnel shared the view that the Department of Native Affairs (D.N.A.) personnel, who are the governors and law enforcement branch of the administration, did not really know the people and that this was part of the problem. Reverend Robbins felt that he had done the administration's job for them by going into the bush and swampland in New Ireland trying to find the people of Lokono and other west coast villages who had been terribly frightened by the appearance of policemen with a tax patrol, and who had had their worst fears confirmed by the behavior of these policemen, none of whom were local.

And yet D.N.A. officials could not help but wonder if the missions were not somehow to blame for putting all sorts of mystical ideas into the native's heads. They noted that many cultists were Methodists, and many spokesmen were Methodist missionaries or local preachers (*munamuna*) and thought that the mission personnel should somehow discipline these members of their organizations.

"Cult Violence"

I report this incident on the west coast of New Ireland at some length for these reasons: the government officials always associated what happened at

Lokono, New Ireland, with the Johnson cult of New Hanover, even though there was no further activity on the west coast of New Ireland, and even though this encounter did not involve the use of the Johnson cult ideology in any way. To government officials, this violent interchange at Lokono was evidence that the Johnson cultists might be violent and that, therefore, appropriate care needed to be taken to meet this potentiality; and also that the Johnson cult was spreading fast and dangerously and that, therefore, government officials needed to be on guard everywhere.

These were fair assumptions for government officials, lacking intimate knowledge of the people they were serving, to make. I myself continued to test these assumptions for years to come, but I began to doubt, early on in my field work, that they were true. When I met D.O. Ken Williamson, in January 1965, I thought that he seemed to have a sympathetic, rather than an authoritarian, approach to government problems with the "natives." I asked him if he thought that New Irelanders were potential cultists, and he said, "All the people of Papua New Guinea are potential cultists." This seemed a reasonable generalization from an anthropologist's point of view. Gradually, however, I came to think it was not true for New Ireland.

Anthropological Perspectives on Cargo Cults

Anthropological accounts of cargo cults emphasize political, economic, social, historical, psychological, religious, and cognitive factors that help to form cults, but they do not agree on how these factors should be interpreted or weighted. Some see cults as rational in terms of the information available to the cultists, who are confused by changes they cannot fully understand. Viewed from this perspective, the natives are sensible people who want things like all the rest of us do: they see what white men have that they do not have, and they are doing what they think has to be done to make the cargo come soon to them, too. By contrast, other students emphasize the need we all have for irrational beliefs that sustain us in difficult times: their accounts try to trace the irrational threads to psychological needs rather than to mistaken information.

Still other anthropologists see cargo cults as a justified outburst of rage by the have-nots against the haves, the latter being an array of colonial imperialists exploiting the Third World. These students are less interested in the details of belief systems or emotional behavior than they are in the analysis of political and economic systems, internal and external, which affect the lives of cultists whether they know it or not. Based on these and other varying perspectives, and with varying kinds and amounts of data available, anthropologists have tried to produce systematic theories that order observations made by them and by others.

Even anthropologists, in private, are not insensitive to the humorous aspects of cargo cults. Making jokes about them is almost irresistible, though it is considered unprofessional to do so publicly outside anthropological circles. The Johnson cult provided grist for many a small mill: for instance, when one of my

American colleagues heard about the vote for Johnson and that I was trying to go to New Hanover to study it, he wrote suggesting that I tell the cultists that "the Americans can't spare him just now." That was when Lyndon Johnson was running against Barry Goldwater for the presidency. Later, after President Johnson had disappointed some of his American followers, that same colleague wrote to me thus: "We are taking up a collection to send Johnson to New Hanover, and we hope they still want him." Only Margaret Mead, an old hand with cargo cults, was not amused: she asked me somewhat contemptuously, when I met her in Port Moresby, why I wanted to go to New Hanover, asserting that "cargo cults are boring."

One point that I think we have overlooked, which reveals not only our personal solemnity and professional sobriety but also our potential for patronizing the people we study, is that cultists, too, may find their cult amusing, and parts of it downright funny. We have not seriously considered cults as satire, as jokes played by the cultists on a pompous administration.

This is not all a "cargo cult" is, but in the case of "the Johnson cult" I think that this is part of the explanation for how it came to pass.

All of the proposed interpretations no doubt carry some truths. I am probably a somewhat "mentalistic" or "cognitive" or "symbolic" anthropologist, at least to start with: what I wanted most to know at first was what the people of New Hanover really thought. What had they done and why had they done it? Did they really believe that Johnson would come? If so, was their belief due to misinformation accidentally transmitted by the American map-making team that had been in the area, perpetuated by inertia and indifference? Or was it a conviction clung to irrationally or desperately? What evidence did they offer? How had they heard of Johnson? Did they have any "standard" beliefs about cargo? Did they believe that the ancestors produced it? Did they think the ancestors and Johnson were somehow associated and would somehow bring cargo to the people together? There was no easy way, I soon learned, to find out.

The first question for which I and all other anthropologists needed an answer was, however, this one: what exactly had happened?

Permission and Practical Matters

In 1968, when I had just returned from the field, I heard an anthropologist[2] lament that most anthropological reports begin when the researcher has been in the field for six months. When the account opens, the language has been learned, the village selected, the house built, transportation and supplies secured. As all the scars, physical and mental, of battle were still fresh for me at the time, I agreed that "Getting There" is a profoundly legitimate part of a report. Some such report provides essential information about the epistemological foundations of anthropological observation and interpretation. During the 1970s and 80s, many anthropologists began to return to the "thumbnail sketch," if not to total Malinowskian candor or lyricism, in sharing with the reader "What Really Happened."[3] Recent trends in theory allow, or even require, us to "Tell

All." With this assertion of both lofty relevance and contemporary vision, I proceed with my account of these matters.

Before we left Sydney, Nic Peterson and I wrote for and received permission from the famous Mr. J. K. McCarthy, director of the Department of Native Affairs in Port Moresby, to undertake our study on New Hanover. With his letter in hand, I felt that we had fallen into step behind our illustrious predecessors who had worked in New Guinea and who had all, somewhere and somehow, met Mr. McCarthy.

Nic also talked to Keith Adam of the Australian Broadcasting Company, who had been sent to Kavieng to do a story on the cult. Mr. Adam summarized for us what he had learned and also gave us a rundown on who to talk to in the administration; and advice on how to butter up Mr. Kappy, the manager of the local hotel, who was married to a local girl.

In New Ireland

Arrival in Kavieng

We arrived in Kavieng on New Year's Eve, 1964, and found the hotel of perhaps twelve rooms completely booked. We were lucky to be admitted to the last beds in town at the local, all European (white) Kavieng Club, whose members were mostly private business employees and plantation owners and managers from the entire Kavieng District. While we were concerned about the "Europeans only" status of the club, I saw the wisdom in Nic's observation that the alternative was to sleep under a nearby big tree; and we checked in. We were made very welcome, and we had an opportunity there to meet many of the planters and government officers who were to play various roles in our future work.

Department of Native Affairs: Permission Denied

On our first visit to the district commissioner's office two days after we arrived in Kavieng, we saw on his desk two great, thick files labeled "Native Thought in the Johnson Cult." Naturally, our anthropological mouths watered. We were told, however, that we would not be allowed to go to New Hanover; first by D.O. Ken Williamson, who was on Keith Adam's list of people to talk to; and then, most especially, by incoming District Commissioner Bill Seale, who was not. We spoke to them first on January 2, 1965. Mr. Seale, who was replacing Mr. Mick Healy, said that it was true that he did not become district commissioner officially until January 5, but he certainly would not allow us even to visit New Hanover.

Because Mr. Williamson and the district commissioner, Mr. Healy, and later Mr. Seale, held the views they did about possible violence in the Johnson cult, all government action was based on this perspective; and one action they took was to rescind the permission we had obtained to go to New Hanover. It was thought that our presence might cause trouble and that we might be in some danger. Mr. Williamson kindly suggested a place for us to stay in New Ireland, in Mangai, a village which was, he said, "very progressive."

Then they excused themselves because they had to go to a court case. Nic asked if we could go to the court, and Mr. Williamson said that it was open, as all court cases are. They did not tell us it was a case in which three New Ireland "Johnson cultists" (the word in common use) were being tried for conspiracy and sedition, though they seemed to assume that we knew that: "You heard the news this morning," one of them said, which we had not. We felt that government officials saw our presence as at least a nuisance, but we went to the court, anyway.

Field Work, 1965

The next day, Mr. Williamson generously arranged for a government Land Rover to take us down the road to Mangai and to the teacher there who became our great friend and mentor, Apelis Kasino, "Kas." We settled down in Mangai for the duration of our study, but every week we went into town to ask if things had changed, if it would now be all right for us to at least visit New Hanover with some of the European friends who had invited us; and every week we were told to come back again the next week. We never did go to New Hanover in 1965.

We did have the opportunity to talk to several government officers whose work in the service departments took them to New Hanover, and we also talked to the few European planters who lived in or near New Hanover. There seemed to be unanimous agreement among them that the Johnson cult had resulted from government neglect and that the only harm that might come from our carrying out a study there would be that we would find this out and publish it.

It was not necessary to go to New Hanover to find out some things about the Australian administration. On January 4, 1965, there was a farewell party for Mr. Healy in Mangai, at the council house where we were staying. I record in the interests of history that there was some confusion about who was to eat first in the gathering, which included local counselors, Australian officials, and people in general, both indigenous and European. What happened was that all the Europeans ate first, while all the local people, even the counselors, ate after the Europeans had gone. We, knowing that all was not well, and not knowing what to do, hung back with our English-speaking friends, young educated people from Mangai village who just happened to be home for Christmas vacation from their jobs in Port Moresby.

Mr. Healy came over to say a word to me, which I appreciated. I said that we were being very well looked after in Mangai, and he said, "Yes, these people are some of the best in the district." More usually, he went on, "The native is . . . "—and he paused to think of just the right word—"dilatory." I did not want either to agree with him or to insult him, so I merely mentioned that there were some, like my new English-speaking friends—to which Mr. Healy responded, "Oh, yes, well, they're ordinary, of course." He then said that one of them had worn a better suit at his marriage than Healy had ever owned and that he'd felt like a ragbag at the wedding. I mentioned, as we were eating, that the people had worked very hard to produce this feast and how good it was, and he said, "If you like it. It's always a bit smoky for me."

I saw him then, and in retrospect even more so, as a gentle man who did not really seem to want to impose his views, or have those of others imposed on him. In his speech that day, he said he had been in the territory for thirty-eight years, and if he had contributed any small thing to the success he was sure lay ahead of them, he left a happy man. In our brief, private conversation, he told me that the United Nations had shaken him till his teeth rattled and that three years ago he did not agree with Sir Hugh Foot when he came here, but now he thinks perhaps he is right. What, I asked, did Sir Hugh Foot say? "Independence," Mr. Healy said, "You must give these people independence."

Field Work, 1966

When I returned to Kavieng and to Mangai in 1966, I continued my efforts to gain permission to go to New Hanover and to be allowed to see the "Native Thought" files.[4] I also continued to listen to anyone whom I could get to tell me what they knew about the cult. Conversations, largely informal, with European planters and other residents of the Kavieng District often took place over a drink at the pub or the club, where the aim of the conversation was to entertain; an occasional crumb dropped, perhaps a name and a crack, from a member of the staff of D.N.A. (which became the Department of District Administration, D.D.A., in 1966). Most of the staff of D.D.A. regarded information about the cult as confidential, most especially not to be discussed with an untested anthropologist. The lower the rank of the officer, however, the more likely he was to be cut out of the higher levels of information and camaraderie, and the more likely he was to give me the bare bones of some incident which provided me with a few names of a few cultists to ask about the next time I met someone who might know more, or know more reliably.

In 1965 and 1966, I had long, systematic and reliable interviews with a few Europeans who were in a position to know something about the Johnson cult. This group of Europeans comprised staff of various kinds of government services (medical, malaria, agriculture and fisheries, welfare) and missionaries. Most of these people acted on a view of knowledge and action quite different from that directing the behavior of D.D.A. personnel. They believed that the Johnson cult in New Hanover was largely a response to the activities and inactivities of the Australian government, to the power relationships of a fundamental nature shaping cultists' lives, and to the large forces of change at work in the world; and that it did not matter at all if one inexperienced American anthropologist wandered around asking questions, in or out of New Hanover. D.D.A. personnel attributed, or pretended to attribute, to this situation tremendous potentiality for significant behavior change. Specifically, I was told that I might be seen as Lady Bird Johnson or as an American arriving in the vanguard to announce that the President was on his way. While this may have been a joke, it was one which carried weight in preventing me from carrying out my research in New Hanover.

Field Work in New Hanover

A review of the practical difficulties I encountered in trying to begin field work in New Hanover, and of the ways in which many people helped me overcome them, will convey to the reader the essential flavor of the various subcultures that were interacting in the Johnson cult events. My interviews with the people of New Hanover, Australian administrators (called *kiaps* in pidgin English, and in this account), other government personnel, missionaries, and others who affected or were affected by the Johnson cult, often took place in a context of complex circumstances in which I had to be as much participant as observer. I needed transportation and hospitality, and I needed help. My sojourn had to begin with the Europeans in charge.

The following brief survey of white or "European" subcultures is no substitute for systematic study, and the reader should take it for what it is: a sketchy account. It is unfortunate that I and other anthropologists did not do the systematic study we ought to have done before the subculture of the Australian administration became subdominant.[5] There is no doubt that their side of the story is not properly represented here: I write from a participant's perspective, sometimes as opposition, sometimes as advocate. The advocacy role is comfortable for anthropologists: we are nearly all advocates for the people we have studied. The role of opposition is less comfortable for me professionally: it is, in fact, inexcusable. It is necessary, however, to give some idea of the context in which the Johnson cult occurred, and in which I tried to find out about it.

Getting There and Getting Around

Visit to New Hanover with the Methodists

My first chance to find out for myself whether or not my presence in New Hanover would be a dangerous spark to riot was given me by Rev. Ozzie Dale of the Australian Methodist mission in Kavieng.[6] The inspector for mission education, Mr. Rex Crabb, was coming in from Rabaul to go on rounds of the Methodist schools in New Hanover with the staff of the Methodist mission station in New Hanover, at Ranmelek. The Reverend Mr. Dale got permission for me to go along on the ship *Daula* with Rev. Allen Taylor, who became a major informant for me about the events and people of the Johnson cult and about the role of the Methodist mission in it; and with teacher Nancy Anderson, who, along with nurse Val Beckett, subsequently helped me in many ways (George, 1966).

During the week of August 26 (Friday) to September 2 (Saturday), 1966, I visited several villages along the east coast of New Hanover with the mission boat, asking questions not about the cult but about traditional culture. I already knew that *malanggan* was a basic institution in New Ireland, one which patterned life in ways that seemed to me to be inconsistent with cargo cult activities; and I thought that its presence or absence in New Hanover would give me a good idea of whether or not New Hanover traditional culture was much like that of New Ireland. Oddly enough, it was not at first clear-cut as to whether or not New Hanover had *malanggan*, because the people I met knew, or thought they knew, or thought they should know, what it was; but by the end of the week I was sure they did not have *malanggan* in New Hanover.

Only one man spoke to me, and only briefly, about the Johnson cult. No one seemed much interested in my being American. The Reverend Mr. Taylor thought there would be no harm in my coming to New Hanover to do a study. He, like the others who could see no harm in it, expressed interest in my study. Europeans who worked with the people of New Hanover found them terribly exasperating and interesting, and I began to see that some of the Europeans were "hooked" in a strange alliance with them. These Europeans paid taxes for them, liked them, and wanted the affection returned. They were glad to have an anthropologist come, hoping I could add something to their understanding of the people with whom they were working.

Miss Anderson and Miss Beckett were the sort of people who are completely caught up in their work, which was awesome in scope but which did not overwhelm them. Everything was taken in stride, a rapid purposeful stride. It was these Australian Methodists who gave me my only moments of panic in the field. On our first day out on the *Daula*, we docked at about 7:00 P.M. near the village of Konemetalik. By "near" I mean about thirty minutes by moonlight over slippery mangrove roots three to four feet above their bed of ooze. Miss Anderson strode ahead in sneakers, while I came whimpering next, and Mr. Crabb and Rev. Taylor, who I believed shared my apprehension, but quietly, came behind me. I simply do not know how or why we made it without accident. I just aimed my thong-shod feet at the shadows that flickered by under someone's flashlight and lived to tell the tale.

This experience prompted Rev. Taylor to elaborate his main theory about the cult: that it resulted from isolation, that New Hanover was more isolated than some other places, and that villages in New Hanover that were the most isolated, like Konemetalik, were also the most cult-oriented. *Of course*, he pointed out, the government officials preferred to stay behind their desks at Taskul government station rather than to risk their physical persons and abandon comfort to join the isolation at the other side of the mangrove swamp.

The Methodist missionaries, of English ancestry, reminded me of something an American friend[7] had once said of our English friends: that they are like little chips of wood floating on the ocean, rising and falling with the waves, always on top. Wherever the Methodists went, their work surrounded them like a haze, a protective buffer; and they went everywhere, rushing, doing, never allowing themselves the purposeless, friendly, idle sitting and chatting that gave welcome high spots, direction, and meaning to the lives of many Europeans of the territory.

During that trip I met for the first time two cultists who later gave me important help, but with whom I did not discuss the cult at all at the time: Makios, a man perhaps in his sixties, of Patekone village, near the Methodist mission at Ranmelek; and Bosap, in his forties, who was captain of the mission boat, *Daula*. I did not realize that Bosap was a local, either in or out of the cult, until I took another week-long trip on the *Daula* nearly a year later. I liked Bosap, and we were always friendly, but it did not occur to me to ask him for help, which he later volunteered, in meeting people wherever we went.

Visiting with Government Personnel

During September 1966 to February 1967, I continued my work in New Ireland, but I talked to people who knew about New Hanover when I met them. On December 20, I had a long talk with Mr. John Lobb, who was just resigning as *"didiman,"* i.e., agricultural officer, in charge of New Hanover. He gave me an interesting account of the failure of the coffee crop in New Hanover and of the influence that failure had had, in his opinion, on the development of the Johnson cult.

In 1965, Nic and I had met Keith Hill of the Fisheries Department. The people called him "Master Fish," an appellation that fit in many ways. He was surely a master of the arts of fishing, an eager student of other people's knowledge of fishing and, indeed, a devotee of fishing. Master Fish seemed always to be thinking and wondering about fishing and sometimes even muttering to himself about fishing. However, he had a rival interest in the human species and juggled the needs and wants, however big or small, of a vast variety of people around his own continual activities on behalf of the development of a fishing industry for the local population. I was one of the people whose needs he fit into his schedule. He knew that I wanted to go to New Hanover, and so whenever he went there he let me know and offered me a ride. I went with him for the first time January 4-6, 1967, just to the government post at Taskul. Many people had suggested that I should talk with Mr. Carroll Gannon, who was the medical assistant at Taskul, about where and how to undertake a study of the cult in New Hanover.

Carroll was as devoted to his profession as was Keith. Both viewed the success of their work as completely dependent on their interpersonal relationships with the people they were trying to serve, and attempts to communicate as part of their job; but, of course, to a person like Carroll, a job is never just a job. He gave away all his money and did not take the six-months' leave to which he was entitled, preferring to spend his holiday with his local friends.

Moreover, Carroll was as willing to talk to the anthropologist as he was to the locals, just as many D.D.A. officials were, by contrast, as unwilling to talk to the local people as they were to the anthropologist. Their silence was partly due to their following orders. A friendly young Australian patrol officer, Cadet Patrol Officer (C.P.O.) Tony Beard, arrived at Taskul just before Keith Hill and I did on January 4, with a letter, in pencil, from Assistant District Officer (A.D.O.) Mert Brightwell, which read in part: "Miss Billings is there against the wishes of the D.D.A., the D.C., and myself." The letter indicated that I was to be given no information and shown no files, including Lavongai Local Government Council reports, which were, in theory, public but which were, in fact, in a file case in the council office.

Tony Beard and I both remembered our first meeting and now, in Carroll Gannon's home, we laughed about it. It was in 1965, when he visited the village of Mangai along with Mr. Brightwell, who walked past Nic and me as though we weren't there, despite my attempts to greet him. Tony kindly reassured me about the letter which he brought to Taskul from Mr. Brightwell and the other government officers. I had come, after all, only for informal chats and to ascertain whether or not local European personnel thought there was any reason to worry about an anthropologist's visit disturbing the peace. I was assured that there was nothing to fear. I talked to some New Hanoverians, who knew I was American but who seemed quite able to grasp the minor import for their lives of my visit.

Carroll often talked to me in the months that followed of the entertainment value of the cult. On this occasion of our first meeting, my notes indicate that he said, "Of course, the blacks aren't the only ones who enjoy the diversion the cult provides—the whites do, too." He also said that he "loved the post-cult period—everyone is so happy." And everyone around Carroll always seemed happy or at least smiling. If you weren't smiling, Carroll kept after you until you were.

This visit convinced me that I could safely and responsibly undertake field work in New Hanover.

Getting Permission At Last

Several Europeans told me that the government could not stop me from going to New Hanover unless they restricted the area. I made an appointment to see Mr. Seale on Tuesday, January 10, hoping to discuss the situation with him. My New Ireland neighbor, planter Peter Murray of Baia plantation, warned me with his usual wit: "Make sure he doesn't make you write 500 times, 'I will not fly in the face of constituted authority.'" By this time, I felt that in my dealings with the administration I had been not only unfortunate, since anthropologists often receive a great deal of help from D.D.A. officers in New Guinea, but deliberately misled.

When I got to my appointment, Mr. Seale saw me briefly in the presence of

Mr. Brightwell and of Bob Hoad, the D.O. at the government post in New Hanover, Taskul. Mr. Seale told me they had decided that the government would help me work in New Hanover if I would go to Lavongai, the village next to the Lavongai Catholic Mission. This area had been in the cult but not as intensely as the Methodist area nearer Kavieng. I was asked not to interview about the cult until I had been there a while and the effect of my presence could be evaluated. Most importantly, the Catholic missions in the Kavieng area were, and are, the responsibility of the American branch of the M.S.C. (Missionaries of the Sacred Heart, headquartered in Aurora, Illinois), and American priests had replaced German ones at Lavongai in the 1930s. Thus, my being American in Lavongai village could be associated with the missions rather than with the imminent arrival of President Johnson. If I would agree to all this, Mr. Seale told me, he would ask the bishop in Kavieng if it was all right with him. I did agree, and gratefully, as I had no better way, at that time of deciding on a place to set up headquarters. I also thought that it was good anthropological policy for me to begin my work on traditional ethnography, and so not talking about the cult was exactly what I had intended to do anyway. The D.C. made a call to the bishop, and I went to see him.

After I visited Bishop Alfred Stemper, M.S.C. (from Minnesota), I felt like Sisyphus would feel if he finally got that rock to the top and started down the other side. The Catholic mission and the individual missionaries treated me from beginning to end almost as though I were one of their own, and they treat their own, and all the rest of us, with tender loving care. Instead of being regarded as a spy, a revolutionary, a nut or, at least, a nuisance, all of a sudden I was a person who had made great sacrifices to come to help the people, and my life should be made as easy as possible to make up for the inevitable hardships. Whenever I went to a Catholic mission station in the Kavieng District, I felt as though everyone there had been preparing just for that moment. Cold orange juice, warm cake, the fatted calf; a chair, a bed, clean sheets, hot showers; a ride into town, a ride out of town, swabs for tropical ulcers, medicines and reassurance; postage stamps, magazines, repair of machines, and any one of possibly one hundred Roy Rogers movies or home movies and slides, were offered along with attentive interest in conversation for as long as the visitor wished. What was most appreciated by me, however, was the welcome and gracious assumption that the anthropologist was a "Good Person." This is a far cry from the lonely status often occupied by members of our profession, who are sometimes greeted by the European population in colonial situations with all the enthusiasm usually proffered itinerant lepers. Of all Europeans, it was to missionaries, whom anthropologists have so often opposed, that I felt most obligated to justify myself. This proved to be completely unnecessary with the Catholics of the Kavieng Diocese.

Bishop Stemper said that of course I could ride on their boats, that they would transport my supplies, and he would let Father Bernard Miller at Lavongai know that I was on my way so that he could make sure the "government rest house" was ready for me. (Months later, one of the patrol officers told me that the "government" rest houses belong to the villages where they are built, not to the government. Since neither the villagers nor the anthropologist knew this, it was necessary to get government permission for me to stay in this house in Lavongai.)

What the Catholic Bishop Thought the Cult Was About

I had a brief conversation with Bishop Stemper about the cult on that day. My notes indicate that he thought the cult lacked leadership: "Often the 'leaders' aren't, as far as the people are concerned." The cult leaders, he thought, were mainly "just young guys." He didn't know how many of the old ones were behind them. When people came to talk to him, it was only the "young guys."

In reference to Oliver, whose name I had heard most because he was always evading arrest, Bishop Stemper said he "just roams around." I had heard this idea from several other people, that the men called leaders just went from village to village. Once, the Bishop told me, they brought money to him, eight to ten men, to buy Johnson's ticket to New Hanover. In response to my question, he said that not just the Catholics came to see him about cult affairs. Once when he went out to Lavongai two years before, a whole group of Methodists came to get his views because, since he was an American, he should know.

Was there religious zeal? I asked and "Oh, sure," the Bishop responded. New Hanover people had had some contact with Americans, but only slight, compared to, for example, Manus. "This was just a cargo cult, and Johnson's name got involved," the Bishop told me.

What the Government Thought the Cult Was About

After my visit with the bishop, I went back to the government office to finalize plans with Mr. Brightwell. He told me that his office would be glad to have my report on Tutukuvul Isukal Association (T.I.A.), a new economic advancement society that Father Miller had started. The members were all the old cultists, and Mr. Brightwell thought that T.I.A. members were working with the belief that their efforts would eventually bring America to New Hanover. Village representatives to T.I.A., called *bord* (board), held lengthy meetings just as, reputedly, the cultists did. "We call it [T.I.A.]," Brightwell allowed with an amused smile, "Father Miller's cult."

Mr. Brightwell took me to see Mr. Frawley, the assistant district commissioner (A.D.C.), who was with the patrol that was attacked on the west coast of New Ireland when they tried to collect taxes. Mr. Frawley told me that the women, and some men, did not know what was going on in the cult. Some enjoyed being made a martyr, he said, with regard to the jail sentences given for nonpayment of taxes. The third time around when they wouldn't pay their taxes, in 1966, they were given six months in jail. When they got out, they talked of their wives and how they had to get along without their men. This was "sheer attrition," Mr. Frawley said. Mr. Brightwell had told them: "You should have thought of [your wives] before you did things to get sent to jail."

Mr. Frawley said the local government council tax had been levied and paid for three years, since the council was established in 1960.[8] But in 1964 they gave as a rationalization for not paying that they did not want the council, that it did not do anything. "A valid argument," Mr. Frawley conceded.

I talked a little to Mr. Seale on this great day about his views of the Johnson cult. He told me that the people of New Hanover did not want their problems solved, that they wanted to preserve animosity. Paulos, he said, was a main leader. (Later, it turned out that he was president of T.I.A. as well.) However, there was "no definite leader or policy," and the cult was "never a stable thing." Furthermore, the "emphasis on Johnson did not affect everyone."

Mr. Brightwell agreed that the cult was a matter of "individuals," that there was "never a policy," and "never leadership." He thought Robin and Oliver, whose names were often mentioned together as cult leaders by Europeans, were never really big in it, but that they just came to administration attention. Robin and Oliver "annoyed Toughy," one of the *kiap*s (government officers) involved in the early stages of the cult, and he cited them in his report.

Mr. Seale said he didn't know what they wanted, and he thought they didn't know either. In 1965 he had said to me with what might have been profound insight or merely a dismissal of the trivial: "They just want attention."

Getting to New Hanover at Last

I was not able to gain an overview of what had happened from Europeans or local people outside New Hanover. Europeans who knew the rumors or something more much preferred to keep the laughs going than to give a dull, straight story to an anthropologist, none of whose damn business it was anyway. But most of them would have helped me, and did, in any way they could. They were not sure, themselves, what had happened.

I had to wait until I moved to New Hanover and began to have long interviews with cultists to learn the chronology of events well known there. It was quite easy then to find out in short conversations from almost anyone who had been there—and almost everyone had been—how the vote for Johnson had occurred.

From Mangai to Lavongai

On Wednesday, February 6, 1967, Sirapi and my other Mangai friends came to help me load things into a car. My notes say we all felt bad about my going. I did, in any case, but wanted to get it over with.

> I took my orange cat in a basket. Got to town and got the Catholic mission boat within a couple of hours. Stopped at Analaua, the leprosy hospital island, not to go on. Stayed with the Sisters, who were very nice. One American, three Germans (one of the Germans had also trained for nursing lepers at Allentown, Pennsylvania). Black and white nuns live separately. I arrived with a Manus

teacher, who was taken to the ward to sleep with other visitors.

Father Jacubco and many here are from Langsford, Pennsylvania, where there is a Missionary of the Sacred Heart convent. Sister Mildred at Lemakot, also Sister Regine at Lavongai. Sister Regine and Father "Jake" are Slovaks, he tells me, and so is Sister Jesofa, the American nun here. There are also Poles and Irish Catholics in Langsford, he said.

I ate separately. Talked to the nuns at "recreation," 7:40 to 8:30. They were tired. I think I kept them up. I slept in a room in the European nuns' quarters. My orange cat ran away when I took her outside and she saw other people, and she didn't come back.

I had become attached to the cat, and her presence kept away rats, a not inconsiderable service from the point of view of the local people as well as, of course, from mine. The next morning, when it was time to leave and the orange cat hadn't come back, the sisters promised to watch for her for me, but thought she had probably been eaten by the Manus patients. One of the local sisters suddenly popped a black and white kitten into my pocket. Father Miller often said, later, that when I showed up at Lavongai at 8:00 P.M. on Thursday evening, February 9, with a kitten in my pocket, he groaned inwardly and thought: "Oh, no, what has the Bishop sent me this time?" He kept all his misgivings well hidden, however, and I was warmly welcomed by Father Miller of Toledo, Ohio; Sister M. Regine of Langsford, Pennsylvania; and Sister M. Liboria of Australia. When I left Sirapi, my close friend in Mangai, I felt like I was leaving home; but at Lavongai Catholic Mission, and later in Lavongai village, I soon felt I had found another one.

Settling In

On Friday morning, February 10, Silakau, the Lavongai village councillor and an active church member, came and got me and my gear in a small boat to take me across the river to the large thatch government rest house, which was near his in the village. The children were anxious to help, to carry, to touch, to tell me things, and then to sing—completely different from the shy children of Mangai. After about half an hour with most of the village on my packed verandah, Silakau said that maybe I wanted to be alone and everyone should leave. They did. Again, something completely different from Mangai. I did not know what was going to happen, but I knew it was going to be different.

Getting to Know New Hanover

Early Interviews

I did not do any systematic interviewing about the Johnson cult or T.I.A.,

"Father Miller's cult," until late July. By then, I had a fairly full idea of the traditional culture of New Hanover, and I and my work had become known, not only to the Lavongai village people but to people from other villages. They had visited Lavongai, I had been to their villages, and we met at meetings: council meetings in Taskul and a T.I.A. meeting July 12 and 13 at Lavongai. I had been away and come back several times, something which I felt somehow made me more a part of the furniture—I wasn't just a one-shot deal.

Silakau

At first, I remained in Lavongai village, mapping and doing genealogies and going along to the bush and doing what anthropologists do anywhere. A few days after my arrival, Silakau, who was from the beginning my best friend and informant, told me the story of the vote for Johnson at Ranmelek, and of his part in it.

Everyone from Lavongai village had voted on Saturday morning, February 14, 1964 at the Methodist mission station, Ranmelek, which was the first polling place. It took all day for Silakau and others to walk there, and they arrived Friday evening. On the way, they passed through the neighboring village, Magam, and found there a meeting where people were saying that they were going to vote for the president of America. Silakau heard this talk, but did not know what to think about it. He was tired, and went on to find a place to sleep and something to eat.

Next morning, Silakau went to the sea to wash the sleep out of his eyes, and then went to stand in front of the missionary's house, where the *kiaps* had spent the night. A great crowd had gathered.

It was from Silakau that I first learned that those who voted for Johnson had done so by setting up a blackboard on which their choice was written, rather than by dropping a marked ballot into the red plastic ballot box which patrol officers brought with them for the election. When the *kiaps* ignored the board, the people shouted a voice vote and ran away into the jungle. Thus, Johnson cultists became known as those who "voted on the board," as distinguished from those who "voted in the (red plastic ballot) box." Silakau said that only he and the missionary and his wife had "voted in the box". He did so because he saw the *kiap's* head go down, his face red with shame, and Silakau felt sorry for him. He did not remember whose name he marked on his ballot.

From there the government patrol had moved west around the south coast, back east around the north coast, and finally out into the Tigak Islands, stopping at eight polling places altogether. The vote was split, Silakau told me, with most of the south coast voting on the board for Johnson and most of the north coast voting in the box. But Silakau was unclear about what had happened and what people thought where he was not present, less clear especially about the more distant polling stations.

Pengai

The only other person who talked to me about the cult in the early days of my residency in New Hanover was Pengai. He gave me my first, and one of my most important, interviews about the Johnson cult. I had been in Lavongai village not quite three weeks when, on Thursday morning, March 2, 1967, my neighbor, Joseph Pukina, came lumbering up my veranda ladder steps at 9:00 A.M. with his friend, Pengai, of Nusawung village. Joseph was, as usual, confident, but Pengai seemed a little nervous. He said he had come to see Father Miller, to show him a notebook he had written—about the election for Johnson.

Conversation was at first somewhat strained, for several reasons. In the first place, I thought the man had come to see Father Miller, not me, and that Joseph had just stopped by to introduce his friend to the odd, new white lady and perhaps to pick up a smoke. I thought perhaps they were staying while they smoked only to be polite, and I didn't want to hold them against their wills. Furthermore, Father Miller was very interested in talking to cultists, and I did not want to divert to my own purposes an informant whom Father Miller had "earned" for himself. I felt an enormous obligation to the mission not to interfere in any way with its operation while I was resting so heavily on the labors, present and historical, of its personnel. In addition, Mr. Brightwell had asked me not to discuss the cult at first; and while I had not obligated myself absolutely to his plan, I felt some respect for his opinion.

Despite these barriers, Pengai and I began to talk. It soon became clear that his talk would flow forth freely and that the use of my tape recorder would facilitate our conversation. Joseph and his wife stayed with us for some time, perhaps until shortly after noon, when my friends Silakau and his wife, Ngurvarilam, called me to their house to eat. Later, Silakau brought Pengai something to eat, too, during our "lunch break," which lasted for about an hour. We then resumed our interview until about 3:00 P.M., when I felt that our talk had dwindled. When my second tape ran out, I did not move to replace it. I walked with Pengai down the beach as far as the river, which he had to cross on a bamboo raft to go to the mission. We stood and talked another fifteen minutes. I still thought he was going to see Father Miller, but he then said that he would not do so, as Father might shame him. I assured him that Father Miller would not do that, and that he would be glad to see him. However, according to Father Miller, Pengai did not come to see him that day. It seems quite likely, then, that Pengai had heard of my work and had come to Lavongai to see me.

In this interview with Pengai, I heard many things that I would hear again from other cultists about what they thought the cult was about. Pengai was the first to tell me the justification for their vote that I was to hear many times from many people later: that the Australian government had brought them projects that were meant to help them develop ways to make money, but that all had failed. "Nothing had come up," as people often said, from the Cooperative Society, from planting coffee, from the local government councils. Big promises had been made for these, but these were "lies, that's all." People wanted a new way of life, not just material goods; and they did not have confidence in any local people, black or white, to teach them what they needed to know. They had merely hoped, not sought to prove, that Johnson of America would come and be able to help New Hanover. Pengai also was the first to tell me that many people, led by Peter Yangalissmat, had wanted America to come after the war; but when Peter Yangalissmat was jailed for speaking out about this idea, other people were afraid to express their true thoughts.

I did not see Pengai often, as he lived in Nusawung, the major Seventh-Day Adventist (SDA) village in New Hanover, near Ranmelek. The accounts of several people suggest that the Australian SDA missionaries in Nusawung had been very concerned about injustice against the local people. This factor may have had some impact in making Nusawung the place where the vote for Johnson was initiated. However, I was not able to closely assess the differences between parishioners who were "Seven Days," and the Methodists or Catholics, except that those who followed the SDA rules had clean white teeth because they neither smoked nor chewed betel nut.

The notes I made that day describe Pengai as I continued to see him in 1967, and during my subsequent periods of field research: "He is a dramatic speaker, with an almost over-polite but also quite sweet smile. He raises his eyebrows, smiles warmly, very polite, like Joseph—but Joseph gives an impression of hidden anger and POWER, whereas this man [Pengai] is sweet."

In 1967 I noticed a "facial twitch on Pengai, all the time—nose, cheek, eye—just slight, continual tingling, not sharp twitches. I thought maybe he was just nervous, but it reduced little if at all." I do not remember whether or not he still had it in 1974, when I spent some time with him but not in close face-to-face interviews. He had spent years at Analaua Leprosy Hospital with leprosy, and the facial trembling, like the weakness in his hands, may have been related to that illness.

I soon found that Pengai's loquaciousness was typical of New Hanover. I subsequently taped all my substantial interviews in New Hanover, whereas in New Ireland I had taped only singing and ceremony, and no interviews: there, verbal statements are brief and without elaboration.

Early Travels

Transport, Meetings, and the Mumps

On Wednesday, March 15, I left Lavongai to go to Taskul for a council meeting on the government ship *Mercy*, intending to return the next day. The *Mercy* had big, deep insides with no windows, and one look down into it was enough to convince me that I should stay on top, even though I had been feeling like I was getting sick and the gray skies started to drop a cold, sharp rain on us; and my raincoat was inaccessible somewhere in the depths. It soon became evident that I was getting the "children's ear disease," i.e., mumps, which my local friends quickly diagnosed. There was circumstantial evidence: lots of children had it at the time, I had never had it, and Mrs. Pat Murray, my neighbor in Mangai, had a severe case.

So I went on from Taskul to the hospital in Kavieng, where they did not want me because mumps are contagious. I was finally allowed to stay when I - made clear that I had nowhere else to go. The European doctor, in any case, thought, or said he thought, I had some kind of infection and gave me penicillin in the early stages of the disease. My Mangai friends came after a week to bring me food and to take me home to Mangai, where they gave me all sorts of attention, hot towels, leaves that make sore skin itch, and the clear certainty that it was mumps because my eyes were pink.

I was glad to be back with my Mangai friends during this ordeal. I already felt sure that tender loving care for the sick was not a Lavongai talent. I returned to Taskul on March 30, spent some time copying files, visited the Ranmelek Methodist mission, and, finally, with great difficulty, got back to Lavongai.

Getting to Know "Kiaps" (Government Officers)

The story of how I got back home hints at D.D.A. subculture, which was, in my view, accurately perceived by the people of New Hanover. The people often said that the Australian government did not want to help them. This often seemed true to me; but what surprised them was that the Australian government did not want to help me either, even though I was white. We gradually worked out together that D.D.A. did not want to help government service officers either; but it took me quite a long time to realize that D.D.A. officials wanted perhaps even less to help each other. Their attitudes toward each other were largely punitive, due perhaps to their high expectations of each other, or high suspicion of each other, or both. Their unwillingness to help is probably partly cultural, the other side of a well-known Anglo-Saxon coin: self-reliance. I will illustrate the evidence for this generalization later, but here I will just tell the pieces that fit with the story of my solutions to the practical problems of field work, most especially the logistical ones.

Mr. Seale had told me that if I cooperated, that is, if I went to Lavongai village rather than somewhere else, I could ride on the government trawler and be helped in other ways with transportation when the government was going my way. It was clear from the beginning, however, that making use of this offer would not be easy. During our January 10th interview, for instance, when I mentioned that Patrol Officer Neil Watts of Konos had said that I could ride along the next time he went to Tabar, Mr. Seale said that I could not and that I should ask him (which I had, in general, many times) when I wanted to go to Tabar. Of Mr. Watts, he said: "He'll have to learn he's not boss of the ship." Mr. Seale had already heard of five going on it, he said, and there would not be room for me.

Regardless of what Mr. Seale said, no one could possibly have gone on the government trawler without the permission of Captain Bill Busch. I first met him on March 17, the day I hitched a ride with him to Kavieng because I was getting the mumps. On that occasion, I had not yet introduced myself when I walked across the trawler to wave goodbye to Steven, the president of the council, who had nearly missed the departure of the *Mercy* for having stopped to talk to me. Captain Busch shouted at me: "Who gave you permission to come on my boat with dirty feet?" (I hadn't made any noticeable mark on his boat, but it is true that Taskul is noted for its clinging, impossible, red clay which, according to some European residents, redeems itself by inexplicably curing tropical ulcers.) One was never sure how much humor Captain Busch intended, but one did not press to find out. I managed to make friends sufficiently during my voyage to be allowed to ride back to Taskul, cured of mumps, on Thursday, March 30, when the trawler was making a trip with the doctor. Captain Busch told me then that he would be going all the way to Lavongai and beyond the following Tuesday and that I could ride along if I had not found a "road" (as pidgin English calls any means of transportation) yet.

Carroll Gannon always kindly let me stay at his house when I was in Taskul. While I waited for a "road" back to Lavongai, I asked A.D.O. Bob Hoad for permission to copy, from files in his office, the minutes of council meetings. I asked only to see accounts of the type which one would think were "public," because the meetings themselves were. He said that would be all right. When I went to his office, however, on Friday, March 31, and reminded Bob that I would like to see the council minutes, he gave me only those for the current year, 1966-67. I then asked Patrol Officer Ian MacDonald, who was advisor to the council, if I could see the files containing minutes of council meetings before the current year. He said he did not know if there were any minutes for council meetings before 1964. He did not know if they kept them, or where they were. He offered parenthetically that there was a big box of something thrown out. He shouted "I don't know" to terminate the conversation, and he and Bob left.

On Saturday, April 1, Ian invited me along to have a beer at his house. (I later realized that this was an enormous achievement.) While I was there, Bob came to the door. The government ship *Mercy* had come in with an education inspector and a bank man and two others, and Bob had nothing to feed them. Did Ian have anything? Two packages of sausages, Ian responded, and some steak. Bob wanted a barbecue, he said, in response to my saying, trying to be helpful, why didn't he open a tin. Then he volunteered that he was up at Ian's hiding. Ian said they were known as one of the two most inhospitable stations in the district, the other being Namatanai, where they all went bush if anyone came. He talked about what a mess the place of one of the *kiap's* was. Bob invited me to eat with them, adding, "but don't expect much." I said I'd better go down to Mrs. Gannon (Carroll's old mum, who was visiting), who was expecting me. I said I knew why I was here, but I could not understand what kept them in this life. "Money!" they said, laughing.

It is not that being hospitable to their mates would have cost them any money. The government issues its employees warrants in generous fixed amounts that they are to give for reimbursement to any station, government official, or private citizen, where they receive bed and board. The *kiaps* could make money on this, as on any expense account, and apparently did. But I heard many planters complain that they gave their hospitality freely, that the *kiaps* did not like to give them their warrants because the *kiaps* were supposed to be sleeping in the villages instead of boozing it up on planters' grog supply; and what really made them angry was that "in ten years, not one *kiap* has ever bought me one drink or had me in his house in town." I bring up these incidents to show that I am talking about *kiap* subculture, both from their point of view and from that of outsiders, to answer questions which should arise as to whether or not the behavior described was related particularly to me (or to an anthropologist). I think it was not.

On Sunday, April 2, Rev. Allen Taylor came to preach at Taskul, and I went back on the *Daula* with him to Ranmelek, hoping to get a ride on to Lavongai. However, no one went by. Monday, on the regular government "sched," i.e., the scheduled radio conversation that takes place every morning among various stations, the Reverend Taylor heard part of a message for me from Captain Bill Busch. As it was the government "sched," not the Methodist "sched," he heard it only by accident and not clearly. He said I could ride back to Taskul with him the next morning on his way around the island. As the next day, Tuesday, was the day Captain Busch had originally told me he would be going my way, I presumed that I would be in time. And as the government trawler, I presumed, usually stopped at Taskul, I thought for once I would be in the right place at the right time.

I got back to Taskul in a pouring and cold rain. Carroll was in Kavieng, and I went right to the government office to find out what my message had been from Bill Busch. The officers, Bob Hoad and Ian MacDonald, were apparently busy. I knocked, and they asked me to wait outside (there being only one room to the office) in the rain for about fifteen minutes. It was on this occasion that it occurred to me that these two, had they been tramping through the jungle for a year looking for elephants and happened to run into Dr. Livingston, would not have spoken until he was out of earshot, when one of them might have said to the other, "That must have been Dr. Livingston." After I mulled this over for a while, however, I realized that this was not a fair analysis. They would never have mentioned it at all, to each other or to anyone else. Each just to himself might have thought: "Bloody Livingston must still be here mucking about." I must stress, however, that this scenario is hypothetical, and hypothesized by me while waiting in the rain. I also remembered a line from a poem by Ogden Nash which had once become famous among a little band of Americans I knew in New Zealand.

> Of defining Anglo-Saxon reserve I despair,
> But I think it consists in assuming that
> nobody else is there.[9]

Additional evidence for the role of "reserve" or self-containment in this behavior lies in the fact that the Australian *kiaps* who had planned the Taskul station, predecessors to those resident in 1967, had deliberately had their two houses built twenty minutes' walk from each other and from the medical assistant's house, though these three were the only Europeans living at Taskul. Furthermore, the *kiaps* from D.D.A. sometimes went a week without seeing Carroll, each preferring his own company.

By the time I was allowed in, I was not in a good mood to hear Ian MacDonald tell me he did not know exactly what the radio message for me was, just something about meeting Bill Busch at Lungatan (Jim White's plantation, near Ranmelek, from which I had just come). Since Taskul was along the way between Kavieng, where the trawler would start, and Lungatan; and since the message was not clear, I said, "Oh—well, I'll wait here then," to which Ian MacDonald responded with, "He wouldn't have told you to go to Lungatan if he were coming here." I then said some angry things about his not making clear to me whether or not he knew what the message was, and stamped out. Bob Hoad called me back. Ian then said, "Do you want to talk to Bill Busch, or what?" I said, "I don't know the system; can he be talked to?" Ian responded with the only thing he ever said that I thought was amusing and which hinted at redeeming possibilities: "Some people have managed." He then said there was radio contact time at 12:05, and I said, "Can you try that?" and he said, "You probably won't get anything, but you can try." I, of course, could try nothing without help from these two, as radio contact was achieved through some complicated manipulation of a large piece of equipment.

However, contact was made with Bill Busch, and he did want me to meet him at Lungatan, as he was not going to stop at Taskul. Ian and Bob both heard this. I asked them if they could direct me to some local who might be able to help me find a canoe to go back around to Lungatan (which would take two to three hours of paddling). No, they didn't know anyone. Could they just tell me one name of one person that I might start with? No, sorry, they didn't know any. Why didn't I ask Carroll to help me? Bob said. I told him that, of course, I would ask Carroll, but he and his mother had gone to town.

This was the only time the *kiaps* nearly reduced me to tears. I trudged down the hill in the rain toward Carroll's locked, empty house, and as I came near the little house of Sering, a fine old gentleman who was Carroll's "boss boy," I decided to throw myself on his mercy. I told him my story, and within minutes he had lined up two canoes, one for me and one for my "cargo," as all white man's goods are called.

Sering's friends brought me on a lovely canoe trip over protected waters to join the government trawler, where Captain Busch and I had a most civilized dinner and discussion. I learned more from him than from anyone else about the Americans who had been there making maps, because Captain Busch had helped to steer the ship on which the Americans came, and to which they returned after work every night, guiding them around and through the reef.

It was very difficult to find out much about the Americans on Mt. Patibung. The planters had scarcely seen or talked to them in Kavieng. They had not spent any time in the villages, nor socialized with any of the government officers, so far as I could gather. Captain Busch told me that the reason there was little general knowledge floating around European conversations in town about who the Americans were, or what they were doing, was that the Americans had generally remained on their ship out at sea. He said that there were some "American Negroes" among those who went ashore on New Hanover, but Captain Busch thought that they were generally left behind on the ship and not often seen. This would explain why nearly all Europeans and natives were unclear on this point. None of the Americans could speak pidgin, he said, a circumstance sometimes also cited to me by Lavongai informants to explain why they knew little about the visiting Americans.

Captain Busch had spent years in the territory and had many interesting stories to tell. He did not take *kiaps* on the government trawler, even if they wanted to go on patrol. Mert Brightwell had said not to. They get £1 5s. a day traveling expenses, and he did not want them to get away with that (as they would have had no expenses on the trawler). "They think only of money," he said. This was the bit of information that made me realize that the government did not want to help anyone, even its own.

To Tsoi and Oliver, Finally

I was glad to get back to Lavongai on Wednesday, April 5, but I had only a short stay, as I had to get back to Mangai for an important *malanggan,* for Sirapi's husband. I left Lavongai on April 17, when I went into town with Father Miller on the *Joseph,* which took six to seven hours; during which Father Miller hid under a big black umbrella, trying not to get sunstruck. I returned on Friday, May 19, when I hitched a ride back with "Master Fish," Keith Hill. He was coming straight to Lavongai village to continue his efforts to teach the people large-scale fishing techniques with the red government nets he had lent to them.

I finally had my second long interview with a cultist, one which I had to seek out, on June 17, 1967. Keith Hill took me along to Unusa, in the Tsoi Islands, where he was checking up on the net he had left, on its repair and on the results the people had achieved with it. From Unusa I could easily walk over to the small island of Mamion, where Oliver lived. In 1965, I always heard the name of Oliver linked with Robin and Samuel as cult leaders, but by June 1967, when I arrived at Mamion, Oliver's name was the only one still regularly mentioned. Robin was not active, and Samuel had moved to Rabaul to work in a store.

Keith Hill and I walked to Mamion after we arrived in the late afternoon of June 16, 1967. We were accompanied by Oliver's teenage son, David, who had been working for several weeks for Keith as his "boat boy," i.e., he operated the speedboat that took Keith on his rounds. David brought us to his father, and I arranged to come back the next day to talk to him. Oliver had heard of me and my work, and his son had had a chance to get to know me over several days in Kavieng while Keith was preparing to set out. Still, I was sleeping over in Unusa in the new corrugated iron house built by the council and under the supervision of Edward, a "loyalist" in government eyes, but, from Oliver's point of view, "the enemy." However, Edward and Oliver had, at least superficially, reconciled, and Oliver came over and sat and talked informally with us, along with his son, in the evening before our interview. Edward was also present. They each told me that they wanted now to work together.[10]

On June 17, I went to Mamion, and Oliver and I had an excellent talk. Oliver was the only person I interviewed who was apprehensive about my use of the tape recorder, so I took notes for about two hours, then asked him if I could turn on the tape recorder while we ate the meal his wife served us. I left it on for about an hour but went on taking written notes, mostly to emphasize for Oliver that the tape recorder was just an aid to me for note-taking. Father Miller had taped several conversations with Oliver, with his permission. I was so pleased with the tape I must have felt that it would glow in the dark, because I failed to mark it right away; and a few days later I erased it, thinking it was empty, while recording a talk with Joseph Pukina. I went back August 3, and Oliver and I made another tape that repeated most of what I needed to know, and I had my written notes. But I did not get again quite the same discourse I had lost on the subject of "belief."

In that interview on June 17, 1967, after having talked to Oliver for over two hours, I finally asked him if he ever really believed that Johnson would come. He reflected for a moment before he answered. Then he said, "I must believe. If I do not believe, I sit down and do nothing." It was at this time that I first understood that by "belief" he meant "faith," faith which gave hope and commitment. We discussed the term *"belip"* in pidgin, and, when he saw what the ambiguity was, he made himself amply clear, both in June and again in August. In these crucially important interviews, Oliver showed me his sophisticated understanding of the power of belief to overcome apathy, and his own attempt to come to terms with epistemological problems.

While I was in Unusa, I had several conversations of substance with Edward, but I did not tape one until we met again at Carroll Gannon's house in Taskul.

A Big House—For Cargo?

I made one more small foray into the bush before I began my systematic interviewing of the electorate about the vote for Johnson. Several Europeans, both government officials and missionaries, had mentioned the village of Bolpua as a hard-core area of cult. The Big Man in that area was a man called Pilikos. It was one place where men met after the vote for Johnson, and it was near Mt. Patibung, where the American map makers had done whatever it was they did. Bolpua was not on the coast, but back aways into the bush, up a river from the coastal villages of Meterankan. It was not easy for Europeans to stop by for a visit, and it remained more isolated from European visitors than coastal villages.

On Friday, June 30, Sister M. Liboria, the nurse at the Lavongai Catholic Mission Station, went "on rounds," as they say, to do infant welfare work near Bolpua, and I rode along. Tolimbe, one of my good friends among the young men in Lavongai village, drove the little speedboat, *Joseph*, and agreed to walk with me to Bolpua to show me the way, while we left Sister Liboria to do her work in Meterankan. We walked for thirty to forty-five minutes to get to the village. Someone was sent to get Pilikos. He came after another half an hour. There was a lot of silence and no easy talk. I asked about traditional culture, the land in relation to T.I.A., and told them I was here to learn about their culture (pidgin: *fasion*). They had heard of me, some had seen me. We left another half hour and walked back. My notes tell me that

> Sister Liboria said almost no Bolpua women came to Welfare today. They never do, but she says she thinks this isn't cult. They never did. The people say it's because they don't all live in the village but are living around and about in the bush. The village is long, stretched out on a flat top of a hill. Big, nice houses, nice breeze, a woman hurriedly finishing sweeping as I came up. Many coconuts. The kids don't go to school, Sister Liboria said. Very few come, to school or to Infant Welfare, but government figures showed this as the largest population of any village of the area: 246, or some such.

What my notes do not record is a big, new house that I remember and that I commented on. It was just a roof, no walls, the kind of house people build for communal purposes, for cooking or meeting, but not for sleeping, as it would not protect from cool night winds. I remembered this house when, a month or so later, I heard that a big, new house had been built in Bolpua for secret meetings among cultists. Or was it a warehouse for the cargo that the Americans would bring? I heard these remarks from Europeans, but not from other local people, who were puzzled about European interest in this common structure. Bosap later explained its innocuous purpose to me: it had been built to house a farewell party for the Americans who had worked on Mt. Patibung. Perhaps a big farewell party is not something *kiaps* could easily understand.

The Anthropologist's "Rounds" to the East

Time was running out, and I was convinced that my presence was not going to be a threat to law and order. It was time for me to mount some sort of systematic interviewing about the vote for Johnson. The missionaries and government people all went "on rounds": it was time for the anthropologist, too, to go "on rounds." Reverend Taylor had told me several names of men who lived near Ranmelek, and I would have to go and find them and really come to grips with what they thought; and I wanted to go to visit the surviving wife of Peter

Yangalissmat, of whom Pengai had told me, the man who had spoken of America twenty years before. She lived in Narimlawa, quite a walk, I was told, from Ranmelek. What bothered me, really, was not the walk but the showing up in remote villages, a strange white lady with no stamina and no immediately apprehendable purpose. I was therefore very happy when Nolis, a young friend of mine in Lavongai, agreed to accompany me. He could, at least, help to explain that I was harmless, if odd, if that became necessary.

Ranmelek and Environs: The First Polling Station

And so, on July 19, we set out for Ranmelek, and points beyond, to interview cultists. Father Miller sent us in the small speedboat, *Joseph*, to start the rounds of the anthropologist. I had assumed Nolis would know better than I did where places were and how to get there. This turned out to be an ethnocentric assumption, based on the general myth that native peoples all know each other, know all the paths, and know protocol. As it turned out, I always had to take the lead; he felt very shy, I think, but I appreciated his company anyway.

Makios
While I worked near Ranmelek, the Methodist missionaries kindly gave me hospitality. It was from there that Nolis and I set off, on Thursday, July 20, to Patekone, only a half-hour's walk, to find Makios. I had met him briefly in August 1966, when I went with the Methodists on their education inspection tour; and again more recently at a T.I.A. meeting in Lavongai village. There, on July 12, we had both attended a meeting of T.I.A. representatives, called *"bord,"* a derivation from Father Miller's idea that there be a "board" of representatives for T.I.A. So Makios knew who I was and knew something of what I was, and we had a full and enlightening conversation, most of it on tape.

Makios was a man of perhaps sixty or more years old who had been a leader of traditional events. He had decorated the bones of the dead for *maras*, a traditional men's event, more than once. Now, when many villages had turned to their young men for leadership, Makios was *bord* of T.I.A. for his area. He told me of the many failures of the past, of the cooperatives, the attempts to produce coffee, and now the council, that had led the people of New Hanover to seek the aid of America. I asked him all the questions that rumors had raised in my mind concerning cultists' beliefs: about the coming of cargo, the role of ancestors, contacts with Americans, and so on. These ideas, Makios told me, were spread by the enemy, i.e., Lavongais who opposed the cultists, and who wanted to make them look foolish by attributing to them beliefs which had been held, perhaps only lightly, by some of the ancestors who were trying to make sense out of the coming of the Europeans. These beliefs, Makios assured me, did not belong to today.

During this interview, Makios used the pidgin term *tok bilas*, which means "ridicule" or "mockery." I had never heard the term in New Ireland, and a review of my conversation with Makios indicates that I did not understand it when he first used it. I was to learn that it is the pidgin term for a concept of central importance in New Hanover.

Saripat

Following Makios' suggestion, I went to see Saripat, who was in the Ranmelek "hospital" so that he could drink the medicine for tuberculosis. He had been councillor for Magam, the village just beyond Patekone, and he was about Makios' age, i.e., in his sixties. I had not met Saripat before. He knew vaguely that I was around, and seemed content to come and sit on the grass with me, talking about things old and new for me and my tape recorder.

My interview with Saripat was a turning point, because he made me understand what I had not grasped at the time in my talk with Makios: that the idea that the Americans or the ancestors were going to bring cargo free was *tok bilas*, i.e., ridicule invented by the opposition, not beliefs urged by the cultists. I asked him solemnly about cargo and ancestors, and he answered solemnly for a while, then laughed and made clear that he was teasing me. Lavongais are great teasers, whereas Tikana are not, and I am not when I am doing serious anthropological business. But I became a tease in New Hanover in self-defense, and, fortunately, I knew something about teasing in New Hanover by the time I talked to Saripat.

Savemat

Saripat mentioned Savemat, whose name I had heard often before, especially from the Methodist missionaries. He was about the age of Makios and Saripat and had long been a trusted Methodist *munamuna*, i.e., local preacher. It was of some concern to the mission that he had joined the cultists. When Saripat suggested that we go to see him, I was delighted. Saripat could show me the way, and, having talked to me for a couple of hours, could quickly indicate to Savemat something about me. Moreover, it was sometimes easier to talk to two people than to one when I was a stranger, and I was a complete stranger to Savemat.

The three of us talked all afternoon, and I returned again for an hour after dinner. Most of those conversations are on tape, though Savemat spoke in a low voice, sometimes glancing at Saripat for reassurance that it was all right to say what he was saying. This interview gave me my best insight into what had really happened at Ranmelek on that great day when most people voted on the [black]board instead of in the [ballot] box, because Savemat actually wrote the vote for Johnson on the board. Savemat was perhaps more reluctant to speak to me than any other informant; perhaps because of his long, close association with the mission, where I was staying. He knew, however, as I did, that the missionaries were not entirely unsympathetic to the "Johnsonite" complaints.[11]

Bosap

On my way back to the mission that night, I had a brief talk with Bosap, the captain of the Methodist ship *Daula*, who was waiting for me. I realized that I would need to have a long, taped interview with him eventually, but I was out of tape and out of energy at that time.

Peter's Wife

The next day, Friday, July 21, Nolis and I started the hard, unknown part of our rounds. Reverend Taylor took us as far as Lungatan, Jim White's plantation, by boat, dropped us off, and then we were on our own to find our way to Narimlawa. We had no trouble as far as the adjacent village of Mataniu. Then we, or rather I, began asking how to get to Narimlawa, where Peter Yangalissmat's last wife still lived. Fortunately, we met two men from there along the road almost immediately, and so we did not get lost. This was part two of my awakening to group prejudice, which believes that people of the other group have great powers of stamina and endurance, which we, whoever we are, do not have. "Nolis made more of a fuss about the road than I did," my notes say. I thought a young, strong, local boy like Nolis would be able to ask directions and pick our way through the jungle, but he appeared to be more nervous than I was about being lost and about the social awkwardness of the situation. Maybe it was not an accident that two men who met us on the road and accompanied us were *bord* of T.I.A.; but, in any case, it was a great relief for us two greenhorns. One of them said that his brother had sent a letter saying that "Dorothy" was coming. So I knew, at least, that I was known.

My interview there with a group of men was not very satisfactory. They spoke a little bit with me, but mostly to each other in their local language. I later asked Nolis about it, and he agreed with me that they seemed apprehensive about talking to me, but he did not seem to understand why. However, he understood one important thing that I missed: one of "the enemy," Nolis told me, a man loyal to the Australian government, was present, and that may have been the main difficulty. Anyway, it was not all in vain when I met Peter Yangalissmat's last wife, who had a most beautiful, warm smile which displayed the clean, white teeth of the Seventh-Day Adventists (who do not chew betel nut or smoke). Peter, too, had been a Seven Days member, and some of the stories underscored a role for this mission in urging people to seek justice. Peter's wife did not have much to tell me, nothing really that I could not have learned from others, except that hearing it from her gave a kind of reliability to it. She also had a kind of genuine quality about her, or poise, which told me, along with her stories, something about her dead husband.

Some men from Narimlawa came most of the way back to Lungatan with Nolis and me in a cold, drenching rain. I did not mind the journey, as I felt that, to some small extent, the mission had been accomplished.

I stopped at Lungatan plantation to talk to Jim White, who also had known and admired Peter Yangalissmat, while Nolis went on back to Ranmelek. Mr. White, whose daughter Nic and I had met when she took anthropology at the

University of Sydney, was the first planter we met in 1965, at the Kavieng Club. He was among the planters whose wit never failed him when it came to lampooning anthropologists; but he, like all the planters, never failed to lend a helping hand, to me and to the missionaries. They expressed boundless appreciation for his services and contributions, about which few people knew. On this occasion, he lent me a shirt and, after a most interesting discussion, took me back to Ranmelek in his speedboat.

Bate

The next day (July 22), Bate, whom I had met the previous October, and who had worked for Jim White for years, walked down to Ranmelek so that I could talk to him there. We sat on a log near the sea and recorded our conversation on tape. Bate gave me a clear view which confirmed that of Makios, Saripat, and Savemat: the cult was about Australia's failure to develop New Hanover, not about free cargo from America or ancestors. He was about the age of these other cultists, and remembered working for the Germans. Makios sat near us, but out of earshot, ready to go with me on two canoes, for which he had successfully arranged, to see Silikan of Enang Island.

Silikan

Silikan was a Methodist preacher, like Savemat, and also a man whose name I had heard a lot from the mission in connection with Methodism and with the cult. Silikan was also a *bord* for T.I.A. Still conscious of my obligation not to start trouble, I always asked to talk to people who were *bord* for T.I.A., and always started my questions with T.I.A. and followed through when the subject of the election came up, as it always did. I always asked about traditional culture, too, partly because I wanted to know about it and partly because I wanted to know how much the cultists knew about it, whatever "it" was.

Silikan was a bright man, perhaps in his early forties—about Oliver's age. He knew of me, but my coming with Makios greatly facilitated our discussion, which took place in front of Makios and a few others, one of whom, Su, occasionally added a comment. I recorded most of the discussion on tape. This interview gave me two memorable incidents: one in which Silikan symbolized the kind of development, or savvy, they wanted by holding up a metal teapot and saying, "I want to know how to make this teapot." The second memorable incident occurred after the recording was over. Silikan asked me about various ways of getting America to come to help New Hanover, ways that startled me because they made sense and were possible in terms of the world as I knew it.

Islands Culture

I talked some more with Makios while food was prepared for us. I already had some feeling that the ambience of the islands was more like New Ireland than like New Hanover, and the preparation of food for me (which almost never happened in New Hanover, or, if it did happen, was "special," not just part of the routine), prompted me to ask about the kinship system here. It used Tigak language kinship terms, identical to those used in Mangai. There was a gentleness, no crying babies, much silence, and slow movement. Other characteristic similarities with New Ireland were confirmed later by the observations of others, Reverend Taylor in particular. Yet the islands did not have *malanggan*, and they did not have Big Men who sponsored them. Still, emotionally, I think their involvement with the Johnson cult was less lasting and differently motivated than that of the New Hanover people.

Taskul and Environs

On Sunday, July 2, I went back to Enang for church services and to take some pictures to send back to the people. My notes say,

> Nolis didn't come. He has a headache. He *pull*ed (i.e., paddled the canoe) some yesterday. Today's lot are really working, but they sent four instead of two.

There was so much opportunity for misunderstanding. I was not able to make sure that Nolis was adequately housed and fed, after all.

I attended the church service at Enang, shook a few hands, and went on by canoe to Taskul, a journey of about a two-and-a-half hours. It was a lovely, smooth ride, during which I wrote notes in my little notebook, but toward the end of which I began to feel feverish; and when I got to Taskul my temperature was 101 degrees, apparently a slight "sunstroke" due to spending too much time hatless in the sun. Now I understood why Father Miller regularly hid under his big black umbrella in the *Joseph*. I recovered in a couple of hours and began my Taskul rounds.

Karol (Carroll Gannon)

In Taskul I had a chance to get two long, recorded interviews with Carroll Gannon. Carroll, bless him, never let me have a moment's peace. He told everyone who the "*missus*" (white woman) was, that they should say "'Good morning' to the *missus*," that they should come and talk to me; and he told me in their presence what side each of them was on in the cult, how they had changed over time, who they were related to, and why they were in jail, or the hospital, or trouble.

When people came to see him, as they did in large numbers, he told them I wanted to talk to them, who I was, that I wanted their stories for a book and would not get them into trouble. On Monday, July 24, I had two long interviews with noncultists: Benson, who was young and did not know me; and Edward, who was old and already my friend from Unusa.

Hoad's Report

On Tuesday, July 25, Bob Hoad kindly allowed me to copy a report he had written which briefly outlined the events of the Johnson cult from the administration point of view. This document is a great help to the European mind, used to hanging things on properly spaced time hooks. There had been three years of jailing men for nonpayment of taxes. There had been turnover in personnel. There had been several meetings with officials, sometimes from Kavieng, sometimes from America, sometimes from the United Nations, sometimes with a few from each category. Some meetings were at Taskul, some at Meterankan, some at Lavongai. From what people told me I was able to locate each event with one described in Bob's report, which had dates attached. I felt then that I had uncovered most of the major meetings, confrontations, and so on, that composed, in the minds of the people as well as in the minds of the administration, the Johnson cult.

Lapantukan

On July 25, I had an interview, arranged by Carroll in his house, with Lapantukan of Kulingei village. Several things about this interview made it distinctive and important. Lapantukan told several stories of his confrontations with the *kiaps* in which he successfully asserted rights that he felt he had and that, when pressed, the *kiaps* had to grant him. He was an intense informant; and, although he often said that he had not been afraid, it was clear that it had taken staunchness in the cause to risk the ridicule to which he had been subjected, and to still feel right about it. Groups of men in jail together could reassure each other and reconfirm each other, but many of the men did have moments when they had to stand alone early in the cult when they were not sure themselves exactly what was going on—as I suppose nobody ever really was or is.

It may be that Lapantukan had especially what we might call "the courage of his convictions," or it may be that he had stronger, or different, convictions than did some of the others. He was the only one to tell me that he thought it was possible that cargo was made by the ancestors. One or two others were noncommittal, but most clearly denied it. This particular aspect of Lapantukan's interview is noteworthy only from the point of view of Europeans (who have found cargo beliefs important elsewhere) because this belief was not stressed by Lapantukan in any way and was not part of his thinking in relation to events of the past, nor part of his program for the future. It was just something that lay there, unresolved but unused, in his mind. After the interview with Lapantukan, I began to think that even if some people had heard of this belief about cargo and ancestors, it was in no way central to the cult. To pursue it would have involved me in the spread of rumors not part of current conversation.

Homosexuality

During the evening of July 25, Carroll capped his services to anthropology and the anthropologist by inviting to dinner a young man who, Carroll said, knew about and would tell me about homosexuality in New Hanover. Carroll himself acted as *"manki masta,"* i.e., cook and house servant for the occasion, preparing the food and serving it to me and Pasingan[12] in the living room; while Carroll himself ate in the kitchen so that our interview could be private, as well as smoothly organized. He, of course, also told Pasingan something about me and my work and what I needed to know about before we met, so that my informant was ready and willing as well as able when he arrived. This was a crucial interview not just from the point of view of obtaining a full description of the culture and getting a good interview on a difficult subject, but also because of what I learned about Lavongai cultural character in relation to the cult. Briefly, the homosexual encounter was usually pederasty initiated by older men with young boys, who might be unwilling participants. As men grew older, they no longer submitted to pederasty, but some continued to initiate it. A respected Big Man was especially able to initiate encounters with whomever he wished. Such men are feared but not respected. The act manifests the kind of dominance-submission relationships which characterize this culture, in spite of a vehement demand for egalitarianism. Far more importantly, this information focused for me what I had only vaguely apprehended: there is no respected Big Man and never has been in New Hanover. To find a "hero," someone you can respect, someone who will help you and not take advantage of your weakness, you might turn to a dead father, or perhaps even to the president of America.

Oliver Again

On July 26 and 27 I had some more systematic interviews with Carroll, during which he told me more about some of the events of the cult and the people and their personalities. I went into Kavieng for supplies and from there got a ride back on August 1 to Taskul and on over to Mamion, where Oliver lived, with Labor Inspector Dennis Shepard. There I talked again with Edward, of Unusa, and I taped a second interview, on Thursday, August 3, with Oliver. I stayed in the big house of corrugated iron, which I could have to myself and which was just next to the house of Edward, the loyalist. Oliver wanted me to come and stay with his family. I felt that I should, even though I could think of lots of excuses, e.g., Oliver was trying to dominate me and "capture" me away from the enemy. All anthropologists have lines drawn around themselves beyond which they do not allow the invasion of their person, even though it may cost their anthropology something. This was a case where I drew a line simply because I was personally more comfortable back in the house by myself. But I felt guilty that I was not willing or able to be a little more easy about this. I tried to comfort myself with the thought that Oliver's being of opposite sex complicated matters, which it did, and that if my major informant had been a woman I might have gone over there to sleep at whatever cost to my physical comfort. It was the social discomfort, not the physical, which determined my decision.

On August 3, when I had my second interview with Oliver, I also interviewed his brother, Anania, who had been in the cult but who was then working with the government and the council. No one seemed angry with him for it. There seemed to be a notion that someone had to make the liaison, reflecting, I think, a tendency to conciliate, rather than to fractionalize, that distinguished New Ireland and the islands from New Hanover.

Robin

I also met Robin and talked with him. I had never seen him before, nor did I ever again. Long before I went to New Hanover I heard of Oliver and Robin, always the two together, and always in that order. Further questioning could produce stories about Oliver, but nothing about Robin, who seemed finally to fade out of the picture. I met him walking along the beach while Oliver and I were walking back from Anania's house toward the canoe which was to take me back to Edward's. Robin and I began to talk, went to stand, then sit, under a little roof in the shade, and finally talked for about an hour. Oliver, meanwhile, had gone on ahead, carrying my tape recorder. Robin's voice was very soft and would not have recorded, I think, anyway. He seemed very anxious and seemed to have the "asthma" that Carroll Gannon found to be relatively common in New Hanover. Robin was more interested than most in what might be called the supernatural aspect of things, phrased in Christian terms.

Farewell to Oliver

I left Robin and caught up with Oliver and Anania on down the beach. Oliver walked back to Unusa with me. He brought along his dog, called "Whiteskin," because it had white paws. He patted the dog several times. He seemed sad. He asked me several times to write to him from America. When we last shook hands, he said, "Dorothy, you can't forget me when you go back to America!" I told him that certainly I would not. And as I walked away he shouted after me, "Don't forget me!"

Certainly I have not.

More About *Kiaps*

When Labor Inspector Dennis Shepard and I arrived in Taskul from Unusa on Friday, August 4, he visited a while at Carroll's but went up the hill to stay at Ian MacDonald's. The next day he came down to join us at Carroll's house. He said he was so angry at the lack of hospitality from D.D.A. at Taskul that the next time he had to come this way he would go around to Lungatan to stay with planter Jim White. He said he had been to many outstations, was a planter in Papua and a labor inspector in the Sepik, and he had never been inhospitably received before.

He must have been lucky, or perhaps he was trying to hold out for the "everyone is good at heart" theory. The night before, he had been trying to politely say that Ian was just young, but breakfast had apparently pushed him too far. He said that Carroll had sent up six eggs to help provide food for Dennis, and Dennis got one egg for breakfast. I asked how much bread he had brought from town, and he said two loaves. And how much had he got for breakfast? One-half piece of toast, with a dab of tinned mincemeat on top. He'd had to bring his own sheets and pillow. He wouldn't have known to do this, but others had told him. Dennis deducted everything he could from the government warrant, but he had to pay Ian $15.50. He said he'd never stay there again. Ian didn't even speak to him—he had four or five bottles of beer, the radio blasting from the time he came in, and read a book. Dennis just turned in at 9:00 P.M.

Mr. Shepard was incredulous when I told him that this patrol post did not sell stamps or cash checks—well, not willingly. I had thought Ian was going to refuse to send my radiogram to Kavieng because I did not have any stamps, but he merely informed me that it "really is a bit of a nuisance to us," that they have to put the money in an envelope and send it to town for stamps. When I first asked him to send the radiogram, he had thought I was asking him to send my message to Mr. Seale on government time. He had answered, "It's not my job." I blew up and said he had misinterpreted my request that he send a radiogram, that I would, of course, pay for it: "Don't worry, you don't have to help anyone for nothing, you don't have to put a toe over the mark." Ian had retorted, "It's easy to see why Mert Brightwell wouldn't help you." I was able to say, then, that Mr. Brightwell was helping me, that he had let me see some letters that had come to him from cultists and had let me borrow his tape recorder to use in copying them. (I felt that this crack was not quite "fair play," as apparently Mr. Brightwell had not informed Ian MacDonald of the change in strategy and/or policy toward the anthropologist.) Mr. Shepard said, upon hearing this story, that it was Ian's job to ask Mr. Seale on the phone or "sched" about my request: "Why, he doesn't even do his job."

What had, I gather, changed government policy toward me was a letter I had written on July 20 to Mr. Seale in which I "blamed" (as they saw it), primarily, not the government but traditional New Hanover culture for the Johnson cult. I had written that I thought the "cult" would not "spread" to New Ireland because the traditional culture was different from that of New Hanover, and "cult" behavior had quite different meanings in the two places. I asked, as I had before, if I might see letters from cultists or other documents. When I went into Kavieng on July 29, I was overwhelmed by the reception I was given. I was offered a chair and a typewriter. Mr. Brightwell sorted out some very important "native documents" for me, including a speech by Samuel to the United Nations. He lent me his tape recorder to help me copy everything quickly, aid for which I was very grateful. I can only presume that somehow my letter to Mr. Seale had made me respectable, at last, in the government's eyes.

Certainly government policy, not just individual personality, played a role in the behavior of its officials. Nor is unhelpfulness just a matter of national character. I once had a sharp exchange of words with an American who was working as a patrol officer for the Australian administration about the role of the government in relation to the people. He had let me ride along down the road in New Ireland to a function which we both wanted to attend. On the way home, near midnight, a woman waved to us to stop. Her baby was sick, and she wanted a ride to the Lemakot mission hospital, which we would pass. My American *kiap* friend was annoyed, said the people should arrange their own transportation, and would have gone on had I not protested. I could hardly believe what I was hearing. One would scarcely have gone past such a person in New York City, let alone in New Ireland, where it was unlikely that there would be another car going by before morning. He finally let her ride along, muttering that I should remember that I, too, was a "guest of the government." There was, of course, no public transportation at that time, and I usually traveled as the people did: by waiting on the road and hailing a passing truck. But the government did not consider that to be among its concerns. Government, as they often said, is not business.

The clearest evidence that government policy favored officials who minded the store in a very narrow way lies in an account of who was transferred in and who was transferred out. Ian MacDonald was the man the government had ready to take over as advisor to a local government council the people had a cargo cult against. Carroll Gannon, on the other hand, was transferred out in about 1968: he had been warned that he was, they said "too close to the people." And in 1967, "Master Fish" (Keith Hill) resigned because the government told him to collect all the big red nets he had been helping the people learn to use for over a year. The government had decided that, after all, it did not lend government property. "Master Fish" went to work helping people to develop fishing industries, first for the Japanese and later for the United Nations.

Something About Anthropologists

Most Europeans that I met had negative experiences with anthropologists, who often made clear their view that they knew more than did any of the local Europeans, or who wouldn't talk to them at all, on the grounds that no nice people, especially anthropologists, associate with "racists." In subsequent discussions with anthropologists, I have found that many of them pride themselves on having had "nothing to do with" the local European population. Apparently, then, the local government officials' dislike for anthropologists was not based entirely on prejudice but reflected actual experience of rejection and conflict.

On the other hand, many European business people and planters, and their families insisted that anthropologists were about the most awful, neurotic, unhappy mob they'd ever encountered, mad as hatters, given to going to gardens and mucking about in the taro, and unspeakably dull and self-righteous to boot; and yet these European residents never hesitated to offer every assistance to body and spirit and even to the crazy intellectual endeavor which anthropologists so doggedly pursue. As Diane Stanfield Grose said to me when I mentioned, admiringly, that I noted that she, with her diamond lapel pin and beautiful silk dress, had been sitting at the bar on New Year's Eve (1966) chatting amiably with a local, perpetually drink-sodden human wreck, a remittance man from England: "I found out a long time ago that if you are choosy about your friends up here, you just don't have any."

And so the local Europeans befriended the anthropologists, if at all possible. I was a pushover: whatever tiny doubts I might have had about mingling with the local Europeans were consumed along with my second peach mousse one night at the home of Peter and Pat Stanfield Murray.

When I was with Europeans in their homes or cars, I respected their etiquette in relation to the local population. (My local friends did not seem to need my apologies: they wanted me to get along well with other Europeans, I thought.) Often local Europeans and their native servants viewed themselves as friends to each other, and yet they could never socialize as equals. When Europeans visited me at my house, they respected the etiquette of the household: everyone here is equal.

I had not expected or tried to make any converts, and so I was very much surprised to find that several local Europeans were glad to have the opportunity to abandon the local caste courtesies at my house, and were very pleased about finally having a chance to talk to the local people. One Australian woman told me she had lived in New Ireland for ten years and had never gone to a *malanggan* until I invited her along to one. Many of the caste barriers for many, but not all, of the Europeans in the Kavieng area were superficial, and disappeared almost without trace when independence came. And when my planter friend John Betheras, who seemed always to be sewing up cuts and otherwise doctoring his labor line, occasionally pointed out that "racist" planters were helping the local population far more than anthropologists were, I argued for anthropology's special contribution; but I could not completely disagree.

Coming Home From the Eastward Rounds

On Sunday, August 6, I got a ride back to Lavongai village with Father Hillary Fischer, an American priest who had come to northern New Hanover from Manus, and who drove a truly speedy speedboat. Carroll rounded up four men to bring my luggage on a sail canoe, as it would have made Father Fischer's speedboat too heavy and slowed it down.

Alipes
One of the four men sailing the canoe, who arrived in a cold rain and who ate and slept in the living room/veranda of the house where I lived, was Alipes, the brother of a well-known cultist and himself probably a cultist. I had a long talk with Alipes, which was important because he manifested a kind of

trembling and intensity of belief that was not at all widespread by the time I came to New Hanover. I never found any evidence that it had ever been widespread in the early stages, or any stages, of the cult. Yet many Europeans referred to the cultists as *longlong*, i.e., crazy. Alipes was the only cultist I talked to whose intensity was such that he could have appeared "irrational" to a European who wanted to see him as such. But Europeans called the cultists crazy for reasons of their own, I finally came to think—not because of any erratic behavior on the part of the cultists, and not even because they refused to accept our views when we white-skins told them that America could not and would not come.

Rounds to the West

With the Methodists on the *Daula*

On Monday, August 7, I started out again on rounds, this time to the west, away from Ranmelek Methodist mission and Taskul to the east. I have the Methodists to thank again for this trip. Once a month, the Methodist ship *Daula* set out to the west taking the nursing sister, at this time Val Beckett, around New Hanover for her regular infant welfare clinics. Val Beckett had a tough act to follow: her predecessor was Doss Pedrick, whom I did not know. She was called just "Pedrick" by the people she served. She had been the Methodist nurse for years, had walked around the island and, according to the people, carried her own box of medical supplies. My friend Ngurvarilam, Silakau's wife, told me that Pedrick was "truly sorry if you were sick, she got tears in her eyes." Sister Liboria admired Pedrick very much, though she said she never saw much of her. I asked if Sister Pedrick stayed with them at the Catholic mission on her way around, and Sister Liboria said, no, she stayed in the villages. She often would not even stop for a cup of tea; she'd just walk on through the mission.

Val Beckett certainly could not have carried all her own equipment. She had a huge metal box containing medical supplies, and she also took a big suitcase full of nice clothes—pretty *laplaps*, blouses, little "trousers" for the babies—that the school girls helped to sew up at the mission and that were sold at cost or below cost to the people. We stopped at two or three or four villages per day. Val always hoped there would be a large crowd of women and children there to see her and was disappointed if there was not. She "shot" them with various things, attended their sores, and gave them medicine and instructions; and sold them clothes. While she was doing all this, I milled around asking to see the *bord* of T.I.A., or the councillor; or I just let myself be found by men who wanted to talk to me. By then many people in New Hanover had seen me and knew something of my work. I'm sure now that the captain of the *Daula*, Bosap, was of more help to me in this respect than I realized at the time. In any case, I had remarkably little trouble finding informants who were helpful. I was always very relieved when I found someone, as I often did, who wanted to talk to me, as I felt anthropology seemed a rather frivolous occupation in contrast to Val's medical work, the usefulness of which seemed very clear.

Mr. and Mrs. Pitts

We stopped at several villages during our first day out, Monday, August 7. While Miss Beckett did her work at Metakavil, I went over to the plantation to continue a discussion begun the night before with Mr. Pitts, manager of the Catholic plantation adjoining the village. He had been to Lavongai for church the preceding day and had told Father Miller some of his criticisms of T.I.A. Mr. Pitts said that he thought that the people would not keep working for T.I.A. While they were working, however, it interfered with his attempts to keep a regular labor supply at the plantation. For instance, some of the men told him that they were not coming to work for a week; and, moreover, that this was on orders from "Father's Association." T.I.A President Walla had told them to split up, that some villages should work for T.I.A. and some for Mr. Pitts so that he would not be left without labor, but he had no control over who showed up for work. "It's the same core group that was in the election," Mr. Pitts told me. "They just go haywire. They can't do anything in moderation."

Mr. Pitts thought Father Miller had let T.I.A. go too far. He should have started it just in Lavongai village. And why the collection of big money? It's top heavy; it's unwieldy. "I would hate to be a father or a *kiap* here in ten years' time," he said. "People will be asking what's happened to the money, and in ten years' time the question will be magnified."

Mr. Pitts had told the people to ask their association for loans with which to pay their taxes, instead of asking him. "Even with the best of intentions, I could not possibly provide enough work or money for tax money for all of them," he said. Some T.I.A. members asked him to oust some men from their jobs so that others, who had let him down three times already, could work for tax money. Then they had the temerity, when he refused, to ask him to loan them money with which to pay their taxes. He told them that since they could find £5 for T.I.A., they could also find £2 5s. for taxes. After all this, they still came and wanted to borrow his spades for planting in T.I.A. gardens.

At this time, the Methodist missionaries also had doubts about T.I.A. When I told Val Beckett what Mr. Pitts had said, she said that he was a very experienced man, good and wise, and that she would trust his judgment.

Meteran, the Second Polling Station: Logo and the "Cement"

Our next stop was Meteran, the village which had been the second polling station at which people had voted for Johnson. A leader in this event, and in this village, was Cornelio Logo, who had been a *munamuna* (missionary) at Lungatan (near Ranmelek) at the time of the election, and had been one of the original participants in the plan. Bosap took me to meet Logo, having told me that Logo had questions to ask me.

Logo said that he had brought the message right away to Meteran, after the election for America at Ranmelek, and everyone had immediately thought it was a good idea. He said that they still wanted America and that they were working hard in T.I.A. President Walla was from their village.

Logo told me that T.I.A. and the council "are not brothers" in Meteran. This split was the basis of factionalism about which I was to hear much more. As to what he and the people of his village expected from T.I.A., Logo told me, "We have hope in our hearts. We do not talk about it. All our thinking goes toward T.I.A., that's all. Walla and I talk strongly to the people, telling them that we must think only of T.I.A."

Logo told me about a brass and cement object that the Americans had put on top of the mountain at Mt. Patibung, that no whiteskins had seen, only blackskins. On it was writing which, Logo said, they had tried to read with their books, but "it is too strong." Then Logo asked me if I had seen one like it near the school in Meteran, which was quite a long walk away from the village and then up a hill. He said that the teacher there had translated the writing for them, but then added that they worried that nobody told them straight what the meaning was. I said that I would like very much to see the brass and cement and that I would try to come back when I had time to go to the school to see it.

As I stood alone for about ten minutes waiting for Bosap to find Logo, I noted again the differences in hospitality patterns between New Ireland and New Hanover, and wondered still, at the time, how to understand them.

Meteselen

We went on to Meteselen, where I soon found myself sitting in a little shelter talking with a dozen or more men who crowded around. Kuplis, who appeared to be about thirty years old, and who had long been the village representative ("committeeman") for the local government council there. He had heard of me and my work, and he and the others of his place seemed pleased that I had come.

They were working hard for T.I.A., and they were still strong in their election for Johnson. They showed me lists they had kept of people who had not voted for him. Factions in this area were well-defined, and remained undaunted. Kuplis told me how the neighboring villages stood in relation to the election and to T.I.A.

I asked them for examples of *tok bilas*—ridicule—and they offered many. When a ship was passing by, those against the cult and T.I.A. would say, "Ah, the ship of America comes, bringing the cargo of America to those who voted for Johnson."

I asked if they had heard of Peter Yangalissmat, and everyone had. He was a Big Man, they said. They knew he had been jailed in Buka during the war, but they did not know why, and they did not know that he had talked of America.

I asked them about the cooperatives, coffee, and the council and heard the same kinds of stories that I had heard everywhere. They used to have a co-op here, but "We were tired of all the clerks that buggared up the money," Kuplis said. Temeke said that they were also tired of the co-op because the *masta* (European boss) of the co-op had told them that the large amount of money they would make, when capsized, would be enough to make a bridge from Kavieng to a nearby island. That was a Mr. Evans. "Now we don't see this money [that we gave] anymore," Temeke said. "Now we think it wasn't a business that belonged to all us natives. It belonged to the Europeans." Another man continued the account of their reasons for not liking the co-op: "The first thing they told us was that the co-op would save us. A man with a broken leg or blind or an old woman. Now we don't see this happening. That's why we want change. We want another country so that we can see their work."

They had planted coffee, but it came to naught. They had sold only a little.

As for the council, they had liked it before, but not now. Kuplis said, "I have worked for nothing for plenty of years as committeeman, and I haven't got paid. I work for nothing, that's all." Temeke added, "I don't like it because it has not got one good fruit." Another man reported his complaint: "I also don't like it because I asked for wire to fence pigs and chickens, and they wouldn't give it." Councillor Willi had told him, "Government is not business!"

I asked if, since the election, there had been any *didiman* [agricultural officer] or *kiap* who had come to see them. Kuplis answered, "We don't have a *didiman* anymore. The *kiap* comes to get us for jail, that's all." Everyone, including the anthropologist, laughed.

When I left, Kuplis asked me not to repeat what they had said as I continued my journey, and I said that I would not. However, I had learned a lot on which to base further interviews.

As we went along to our next stop, I felt pleased that I had been able to have such an informative interview with people whom I had not met before. It seemed that my waiting several months to begin systematic interviewing had given people a chance to get to know me, albeit at a distance: during that period the news of my work had been spread and, apparently, favorably received.

Baungung, Transition Area

We spent our first night at Baungung, the transition village between cultists and noncultists. We slept at the house of the local pastor (*munamuna*), and he fed us very well. My being a "guest of the mission" gave me much more than just transportation: it gave me status, definition, a manageable identity—and a place to stay. Here, as elsewhere, no woman, or doctor boy, or anyone, said "Good morning" to me (though they responded to my greeting), nor offered me a place to sit or conversation. The children, like those of Meteran, seemed a little afraid of me. They ran away and cried, but then their curiosity won out, and they came back, one at a time, to stand near enough so that they could look at me.

One man sought me out. He had gone to Meteran to vote, for Johnson, rather than west to Umbukul, where his village was supposed to go to "vote in the box." He told me he is a T.I.A. member here, and they have planted 300 coconuts. Paulos had been to see their plantation, and had urged them to plant more.

This man, whose name I never learned, canoed me back to the mission boat to get something I had forgotten and told me about himself on the way. He had been a little boy when the Japanese were here. His mother had died when he was little, his father in 1954. He has one brother "but he doesn't help me, with a little money or something." His wife had left him and said it was because he would not help her look after the children. He told me that he did not want to help her "because they belong to her, not to me," though she bore them while she was married to him. In my notebook, I have noted that this informant was typical of many Lavongais I met in his preoccupation with the isolated figure, helpless, in need, and not being helped. I wondered which is cause and which effect: do they feel defenseless and helpless in relation to external circumstances because their families do not help them, or do they attribute their sense of abandonment to their parents being dead or their siblings not helping, when it is really external circumstances on which they should heap blame? In any case, my canoe friend gave me the whole ideology of neglect and failure that I had by then heard many times—the co-op, the coffee, the council—as he paddled me to and from the *Daula*. "We worry because Australia does not give us a good way," he said. He asked me to clear up his thinking: "What country can come to help us?" I gave him the answer I had learned from Silikan, of Enang Island: "After you have independence," I said, "you can ask all countries to come and help."

Belewaia

On Tuesday, August 8, we stopped at Belewaia. A group of men came and stood around me. We stood on first one leg and then the other for some time, until, finally, Nasson, the councillor there and a big, friendly man, invited me to come and sit down.

Of the election for Johnson, Nasson said, "We didn't go in. We went to Umbukul [a village, which did not vote for Johnson] to vote." They had "stayed with the candidates," but he did not know who he had voted for or who had won. There was no ridicule, he said, for those who voted for America, and they might have done so had they heard about it earlier.

This village also had not gone into T.I.A. Nasson said it was a good way to develop New Hanover, but they had not had a meeting about it and "it's no good for me, alone, to talk."

Nasson's interest was in the council. "It's a good thing. It's the little [part] of the big government. It's the main thing we have to help the people." I asked what he thought of the idea that the government was business, and he laughed. "I'm crazy now," he said. "You cannot borrow from the government. It helps people with medicine, hospitals, water tanks." I said that I thought people were confused about what the council was supposed to do. In any case, I said, I was confused. I suggested that people should ask questions without being ashamed, and find out how the council might help them. Nasson was very interested in my remarks, and thanked me. He said that he, too, had been ashamed to ask questions in the council and that what I had said was true: one should not be ashamed to talk and ask.

One thing bothered Nasson: "Why does everything go to the places that disobey the talk of the council?" He felt the government was giving things to those who voted for Johnson instead of to those who had continued to support the government. He noted, however, that the new hospital helped Taskul to "look good. Government comes up strong there now."

One of the most important things I learned from Nasson was the story of their former paramount *luluai,* head of all the other *luluai* in New Hanover, Iguarangai: he had had "one hundred wives." He would take a young girl who was a virgin and sleep with her only once. Then he would send her out to the fields to work in his gardens with his other wives. Nasson told this story jokingly, but it was here that I began to realize that the Big Men of New Hanover, in this case one backed by the Australian administration, had not served their people. Did they respect him? I asked. Not really, Nasson told me: they pretended to respect him, but really they felt only fear.

The North Coast-South Coast Split Vote

In Belewaia, from Nasson, I found a man who was committed to the council as an organization for helping the people in general. However, I did not gain much insight into the main question I hoped to answer on this trip: why had the southern coast voted on the board, and then, when the election patrol reached Baungung, there was a split vote; then on around to the west coast, everyone who voted in the big progressive village of Umbukul voted "properly," in the ballot box. This was the case again around on the north coast in the large village of Noipus. In Ungalik there was division, but around on the east coast, at Taskul, there was a unanimous vote on the board again for Johnson; as there was in Nonovul, the last stop, in the Tigak Islands.

Had the north coast not heard about the vote for Johnson? Were they a different ethnic group? By this time, I knew that they spoke the same language that the south coast spoke, Tungak, and that they were considered to be the same group. I also knew that people from the south who happened to be in the north voted as the north did, and people from the north who happened to be in the south rebelled with the south. Clearly, then, some kind of situational factors were at work.

I had only one hypothesis when I started out along the south coast toward the noncult west and north: New Hanoverians seemed to enjoy a good argument, enjoy opposition, and the cult did seem to be something of a game. Could it be that since the south coast had rebelled against the proper election system first, the north coast voted properly mainly in order to take up a position against their south coast fellows? This is how I said it in my notes: "Saturday,

August 5: The only way to get the other side of the island accounted for is to count them as in The Cult—The Opposition. By the time the news got to them, the best way for them to get into the Act was as the Opposition."

This was my greatest leap into a kind of abstract, technical theory: like the Age-Area hypothesis in archaeology, it was based on a gimmick, i.e., a simple, single-factor "theory" about distribution that looks at results, not motives, or meanings, of behavior. I did not know quite what to look for, but hoped I would know it when I saw it.

Umbukul and Boski Tom

When we got to Umbukul village on Tuesday, August 8, I finally met a man about whom I had heard a great deal: Boski Tom. Europeans always cited him as an outstanding example of a "native" who understood the European way of life and spoke English very well. Europeans found it easy to be with him. Born in 1911, he had been a government school teacher for many years, and was about to retire.

I asked to see him and was taken to his house. We sat with several other men and talked for over an hour about things traditional and modern. He had some trouble speaking, having just had a large portion of his cancerous jaw removed. Many of his compatriots suffered from the same affliction, which results from the Melanesian habit of inserting lime into their mouths on a green leaf or pod, always in the same spot in their inner jaws, to chew along with betel nut. Unlike some of his compatriots, he had declined cosmetic surgery. Silakau had told me of Boski's attitude toward his sickness: he did not worry about the pain, or that he might die of it. He just thought that God had made this, and that he would gracefully accept God's will. When the doctors held a glass to it and said they would fix it after they had cut it, Boski said, "No, I don't want you to. What, am I a boat that I bugger up and you make me good again?"[13]

Boski received me graciously and my mission with understanding. He knew about anthropology. He had seen Chinnery, and W.S. Groves had been one of his teachers. He was sorry to hear the news on the radio that Groves had died.

When I asked Boski why the cult had not spread to the north coast, he said firmly, "I stopped it." He had also sent a note along to Councillor Barol, his friend, of Neitab and told him to stop it there. Why had the cult started? He said that he thought the people had some "discontents." He did not deny that they had cause: their own leaders, Singarau and others, had gone around to the villages, along with Europeans, promising more than they could deliver from the cooperative society and other ventures. Still, Boski told the people that they would get nothing but trouble for voting for Johnson. When he first heard of the vote, he wondered who this Johnson was: "Is he a half-caste or who is he?" Did they really believe that Johnson of America was going to come? I asked. "I don't think so," he said. And were they crazy at any time? "No," Boski said, "they weren't crazy. They were just trying their idea."

Sosson

We arrived at Sosson, half an hour along the coast north of Umbukul, before 8:00 A.M. on Wednesday, August 9. The men here told me that they did not vote for Johnson because they did not want to, and because they did not understand well. Some of them had worked with the Americans and with the Australians during the war, and said both were good to them. One man, the councillor, had worked with Peter Yangalissmat, and remembered his talk about America's coming.

This was the only place I went where people seemed a little suspicious of me. They were busy gathering sea slugs to sell to the Chinese. They said they were planting coconuts, but not as members of T.I.A. One man asked me if the election started in New Hanover or in America, and I answered that it started "here." He asked: "Is it true?" I said, "No."

Nekonomon

Nekonomon is up the river from the big northwestern village of Noipus. On the way there, I noted that there were coconuts only at the villages on this side of the island, and plenty of bush where nothing had been planted.

"We get off at Noipus and canoe up the river to meet Councillor Temesavung and the Nekonomon women," my notes say, "but the women did not come [to see the nurse for Infant Welfare, Miss Val Beckett]. Val was sorry, but she knew that they had come twice when she missed them because *Daula* [the ship] broke down."

There are very few inland villages left in New Hanover. Nekonomon is one of them; Minn, further inland, is another. Both went into the election and also into T.I.A. Temesavung told me that they were cutting bush, but would wait for Father Miller to come and look at their place before they planted coconuts. "I don't know if others think about America," he told me. "We just think about working."

Noipus: Logo's Question, Daling, and Two Teachers

As we disembarked from the *Daula* dinghy at Noipus, I by graceless and unplanned somersault, I asked Bosap to wait and talk to me. He had told me that he wanted to ask me something, but not in front of everyone, upon our return from Nekonomon. We went to sit in a little eating shelter built for the mission. After a couple of minutes of idle, slightly awkward chatter, Bosap moved closer and said in a low voice, "Cornelio Logo asked me to ask you this question for him if I got a time while we are going around: what month and what day will he see the fruit of T.I.A.?" I was surprised and a little disappointed and finally said, "I think there's a hidden meaning there." "Yes, I think so," Bosap said.

I explained prosaically what he knew far better than I, i.e., the rudiments of coconut production: it takes seven years for them to bear, and so on. I said that I did not know of another fruit Logo was thinking of, if any.

Bosap then said, "You see, plenty of men *tok bilas* [make fun] of T.I.A." I got the idea that my information would give them some ammunition with which to fight back. "You're on our side now; tell us the truth," he seemed to be saying. He, like Oliver, I thought, felt there was more; and either I did not know or did know and would not tell. When they saw this, they went into respectable gear again and smoothed over their probe.

Bosap continued, "In the next House of Assembly elections, *Tutukuvul* [T.I.A.] will vote for America." He said this with an air of "You can count on us not to break our promise." One more thing he wanted to ask: "Does Moresby Headquarters know of *Tutukuvul*?" I said yes, I thought they did. They had been sent letters. "Anyway, they can know; there is nothing to hide," I volunteered.

The question about Moresby could have been a respectable cover, or it could have indicated that the occasional "mystical" intensity I encountered about the cult had to do with secret political plans, rather than secret "cargo" beliefs or something else that Europeans might regard as bizarre. Or perhaps it had to do with both, or neither. The New Hanover people would certainly be among the last in the world to claim they had glimpsed Absolute Truth. I felt sure about this in general. However, concerning what relative truths they considered in sorting through possibilities following the election, I was not sure. At this point, they were certainly considering one political action of which outsiders, including myself, were not aware: the elimination of the council and the establishment in its place of T.I.A. And in 1968 they accomplished just that. Who is it, then, who is bizarre, naive, or crazy?

At Noipus I met Daling, a man past middle age, and his wife Leia. I had heard about them and their activities from Alette Leysen of the Department of Welfare, because they had managed to direct funds which she gave them to start a women's club into a store, which they ran. Miss Leysen and others knew that Daling had not used the funds as he was expected to, but he seemed to be helping the village, so this was overlooked—and monitored. The situation was at an impasse, as some of the women wanted to use the money for a stove; but Daling pointed out to them that it would "have no work." Women's club, he said, despite the opinion of some Europeans, was "a business." Clearly, the people of Noipus were as interested in development as were any of the cultists, but they did not vote for Johnson. Daling said, "I didn't like it. When they schooled us, they didn't talk about voting for America; they just talked to me about voting for Australia. I told all my men to follow what I said." He was not sure who had won.

In the evening I talked with John Dipros, an Australian teacher in the Noipus school, who was formerly a Baptist minister and who had previously taught in New Ireland. In response to my questions, he said that he had no trouble getting people to bring food for the school children in New Ireland, whereas here the attitude is, "Why should we provide food for our own children?" True, he said, some people from the islands brought food. He had more discipline problems here than in New Ireland: "Behavior [here] is atrocious." Still, he enjoyed the people here very much.

The next day I met Michael Pajaen, a teacher from Manus who remembered riding on a truck with me in New Ireland, where he had previously taught at Ngavallis village. There, he said, the children did not come even though it was close. "Here, they paddle in from the islands." They love to come to school. "They may be a bit cheeky, but there is not much imitation [here]," he said. I asked him about discipline, and he smiled and said, "True, only one thing [is a problem here]: discipline."

These two, then, from their arenas of contact different from mine, saw differences between New Ireland and New Hanover which I thought were comparable to the ones I saw. The Australian teacher emphasized the unhelpfulness and the discipline problems in New Hanover, the Manus teacher saw the greater intellectual quest.

On the Way to Patiavai Plantation

For Thursday, August 10, my notes say, "About half an hour out of Noipus. All mangrove. Don't see a single coconut." Reflecting on the similarities and differences between the people who voted for Johnson and those who did not, I wrote, "The human dilemma [is] expressed here in terms of cargo . . . They want a Good Work, purposeful, just as we do, and they think working to provide cargo is it now."

Patiavai Plantation

While we stopped here briefly, I spoke with Pasingantumese, the committeeman here from Meterankasing village. Of the election, he said: "We wanted to go inside this work, but Boski and Barol held us back." I asked why they did as those two said.

> Pasingantumese: Because we were afraid.
> DB: Of what?
> P: Of the government.
> DB: Of jail?
> P: Afraid of the government.
> DB: That they would be cross?
> P: Yes, no good they are cross with us.

In retrospect, I think that it is this kind of fear, of being ashamed, and ridiculed, and scolded, that the election overcame. There is no evidence that the government caused fear through brutal or severe behavior generally.

Pasingantumese then surprised me by saying that Barol, too, had wanted to vote for America, but he got a letter from Boski and changed his mind. "We have been with Australia for plenty of years, and not one good thing has come up. Now we want to try another country," Pasingantumese said. He and Barol and two others joined T.I.A. because the council was not helping them.

Neitab Island and Barol

We were hospitably received by Barol and his wife, Lucia, on the island of Neitab, a small one of the kind one might see in a movie setting: covered with coconuts, and the sea showing through all around. Lucia told me that she had at first insisted that Neitab should vote for America, but Boski sent a letter recommending against it, and Barol agreed. He stood firm despite efforts by some from nearby islands to persuade him and others at Neitab to vote for America.

All use the ground together here, Barol told me: it is not divided into clan-owned segments. The same matrilineal clans are present here as on New Hanover; and, like New Hanover, marriage is virilocal. I had already come to think that the conjunction of matrilineal clans with virilocal marriage was a key difference between New Ireland and New Hanover; so even though I felt here, as I had on several other islands, a more gentle, giving ethos than that which greeted the visitor on the "Big Place" [New Hanover], I thought that the major structural basis for the individualism that underlay the cult was here. The fact that the north coast had stayed out of the cult was beginning to look like an accident of small historical differences, including the presence of a long-time respected compatriot, Boski Tom. So much for my "Grand Hypothesis" about "Oppositional Forces."

Ungalik

I had heard much about Ungalik Island from friends in New Hanover who were from there, and I was anxious to get there. But I had almost no chance to find out anything about Ungalik, because when I got there I found myself almost immediately held in conversation with a blind woman who had brought her child to Val's infant welfare clinic. At first, I was anxious to find some way to end the conversation, thinking that I must go and find the men who knew about the election and T.I.A. But as we talked, I began to see that this was a key incident in my understanding of Lavongai culture. I had already realized that children have to struggle for themselves much more here than they did in New Ireland. Here was a person whose handicap would have elicited aid and concern in New Ireland, who, like the children, had to fend for herself. The women around her clucked with disgust, and I helped her to some chairs where we sat and talked. It was at this time that I realized that children and the handicapped occupy a single status: the weak. And that the attitude toward the weak in New Ireland and in New Hanover was systematically different.

Upuos

We sailed on to Upuos on Thursday afternoon. Here I talked with Ekonie, the man who had wanted to talk about the cult when I was on my "pilot" journey to this area in December 1966, and did not feel free to respond to his interest. This time he told me about the vote for Johnson and about the work they were currently doing for T.I.A.

In the evening there was a church service, and our boat captain, Bosap, also a Methodist preacher, gave the sermon. In his dramatically delivered message (spoken partly in Tungak, partly in Methodist Kuanua, and partly in pidgin), he said: "Something that we believe strongly in our hearts that we would like to win, if we believe strongly, we can win. If we look at something and [think] it is too big, I can't do it. But if I look down on it, I will hold its fruit."

Mossuang

My notes for Friday, August 11, include the following:

Waiting at Bolpua [village] No. 2 for people from here and from the nearby island Mossuang. No women came. The two men who finally walked over to see us seemed gradually to relax their hostile stance. They had gone inside the election at Taskul. However, they will now pay taxes. 'You are tired of jail,' I offered. No, not tired of jail: they will pay taxes following the talk of the Fathers, who made payment of Council taxes a rule of membership in T.I.A., for which they are working hard here.

The council had brought a corrugated iron tank for rainwater collection here, but it was already no good. Where did they drink? I asked. "We drink around and about at all little streams."

We stood the whole time we were there and finally left, discouraged.

Patipai

When Val Beckett and I got around to Patipai, nearly back to Ranmelek, Bosap brought me to an old man "who has savvy," he said; but it was his son, Isaac, who gave me an important interview. He was a noncultist in a cult area. Everyone from Patipai and neighboring Konemetalik (the site of my memorable moonlight mangrove walk) had gone into the election except Isaac, his wife, and three others. Isaac did not go in because he had not heard it explained. He did not understand, he said; he had not heard the story, and it happened suddenly. The Patipai people had gone to Ranmelek to find out about the election, and then this had happened.

They all voted later at Taskul, where the election was split between two groups, those for Australia and those for America. Those who voted for America went by canoe afterward to nearby Kulibung Island to hear the talk; but they were apprehended at sea by government officers Benham, Brightwell, and Spencer, who "ran" them with the government trawler. This was before anyone had refused to pay taxes. The government ship disgorged police, who held them, fastened them with rope around their wrists, and pulled them all onto the government ship. They were taken to Taskul, and without any hearing, they were jailed for two months in Kavieng. One man here, Lapanmal, who was with this group said that they did heavy work in Kavieng, cutting bush and making roads. When he came back from jail, he paid taxes.

Lapanmal and Isaac were both working hard for T.I.A. at this time. They said there was no antagonism between the council and T.I.A. here and no ridicule of either. Isaac said that when T.I.A. first began, there was some talk, both inside and outside. Now the councillor was in T.I.A. However, he did not go to council meetings. "Everyone sees that he does not go and won't put him in again. He does not go there and tell them what we want."

I asked Isaac what he wanted to do with the T.I.A money. "I don't know about everyone," he answered. What if it belonged to him alone? In that case, he said, "I would buy a plantation or a boat to go with people and goods to Kavieng."

The most important thing Isaac told me that I heard from no one else (but later confirmed with others) was about Peter Yangalissmat: as *luluai*, he had used his position to exploit his own people by charging them "rent" to live on their own land, which he said he "bossed." Isaac had not heard of his talk about America, but knew he had been in jail in Buka. "Did the Japanese do it?" he asked.

Boas, a cultist whose suggestion to the *kiaps* that they quit trying to collect taxes until people "finished their liking" got into a government report, was present. He told me everyone had liked America along with Peter, but had "put all this talk on Peter's head" because they were afraid. This was one of several contexts in which the idea that people cannot be moved from their "liking" seemed common sense in New Hanover.

Coming Home from the West

We sailed home to Ranmelek on Friday, August 11. As the *Daula* drew near, one of the young boys who helped Bosap began to dance on the back of the ship. Val and Pising, the young nurse who helped her, told me this young man was always in gay spirits when we got near Ranmelek, adding that "We're all glad to get home." Bosap put on his hat and blew the conch shell—supposedly to bring people down with lights (as it was getting dark) and to help unload the ship, but also to celebrate our return.

Jim White

The next day, I went by canoe to Jim White's place. We had talked several times before, but this was our most lengthy interview. Once before (on Friday, Judy 21), he had told me he knew Peter Yangalissmat, found him a "big, powerful man" and also "extremely sensible, very down-to-earth." This time, we talked mainly of Jim's attempts to alert the administration to the need for regular patrols in New Hanover. He referred me to the minutes of the district advisory council for 1962, which reported his concern, and the administration's response: no funds, no personnel, and nothing to worry about. Mr. White and another planter, Jim Grose, argued their views to no avail.

Jim White had been a *kiap* early in his career, but quit so that he could stay at home with his two young daughters, whose mother had died. He remained very interested in the development of New Guinea. The Methodist missionaries had great praise for his contributions to them and to the people, manifestations of concern which were hidden behind a gruff exterior.

Local people always imagined that the planters were terribly rich, which most of them were not. It was not an easy life, but one which had appeal for those who, like Jim White, were comfortable with a rough, adventurous routine.

Bosap

Back at Ranmelek that evening, I finally had a long, enlightening interview with Bosap. He had been a much stronger supporter of the cult than I had realized, but he was quiet about it because he worked for the mission. He had clearly played an important role in bringing people to meet me as we made our rounds.

On this occasion, Bosap told me of his close friendship with Peter Yangalissmat. Bosap was with him when he was arrested, and knew well that everyone else wanted America as much as Peter did. But Peter had enemies among men, Bosap said, partly because he had so many friends among women.

A Last Chance to See the Cement

During our interview, Bosap reminded me that he wanted me to go with him and Pilikos to the top of Mt. Patibung to see the cement there. If I went without him, he said, and did not see him again afterward, I should send him a letter and tell him the meaning of what was written thereon.

Several people had talked to me about cement, describing with some detail a kind of cement peg with writing on it in metal. On January 22, while I was still living in Mangai, Laksia had told me something about cement pegs. Now it was nearly time for me to go back to America, and I had not yet seen one. I was very curious myself about what these could be.

I had almost given up hope that I would see a cement peg when Carroll Gannon gave me my chance. He stopped in Lavongai to take me along with him to Meteran on Sunday, August 27. Cornelio Logo's three-year-old child had died suddenly the day before, and Carroll wanted to check on the death. This was my opportunity, come just in time, to see the cement and brass, as Logo had asked me to do.

When Carroll and I arrived in Meteran, we sat a while with Logo, who was mourning his child. Then I asked if I could go to see the cement, and Logo sent Maris, with whom I had talked before, to take me. I must admit I was quite alert with the excitement of finally seeing the cement peg by the time I came, huffing and puffing, upon it. Maris and another man, Tude, watched me with anticipation as I read the writing on a metal plaque on the top of the peg. I photographed it twice, then drew a careful picture of it in case the photographs did not come out; which was fortunate, because they did not. All the while I was photographing and drawing, I was trying to think of how to tell these men what it said on the peg. Logo had told me everyone knew of the pegs, and "we have tried to read it with our books, but it is too 'strong.'" Bosap had said they were worried that people were not talking straight to them about the meaning of these words. How could I tell them without losing my credibility? Being half in the cult in my heart myself, I was surprised and a little disappointed to read, on a round bronze plate embedded in a round peg of cement, about six inches in diameter and a foot high:

> U.S. Army - War Department - Corps of Engineers
> Bench Mark
> $250 Fine or Imprisonment
> For Disturbing This Mark

On the Way Out

During my last week in Lavongai, a *didiman* (officer of the Department of Agriculture, Stocks, and Fisheries) finally came to a meeting of T.I.A. to give a talk. He had been invited to come to help the fledgling organization more than a year earlier but had not been able to fit it into his schedule previously.

I bid my final adieus to Lavongai after that meeting, on August 30, 1967, and rode back to Kavieng on the mission boat with the *didiman*. I took Silakau along with me so that he could visit Mangai: he wanted the diversion, and I wanted to hear his anthropological insights into his experience there.

When the time came for me to go back to America, many of my friends from Mangai came into town to see me off at the airport. On that final morning, September 13, I made a courtesy call at the government office to express appreciation. I was taken completely by surprise when Mr. Seale handed me the two folders labeled "Native Thought in the Johnson Cult," which Nic Peterson and I had seen on our first visit to the district commissioner's office in 1965. I spent about two hours going through about 400 pages of papers that filled and overflowed these long-sought documents. This important task, undertaken in such haste, nonetheless added a crucial dimension to my understanding. I found out that there was no incident reported, no evidence of any encounter, that I had not already learned about, either from the cultists, or from Europeans and other noncultists. Of most significance to me at the time, I found no reports of any "bizarre" psychological states, any "irrational" behavior, any physical or psychological events beyond the ordinary—no trances, no shaking, no crowd frenzy, no prophet leading blazing-eyed believers. Government officials and others had maintained that the cultists were *longlong*, crazy; and if I said they did not seem crazy to me, people replied that I had not seen them earlier in the cult when they really "believed." I was never able to elicit from such informants any examples of the alleged crazy behavior. My hurried, but page-by-page inspection of the "Native Thought" files, wherein I found nothing I did not already know (though partly from a different perspective), reassured me that I probably had not missed something fundamental and unrecovered by missing the first two years of the cult.

When I got to Port Moresby, I went to the government library at Konedobu, where I was allowed to see annual reports and progress reports from the Kavieng District. I was startled to see my own letter as part of the annual report for that year. This convinced me that my letter to Mr. Seale, seemingly exonerating the government from major blame for the cult, was what had finally gained me government assistance. After I had spent several days copying from these documents, the librarian came to me and said that she was sorry, that she was not supposed to have shown them to me. I had nearly finished them, and I relinquished them.

I found that it was difficult to ascertain whether or not particular documents were meant to be accessible to the public. The clearest case illustrating this point involves the obstacles I encountered in seeing old press releases, which, one would think, were born for the public eye. I went to an office of communications to which I had been directed by the secretary of Mr. J. Keith McCarthy, then director of the Department of District Administration, but also a celebrity of the early days of exploration in New Guinea.[14] When I asked to see press releases concerning the Johnson cult and New Hanover, my requests were treated as incomprehensible. I said, as I left, that I would have to trouble Mr. McCarthy to find copies of the press releases, since this office seemed not to have any. When I got back to Mr. McCarthy's office, the secretary was on the phone. As she hung up, she told me that I was to go back to the office whence I had come, that they had found the press releases, after all. When I returned to the office, I was directed to a chair in front of a shelf of bound volumes five feet from where I had stood before. Mr. McCarthy's name had been the magic word which suddenly made these volumes available to the public.

Two comments convey the essence of the problem of gaining permission to see documents in government offices. One man in an office said to me, "I don't think I can help you. I push the paper at a very humble level." And Margaret Mead, whom I happened to meet at the YWCA (on her way home from Manus), told me, in her usual no-nonsense manner, "You have to learn the subculture of public officials. That's part of an anthropologist's job." Thirty seconds later, the YWCA dog bit me and then wagged its tail, which I could not help but take as some kind of double-whammy reinforcement of this message.

Notes

1. The literature on cargo cults is reviewed in chapters 4 and 5.
2. My colleague at the University of Minnesota, Professor Luther Gerlach.

3. Many contemporary students do not cite Malinowski (1922, 1944), who is, of course, the original advocate of the "thumbnail sketch" and the recording of "the imponderabilia of social life." Mead has been scathingly criticized by some who are willing to try to discredit her work by reference to a small part of it, and who appear to be unaware of the tradition of the First Chapter as thumbnail sketch. Laura Bohannon first wrote under a pen name (Bowen, 1954) because of the taboo on "revelation," and she then republished using her own name (Bohannon), after Powdermaker (1966) led us into the present era with *Stranger and Friend*. Several field work books have followed, including Malinowski's *Diary* (1967), and First Chapters have reappeared. A particularly wonderful example is a recent work by Jane Goodale (1995).

4. Nic Peterson pursued work in Australia, gathering data for his Ph.D. and working with the Australian Aboriginal Institute Film Unit. Throughout the years we have continued to assist each other with our respective works in many ways.

5. Dean Fergie, who did her field research in Tabar, did interview European planter women.

6. I did, after all, hope to survive my first field work.

7. Susan Thiemann Sommer, a musicologist and now Chief of the Music Division of the New York Public Library at Lincoln Center.

8. It was 1961, according to some accounts.

9. Yvonne Zacharias (now DeMonte) was my collaborator in this interpretation. We were American Fulbright students together in New Zealand. The quote is from Ogden Nash, "England Expects," which may be found in *The Penguin Book of Comic and Curious Verse*, selected by J. M. Cohen. Harmandsworth, Middlesex, Penguin Books, Ltd., 1952. One young English patrol officer told me he thought I was very lucky to be able to laugh with the people, which he felt would be out of line in his job.

10. I found people in the Tsoi and Tigak islands somewhat different from the people of New Hanover. They were more likely to be uneasy about conflict; more like New Irelanders.

11. This is the term Fr. Miller used in his article (1966) on the subject.

12. Pasingan is a common name in New Hanover.

13. Later I thought that this view fit in with the New Hanover aesthetics, which prefers the natural over the highly processed (Billings, 1987). Cornelio Logo had a child with a sixth finger which dangled from his hand, but Logo did not want the doctors to remove it as they had offered to do, because God had given the child the finger for some reason, and who was he to remove it?

14. See his own book, *Patrol into Yesterday* (McCarthy, 1963).

II

Interviews and Documents

3

The Johnson Cult

The following summary of the cult is based on the interviews and documents referred to in the previous chapter. The general outlines of events were considered common knowledge, and were not in dispute.

I have divided this summary into the categories which I came to see as the most significant ones for an understanding of what was going on: the events of the election itself, subsequent interactions between government officials and cultists, factions among the Lavongai people and among Europeans, ideologies pronounced on different sides, beliefs which people actually held in their hearts, and, finally, the emergence of an economic development organization from the cult. I present examples of various viewpoints in each of these categories, using the words of people involved. These words come mostly from interviews with me and from documents prepared for government reports.

The Election

Events: How the Vote for Johnson Came About

The election of representatives to the House of Assembly in February 1964 required that patrols be sent all over the territory twice. The first patrol explained the election to the people or their representatives (councillors), and the second accomplished the voting and collection of ballots. For this latter purpose, patrols carried locked red plastic ballot boxes, separate ones for each polling station.

No European government officer made an initial explanatory patrol around New Hanover. Instead, two weeks before the balloting was to begin, an official came only to a Lavongai (New Hanover) local government council meeting in Taskul, explained the election to the councillors of the area, and entrusted them with the task of carrying the explanation back to their villages.

Later, Europeans and Lavongais alike were to say that the Lavongais did not understand the nature of the election and the concept of candidates; but there is ample evidence that they understood well enough to have carried out the instructions of the administration. In fact, half of them did so.

The other half did not. The *kiaps* who were conducting the election in New Hanover arrived at Ranmelek, the only Methodist mission station on the south coast of the island, on the evening of February 14, 1964. Ranmelek was the first of six polling stations in New Hanover, at each of which the officers were scheduled to remain for three days.

Early the next morning, Saturday, February 15, the *kiaps* came outside the missionary's house, where they had slept, to begin collecting ballots. On this first day, however, they found waiting for them a blackboard on which was written in pidgin a short message: "We want to vote for Johnson of America. That is all." The patrol officers turned the blackboard around, with its back side toward the people, and continued their preparations. They called for Lavongai village to come forward first. A young man from Nusuwung, Yaman, then stepped forward and restated the message. The people gave a loud voice vote for Johnson, and then left the area.

On February 19, at the second polling station, which was in Meteran village (like Ranmelek, on the south coast), the people proclaimed themselves to be for Johnson, in a similar fashion. At Umbukul, on the west coast, and at Noipus and Ungalik island, on the north coast, people voted in the ballot box provided. Finally, on the east coast, at Taskul (the government station) and at Nonovul (in the Tigak Islands), the people again presented themselves for Johnson. Polling was completed on March 2, 1964.

To most Lavongai people, the vote for Johnson at Ranmelek was as much a surprise as it was to the patrol officers in Ranmelek. Most of those who were present at Ranmelek had only heard that there would be a vote for Johnson on Friday, February 14, along the way to cast their ballots. The few whose idea it was, Pengai and other residents of Nusawung village, sent out a few men with the news. Friday night there was a meeting in Magam village, near Ranmelek, at which people expressed their approval of the idea of voting for Johnson. Savemat, a mission school teacher who had access to the school blackboard, was designated to write their message on the board, and to set it up near the polling place, where the patrol officers found it Saturday morning.

Pengai

I begin with Pengai, who gave me my first long interview in New Hanover. Pengai provided the fullest account of what had happened immediately before the election that led to the vote for Johnson, because he played a pivotal role in these initiating events. I recorded our conversation in the Lavongai village *kiap* house, where I was living, on March 2, 1966.

> *Pengai*: All right now, all the men among us just study this. We study now, among us who are big (adult); we don't see one thing yet. All right, we say: "Oh, Australia, what is it doing with us? Why do some black men—like the Negroes and the Africans—now, they already know about doing all work.

America has taught them all. Now, why hasn't Australia taught us, so that I can understand, too, how to make—anything! Oh, now, we sit down, we sleep inside under the leaves of a tree [in thatched houses]—what is this?"

Pengai said that people felt that none of the local candidates could help them if they were elected; so they decided to vote for Johnson.

P: The mouths of all of us, everyone around, in New Hanover, all said: "We cannot vote. Suppose we vote for one black man, he will show us about what? And suppose we vote for one Australian, will he show us anything more [than the Australians already have]? Because now we are really crazy." All right now, this thinking came up in me and said: "All right, I think I will ask this man for the name of this man who is president of America."
DB: Ask who?
P: I asked my brother, my little brother.
DB: Bosmailik.
P: Yeh . . . he had stayed together with the Americans.
DB: On top on the mountain.
P: Yes. All right now, me, I went and asked him, "Do you know this man who replaced President Kennedy?"
DB: And Bosmailik said what?
P: Bosmailik said this: "President Johnson." All right now, I got up, and I said: "All right now, you and I altogether are crazy inside about this. And all men—that is, you and I altogether—are afraid of the government of Australia, that's all. I think, never mind, me, I can let my body go to Australian hands for the thinking of all of you. Now, never mind, I alone will carry [the blame for] this. All right, never mind, me, I put my name on this." All right now, me, I got the name for this and, me, I said, "We vote for President Johnson."
DB: And all the men said what?
P: They said: "We altogether, it's all right; we like it." All right, it was something that belonged to us, to Nusawung [village].
DB: Just Nusawung, they all heard of this first.
P: Yes. All right, and later, then, all places came and heard—inside of one week only, now, they all heard.
DB: Just in one week. All the talk ran quickly.
P: Yes. All right now, they all said this: "Nusawung will vote like this." All right, everyone said: "Oh, we, too, we like this!" This is how it was. Because at the time they had this election, thinking was not standing up straight. [He is stuttering slightly.] Thinking stayed just with America. All the way around [the island]. All right, at the time when we had this election—all right, in every place it went, we did not do it [vote in the ballot box]. We did not go with it. But the board—a board [blackboard] we made—we voted on the board. We wrote all this talk—all right now, we went and put it on the board. Me, I myself composed this to go on this board.
DB: You! Many times I've heard this talk of this board, and I didn't know you, you wrote [the words for] it.
P: Yeh, just me.
DB: Now, you wrote what for this board?
P: I wrote this, like this: "We vote for President Johnson of the United States."

This, here, we wrote on the board. All right—just that, that's all. [His tone is deliberately casual.]

Boski Tom, Leading Noncultist

Boski Tom told me he was born in 1911 and was one of the first teachers in the area. We spoke English in his house in Umbukul when I recorded the following interview.

DB: You didn't have any idea that this election was coming up. It came as a surprise to you, did it?
Boski Tom: Yes. I think the first meeting was held on Thursday afternoon. [At] Nusawung . . . I was up there. I was Councillor of that area. . . . So I sent a note up to try to contact Mr. Beresford—I think Mr. Beresford was our school inspector here—to ask permission, him and the D.C., if they allowed me, I stay for the first election there. But I waited, and no answer; so I got my canoe and came down to [Umbukul]. I think the man who took my note up did not give it to Mr. Weston [one of two European planters on New Hanover: Mr. Weston was at Metakavil village]. I do not know. I didn't check. So I came here, and that thing happened. It happened then, and when they [the *kiaps* with the ballot box] came down to Meteran, the same thing happened; and when they came here, nothing happened. I sent word around.
DB: How do you explain it's not happening here [at Umbukul]. You were here at the time, were you?
BT: I stopped it.
DB: You stopped it. Were they ready to go in?
BT: Yes. Many of them came and asked me, "What are we going to do now?" And I said, "We'll follow what the government wants us to do, that's all."
DB: But many of them came and asked, did they?
BT: They say, "What are we going to do now—they election for America, and what about us?" They sent two letters to me. Councillor Willi (of Baungung) wrote to me and asked me. He asked me to write a letter and send it around New Hanover: "Tell them to elect Johnson." Not "President Johnson," just "Johnson." And I was wondering, "What Johnson? Is he a half-caste or . . .
DB: [Laughs]
BT: Then the next letter came, from Willi again, and he told me, "President Johnson," and he mentioned Father Kelly [Fr. Philip Kelly, the American Catholic priest at Lavongai in 1964, who was subsequently transferred to New Ireland].
DB: What did he say about Father Kelly?
BT: He said that Father Kelly said that we are going to make our election for Mr. Johnson. And I said, "No, I will not follow that." I told the people here, "We will follow the right. We will not follow their talk. We do not know what is going to happen. There might be trouble." I wrote a letter to my [council] vice-president, Barol. He sent word out to Ungalik, but the news about this Johnson cult had spread up to an island called Nusalik. That's how the Johnson cult got into . . .
DB: . . . the Tigak area.
BT: [Yes.] Baungung [village] came here and asked me, "What are we going to

do?" And I told them this cult idea about Johnson [is no good].
DB: So you were able to influence Baungung, too. I believe most of them followed you, too.
BT: They came and asked me, two of my uncles. [I told them], "If you try to follow them, there will be trouble. I can see it. There will be trouble because Australians are looking after us—so we must follow what the Australians want us to do. It's a safer way, and a peaceful way."
DB: What prevented Noipus and Neitab and Ungalik from going in?
BT: [Firmly] I wrote to them.
DB: Who did you write to—to Barol [councillor at Neitab]?
BT: To Barol.
DB: I did talk to Barol once, and he told me some people came from another island by night once, and he told them to *raus* [get out]!
BT: Us, that's right. We had the same idea, Barol and I; we worked together.
DB: He's a very good man, isn't he?
BT: Very good man. He's been doing work for the Catholics for a long time.[1]
DB: But you think the idea could have spread all over the whole island if you and Barol and perhaps a few other people hadn't stopped it.
BT: Oh, yes, yes, yes. It would be worse. There'd be somebody—if the idea spread all over the island, nobody will listen to the government; everybody will get together, and there will be somebody killed, I think.

Background: The War, Yangalissmat, and the Americans

The men who had originated the idea for the vote had worked for a U.S. Army survey team which had recently spent several months in New Hanover establishing points of reference for some reason: "for map-making," most Europeans guessed. The Americans had spent most of their time at Mt. Patibung, in the mountains above the village of Meterankan. They required local labor to help mainly in carrying equipment up the mountain. They worked from a large ship that remained at some distance out at sea. They had helicopters, and they poured cement on Mt. Patibung to make a landing area. Their work required them to put into the ground small round cement markers like the one I saw at Meteran. The local people had seen similar cement markers in the nearby islands set up by *Masta Mak* ("Master Mark," i.e. officers of the Australian administration) to designate areas claimed by the government or by particular people.

Local Europeans seemed sure that the vote for Johnson had somehow been the result of Lavongai people's contact with this U.S. Army team. The standard joke was that the Americans, about to face an election back home between Goldwater and Johnson, had playfully told the local men who were carrying supplies and otherwise helping them, to vote for Johnson. In a government document[2] it was reported that D.O. Ken Williamson "thinks [the cult is a] result of influence from a U.S. Army team which has recently finished operations on a signal station in the area."

Lavongai informants also told me of the role these Americans had played in their election, but from their point of view it was minor. The experience that the Lavongais had with these U.S. Army men was a good one: high pay and friendly relations. But this was not the first time that the Lavongais had been favorably impressed by the "American way" (pidgin: *fasion bilong Amerika*). They had also experienced it during the war when some Lavongais worked with the U.S. services in neighboring Emira and in Buka, Solomon Islands. Most of these men were now dead, but their descendants remembered the stories. The points especially noticed about the American fashion were these: the Americans had "plenty of cargo," and they gave it away freely and with good will to the local people. Furthermore, they treated them as equals, sharing food and clothing with them, and sitting down together with them in easy conversation (pidgin: *sidaun gris wantaim*).[3]

However, many who were in the cult either felt that Australians (especially those from "outside," who did not know about the customs of the territory) were equally friendly during the war, or else they had no opinion of Australians or of Americans, having met few of the former and none of the latter. They claimed to be merely taking a chance, willing to "try" a different country.

The Lavongais had been thinking about "trying" America as boss for more than twenty years, since Peter Yangalissmat had suggested it to them. He had been in a high position as a native soldier for the Australians, and had ample opportunity to observe the Americans. He began to talk about the idea of getting them to come and boss New Hanover after the war.

The Lavongais thought this was a very good idea, but the government did not. Australian military officers came to find out whose idea it was, and to arrest him. Peter Yangalissmat was sent to Buka to jail for a year. In 1967, many Lavongais said they were ashamed of themselves for having let all the blame fall on Peter, when it was an idea that belonged to them all.

The talk of the Americans had not disappeared entirely during the twenty years after the war, but such talk gained new vigor in 1962-63, when the U.S. Army team came to work on Mt. Patibung.

Bosap: Peter Yangalissmat and Wartime

I interviewed Bosap outside his house, with his family present, the evening we returned from our trip around the island. The following account of Peter, given by his friend, Bosap, suggests that when Peter began talking about America, he needed to shore up his own reputation, sagging among men under the weight of his popularity with women. The men then turned on him and told the officials that Peter wanted what, in fact, they all wanted: rule by America.

> *DB*: You tell me the story: why did they jail Yangalissmat, do you know?
> *Bosap:* All right, the story of the work of Peter—[or] Yangalissmat—one thing: he liked America. Second thing, he used to marry around and about. He didn't pull women [from other men]—because this man, he was another kind of man [he was "something else"]. His skin [body]—suppose he talked to a woman, right away this woman wanted him. Now one thing, too, what he liked,

he really liked women because—that's what he liked. This thing, women, this is what he liked. He didn't pull women.

DB: He just stood up, and the women came to him.

B: He knew how to talk, and he knew how to *sing* [sing words with power] over all those things of the ancestors.

DB: Oh, he knew how to sing to pull women.

B: *Nounem* [You bet]!

DB: All right, go on now. Two things Peter liked, America and women. One thing I asked Isaac yesterday: did he just pull young women, new women, or did he pull women who already had men?

B: And he [Isaac] said what?

DB: He didn't know. He asked Boas, and Boas said: both. New women and women who already had men, them too.

B: He spoke the truth.

DB: Yes, Mr. White told me that Yangalissmat was a really good man, but he had plenty of trouble with women.

B: The master told you he was a good man, had a good head, good savvy, but one thing, about his likes, he liked women, that's all. Suppose he came up to Lungatan, and he came to sleep here, he would get a woman in Patekone. Suppose he came up to Magum, he got a woman in Magum. [We are all laughing.] All right, all the *luluai*, all together they all told him to make this thing happen. Everyone liked America. This came up later in court, and all men, all together, they put it on Peter. He was the only one who liked [America, they said]. All right, they jailed him then.

DB: But all the *luluai*, they, too, liked America?

B: They themselves liked it.

DB: And all men who were nothing [not *luluai*] or some other official, too?

B: All men who were nothing, too, they liked this thinking.

DB: And did they all used to sit down and "grease" about this?

B: It was like this. He [Peter] was a "gold medal" of the army [a sergeant]. He walked around among us, and he used to ask all the *luluai* [what they thought] and sent their talk.

DB: Who reported on Yangalissmat?

B: Akule and another. Two soldiers. Akule is from near Baungung and was second-in-command to Peter. [He names others from other villages.] Gapi, who was "white-hat" [paramount *luluai*] of Lavongai. Gapi got a name for finding things—he had rifles, he had cartridges. I also had all the things of a soldier.

DB: Did Japan give them?

B: No.

DB: America.

B: America.

DB: And Australia?

B: Australia, too. This master, they called him Master Bell;[4] he was captain of this ship. We two [Gapi and Bosap] were here when Master Bell came up. Master Bell knew Peter Yangalissmat. Peter had been his cook when Master Bell looked after a plantation. All right, he sent word, came and got Yangalissmat, went and gave him a rifle, gave him cartridges, he gave him all the things, and he said: "You 'sweep up' all of your people, and you bring them to one place, and talk good to them all." All right, Yangalissmat came back, he put out the word, he "broomed" all the people that already stopped in the bush like wild pigs, like wild dogs. We came back, stayed back in [our] places. Came and cleaned the place, fixed up our houses. The fight came up then. All right, Gapi, Yangalissmat, the two, like, held the place then. The two were boss then here. All right, we walked in the middle, between the two. The two got all the things and came and brought them to our places, and they came behind. All right, Gapi saw that the *fasion* (fashion) of Peter was another kind, with regard to making trouble around and about with all the women.

DB: And Gapi didn't have this [trouble], huh?

B: Unn [Yes]. Because Peter had plenty of things at this time that people needed: tobacco, *laplap*, all kinds of things. All right, he got plenty from his master [Bell] because he was number one among us. He would get a woman, "grease" with her; he would come up to a place, "grease" with a women, give her tobacco, something would happen. All right, trouble now. All right, then he married two women, sisters, just one mother of the two. This thing, they didn't like to report Peter. Peter still walked about. Now, one thing, like this: people didn't like Peter to be number one for us because he had got into plenty of trouble over women. They wanted one good man to carry this work. All right, Peter worked along with us, on and on. All right, this thing [about America] started with him. Peter didn't start this thing [wanting America]; it was the people of the place here who asked Peter: "Why don't we want all these men to come boss us?"

DB: All America, eh?

B: Unn [Yes]. Because they came up and saved us with a good life. They [Japan] had pulled us to a bad state. All right, when they [America] came, we stayed in our places [i.e., we didn't hide in the bush]. All right, Peter said: "[This is] the thinking of all." All right, he went and made it happen. All right, the *kiap* of ANGAU[5] heard this and said: "Better go to court." All right, they all said Peter was crazy, his head was full of *pekpek* [feces, colloquial in pidgin], his head was crazy. They fastened him with a rope, they jailed him, he went to Buka. That, that's all.

DB: No! They fastened him where?

B: In Kalasau. We two stayed there; they put him in court under the sun. He stood up like this [where I am], the *kiap* stood up like you [where you are], one policeman put a bayonet to his breast, this one who stopped at the side put his bayonet here, one stood up here and put his bayonet here, one stood up behind him, he put his bayonet [here], and him, he stood up in the middle, and they held court.

DB: Oh, no, they held him in "court" with bayonets.

B: Yes, during the time of the fighting [he speaks urgently], it wasn't during a good time that they held him in court. Me, I stood up; I was his "second" [second-in-command]. His brother was there, too, his number one brother—he wanted that they two should go back. Because, at this time, they all talked like this: if he didn't win the court case, they would cut his neck. For liking America. Just that. Now, this thing, Dorothy—they all tell you about this man that he liked women all the time—one thing: he was rich with what we ourselves had need of during the time of the fight. We weren't able to get anything. All right, the woman herself wanted—she wanted something from Peter; he brought this thing. Later [when] he brought it, then this thing happened. The woman wanted it herself. It was not Peter's wrong. Peter didn't do anything wrong.

DB: Peter didn't do anything wrong.
B: Peter didn't do anything wrong; the woman herself wanted it
DB: The woman wanted it.
B: If it were Peter's wrong, he would have fastened the woman, fastened her with rope. But it was what the woman wanted.
DB: The woman's wishes; she wasn't forced with anything.
B: She needed something and asked Peter for this thing. That's all. The second thing, they all brought together all the talk against him. With regard to stealing women, I ask the law: if I steal, I fasten this woman and hold her fast. But the woman wanted it. All right now, they all get up, and they say: "He likes America to come boss us, and he makes fun of us." There now. This bit of talk they brought with nothing [without evidence]; it did not come up from Peter's mouth. All right, Peter got up, and he said: "During the time I have worked at the work of the soldier, it has been the wishes of the people of the place themselves, and of all the *luluai*, that by and by this country [America] should help us, because it sang out for us [American soldiers came and called us back from hiding] in the bush. In a little time, we would have died altogether, and now we come and sit down well, and they themselves fight, and we like them. All right, everyone sees this *fasion*, and they like it. Now we all together like America. But they are all afraid of court, and they all put it on me. I think it would be better if I go to jail. This is something for jail." All right, they all said: "You bloody snake-head [in vicious tone of voice], crazy, you must go to Buka! You work with cargo till you die!"
DB: Did you follow him to Buka?
B: He went to Buka, and, me, I stayed then. They got the musket from my hand, they took off the cartridges from my body, they went back. All right, me, I came and stayed here. They took everything belonging to a soldier from my body; and, me, I stayed in the big house where I had worked along with Peter. All right, we, plenty of men, came and stopped and did nothing in our places. Later, I was surprised when they sent a book, and there was my number, and there was my name, and there was money for me from this time. [He means he got a pension.]
DB: Peter stayed how long in Buka?
B: I think about one and a half years. He didn't go to the jail; he carried cargo, that's all. He was a cargo-boy for all the soldiers. In Buka.

Thus, while Peter Yangalissmat had been a controversial figure for some, the idea for which he had been jailed, and the complicity of other Big Men in this injustice, had not been forgotten by those who had known him.[6]

Makios: The American Way Is Good

DB: Tell me a little about the ways of the Americans. What do you like about them?
Makios: Their ways are not the ways of all men. Their ways are very good. They invite plenty of men and sit down together to eat and whatever thing—they give everything to them. That now, this way we have seen, and our liking remains.

Oliver: Wartime Fellowship

> *DB*: All these soldiers, all those that talk English, were they good to you at this time?
> *Oliver*: Oh, during this time, all soldiers of Australia, all soldiers of New Zealand, all soldiers of America, or all Africans, at this time we were good friends, during this time. We made good friends at this time. It was a time for us all to be brothers, this time. It was a time for us to eat together, this time. It was a time for us to stop together, this time. Absolutely everything we did, we did together at this time. Australia or New Zealand or Africa or America, they were not "masters" at this time; we were together—we were together, that's all."

Leadership: Each Man His Own Leader

The memory of Peter was part of the reason cultists knew it was important to refuse to name leaders of the Johnson cult: they felt they were each acting individually, and they did not want to make another man a scapegoat for the views they all shared.

Still, Pengai told me (and other informants supported his view): "I am the one who has a 'name' for this cult." He meant that he had decided to be the one who took the blame, as Peter Yangalissmat had, many years earlier. People seemed to agree that it was Pengai who first said: "You do not want to vote the way the Australians are telling you to vote; so let us vote for America." He said, however, that he was just the "mouth" for all, that all wished it to be so.

Pengai had asked his younger brother, Bosmailik, who was working for the Americans, to find out the name of the man who had replaced Kennedy, of whom they had heard because of the wide publicity given his death. They may have heard the news on village radios, as well as from local Europeans, including Americans at the Catholic mission stations.[7] This is how Bosmailik's name became known, and how it happened that it was he who was sought, and found, by the administration; and cited in *Newsweek* magazine. The administration soon lost interest in Bosmailik, and turned attention to Oliver and Robin of the Tsoi Islands. Oliver was the nearest thing to a prophet that this cult had. He viewed himself as guided by God, the God about whom the Lavongais learned from the missionaries. He wandered through the bush evading arrest, telling people to pray to God, to hold fast to their election for America, and collecting money to send to Johnson. He subsequently acquired a radio worth $400, a wristwatch, and many women. Like many other Melanesians, however, Lavongais are slow to speculate, and only a few felt sure that Oliver had "eaten" the money he had collected to send to America.

The administration and native noncultists said that Oliver made prophecies about the coming of America, but he and other cultists never admitted to me that this was true. It was common cause, rather than any leader or leaders, that kept the Johnsonites together. Each village within the cult area had several men who were stronger than most in their interest in the cult and more assertive in their pronouncements; but many men said that the cult had no leaders, that it belonged to everyone. Even government officials began to say that there were no leaders, but not until they had spent considerable energy chasing men who occasionally emerged from the crowd.

Pengai

Pengai pointed out, as did several other cultists, that different men were "big" in the cult at different times.

> *Pengai*: Yeh. But I mean, me and many, many, many more men carried this election, and it truly is on top [dominant, or winning]. There are plenty more men, many, many. Suppose—it's like this, we replace each other in the work, eh? True, it started with me. Suppose it happens that I go down, suppose they all put me down; all right, there's a man to get up [the election]. All right, they down another one, all right . . .
> *DB*: . . . another . . .
> *P*: . . . another comes up. Um. All right, they all down another one, another gets up. All right, down he goes; all right, this first one gets up. All right, it keeps on like that, that's all. [Pengai moved his hands up and down as he talked.]
> *DB*: Up and down.

Oliver

I asked Oliver how he had heard about the vote for Johnson, or how he knew what to do about the election. He said no one told him about it: "I got it by asking, that's all. I lay in my house for a month, and I thought, and I asked."

Government and Cultists

Patrols

At first the administration responded to the vote, two weeks following the polling at Ranmelek, only with extra patrols and verbal explanations. Johnson, they told people gathered to hear them in their villages, was a busy man, and America was far away and occupied with a war in Vietnam. Never mind, said the people, we will wait. After some "truculence"[8] on the part of the natives was reported in one of these encounters, police accompanied some patrols. From the government officers' point of view, the police protected them and enforced their authority; but from the peoples' point of view, the policemen were a provocation. Repeated attempts to explain that Johnson was not a candidate met with refusal by the people to change their vote. The government decided to change its approach, and to concentrate on tax collection.

Collecting Money, But Not for Taxes

The collection and disposition of tax monies was an issue from the beginning of the cult. In fact, some tax defaulters had been jailed in 1963, with the election not yet in sight. After the election for Johnson, cultists said they had voted for America and would pay tax to America, but not to Australia or to their own council, which had done nothing for them. On March 18, 1964, there was a local government council meeting at Meterankan village, attended (according to an administration report) by seventeen councillors and about seventy members of the public. One among the public was Joseph Pukina of Lavongai village. According to a government report, he gave an emotional speech in which he said, "You can hang us all from the rafters of this council house, but we will not pay tax!" According to his own report, corroborated by others, Joseph Pukina said more at a meeting two weeks later with the *kiaps* and some Americans present.

Many people claimed that they had no money, but money was collected from the people immediately following the election by the Johnson cultists. On March 20, 1964, £443 9s. 11d. gathered in this way was given to Mr. Healy, then district commissioner, with the request that he send the money to Johnson to pay his fare to New Hanover. Bosmailik presented the funds to Mr. Healy when the D.C. came to Taskul to explain to the people that Johnson could not come.

Mr. Healy refused the money and returned it to various Lavongais and administration personnel with instructions that it be given back to those from whom it had been collected. (Later, some people said that their money had been returned, and some said that theirs had not been returned.)

Of the total sum, £200 was said to have come from the Tigak islands. Later, money was given to Fr. Kelly, the American priest at the Lavongai Catholic Mission, who was also asked to forward it to Johnson along with an explanation of what was wanted. He refused. The cultists took the money to the bishop, who also turned them down.

Warnings: Planters Warn Government

There had been warnings that all was not well in New Hanover. The minutes of the District Advisory Council, Kavieng, 1962, show that planter Jim White stressed the need for the administration to resume regular patrols of the island, which had ceased. The administration pleaded shortage of personnel and funds, and no changes were made. At the time of the cult, there was no government station on New Hanover, and patrols occurred only with regard to specific tasks which the administration wanted to accomplish.

District Advisory Council: Minutes, 30th November 1962

> Jim White suggests a Native Affairs Officer should be permanently posted at New Hanover. Since the establishment of the [Lavongai Local Government] Council and suspension of luluais, the young men were becoming "contemptuous of law and order" and were "disinclined to accede to the dictates of the Council."
>
> Mr. Williamson [District Officer] outlined staffing problems. There were time-consuming operations in Land Title restoration. He said that a population of 7,000 could hardly warrant one experienced officer and that he considered that progressively the Council would overcome the difficulties that now exist.

District Advisory Council: Minutes, 14th May 1963

> Letter from Mr. Healy to Director, DNA [Department of Native Affairs], Mr. J. K. McCarthy: Mr. Healy says [in his letter] that he cannot agree entirely that New Hanover is understaffed with one officer. Whilst during the last two years or so there has been an increased incidence of larrikinism amongst the young men, and an indifference to some extent to local authority, it cannot be said that these people are lawless as the pattern is much the same as in other parts of the District where Councils have been established and traditional authority has been relaxed.

Census Taking

On March 29, 1964, administration personnel decided on "a policy of regular patrolling" and enforcement of rules and regulations, including longstanding rules that require the populace to line up for census-taking, preparatory to tax collection. Patrols were accompanied by police, and in most places found resistance to census-taking and to tax collection, but no one to arrest. However, in April, mobs, mainly in Tsoi and mainly led by Oliver, prevented the success of arrest attempts. Finally, on May 6, according to a patrol report, "The D.O. [District Officer], Spencer and Corporal Korau proceeded down a track and at a garden one census defaulter was pointed out and arrested."[9]

The arrests for census defaulting began the cultists' jail sentences which soon thereafter derived instead from failure to pay taxes. These failures and subsequent jailings occurred in large, but decreasing, numbers in 1964, 1965, and 1966.

Meetings: People and Government

The administration did arrange some meetings in which explanations were attempted. Mr. Healy's attempt on March 20, 1964, did not convince many to change their votes, though there were some notable exceptions (e.g. Edward). A major meeting with outsiders occurred on August 8, 1964, when 400 people assembled at Meterankan village to hear speakers invited by the administration: Jim Grose, newly elected M.H.A. (Member, House of Assembly);[10] several administration officers, and two American soldiers. Thirty-five policemen, who were native to other parts of the territory, were present. A widely publicized meeting with United Nations personnel at Taskul, the government station in New Hanover, did not take place until April 1965, more than a year after the vote at Ranmelek. It was at this meeting that Pamais, of Lavongai village, spoke in English about the grievances the people had against Australia, and why they had voted for Johnson. People came to the meetings, listened, returned their own arguments, and refused to change their vote.

Edward: Noncultist

> Edward was one of the few who changed his mind after Mr. Healy told them on March 20, 1964, "The election is not true. Australia is boss. America cannot come up." Edward believed him and "lost his thinking" about Johnson, he told me. He came back to his place and told people that it was rubbish talk, that Australia and America were brothers, good friends. "You cannot make war between the two countries; the two are brothers." Everyone heard him, and some believed. "Some wanted to hit [me] and the teacher who helped me talk and the former councillor. They hit the councillor of Unusa and swelled up his cheek. Some still followed Johnson. Plenty followed me."

Bosap: Cultist

> *Bosap*: All right, we held a great big meeting at Meterankan. They had written a blackboard again [proclaiming their vote for Johnson]. They didn't talk with their mouths; they went and set up the board. All the Big Men [Australian government officials] went and sat down, and they said: "Who is the cause of this election?" Bosmailik got up then and said: "Me." [The Australian government officials] then asked: "All right, what is the source of this savvy, then, that you bring to plenty of people?" He got up, and he said: "There is no source of it, only our liking, that's all, that President Johnson will eventually be boss over me. The liking of us, ourselves. We aren't throwing out law; we are following law. You talked of election; we voted. Just that, that's all."

Joseph Pukina: Cultist

> *Joseph*: Master Seale [the district commissioner] has been here [to Lavongai village] and sat down here and called us all together, and Mr. Seale, he knows all about me. Now he came up, and he said, "You, this man, you come here." I came here, I came and stood up, and he said: "Do you have something to say?" "All right," Mr. Benhem [Acting District Officer, A.D.O] said, "You wait first," and he talked to the D.C. first, and he went and marked a mark on the ground, like a snake.

DB: Like a snake.

J: In the middle of us all. All the women sat down along with all the men near my house. All the line of policemen, they stood up by the roots of the betel nut tree. All right, the policemen lined here, and they had the sticks they use for fighting with them. The police master from Rabaul was there. Now a line of policemen [came] from Rabaul and from Kavieng. Those from Taskul, too, they all came along with them. They all came and lined: they readied all their things for fighting; they all stood up. [Mr. Benhem] marked this line like a snake, twisted around, then said: "This mark here is a crazy election. Now, this straight mark, this, a good election." All right, he talked to us: "All right, you, all women and all men, you get up." Everyone got up, and he asked, "You see now, this mark is like a snake—it is a crazy election. Now, this mark, it is a good election. All right, who among you likes this straight one, all right, he comes by the straight one. Whoever likes this which twists like a snake, he must go by it." All right, me, I go over to this election that's like a snake.

DB: Snake. Good. [Laughs]

J: I stand up over it.

DB: You aren't afraid.

J: All the people come, women, men of New Hanover, around to this part [the "snake"] here.

DB: They all follow you.

J: They all follow me. [Tone: slightly breathless—rough.] We stand up over here. "HUH! [very surprised, as he enacts the *kiap*], all like a crazy election? Ahh [sigh]." Mr. Seale is cross, and he stands up. Master Benhem said: "All right, you go sit back down." We went and sat down, and he said: 'You talk—you got talk, you talk." Now he says to me now: "Go on, you talk." [Joseph then said], "Yes, I have talk." All right, he translated my talk [from pidgin]. I talked to the three like this: "You, you D.C., and you, you *kiap*, this [ground] in New Hanover belongs to me. I wasn't born in Australia. I wasn't born in Russia. I wasn't born in Vietnam. I wasn't born in America. I wasn't born in Manus here, or in this part that belongs to us here, in New Guinea. I was born here in New Hanover, here, on this piece of ground here that you see. I prove it. Now, this election which you say is crazy, it belongs to me yet, on my ground. The craziness of Australia belongs to Australia. The craziness of America belongs to America. The craziness of Vietnam belongs to Vietnam. The craziness of me here, it belongs to me here, on my ground. This isn't your ground. It's my ground." Look, this book that I hold (I put a little book), I said, "Look. Paul has said the same in the Bible. At the time when they asked, 'Why do you make law on this ground here, in Rome?' Okay, he got up and said, Paul said: 'This place is where I was born, and it is my ground. My father belonged here, my mother belonged here; me, I make law because this is my ground.'"

Service or Control?

Two months after the vote at Ranmelek, when arrests began, regular patrolling had still not been established on New Hanover, and contacts between officers of Department of District Administration (D.D.A.) and the people of New Hanover were limited to special meetings. A patrol officer was eventually reassigned to Taskul, but patrols around the island were still few and far between. In a meeting of the District Advisory Council eight months after the cult began, Mr. White and M.H.A. planter Jim Grose insisted in vain on the need for more frequent patrols, especially by an agricultural officer. Then District Commissioner Mr. Healy said that "law and order should be reestablished within the next two months and it might be possible to implement" some of these suggestions about improving services after that time.

Some officers of the service departments (Public Health, Malaria Control, Agriculture and Fisheries, Labor Relations) continued to do their work against the orders of D.D.A., and D.D.A., ironically, continued over the next three years to depend upon service personnel for reports about what the people were doing. Perhaps the different functions of the two categories of officials provoked different responses, but it was clear that different parts of the administration worked in opposition to each other.

On three or four occasions, D.D.A. personnel feared violence (as service personnel never did), but none occurred. It almost occurred in Metakavil village once. A.D.O. Mr. Benhem had ordered a line of men to carry a felled coconut tree, and one of the men fainted. The men were angry that one amongst them had been overtaxed physically, and began to close in on the A.D.O. In the nick of time, the Catholic mission boat, carrying nurse Sister Liboria (an Australian) came into view, and the threatening mob dissolved. This account was given to me in this same way, with some laughter, by the men who were present, by Sister Liboria, and by A.D.O. Benhem, who admitted good-naturedly that Sister Liberia had "saved" him. The Lavongais said they were "ashamed" to fight in front of her: they respected her.

All violent actions came, in fact, from the administration, and the two known instances of it came from the police; most of it without the knowledge or approval of European D.D.A. personnel. Except in the case resulting from the confrontation on the west coast of New Ireland, no one was hurt. Mr. Benhem, explained his own aggressive actions, including shooting at coconuts and instructing a young man to stand in the smoke of a smoke bomb, as "demonstrations of strength."[11] He said that the government had power, that they would use power, and that it was only fair to demonstrate this to the people. One fleeing native was, in fact, shot and wounded, though not seriously.

Orders, explanations, and "demonstrations of strength" all failed to accomplish the aims of the administration: tax collection, and the restoration of law and order. Since the creation of the Lavongai Local Government Council in 1961, taxes had been set and collected by the council: that is, by New Hanovarians themselves, not by the Australian administration. However, the council was often viewed by Lavongais as an arm of the administration, and they refused to pay taxes to "Australia's Council" on the grounds that they had voted for America.

Arrest: Trying to Arrest Oliver and Defaulters

When the people refused to pay taxes, they allowed themselves to become "tax defaulters." They had broken a law: they could be arrested. And they were arrested, in large numbers. Tax patrols much larger than usual startled the villages. Sister Liboria said that she looked out the window at the Lavongai mission one day and saw "the Spanish Armada" coming around the corner. Eighty police, along with several European officers, disembarked, set up tents, and set up court.

I have no account indicating that native councillors performed their proper function of tax collection on these occasions. Many of them had gone into the cult. At that time, the administration may have considered it dangerous for councillors to come along for this work.[12]

Each man was asked individually to pay his tax. Each individual said no. Each was either given exemption (too old, too young, sore leg, TB, bad back, just fell out of a coconut tree, too many children, and so on) or taken to jail at Taskul. When the jail at Taskul was full to capacity, men were taken to the Kavieng jail: and when that structure was also full, they were taken on down the east coast road in New Ireland to the Namatanai jail. In Kavieng and in Namatanai they broke rocks and did road work. At Taskul, Carroll told me, they "beautified the station."[13] He felt that they could have been given work more useful to themselves.

In the Tsoi Islands, the attempts officers made to arrest Oliver made him famous, but they were never successful in making him a prisoner.

Progress Report, 6th May 1964 (Written by Patrol Officer Toughy)

> [Several government officers] went . . . to Mamion, where [District Officer] Spencer pointed out Oliver, who had prevented the arrest [of census defaulters] on the previous Monday. The D.O. informed Oliver that he was under arrest and would be charged with interfering with the police. He protested, and the D.O. took him by the arm. Oliver broke loose, grabbed a stick, then, flourishing it wildly, ran to a canoe and crossed the channel to the other island.
>
> Loud calls on a conch shell were heard and taken to be a general call to arms. The patrol party returned to the Tsolik rest house . . .
>
> At 10:30 A.M. there was some movement, and Oliver approached, followed by some 30 men. The two officers met them on the track and told them they would speak to six people but not to a rabble. However, all went to the rest house. Oliver delivered a tirade about their Johnson election, and said Government Officers were white-skins and did not understand them. He repeated himself, worked himself into a frenzy, jumping and swinging his arms to supplement, no doubt. the shortness of his ideas. Mostly, he was unintelligible. Boski Tom, Councillor Sumain, Perevaitas and Committeeman Fredi, all could make

little of his speeches. D.O. repeated that he was under arrest. To prove it, I grabbed him by the shirt, he stepped back, and the front of his shirt fell out—by the feel of it, the material was rotten. The mob closed in, making arrest impossible. The meeting broke up when I asked who supported this madman. They could pay for the cost of the extra police to be brought up. With that, Oliver, with 24 supporters, got up and stamped off, leaving about 15 government supporters, mainly from Tsoilik.

The position was assessed as being at this stage as bad as it could be. The direction from Native Affairs headquarters instructing that sufficient police be employed to allow Courts to operate had not been followed, through an error of judgment as to the police strength required.[14]

Oliver

Oliver told me about this encounter in which his shirt was torn the first time I talked with him, when we sat down for several hours at his house at Mamion. As it was this interview which I only partially recorded and which I accidentally erased from a tape, the following account of his version of the story is based on my notes written as we talked.

The government ship, *Mercy*, arrived at Oliver's island, Mamion, carrying government officers, police, Lavongai councillors, and New Ireland's elected M.H.A., Nicolas Brokam. Two policemen came to the *kiap* house at Mamion [where Oliver lived]. They rounded up all the men who had failed to line for census-taking two weeks earlier and said, "All right, now you have court." As Oliver related the story to me, the following partial exchange occurred.

Kiap: This election was rubbish. We returned the money. It is dead.
O: All right, you returned the money. Money is something that belongs to you. You took it back. All right, something inside a man, his thinking and his liking, is something inside what is just skin. You can't take that. God put it there, and you can't [take it]. This election will remain, and it cannot change.
Kiap [probably Spencer]: Rubbish. You have no road to go for Johnson.
Kiap Toughy: You are the one who held back all the men who had court?
O: So what?
Kiap: All right, now you're going to court. [They then indicated that they planned to take him away.]
O: I will go to court to whom? You are what? Stay here; you take me to court here. [He was asking them: who shall I go to court to if not to you? Aren't you a court?]
Kiap: No, you must go to the D.C. [in Kavieng].

Oliver was then lucky, he said. His little girl came up, hung on him, and cried; and he said: "Wait, let me go take my girl." He turned and went away with her, and, at this point, "this thinking came up," and he said to them:

O: You can't do this! You can't do this! You can't do this!
Boski Tom: We can.

Boski had been a teacher at Unusa and knew Oliver. Everyone stood around not knowing what to do.

Then Oliver jumped on a canoe and started away [toward Tsoilik Island]. Spencer and a policeman came behind him in another canoe. Oliver said again [from the canoe]: "Go to court in the *kiap* house—let's not just stand up here on the road. Come on to the *kiap* house to straighten this out." Plenty of men all crowded toward the *kiap* house. Robin was there and "plenty of other men" were with him. Oliver said to all those standing around: "You all must think of God, because I stand by for talk" [i.e., you all must pray, my mind will be occupied with other things].

They all went and sat down in the *kiap* house. Two *kiaps*, Spencer and Toughy, came and held him again:

> *Oliver*: "Just you have court" [they said]. One put out his hand to hold me, missed, and broke my shirt. Now, me, I stood there. Everyone surrounded the three of us. [His voice rose in volume with the excitement of the chase.]
> Why this new law? [I said]. You want to bugger up all ordinary men for what reason? You used to send a letter [informing us that you would come to make line for census]. Now you don't. Are you just downing us about the election so that all will be afraid? You can make my skin pain, but you can't touch my spirit. This is something that belongs to me, a liking that belongs to me.
> *Kiap*: The election is dead; it was rubbish.
> *O*: You said the election is dead, and now you come and find it with me. Suppose you go over there, you will find it again; and if you go over that way, you will find it again.
> *Boski Tom*: Do you know that America kills all Negroes?
> *O*: Boski, you are clever. But your savvy belongs to you. And you haven't got a good way to save us.
> *Kiap Toughy*: I laugh at you. America can't come.
> *O*: I laugh at you. America *will* come.

Oliver prevailed on this occasion and remained at Mamion; but it was deemed necessary to continue to try to arrest him.

Jail

The time in jail unified men. They had a great deal of time to spend together, to talk, to exchange ideas, to compose songs and sing together, and to develop esprit de corps. Some say they did not suffer, because it was a time of commitment when they did not worry about pain. Others say it was a time of pain: they had to work hard, they had no betel nuts or smokes, and there was not enough to eat. The greatest pain, however, was the pain of humiliation suffered as a result of continual police taunts, sometimes accompanied by a hit or kick.

Jail terms were from two to six months. The first year of the arrests, 1964, both Lavongais and European administrators emphasize that in the affected villages virtually every able-bodied man was jailed: "Women, children, a dog, a few chickens were left in the village," Thomas of Lavongai village told me. In 1965, a few men paid tax, and in 1966, a few more. Administrators, missionaries, and service personnel were all paying taxes for men who refused to pay for themselves. They knew that jail was making martyrs and creating unity, and they wanted to prevent that. In addition, many Europeans wanted to appear as "good white people" by giving their own money to help. Many were genuinely moved and/or charmed by individual Lavongais, and acted from these motives. Many wanted to save face for what might be viewed as their own failures by keeping mission workers and other locals associated with European endeavors out of jail.

Factions: Cultists and Noncultists

Factions began developing simultaneously with the balloting, as those who voted on the [black]board and those who voted in the (red plastic ballot) box chose sides. Without exception, wives supported their husbands (and children, too young to vote, their fathers). The nuclear family emerged as a unit in the cult, as in other aspects of life in New Hanover. Not a single woman took a position which she regarded as her own, because the cult was regarded as men's business. Most women were, however, clearly emotionally involved, and on their husband's side. But it was not unusual for adult brothers to be on different sides of the election issue.

Three categories of persons voted in the box: the first included councillors, committeemen and others who viewed themselves as especially responsible to the Australian administration (e.g., the occasional former government employee or policeman). The second was composed of their wives. The third category of persons who voted in the box is defined strictly in geographic terms, in relation to polling stations. If a south coast resident was on the north coast for some reason at the time of the election, he was able to vote there, and he voted in the box along with the others. Conversely, people from the north coast who happened to be on the south coast at the time of the election "went inside the election," as they said, and "voted on the board."

That the north coast remained outside the cult reflects the influence of small accidents of circumstance rather than any basic distinctiveness of the area. Boski Tom, a long-time teacher and the best known man on the island, was able to stop the north coast from voting for Johnson, but a month later he probably could not have. Religious affiliations functioned partly in relation to geographic boundaries, but the latter took precedence. New Hanover is mostly Methodist on the north and southeast coasts, Catholic on the southwest coast. The cult drew its adherents entirely from the south coast and the Methodist Tigak islands. The idea of voting for Johnson was first formulated in a village that is Seventh-Day

Adventist. These affiliations with different missions were not fundamentally related to the cult, though they affected a few individuals. Europeans sometimes concerned themselves with this possibility, but cultists did not.

There were very few persons on the south coast, then, who voted in the box. Some of them felt that their lives or welfare were threatened during the first few weeks after the election, and the administration brought them to Taskul for a while for their own protection.

Partly because it was the councillors who were "loyal" to the administration; and partly because grievances against the council were among the major justifications for their actions continually recounted by cultists, those who voted in the box evolved into a clear pro-council faction (even though individually they also had grievances against the council). The cult meant personal humiliation for councillors when cultists refused to obey their orders: first with regard to the election itself, then with regard to "lining up" for census-taking, then with regard to taxes. And of course there were a multitude of small, angry interactions in connection with these larger issues.

It was these loyalists[15] to the government who regularly reported on[16] the cultists to members of the administration. As they became increasingly separated from their fellows by an accumulation of antagonistic encounters, they increasingly depended upon the administration to give them moral and physical support. Conversely, the administration depended on these men to give them information, and to give legitimacy to the administration's punitive action against cultists.

Edward: Former Government Employee, Councillor, Noncultist

Edward accompanied Mr. Seale to Buka and to Port Moresby and said of him, "Oh, he is just too good; he is like a father. He calls me 'child.' He is a good friend of mine." Edward talked with Mr. Seale during the election, and Mr. Seale came to get him personally to take him to Taskul on one occasion.

Edward had been elected councillor of Unusa Island in 1963 and continued to be councillor during the cult. He saw many problems for his people with self-government imminent, but he did not join with the cultists because he believed what Mr. Seale and his predecessor, Mr. Healy, and other Europeans said: that the Americans were not going to come.

Silakau: Councillor, Catholic Mission Worker, and Noncultist

Silakau voted in the box and was actively against the cult, at least for a while, he told me, primarily because he had close contacts with Europeans and he believed what they told him. When I met him, he was a peacemaker. He was a councillor at the time of the vote; furthermore, he had been a catechist when he was younger and remained active in the Catholic church, especially in the Legion of Mary. He joined T.I.A. and became an enthusiastic member, as did many anti-cultists who were Catholic.

Silakau, who was intelligent and entertaining, always made a good story of the conflicts he had survived. He laughed when he told me in 1966 about his being one of only two men who voted in the box at Ranmelek in 1964, though he had not found the consequences of his act amusing at that time. His friends were angry with him, and told him America would slit his throat when it came, he said. Silakau said he cried at night because he was afraid, and he could not sleep: "You can ask my wife, she'll tell you." His wife confirmed this.[17] Nonetheless, Silakau told his cultist friends, "I am boss of my own thinking; I don't like to follow another man." Even though Silakau did not join the cult, he never had any money and he never paid taxes. He was one of those taken for their own safety to Taskul, where various members of the administration paid for him, which made him feel proud and pleased. Cultists did not want to be paid for, lest their credibility be damaged.

Saripat: Former Councillor, Cultist

> *Saripat*: Look, one of our teachers, Boski, a good man for getting up the place now, with regard to school and everything—and, you look, he doesn't stand along with us. For a long, long, long time, he hasn't talked along with us about anything.
> *DB*: Ah, following the ways of the *kiap* now. Just "big head" [arrogant].
> *Sr*: He goes behind all the whiteskins, and they [those natives, like Boski, with higher status] all go stand up along with the whiteskins, and they all go and talk together.
> *DB*: That's not a good way.
> *Sr*: Now, afterward, all the work, it comes for us.
> *DB*: Now, this new president of the council, Steven, does he help you, or no?
> *Sr*: He helps us with what? [Rhetorical, sarcastic] No.
> *DB*: No.
> *Sr*: Him, all men voted for him. And afterwards, as is the way of all councillors, like this: everyone votes for all the councillors, and afterward they all go and turn their backs on their people. Then they go stand up along with all the masters, and afterwards they go and report all the people inside the place. These councillors don't think "Ach! I can't go and stand up along with all the whiteskins; the whiteskins didn't put the vote on me. The people put this vote on me, and I am their boss."
> *DB*: They just think of standing up with all the whiteskins.
> *Sr*: [The councillors think,] "I can stand along with the whiteskins and get rid of this rubbish thinking of my *kanakas* [country bumpkins]. I will bring them all to court; they will all go to jail; by and by, they will all be in jail and will lose this rubbish thinking of theirs."

Makios: Cultist Interprets Noncultists' Accusations as Tok Bilas

It was Makios who first made me understand that the apparently "crazy" beliefs attributed to cultists originated as ridicule (*tok bilas*) among anticultists, "the enemy." Cultists claimed they did not hold these beliefs either as part of the election or as part of their membership in Tutukuvul Isukal Association (T.I.A), the economic organization that grew from the cult.

Makios: Some men who voted in the box talk like this: "*Maski* [Never mind], you are the ones to stop and we are to die—if America comes, it will kill us."
DB: Ah—and they are just making fun.
M: Yes.
DB: Ah, just making fun!
M: Now, some of their talk—those who voted in the box—they talk like this: "Now, we stay like this, and you will stop and wait. Now, why does the road remain [unfinished] like this? All these rivers—by and by America will come, [and] it will put a bridge over them."
DB: Oh, I see! This is the talk of all who did not go inside [the election].
M: That's it. Then they talk like this: "You all wait for America, by and by it will come and give you something free."
DB: Oh, making fun, that's all!
M: Making fun!

Meteselen Village Cultists: Tok Bilas[18]

When I asked the men with whom I talked at Meteselen village for some examples of *tok bilas* in the cult, they readily provided examples. One man said that noncultists would see a plane and say, "The plane comes to bring your cargo!" Those who voted for Johnson were told they were crazy. "Where did your strength go?" they were asked. "You have no power." If they went to buy something at the store, they were told to go to Johnson's store. Why didn't America open the jailhouse? The men who went to jail, why don't they bring the cargo now? "We like Americans," one anticultist mocked, "but they aren't truly men; they are *tambarans* [dead ancestors]." One barbed remark that must have given these men pause was this: "You bring a lot of money, ten dollars, to T.I.A., and what will come of it?"

I asked if any at Meteselen had believed the talk that Americans would bring cargo, and these men answered, "No! We were just ashamed [to hear this talk]."

Among the native population of Papua New Guinea, no one outside New Hanover supported the cultists. Members of the House of Assembly were, structurally, with the government, and they vigorously supported anticult actions, including those by the police. Native police from outside New Hanover, and even one who was from New Hanover, were more visible in their opposition to the cultists than were the Lavongai noncultists, who expressed their opposition primarily as ridicule.

Similarly, amongst Europeans no one really supported cult activities, but many did not really support the administration either. The positions taken by various European groups varied with their tasks in relation to the local population, and with the ideologies which supported them in their diverse purposes.

Chapter Three

Ideologies

Ideologies evolved and became known through public statements about beliefs and stances. Not only cultists and noncultists, but also various European groups developed positions which they justified.

Cultist Ideas: Colonial Countries Have Failed

The ideology of the cult was well-developed before the election. These central ideas were repeated, in whole or in part, by many cultists: First, the Germans came, then the English, then the Australians. They have not helped us to develop. They have brought us schools, the cooperative society, coffee, and the council, each time telling us that these things would give us money, "save" us, and give us "savvy." But this has not happened; our lives are the same as the lives of our ancestors. Now we want to try the Americans.

What kind of "savvy" do they want? They want know-how in relation to producing cargo—that is, material goods of the white man. When I asked them what kind of cargo they wanted, they usually said, but only with prompting, planks for a house, iron for a roof, and perhaps a speedboat. They want the cargo, but they want the "savvy"—the understanding—more; and the "business," the enterprise, the productive occupation. And they want money. People always want money for something, and Lavongais want it for the self-reliance it can buy them. They are more dependent upon money for carrying on their relationships than are some other peoples traditionally in Papua New Guinea. Money allows impersonal exchange and freedom from dependence or obligation.

Some cultists had quite simple and specific wants, according to their own statements. Others had a broad view of the "savvy" that they wanted: they wanted to know how to build a way of life for themselves and their progeny, and they said so. Pengai was careful to distinguish his broader aims from the simple ones sometimes attributed to their election: he said that it was not cargo that he wanted, but a new way of life. They wanted to understand history, historical forces, and power well enough to maintain their place and their ability to control their lives. Those with the broader view did not like being considered ignorant and poor, and did not like feeling constantly humiliated by white people and by their own educated compatriots. They wanted equal status, and equal knowledge, in the modern world.

Their election began as a simple statement of preference—or so they say. In fact, they knew that they were confronting the administration and that the administrators would be cross (pidgin: *kros*). They claimed that they were not cross with the Australians until the Australians became cross with them. The cult ideology was not really anti-administration, although it appeared sometimes to be so. It was certainly not anti-European. It was impersonal, and dealt at length and intellectually with issues. It expressed a great impatience to know, to understand, to be on the move, to be going somewhere, to be in the mainstream.

Samuel's Speech to the United Nations Visiting Commission, April, 1965

> The Australians have been here many years and have not changed us. We are still like our grandfathers. When the Germans came, they developed the land. They planted all the coconut plantations. That was their work. Then the English-speakers came—first the English, then the Australians. They taught us to read and write. That is all. They said they were going to help us develop our place and get money, but that has not happened. First they gave us the cooperative society. They said our store would soon have plenty, and old people and sick people and young people with no parents could take things free from the store. But they were lying. That never happened. Now the stores are closed and we never got anything free. Then they told us to plant coffee. They showed us how to plant it but not how to take care of it. It is all bush now. (A variation of this complaint involved the accusation that Lavongais got but a fraction of the promised prices for the coffee they produced, so they ceased bothering with it.) Then the Australians gave us the Local Government Council. They said it would save us. They said it would help us develop our place and help us get money. But we do not see this happening. Now who will save us? We do not want the Australians to govern us any more. It is time now for the Americans to come. They will give us "savvy."
>
> We do not want the Australians because we have been with them for many years and haven't got changed in our lives. We do ask the Australians not to govern us any more. We must wait for the U.S.A. has his turn. We do like the U.S.A. to teach us the best way how to live good, happy and useful lives.

Pamais's Speech to the U.N. Visiting Mission in April 1965

In 1967, Pamais allowed me to copy the notes he had written from which he composed his speech to the United Nations Visiting Mission, which he gave at Taskul. He was chosen to speak partly because he could speak English. This is a brief excerpt from his notebook.

> This bad election was started among the people, because the people knew that the Australian people tell so many lies to them. . . . First of all the cooperative [which started in 1950] said if we will help the cooperative well, we will stop giving tasces [taxes]. . . . They told the people not to pay taxes anymore. . . . Cooperative said like this, those who are poor, old man old woman widow or a child who has no father is going to be help by a Cooperative. They said they will give them good dresses. Dressed up like European by putting good laplap and good clothing and also clean trouses [trousers] and shirt. You can see some people around New Guinea dressed a bit like European because they had job around the towns or a teacher's job. But what about the poor people? We don't see the cooperative helping these people. They only telling lies to us and they don't keep their promised to us. In 1961 the Local Council was started in N.H. the Government gives you Council because it's a good thing really to save the

people. Those who are poor, poor woman and poor man are going to be save by Council and also to make them happy later on. And the Council did not come to pull your own money. You are the chief of your money. Its your own thing if you want to give taxes for how-much. It's your own wish.

We see this now at the present moment we don't see those things that the Council has promised us. You know . . . there is a rich man and a poor man among European and native. And how they push poor native to jail? Is this good? If a poor man went to jail and also if he has a wife and children, who is going to help his wife and children with money. Where is the Government to save the children and the wife of that poor man, who went for Jail?

This the people saw and their minds are not good at this. That's why we are worrying about the Government because he told so many lies to us.

Joseph Pukina's Notebook:
Joseph, who did not speak English, wrote the following notebook, which he lent to me, to help Pamais prepare his speech for the U.N. delegation.

> Because if Australia has a real love to us he could help us and take the snake off our heads. So Australia doesn't want to take good care of us then we can let him go away from us. In the minds of us the people of N.H. want to ask the love of this country America if he loved our wish to him he could come and care of us now. But if America doesn't want to love our wish to them then we say okay. And after this we don't want any of the European countries to govern us anymore. If America doesn't want to obey our election to them, then we had to live like our grandmothers and grandfathers from the olden times. But we make our vote to America that we want America to care of us at the present moment.

Pengai: Australia, Aborigines, and Savvy
Pengai knew that Australia had once belonged to the Aborigines, and he was afraid that Australians would push the people of New Hanover off their land in the same way.[19]

> *P*: Yeh. I mean, "understanding"[20] brought this about. It was like this: one man got his book, his "school"—all right now, he came and said: "This, too, I learned of this." All right now, one man he came and said: "Me, too—I learned in school of this." All right, another, he came now, and he said: " Me, too—I learned of this." All right now, this: when we were in school now, we studied Papua New Guinea. All right now, we studied; now it [what we learned] was not very straight [correct]. For a long time, Australia has stayed with us, and we are completely tired of this kind of school: "A, B, C . . ." [Pengai mocked a teacher's tone]. Plenty of men have savvy about English, and what have they done? They know English for nothing, that's all! It's for meetings, that's all—then we finish talking, and the master goes, and we come bac *Pengai*: Oh, I have heard this: all the time all the men got up from England, and they put them [Aboriginal people] all in prison. They put them all in jail in this place. . . . All right then, they moved all the natives of Australia just to this place

[prison].
DB: And you think Australia is doing the same thing to you all, putting you altogether in jail.
P: Yes. No, it's like this—I think this: suppose we—suppose Australia does not give us savvy—all right, at a later time we will be stupid, that's all. We cannot know how to make anything. All right, Australia will make us like this. By and by, it will move us; by and by, it will get up and go put its mark [cement peg], and it will say: "Me, I will take this place. Me, I will take this place." All right now, we have no power to enable us to talk. Ah, no. "We have already put cement [they will say]."[21] All right, it will surprise us; it [Australia] will take us and put us in jail.
P: All right now, this [story], it's not just me alone who knows of this story [about whites taking Australia from blacks]. Every last man knows this story—this election got up, and all our knowledge came together.
DB: All knowledge came together at this time. k. But there is not one good thing that comes up. English is not a true savvy; it has to do with the mouth, that's all. But savvy for my hands, where is it? This is the talk we have.

Pengai: America Helped Other Peoples Become Self-Reliant

Pengai: All right now, I said—I mean, this is all talk that I said to [Boski Tom] here: Negroes, and Africans, they all sit down well. They sit down well, as though they were half *masta* [white]. Because America, now, America holds all this line of black men. All right now, we, too, see this; now, I mean, it would be good if Australia would straighten us out. Oh, it's not strong. We can't keep zigzagging about. But Australia has not straightened us out: all right now, this now, you can see. I mean, we—you [Boski]—sit down in the hands of the government, the government holds you, and you say that you are a man. You are a man on Australia's money. But about your situation, if you lived as I do, you're not a man—you are nothing. You aren't able to get rich; you aren't able to do anything like a *masta* [white man] does. All right now, he [Boski Tom] was finished; he didn't talk to me anymore.

Saripat: Savvy About Good Work

Saripat: [The councillor] has no work [for us], just this kind they all make, that's all—do work on the road [and so on].
DB: He hasn't got good work, that something good will come from it.
Sr: Unn [yes]. Just work on the road—find money for tax.
DB: Find money where! [Laughs] . . .
Sr: Un [yes]. It's true. It's true, Dorothy. You look, there [is] no business with sago—no. Just "go sell it again to all the blackskins," just like us, "in the islands." Then we get the money and bring it back, then we send it again for taxes.
DB: And this blackskin in the islands you sold sago to goes to jail because he has no money.
Sr: *Naunem*! [You bet!] You look. Too much work and too much sadness because I work for the money of yours, just as you say to me, in order to pay taxes.

Lapantukan: A New Laplap As Metaphor

Lapantukan: We want—it's like this: ah, the *laplap* we put on are already old with us. All right, we want to throw them away, get new *laplap*. It is the same with this. We know already about all the ways of Australia, because they have already held us. . . . All the fruit [of our hard work] belongs to all of them, that's all. We are like rubbish, we sit down like pigs around and about, we are like dogs, we are like cattle, we just pull the paddles, that's all. . . . Everything that you see, we "pulled the paddle." All right, we want something new for us.

Abo, Mission Worker: "They Kicked"

Abo, a longtime Catholic mission worker from Neitab Islands, where his sister is married to Barol, supported the cult quietly, and without an elaborate ideology. He was a quiet, firm man. He told me this:

The reason for this election is this: a long time has passed, and we haven't got up. Everyone looks at the news and knows that some places get up. Everyone thinks: no good that we go, go, go and take orders, take orders, take orders. So they kicked first. That's what this election was, that's all. They kicked a little; that's what makes a man get up. They wanted to kick, that's all.

Family Metaphors for Help: Bate, Edward, Tombat

The expectation of help from Australia or America which cultists expressed derived explicitly from the conception of obligations within the Lavongai nuclear family. Both countries were referred to metaphorically as "papa," and evaluated as good or bad to their "children." The colonial countries were also seen as "husbands" who were not good to their wives.

The following conversations illustrate the New Hanover symbolic usage of the term "papa" in the Johnson cult.

Bate: It was always the same. Our way of life, in all places, was not straight. All right, then church came. Everyone got understanding from the Bible. It gave us this talk about *marmari* [mercy, pity, being sorry for others who have less than you do]. This is a big thing. For instance, me and Makios, he must *marmari* to me, and I to him. This wasn't something of mine; I didn't know about it. I didn't know about church. The missions taught me. I heard this good talk. The English came and taught us about this thing, church, but they do not follow this talk of the Bible well: *marmari* [said with conviction]. I am so sad. I am just nothing in the eyes of the English [English-speakers]. My way of life, it is as though I've got no father.
DB: You have no father?
B: No, I have.
DB: Oh, you are speaking figuratively [pidgin: *tok piksa*].
B: Yes, I speak figuratively. A man with a child, the child must cry to the father for all good things. You want to know the root of this thing [the election]? This thing which we want, they all say this thing is to help all men who don't

have anything, or a man who is not all right; or an old man or an old woman, later they can sit down well.

Edward told me that he is not afraid, as some are, to stay out of T.I.A.: "Australia, papa to me, is here. I am like a fish inside the fence of Australia—I eat good, sleep good, play good under Australia—I know, we are under the United Nations."

Tombat explained another family metaphor for me. Cultists saw themselves as child to a "papa" country, but also as women leaving an unproviding husband. In the following examples, their fear that their wives will leave them if they do not become better able to provide is also mentioned.

I told Tombat, my good friend from Lavongai village, I was worried that I did not really understand the election. He very kindly tried to give me some savvy. I asked what the women thought of the election, and he said all the women had no talk. They followed all the men. I asked if the women had been cross, and he said, "No, they weren't cross. They said: 'Let all the men finish their liking.'" No, he did not hear of ancestors or America bringing cargo. When I asked if they wanted savvy, not cargo, Tombat replied, "They wanted savvy and cargo."

Tombat said that, "If I don't look after my wife well, she'll run away to another. This is *tok piksa* [an analogy]." He then used a local word, *sol*, which means a great anger and jealousy. Tombat described the word thus: "I am cross because I want something and they don't give me anything good." The election got up from this, he said. We thought, "One hundred Christmases go, and they don't show me about one good way. Plenty of years since the ancestors, we were all young then. What, are we to sit down like rubbish, on and on? I want a good way to save my wife so that she will like me. Plenty of men suffer about this. We stop, stop, wait, wait, and Australia doesn't get up one good way."

Help and Equality First, Self-Government Later:
Oliver, Savemat, Saripat, Silakan

Cultists were afraid that they would have self-government thrust upon them before they were able to be self-reliant. In order to maintain equality among themselves and with outsiders, they wanted help with economic development, which they hoped they could get from America.

Cultists and noncultists alike saw self-government as the loss of the little help they got from Australia, the loss of the hope they had maintained of gaining savvy so that they could become equal to other developed men.

Oliver: Now, suppose self-government must come to men who haven't got - money for everyone. And there is no good road to find money, or there is no good road for all men so that they all must be equal in buying everything or getting money from whatever kind of work. And everyone must have good money, have big money: all right [when that happens], self-government must come, and it's good, too lucky. But we have not got this. Some men are well

off, some are not well off. And all men of savvy savvy well, and one man, he does not savvy—he is just the same as one man shit-nothing, that's all. Later, when self-government comes, it buggers up again this man who is already buggered up. Before, he was buggered up; then self-government comes, buggers him up again. About money, that's all.
DB: Yes, true.
O: But who will straighten it first, the road? Because—you, all whiteskins, you have another kind of road, and another kind of law. Now, with us, all black men, another kind. That is, we are down more yet. Now, a man who has got savvy, he goes and jumps up a little, he goes and jumps up a little on the step; he goes together with you all. But we, some of us, we sleep truly no good. Down below. And what road will you—will they make so that, by and by, all men who are not well off, and all men who have savvy, all must be equal?

Savemat: Now, too, the talk we have heard from the mouths of all [pause] who go first [leaders], they all say: "This day is a day for you and me to be one! [emphatically], that's all. That is to say, you and I cannot divide ourselves, all black men and all whiteskins. This day is a day for you and me to be equal, that's all." But we look, according to the thinking of plenty of us, we see that the meaning of this talk is not true. It's . . .
Saripat: They lie.
Savemat: Lies, that's all.

Silakan had thought of a way to get more rather than less help from the civilized world after self-government. Following my interview with him in front of other men, he drew me aside and asked me quietly in what way they could get America to come. I told him all the reasons I knew why America could not come. He then said, "We are to have self-government, aren't we?" I said, "Yes." "When we have it, can't we oust the Australians and ask some Americans to come and help us?" I was startled and chagrined. 'Yes," I had to admit, "you can."

Why They Liked America: Savemat, Saripat, Makios, Pengai, Rev. Taylor
Europeans close to the cultists thought that they were more interested in savvy rather than in just cargo, and that they wanted savvy about cargo in order to achieve equality. It was the attribution to America not only of savvy about making cargo, but, much more, of having egalitarian relationships with native people that led cultists to vote for Johnson. The following statements made in separate conversations all underscore this idea.

DB: Now, Savemat, you too, have you heard talk about this, about the ways of America?
Savemat: Yes. And they used to say of them [the Americans] that they used to be like good friends together with them.
Saripat: A man would come up. Now, they themselves would get food and put it out for all these men, and they ate together with them. They used to sit down together with them and eat along with all the natives. [Pause.] And we see it like this: I think they are better about this bit of talk now, about you and I are

brothers, and you and I are one now.

Makios: Their [American] ways are not the ways of all men. Their ways are very good. They invite plenty of men and sit down together to eat; and whatever things—they give everything to them. That now, this way we have seen, and our liking remains.

DB: Now, Pengai, I want to hear a little more of the story about how you all know about America, about your thinking America has a lot of savvy. You saw America just at the time of the war and [later] at the time they all went on top, on the mountain [Mt. Patibung], that's all, right?
Pengai: [It was] not us [who saw them in wartime]—they all saw them among all the Big Men. . . . We are not of this line—it was other men at the time of the war, because we were little [children at that time]. All right now, they came back. . . . They told stories, and they all said: "Suppose America sat down together with us, I think it would be very good. Because their ways are good. For instance, when they prepare food, it's not like the way of Australia—they [the Americans] prepare food, you and I together sit down, and I eat now. Now, Australians—they see us, and they tell us to get out."
DB: All the Big Men of before—did they eat the food of Americans?
P: Yeh. They used to sit down together with everyone.
DB: And did they like this food?
P: It's like this—they saw this way, that's all; they did not like the food, just the way.

Rev. Allen Taylor, nurse Val Beckett, and teacher Nancy Anderson ate their Sunday meal with the local teachers and nurses. When I commented that I thought that it was this kind of social equality rather than cargo that cultists wanted, Rev. Taylor said, "I'm sure of it."

Noncultist Ideas: Crazy, Lazy, Disobedient, or Right?

Noncultists among the Lavongai shared administrators' view that cultists were "crazy" men who refused to yield to more "reasonable" beliefs. These irrational beliefs were held to be common to "cargo cults," about which the "loyalists"[22] had perhaps learned from the Europeans, and they included such beliefs as these: that a passing ship was full of Americans who had come to take over the island, or that a cultist had been talking to an American in the bush.

All cultists said that these ideas originated entirely in ridicule (*tok bilas*), and that they had never held these beliefs. Thus, for instance, a policeman at the jail in Taskul shouted out, on seeing a ship out at sea: "Here come the Americans, now you can get out of jail!" Cultists told me that they felt it to be a matter of pride to restrain themselves from responding to these taunts; but sometimes they would say, "That's right, just wait, you'll see! The Americans will come!" Their silence was taken as acquiescence, or their remarks as offers of proof: and all this was ultimately reported by a noncultist to administration officers. Oliver told me that when an administrator challenged him to produce proof, he responded thus: "You'll see, a ship will come." Oliver said he was just talking *gamon* (fooling), and he laughed about it when he told me. These kinds of contacts were the major source for these rumors.

The native noncultists' view that the cultists were "crazy" was founded on a basis quite different from that of the administrators. Cultists and noncultists agreed that they lacked information on which to judge whether or not it was reasonable for them to believe that the Americans would come. Noncultists had grievances against the administration, too; but they thought that the Europeans knew what they were talking about, and that it was silly for the natives to place their own savvy against that of the Europeans. However, more to the point, they saw that cultists were disobeying the Australian government, the only government they had, and the only one from whom they could realistically expect help. For native noncultists, the idea that the cultists were crazy was secondary to the idea that the cultists were confronting the power structure, which they felt it was in their interests to support. When pressed, some noncultists, including the leading figure amongst them, Boski Tom, said that the cultists were not crazy. When noncultists believed that cultists were starting "crazy" rumors, what their reports to the administration amounted to was a warning that these cultists were starting trouble, not that they were crazy. Noncultists agreed that development had been slow and inadequate, and they noted, with some annoyance, that the cult had brought about some benefits.

Edward's Report

I asked Edward to tell me some of the ideas the cultists had. He told me of Cornelio Logo, of Meteran, who saw an American when he slept in the church. He dreamed, and God told him that America would come. I asked Edward who told him that, and he said Silaupara, a councillor of Lungatan, told him this at a council meeting. Silaupara himself followed Australia.

Progress Report, 19 June 1964

Rumor: *Queen Mary* would arrive off Lavongai Catholic Mission with 700 American troops on 16th June. Also thought that helicopter pads were being secretly prepared to be used in this rumored operation.

Cultists Lazy, Not Crazy: D.A.C. Minutes, 1st May 1964

Both Europeans and native noncultists thought that those who had voted for America were looking for an easy way out of their problems. Most native noncultists did not really think cultists were crazy.

Boski Tom refrained from ideological accusation and remained the "scientific observer," but did not resist a sarcastic remark at a district advisory council meeting, as reported in the minutes:

> Mr. Needham asked Mr. Boski Tom's opinion of the cult. Mr. Tom replied that he was unable to offer any solution.

Mr. Healy said the two patrol officers on the island had had only partial success in bringing the people to normal thinking.
Mr. Grose asked Mr. Tom if, in his opinion, the American survey team previously working on New Hanover could have had some bearing on the outbreak.
Mr. Tom said it was his opinion that Bosmailik, having no house or garden, had too little to occupy his mind.

But in his interview with me, Boski Tom also agreed that some of the accusations which cultists made were true. They had, he thought, been misinformed and led to think they would get much more than they could from the projects they were asked to undertake.

DB: You were here at the beginning of the cooperative. Do you think their complaints had some justice about the cooperative movement failing here? Do you think the cooperative movement has failed here?
Boski Tom: Yes, yes, because of some of the leaders. They went around telling the people propaganda, and the people . . .
DB: believed it.
BT: Yes, they believe it when it was said, but later they could not see what had been said.
DB: Some of these leaders did tell them false things, then did they?
BT: Singarau.
DB: Tell me a little about Singarau.
BT: He said that the cooperative came here to help everybody, small and big and weak and strong and old and young.
DB: He said all that?
BT: Not he only.
DB: This Mr. Evans that I keep hearing about, did he say all this? Did you meet him?
BT: I've not been with Mr. Evans when he went around with the people, but I've heard from some of the men in the village. We cannot see what these, all men, leaders of the cooperative, told us before. I think once one director—I knew one director who asked them a question based on what those Big Men were talking about, that co-ops will help everybody. I've been thinking about what Singarau (he was a nephew of mine) and other people said—when they came around and said, "The cooperative is going to help everybody." How will it help us? And I said: "You're going to work. You have to work for everything. Have a meeting and try to find out whether it's a good idea, and then you're going to work for it. You work hard, and you'll get your money. There's no other way you can get money to put into the aid post to help everybody. You can get money to build an aid post in your village, or a tank."
DB: Ah—[and now they see] no tanks.
BT: [Sadly] No tanks. I think this is what they were discouraged about, because they didn't see what these leaders told them before.

Edward admitted that the election brought about some good things, like the new hospital at Taskul. "Before," he told me, "it was no good, just bits of wood, that's all. . . . The government had turned its back on us. This election turned the face of the government to look at me." He demonstrated by first turning his back to me, then turning back around to face me. "Now I eat along with you; I sleep along with Bob [Hoad] and Carroll [Gannon]—just *after* the election. Before, it wasn't like this. Before, I was just rubbish."

> *DB*: Self-government. Edward, what do you think—do you know about self-government, or is it just talk?
> *Edward*: I know about it. But it cannot come up quickly.
> *DB*: It cannot come up quickly. Why, now?
> *E*: Because we haven't got a good thing that has come up in our place: there are not plenty of things that we have planted, for this thing, self-government, to come to us.
> [DB notes in English that the value of freedom is relative to context, then explains to Edward in pidgin what the talk in English for the recorder was about. He responds thus:]
> *E*: Just to be boss, with nothing—by and by, it will be no good.

Administrators: Ideas, Policies, and Ideologies

Because everyone in the administration, as well as other Europeans who were knowledgeable about the situation (e.g., planters), agreed that New Hanover had (for various reasons) been neglected, administrators were defensive about their role in creating the cult. They viewed the failure of the election in New Hanover as damaging to their official reputations as administrators; and, thus, they had a vested interest in viewing cultists as "crazy," and their protest as "just another cargo cult." Noncultists found administrators particularly interested in "crazy" rumors because if the whole thing were viewed as "just another cargo cult" with the usual "crazy beliefs," administrators felt that they could not be blamed for what happened in New Hanover. Most of their superiors had also been in charge of areas where cults had occurred, and most of the natives of the territory were viewed as potential cultists.[23]

Progress Report, circa June 1964

> A.D.O. Toughy reports [from New Hanover election patrol] this a cargo cult. They think they will get more free from America than from Australia. No anti-Australia feeling, only pro-America. His patrol proceeded without incident.

Progress Report, October-December 1964

> Cult activities continued, and it was reported that Oliver and Robin (warrants issued) had held a meeting at Upuas 6 December 1964. However, it was significant that only 7 males out of a possible 100 attended the meeting. One person was convicted and sentenced to 2 months for assisting escapee Oliver, on evidence given by the Tsoi Councillor [Edward] and two other men. They also told P.O. Mr. P. J. Power that at the meeting cult leaders Oliver and Robin

stated that the Americans would arrive to take over New Hanover on 25 January 1965, providing the Australian Administration had left by that date.[24]

Central Administration: Mr. Fenbury

Mr. Fenbury, an official of the Central Administration, visited the Kavieng District in order to evaluate antigovernment activity there and stated his views in a press release. He saw the cult as basically rooted in the character of the people, who were slow to realize that they had to change, whether they wanted to or not.

> Mr. Fenbury said that while political disturbance in slowly evolving Melanesian societies frequently exhibited elements that, from a Western viewpoint, were illogical and irrational, such phenomena were rarely as simple as some people imagined. In the existing New Hanover and West Coast [of New Ireland] situation two important elements appeared to be apathy toward economic development and a withdrawal from the increasing complexity of modern life. With this there was an emotional regression towards anarchy.
>
> While emphasizing that he was stating a personal view, Mr. Fenbury said he felt such people now needed to be told that while nobody enjoyed paying taxes and few people liked hard work, time was running out for the target working villager who was resistant to change.... Unless they developed their own land and their own institutions much more rapidly than they were doing at present, history would overtake them.
>
> The island was economically retarded, mainly because the people were disinclined to make the necessary effort.... The problem was one of motivation.... This, in essence, appeared to be the crux of the New Hanover situation. Similar lotus-eating attitudes appeared to be current in the Namatanai area, which, while the ancestral home of the Tolai people, exhibited none of the Tolai progressiveness.

Service Personnel: Ideas, Policies, and Ideologies

People advocated various kinds of attention or inattention in stating their views about what should be done to end the cult. It is clear, however, that there was a massive increase in attention from police and Department of Native Affairs (D.N.A.; later, Department of District Administration, D.D.A.) personnel, and that there was a decline in service activities. Throughout the early months of the cult, the administration not only did not try to improve services (despite the urgings of some members of the District Advisory Council), they gave orders to service personnel to stay out of New Hanover.

Some service personnel (notably in Public Health, Malaria Control, Education, Agriculture, Stock and Fisheries, Labor Relations), nevertheless, continued to do their work. The official position of D.D.A. was that contacts would create trouble, and D.D.A. personnel feared violent reception for themselves in New

Hanover. Service personnel, however, said that they never feared violent reception: they thought that D.D.A. was overly fearful and overly punitive, and they saw no violence associated with the cult.

Ray Sheridan, Malaria Control

Ray Sheridan, a Malaria Control officer who seemed particularly close to the people and who had produced a record of New Guinea music which he had himself recorded, scoffed at the idea that the New Hanover people were violent. He had conducted a regular patrol there after the election (against D.N.A. wishes, or even orders) and had had no trouble.

Brian Campbell, Malaria Control

Mr. Campbell had previously worked in Manus. He found the people of New Hanover more open than those in Manus and said that they talked more easily. He found no resistance to his service patrol. In fact, there was a party in every village, and he was made very welcome.

He thinks the cult was due to neglect, genuine neglect. The administration asked a Manus Malaria Control team, led by Mr. Campbell, to come to deal with New Hanover, because the present experienced officer (Ray Sheridan) was leaving. The people have been neglected by Agriculture and the co-ops. Mr. Campbell told the people to send a delegation to the D.C. They said: "We did, Master! We were pushed from one *kuskus* [clerk] to another. At the end we were told, 'Your *kuskus* stole all your money.'" No co-op officer went; no *didiman* (agriculture officer) went to show them what to do with their coffee. "They're thinking people," Mr. Campbell told me. "You could do more with them than you ever could here [New Ireland]. I was very sympathetic, I'll admit that. Peter Pouwer [*kiap* during the height of the cult] was transferred from Milne Bay to New Hanover, and he couldn't even speak pidgin except for, '*Sapos iu no harim tok bai iu kissim sikis mun long kalaboos* [If you don't hear (obey) my talk, you'll get six months in jail]."

Keith Hill, Fisheries

Keith Hill, of the Department of Agriculture, Stock and Fisheries, continued to make contact with people throughout the cult. He began an ambitious project in 1966, lending large red fishing nets to villages, and teaching villagers to use and repair them. When I traveled with him, I saw him during his long, patient hours of teaching, often waist-deep in the sea. His efforts were very much appreciated by the people. When the government instructed Mr. Hill to retrieve the nets, he, instead, resigned his position and went to work for the United Nations.

He had also been unable to interest the government in creating a fish canning factory, one where the fish would be packed in coconut milk, a widely used native recipe, rather than in the tomato or mustard sauce in which tinned fish from Japan were packed. He wanted to provide a freezer ship that would pick up the catches of the people who were learning to use his nets. The administration gave him no support for this project which was, however, carried out by a Japanese firm in 1972. "Neglect" is probably not a strong enough word to describe Mr. Hill's view of government inactivity. He himself never wasted any time in complaints or regrets, however.

Carroll Gannon, Medical Assistant

Carroll Gannon was transferred to New Hanover by Mr. Seale, who had seen his work before and thought he would do a good job in New Hanover. Carroll saw the real problem as one of being happy, and he tried to be happy with the people without worrying about getting jobs done. But he said that work is good medicine, and found work for people to do: most notably, the construction of an aviary to house birds from all over New Guinea. He had three rules, he told me (and everyone else): 1) work hard, 2) help others, and 3) don't get cross quickly. "Are you happy?" he called out as he greeted people he met and kept up a steady stream of words. "Talk is Carroll's food," one young man told me with a smile.

Carroll was pleased that a doctor (Ph.D.) from New Guinea, anthropologist Ted Schwartz, and the missionaries praised his work, but he was quick to point out that his way was not necessarily the right or only way. Jailing cultists was not his way, but, he said, jailing cultists had been effective. "Bob [Hoad] has done a good job. Maybe he was the right man in the right place at the right time. He's sadistic—he put the old ones in for six months to make them savvy. But this worked."

Like a good scientist, and therapist, Carroll balanced his views and concentrated on keeping people doing things. "Those that say they enjoyed their martyrdom in jail have a chip on their shoulders still. Those who say, 'We were silly' and laugh are over the border." Carroll constantly gave pep talks to try to get people working together, to try to end factionalism, within Lavongai and between the people and the government.

Carroll had his own differences with the government. In response to the continual efforts to label the cultists crazy, Carroll asked for a speedboat in which to visit his "mentally ill" population on New Hanover. His request was declined, and he wondered aloud if the government really thought the people were mentally ill, or were just making excuses for their own neglect.

Carroll's greatest material accomplishment was the new hospital at Taskul in 1967, and he walked around the island to invite people to the party to celebrate its grand opening. Only 500 came, and he was a little disappointed, although everyone else thought it was a grand success. Afterward, Carroll was cheerful and philosophical, as always, about the party: "It was just like the cult," he told me. "Those who were in it had a wonderful time, and those who weren't always wondered what was going on." His insights into the cultists were very interesting and enlightening to one who, like myself, tended to be brainwashed in a puritanical social science which, at that time, rarely mentioned that one thing people do is have fun. On another occasion Carroll said, "Do you get the impression that they're just acting? They're all actors here, all Academy Award

Winners." After years of pouring over my notes, I finally made that observation a fundamental part of my analysis of the Johnson cult.

Jim Hancock, Teacher

Jim Hancock, an Australian teacher at the Meteran school, independently made the same observation Carroll Gannon had made about New Hanoverian acting ability. He said that he thought many men had wanted to buy out of the cult long ago, but their pride would not let them "They're very damned proud," he told me, "and they're great actors."

Planters: Ideas, Policies, and Ideologies

Government (D.D.A.) officers' attempts to take an optimistic view of the cult as in decline, of the results of their efforts to stop the cult as successful, and of the irrelevance of their own role in its origin were rejected by planters Jim White of New Hanover and Jim Grose of New Ireland. These men continued to insist on the need for more frequent patrols, which, up until 1998, still had not been initiated.

The cultists probably would have been very much surprised had they ever found out that one of the staunchest defenders of their view that the government had neglected them was planter Jim White, whom they often saw as an adversary. M.H.A. (Member, House of Assembly) Jim Grose was not known in New Hanover but was generally on friendly terms with the people of New Ireland, where he had grown up in a hardworking Australian plantation family, and where he had just been elected at large from the Kavieng District to the House of Assembly. He agreed with Mr. White.

District Advisory Council Minutes, 6 November 1964

> Mr. White said that in his opinion [the cult] was due to four things: 1) that there was no patrol officer stationed at Taskul for some time; 2) that the hospital had been removed from Taskul; 3) that the Public Health Department had built an Aid Post at Baungung against the wishes of the Council, the D.A.C. and all Europeans in the area; and 4) that water tanks had been built but not installed, and the Public Health Department subsidy stopped.
> Mr. Healy said that the P.H.D. subsidy had not been stopped; the people simply did not want those things.
> Mr. White referred to the coffee scheme initiated on New Hanover by the Department of Agriculture which had foundered and said this was another cause of discontent.
> Mr. Grose suggested posting a D.A.S.F. (Department of Agriculture, Stock and Fisheries) officer to New Hanover for twelve months to salvage the coffee scheme.
> Mr. Healy said the current D.A.S.F. staff situation would not permit posting an officer to New Hanover.

Mr. Grose said that an officer could be transferred in.

Mr. Healy said that law and order should be re-established within the next two months, and it might be possible to implement Mr. Grose's suggestion then.

Planters Birch and Walker

All of the planters were solidly anticult and certainly wanted to see an end to it, as it threatened their own work. Many of them believed the government had neglected New Hanover (and many other things), and they were concerned that their own criticism of the government might have stirred up the cult activities.

Jack Birch of Enuk Island and Jimmy Walker of the west coast of New Ireland told me when I asked them one day that there was nothing religious about the cult. "I would not have thought of that," Jack said. It was anti-*kiap*. Jimmy Walker, who was English but had been raised in the colonies (India), thought the planters were partly to blame: "We all spoke anti-*kiap* to them," he said.

Planter Betheras

John Betheras, manager at Medina plantation on New Ireland's east coast, was a gentle man who, like many planters, spent a great deal of time sewing up wounds and administering medicine to his labor line. Most of these men were, however, from other parts of the territory and had little involvement with local people. John criticized his compatriots generally for talking too frankly against *kiaps* to the local people. "You know I can't stand most of these *kiaps*," he told me, "but I stand up for them to the natives."

Mr. and Mrs. Pitts

But some plantation managers thought that the cult was the result of too much attention, rather than of neglect, from the government; and that the roots of the problem lay in the character of the people themselves, and in their lifestyle. One manager told Mr. Pitts that if the government had not kept up their activities against the cult it would have long been dead. He told me that he thought there was not enough to do, and that that was the source of the cult. "A lot of what the cultists do is to upset people," he said, "and they have had too much attention for doing that." Both Mr. and Mrs. Pitts said that the people here were like children: they try to annoy you to get your attention. Mr. and Mrs. Pitts do not give in and get cross because then the people have won.

Mr. Pitts thinks the people are still in the cult, "still anti-administration," but that some would like to get out but cannot: "They have so much pride they won't climb down." Mr. and Mrs. Pitts look back nostalgically to their earlier years as plantation managers in Tanganyika, where people were friendly and polite, but where protest was more serious: "This is childish compared to Mau Mau," Mr. Pitts observed.

Missionaries: Ideas, Policies, and Ideologies

The missions were in some ways on the side of the administration and the noncultists. Cult activity was most fervent in Methodist areas, and the European Methodist missionaries spent a great deal of time talking to cultists, trying to "explain" various things. On at least two occasions, Methodist missionaries convinced cultists who had evaded arrest that things would go better for them if they turned themselves in at the district office.

The missions, however, disagreed fundamentally with the approach of the administration to stopping the cult. Administration action was punitive and aimed at reestablishing authority; while missionary action was educational, aimed at reestablishing communication, confidence, and constructive activity. Each felt that its own approach was sufficient in itself to stop cult activity, which was considered disruptive of order and daily work, and potentially violent; as well as threatening to the legitimacy of both mission and government as structures of order with various kinds of authority.

Rev. Allen Taylor, Methodist Missionary

The Reverend Mr. Allen Taylor of the Ranmelek Methodist Mission said that the cult was a communication problem. It could be related to relative isolation of villages and inaccessibility by boat. Umbukul had no cult, and it has a beach. Ships can and do go to it. Cult villages are villages, like Konemetalik, with no exchange—of goods or ideas. They heard this one idea, and they followed it.

Reverend Taylor spent quite a bit of time, when he first came to Ranmelek in 1965, going around to the Methodist villages in his area and telling the people that Johnson was not in "the line" of those they could vote for in the election. He also told them that the council was a new road, inside the road of the government. By and by, the little road will "eat" the big road, and they will be the same, one road. They must not, he told them, put a fence on the council road: "If you do, it's your children who will suffer." Of their thinking about Johnson and the Americans, he advised them to "throw it away." He did not call it "rubbish" or "crazy," he said, because these words had acquired an emotional meaning, and it was best not to use them.

Reverend Taylor thought it was harder for the people in New Hanover than in New Ireland. They did not hear what goes on. In New Ireland, if you go up and down the road, you can see that things are happening. I asked, "Like what?" The Reverend Taylor listed better houses, copra houses, tanks, and a general sense of busyness.

Reverend Taylor thought that the government did not know how to talk to the people. They sent a paper around telling the people that the councils had "power." He thought that the government was overly concerned with this concept.

Fr. Bernard J. Miller, Missionaries of the Sacred Heart (M.S.C.)

On my way to Lavongai for the first time, at the Analaua mission station, I read an article by Father Miller before I had met him; and I thought it was very good. Since then, Father Miller has gained not just intellectual but substantial confirmation for his views as he applied them in his work as an "action missionary." Here follow brief excerpts from his article:

> We often underestimate the pride of this man [the Lavongai]. He has a deep pride, but is constantly being humbled by the knowledge, superiority and often the scorn of the white man. The Lavongai's pride is not being destroyed, but simply being overwhelmed by all he sees and hears of the European world. He does not hate the white man, at least not yet, but is simply ashamed and humbled in his presence.
>
> Most white men approach the natives as liberators from ignorance, primitive societies, fears, diseases, and hunger, or for cheap labor and quick profit, but they do not consider the pride of the man they classify as primitive. Yet the pride is always there like a spring being wound tighter and tighter. It must release with force from time to time.
>
> PROGRESS THROUGH RESISTANCE
>
> The Lavongai has developed an expression of resistance that is positive and for progress. He is not against the present government. He is not anti-Australian. He is pro-American. I have given up trying to reason with the people about Johnson, about the elections and the Americans. It is useless. To the Johnsonites reasoning is useless. You have to show these people.
>
>> I try to show them how they can make their own country into something to be proud of. It will not be Americans, Australians, or anyone else who will bring progress to their country. They themselves must do it. . . . "Use your ground," I tell them. "Where are your coconuts? Where is your copra? Why don't you have cattle?"
>> This is what I preach to them. "Use what you have received from God. Use this beautiful land where things grow so easily." I try to back up my words with actions. There is timber on the island. I have managed to acquire a saw mill. I hope to develop this into a small operation that will show the people the value of building a saw mill, or planting cocoa, or raising cattle. It is not easy to show these people the value of a long-range operation. It is a complicated work, but I believe this is honest missionary work.
>> We missionaries have to be leaders not only at worship but in the copra plantations, on the trading wharfs, and in the village meetings. Deep inside the people of Lavongai there is a respect for truth. We have to help them understand truth in a confusing age. We have to lead them not only to eternal truth but to worldly truth. . . . Our aim is to help them not just to be good People of God, but to be good People of Lavongai (Miller 1966, 20, 22, 24-25 *passim*).[25]

Catholic Missionaries: Discussion

When Carroll Gannon sent his medical report to Port Moresby, in which he said he thought the cultists were "mentally ill," both Father Miller and Sister Liboria objected to the diagnosis. Sister Liboria thought that Carroll's report might be misunderstood in Konedobu: "It's all right for those of us who know them and know what he means," she said. Father Miller said that he would say "fanatic" rather than "mentally ill."

Father Miller told Father "Jake" Jacubco, "They're not mentally ill; it's just like a religion." Father Jake said, "No, religion is logical; we have systematic arguments." Father Miller replied, "But this is logical. Look at their evolution idea. It's just like Marx. It's terribly logical."

The reasoning, if not the premises, of the cult was often compelling. "I don't know why they call these 'cults'; I think they're very intellectual," Father Miller said one day, an opinion he often expressed in various ways. On one occasion when I said that I thought they did not really "believe," that there was no misuse of evidence, that they just had "hope," Father Miller said, "Oh, yes, it was a matter of hope. They hoped the Americans would come. Just like me, I have hope of eternal life. Otherwise it would be pretty silly for me to be out here doing what I am." In response to my request, Fr. Jake, who was often visited by Oliver and spent many hours talking with him, wrote me a long letter about him in which he stated that the question was not what did Oliver believe, but what was *bugging* him.

Father Miller and his colleagues in the mission had a great tolerance for diversity of belief which their predecessors may not have shared. Of my agnosticism, Father Miller merely commented, "Well, I sure hope you guys don't turn out to be right." He kept in his house carvings which an earlier generation of missionaries had called pagan images; and, after a while, he listened to the cultists without trying to persuade them to abandon their ideas. When we were discussing exactly what cultists did mean by "belief," Father Jake noted that "Truth or falsity does not seem to be the issue." Father Miller agreed that cultists did not try to offer "proofs" for their beliefs: "*Laik bilong mipela tasol* [It's what we would like, that's all]."

Fr. Miller: A Musical Comedy

Like Jim Hancock and Carroll Gannon, Father Miller noticed the dramatic quality of the cult, as well as its humor: "You're not going to write this up as a dissertation, are you?" he said one day. "You should write this up as a musical comedy."[26]

Beliefs

What did the cultists really believe about their election for America? There was an ideology, developed partly for its political effect. There was the residue of contemporary verbal assault and counterassault between cultists and noncultists, and of the ridicule of the police, received in suffering silence. But beneath all the politics and insult, did the cultists really believe that Johnson would come? What did they believe about America? And did they believe that cargo would arrive in ways mysterious to Europeans? What did they believe about the supernatural, and the effects, if any, of ritual? Many outsiders thought that the cultists rested their faith on some kind of empirical evidence, but none that I met offered any kind of proof that could be debated or refuted. Nevertheless, as it always seems simple to those outside a cult or movement to refute with facts the expectations and claims of the True Believers, so here, in New Hanover, most Europeans at first offered "facts." Details of history and current affairs from widely accepted current world views or mythologies were patiently, or sarcastically, offered as "evidence" that the Americans would not come. This approach sometimes had unintended consequences: cultists were skilled at argument, and sometimes were able to construct a scenario in which, from the European point of view, the Americans could, in fact, come. But did they believe it would?

America

With a few exceptions, virtually all Lavongais, within the cult and outside it, believed that it was possible that America might come. However, it is not clear that this belief looked to processes outside those to be found functioning on the world stage.

Joseph Pukina
One day Joseph Pukina told me that that very day he had heard on the radio that America had wanted to come to New Guinea but that the Australians would not let them. On the trail of a current rumor, but wanting to avoid causing trouble, I questioned him further. I found that he referred to the fact that that day it had indeed been announced on the radio, in pidgin English, that the American Peace Corps had wanted to send 400 people, and that the Australians had turned down the offer, saying they preferred to try to do the job themselves first.[27] Pukina seemed to have a "realistic" understanding of it, that this was not the government of America wanting to come to boss as a result of their election. The fact remained that some Americans had wanted to come, and the Australians stopped them. I never heard this incident discussed, however; it was not, somehow, the heart of the matter.

There were a few cultists that I found (and no doubt some that I did not find) that I think really believed that America was coming, but none so unambiguously that they did not want to know what I thought about it, though they did not ask directly very often. All they really wanted to know was that I agreed with them; if I did not, these firm believers were not really interested in my views.

Most, I think, did not believe literally that America was going to come. I think they would have been very surprised, and probably pleased, if it had. They did not "believe" because they thought they had evidence, but because it gave them hope. There was never any standardization of belief, no clarification of exactly what their faith was in, no catechism offered by which outsiders could join the cult. The content of belief was clearly secondary to the ideology that grew from it, which was stated in terms of the relationship of the people of New Hanover to the government, and which was rooted in all the problems of their daily life which seemed to make them so helpless and unfulfilled.

Oliver

> *DB*: Now, in your thinking, is this one reason America did not come, because all did not believe strong?
> *Oliver*: I do not know about things related to the United Nations. Or everything about them. Just believe, that's all. Believe in God, or believe in this thing, or believe that this thing will come up later—that [the decision] is for God. Now, what idea He makes in whoever is boss of the world, so he [the boss] brings whatever kind of idea, or he does whatever kind of work, or he brings whatever kind of thing that is strong that something will come up, so as to support this thing.
> *DB*: Yes, I understand.
> *O*: Just like, like, it's just like, like, that's all.
> *DB*: Yes, now I understand, but I wanted to be clear.

Ritual

Many cargo cults are said to have produced ritual acts that western science views as futile in relation to the accomplishment of the purposes for which they are explicitly performed. I know of no such acts in relation to the Johnson cult.

The cement pegs left by the U.S. Army were viewed apprehensively as perhaps more than what they were (although who knows what they, property of the United States Army Corps of Engineers, portend?), but there is no evidence that their significance was exaggerated in the direction of "magic." I think people viewed them as signs and symbols of the intentions of Americans, and not as objects of power that might be ritually invoked.

The term "ritual" has a range of meanings, and in another sense there was one act performed by many of the cultists that I would call a "ritual" act. This occurred when cultists "promised to God," or to themselves, that they would vote for America. They made this promise when, at many different meetings, a local spokesman asked those present to raise their hands if they would vote for America. The first meeting at which this hand-raising occurred was at Magam village, the night before the scheduled balloting at Ranmelek. Those who raised their hands at that time later interpreted their own act as a commitment. I never found out that anyone asked people to commit themselves through this act. Each individual merely interpreted his own act in this way, no doubt influenced by the opinions of others. This was a ritual act in the sense that it marked a transition point in their lives, a "bridge-burning" commitment (Gerlach and Hine, 1968) after which there was no turning back. Many took their own commitment to mean that they would vote for America forever, no matter what happened, and that their children and grandchildren would follow them.

In 1967, there was still evidence in behavior of a commitment to the election, to America, and to a better life for themselves. And this single act of ritual was often given as the reason why they could not change their attitude toward paying taxes. However, when something else came along that allowed them to honorably reinterpret their commitment, they quickly changed. The ritual act had little power in itself. Ritual acts were not characteristic of the cult, and from what I could learn they were not characteristic of New Hanover's traditional culture.

Pengai

    Pengai: All right, I did not worry about this [being jailed] because, it's like this: I had already promised.
    DB: You promised to all men.
    P: Yeh—no, I did not promise to all men; I mean [in] my thinking.
    DB: You promised to yourself, that's all.
    P: Yeh—I promised to myself.

The Supernatural

The only "supernatural" agency believed to be active in the cult was God, the God of whom the Lavongais had learned from the missions apparently, but perhaps the same one in which they had always believed. The beliefs of Lavongais about God were certainly in the same realm of discourse with the European Judeo-Christian beliefs about God.

God was mentioned primarily in three contexts. The first was with regard to the election itself, particularly the balloting at Ranmelek. Unity is not a common state in New Hanover, and is not expected. Not without sorrow, the people joke about their characteristic inability to act in concert. The unity achieved in the vote for Johnson was surprising to them, which partly explained their invoking the supernatural to explain it. They said God must have come at once into everyone's mind, else why would all have had the same thought at the same time?

The second context in which God was regularly mentioned was with regard to the "promise to God," which has already been discussed in connection with its ritual aspects.

Third, a firm faith in a loosely defined God did sustain many cultists to whom I spoke. When they were suffering in jail, or afraid upon the arrival of the police to arrest them, they asked for God's help, and felt that they had perhaps received it.

I found no suggestion that traditional beliefs about particular supernatural agencies, or any amalgamation of the new and the old, were involved in the cult. I found no formalized traditional beliefs easily categorized as "religious."

Savemat: Promise to God

> *Savemat*: Silaumirigen asked us [after the vote for Johnson] altogether, "Suppose you altogether agree in this liking, then you and I altogether, our hands on top." All right, this: all of us came and put our hands up for this. This, all the time we refer to this, our hands up at this time. [Pause]
> *DB*: If you all put your hands on top, the meaning of it is?
> *Savemat*: Arm goes on top, to [pause] to God here.

Lapantukan: God Helped in Hard Times

Many cultists felt they were receiving help from God when they were suffering from physical pain, fear, ridicule, or uncertainty. It was in this context more than any other that reference was made to a supernatural agency when cultists talked about their views to me. Lapantukan was more interested in this subject than most, and I used a more directive mode of questioning than usual, in case it was I, and not the cultists, who was avoiding the supernatural.

> *DB*: Now, at this time of the election, you all were strong, and you believed that God was helping you with this?
> *Lapantukan*: Um [Yes].
> *DB*: God helped you.
> *L*: Yes, yes. Then I felt my strength; and my beliefs, I saw them.
> *DB*: You all no longer believe still that God helps you?
> *L*: I believe now that God helps me—now. In this work I hold, and with this thing, I believe yet that God can help me and show me about this thing.
> *DB*: I just look at you all working very strong in *Tutukuvul*, and I think plenty of men think God stands up along with you in *Tutukuvul*, right?
> *L*: Um [Yes].
> *DB*: Now, suppose you all pray to God, what would you pray for, that He would help you with what?
> *L*: That He should help us in this election of ours.
> *DB*: That America will come.
> *L*: Unn [Yes].
> *DB*: Another thing you prayed for?
> *L*: That He should help us with this kind of thing—that the police come up to us with.
> *DB*: Oh, help your body so you can stand up strong—all the policemen hit you all? Or did they make fun of you, or what?
> *L*: They all said I was Councillor of America—ah, I was President of America. Oh, all kinds of talk, oh . . .
> *DB*: You cried at this time.
> *L*: What could I say? The "black hats" [police] truly . . . they all said Johnson will come along with cargo for us.

DB: Who said?
L: Them, all the police.
DB: They just made fun, that's all.
L: Unn [Yes], made fun of us. The police, they kicked the asses of some, they hit the asses of some, they said, "Him, Johnson comes in a plane here, he will come to you all, he comes to help you with your work." All kinds of talk, all kinds of talk.

Cargo

There were no rituals to magically produce cargo. All cultists interviewed, with two possible exceptions, said that cargo comes about through work of a practical sort rather than through ritual actions or reliance on supernatural agencies; and the two possible exceptions merely thought that the spirits might help human beings mentally, not that they could do the job themselves.

Because of persistent rumors among Europeans and native noncultists that cultists believed that cargo was made by and would be brought by the ancestors, I asked for information on this subject. I finally found informants who told me that this was an old story amongst their forbearers who first had contact with Europeans. These people of before did not understand. They did not really know what to believe, and they told stories in which they suggested that perhaps ancestors made the cargo. They were just guessing and wondering (pidgin: *siut nabout, tok nabout*), it was said, not asserting a belief. This was in the old days when the local population had not yet seen the light, they said. I did not evoke a connection between this story and contemporary actions, even from the one passionately involved cultist who admitted that he had heard the story and that he did not know whether or not it was true. He treated it as irrelevant. In any case, he indicated, whether or not ancestral spirits knew how to make cargo, it was clear that Americans knew how, that they could teach the people of New Hanover, and that it was important to keep working hard and believing that your work would bear fruit.

Barol: Noncultist

I asked Barol why he thought some people had voted for America, and he said, "The main thing that made them vote for America was this: America will come up; they will give to everyone for nothing." He knew, he said, that "all things do not come from nothing: they come from strength."

Saripat: Cultist

The following excerpt from my long interview with Saripat was a high point in my investigation of the question of whether or not cultists had really believed they were voting for free cargo. In it, I was, and am, unsure whether or not Saripat was teasing me at first. I believe, however, that he changed to a literal mode when he saw that I was confused, and that he was talking "straight" when he told me that beliefs about cargo and ancestors belonged to the old days. He probably assumed, since I seemed to be interested in the Lavongai point of view, that I knew this. Because of the centrality of this point in conversations with local people outside New Hanover, anticultists, and Europeans, I pursued it more than was comfortable for me in this conversation.

> *DB*: Makios explained well about talking around. I heard there was talk around, at the time of the election, "By and by, the ancestors who are dead, they themselves will make cargo for you all." Now, Makios said: "This talk does not come up from us of the election; this comes up from making fun, that's all." Is that true?
> *Saripat*: Um [Yes]. This talks it doesn't belong to us. This talk, all these men make fun. Now. this talk—did you ask Makios about it?
> *DB*: I just asked him about this . . .
> *Sr*: . . . talking around.
> *DB*: Talking around about, by and by, the ancestors will bring cargo.[28]
> *Sr*: You heard where?
> *DB*: He asked me, too, I heard where, and I said one . . . I heard it around from some men in Taskul. Carroll [Gannon] told me that some people talk like this.
> *Sr*: *Kiap*?
> *DB*: Carroll—doctor boy.
> *Sr*: Ah, ah, ah—he told you. [He is really pressing and interested. I wonder why. Is it because they want to know who to blame for revealing their secret to the anthropologist? Or because they want to know who is ridiculing them? I now think it is the latter. I am guilty of almost spreading rumors.]
> *DB*: Yes. I think—yes, he told me he heard this talk around. Are there plenty of men who believe about this thing? Plenty of men believe by and by cargo will come up from the ancestors?
> *Sr*: I think—I don't know well, Dorothy. I don't understand well about all men, they believe . . .
> *DB*: whatever thing . . .
> *Sr*: about all the ancestors. About all the ancestors, about cargo comes up from all the ancestors, I don't understand well about this.
> *DB*: Now, you yourself, just you alone, do you believe in this thing?
> *Sr*: In?
> *DB*: By and by, cargo will come up from the ancestors?
> *Sr*: I [laughs] am not talking clear [laughs] to Dorothy [laughs], that's the truth!
> *DB*: You don't know well. [I have misunderstood. He is laughing because he sees that the naive anthropologist thinks he may be a naive native.]
> *Sr*: I don't know well. No good I pretend to you. [He is just being a careful empiricist here.] Because it [this talk] doesn't belong to now, the time of the election—it belongs to long before, to all our ancestors.
> *DB*: Yes, I want to hear about this. What did all the ancestors teach about this?
> *Sr*: When all the ancestors were still alive, they said: "When a man dies, he is completely dead." And [or] they said, "A man goes to *Mait*," this here, a place which we call *Mait*.
> *DB*: Oh, that's the place where they made *mias* [red shell currency] before, I think. [Mangai people say *mias* is made in Djaul Island and, with a smile, in *Mait*.]

Sr: Just that, in *Mait* here! But—they asked, "What do they do in *Mait*?" because *Mait* is down below, [where] they buried this man who died. "What do they do in *Mait*?" What do they do? They go to make *laplap* (wrap-around cloths worn by all). And they go make blankets for us. [Thus people mused about what might be the activities of the dead, some of whom had been known and loved.]

DB: Oh! Who talked like that?

Sr: They did, all the ancestors. This bit of talk belongs to all the ancestors themselves.

DB: Oh. This bit of talk belongs to all the ancestors themselves.

Sr: Them, they said: "It was them, all your ancestors who died and went [and made these things]." Now, they didn't understand well where all these things came from: *Laplaps* come from where? And whatever kind came, whatever kind, whatever kind, whatever kind of thing came up, they all said: "Oh, I think all these men of ours before who died went and made this thing for us now." Like that. This talk doesn't belong to us!

DB: It belonged to the ancestors before.

Sr: It belonged to all the ancestors here!

DB: You heard it when you were a young man?

Sr: I heard it when I was still a young man. It's not now! It's not now that I hear this talk. This bit of talk belongs to long before.

DB: To the time all whiteskins were new along here.

Sr: Umm [Yes]!

DB: And *laplaps* were new things!

Sr: *Naunem* [You bet]!

Bate: Cultist

Jim White directed me to Bate, an old man who had long been a faithful employee. Bate was in the cult. After I had talked with Bate for a while, I asked him if there was a belief, as some people had suggested, that the ancestors make cargo. He laughed and said, "I think they are joking, that's all."

Lapantukan: Cultist

DB: Another bit of talk I have heard: by and by, the ancestors who have died make cargo and will bring it to you all. This bit of talk, is there someone who believes it? Or is it just ridicule?

L: [Pause] Here? Um [Yes], I have heard it, too, from some; they got this bit of talk, and they say it's all right. I [am one who] hears it, that's all.

DB: Do you believe this talk?

L: [Nervous laugh] Do I believe it?

DB: Yes, you alone, do you believe in this talk, that the ancestors will bring you cargo? Do you believe a little?

L: Um [Yes: talks slowly], I believe a little. I haven't got anything to hide from you.

DB: No, don't hide it from me.

L: [Matter-of-factly] I heard this thing, and I believe a little in it.

DB: Who first gave you this bit of talk?

L: [Very quiet] I have forgotten.
DB: When you were a little child, did you hear it?
L: No, no.
DB: It came to your ear now, that's all.
L: [enthusiastic now] Now, that's all. It came up—from this work of ours that we've done. But long before yet, I didn't hear it. It's like new talk, yes.

Alipes: Uncertain

DB: Did you [hear this talk] when you were a child?
Alipes: I heard that, by and by, Papa will come. He died when I was little. I have heard of the ancestors, but I don't know, is this a riddle [*tok bokis*] or a figure of speech [*tok piksa*], or is it true? I think it is true or [not true]?

Oliver: Cultist

DB: You told me before—you said if you did not believe strongly this thing cannot come up, right?
Oliver: It cannot come up, because I just play, or I just go around for no reason, or I do not believe in this thing; and, thus, God looks—and he knows about me, right? He knows about me, and he watches my thinking just playing for nothing [my insincerity], and he watches my thinking just do things easy, for nothing—this thing, do I want it, or do I not believe? All right, it will not come up. Or He will not bless this thing. All right, it will not come up. If I believe in something, and I am strong in believing, all right, God knows this; he knows my belief—all right, he must . . . [does not finish sentence]
DB: And this is the reason you went around to all men, right, to strengthen belief?
O: Yes.
DB: Yes, now I understand, but I wanted to be clear. You told me before. Because you know, plenty of people outside are not clear, and they make fun of you, because they do not understand the meaning of belief [to you]. "Belief" is something to strengthen you all, and, by and by, God will know that you truly believe.
O: You look—suppose there is something that I have not seen, I must believe in it, right? I must believe in this thing I have not seen.
DB: For instance, heaven.
O: Yes. Heaven I have not seen either; God I have not seen; but I must believe without evidence . . . I don't know what time I will find this thing I have believed in. Now, something I have seen, and I believe in it, that is not straight. That is not true [belief]. But something I have not seen, I must believe [have faith] in it. It must come up, or I must find it. That is true belief [faith], this one. But look at something, then believe in it—that is not true belief [faith].
DB: Ah, now I understand—just like Doubting Thomas, in the Bible.
O: Yes, yes.
DB: I had forgotten about that. [Pause] When you were a child in this mission school, did they teach you about all these things?
O: No.

DB: It just came up in your mind.

O: It just came up in my mind—the reason for it was my asking.

DB: Yes, you have told me of this time when you waited, and thought, and asked. [Pause] When you were a little child, did you believe strongly everything that the Church taught you?

O: I heard, that's all—I believed, I heard, but I believed—but I found it [for myself], too.

DB: You found it, too, later.

O: Yes. I must find it. I cannot just hear it. I must find it, too.

DB: In your own thinking.

O: Yes.

DB: Now, you mentioned the work of the spirit. What is the work of the spirit?

O: The work of the spirit: I know how to think, that's all. Suppose I sit down, and I think of something. For instance, I sit down with nothing, I haven't got anything—I haven't got food, I haven't got anything. Now, it's something like the mind—now, it's like this: I know that all spirits must work inside and turn my thinking. They show my mind how to do something, and I do it, and I eat, or I have got one shilling. Now, I call this the work of the spirit.

DB: To help you with this . . .

O: With all my life, for all time. Now, every little thing that I find or that I make or that I think is the work of all spirits, because the spirit comes down to work. It does not come down to sleep and do nothing in all places everywhere. It comes down to work. To straighten all men, or to show all men.

DB: Yes, I understand. I had thought [at first] that you meant something else. I think that you know that plenty of men in the old days, and today, too, they think that the work of the spirit is to produce the cargo that belongs to you and me now.

O: Cargo?

DB: Umm [Yes]. Plenty of men believe that the work of the spirit is this kind of work.

O: Plenty of men believe in the spirit, that it shows all about some good thinking, so that they will find out everything, so that there will be enough for the bodies of all in their lives.

DB: But with regard to making the cargo? Does the spirit work it straight [directly]? Not so, huh?[29]

O: Spirit—in the mind, that's all. The spirit, its work is to give ideas, that's all. But as for working [making, doing things], it is not able [*i no inap*]. Now, the minds of all men know plenty of things. And they all know about plenty of things. Plenty of things in the ground, plenty of things in the bush plenty of things in the sea. But their work [use], there is no man to teach everyone about it. Suppose the spirit were a true man, a man who belongs on the earth, it would be better if he showed everyone about all this. God must talk to all; he must show all about the work, as he showed Jesus first. All right, all would be able to do it. But Jesus, he went back, and the Holy Spirit comes down in order to work, so that thinking will be clear, because the spirit clears the thoughts. But its work is strong [great]. But—who will show everything to everyone?

Suppose I find some trouble. I find a woman. Now I don't forget about God with regard to this. I must thank God for this. Or suppose I find whatever kind of thing. I find fish. Now I have what kind of fish. Or I come and eat. I must say thank you for this. Or suppose I find whatever. I go to the garden, I must say thank you for this. Because I know, everything, God put it on the earth, and it does not have no purpose. I must see Him at the time, say thank you. Absolutely everything belongs to Him Himself. And my little time [of life], too. It does not belong to many men; it belongs just to me.

DB: You think of God all the time. Why don't you go to school to be a missionary, Oliver? I think missionary work would be good work for you.

O: Missionary [work] is good work for me, but missionary—God does not stop just with missionaries. He must be with me, too, if I am a man who is not a missionary, or if I am a man who is not straight. God stays with all men who hold His law, and God stays with all men who believe true. And God stays with a man who does something bad, too. All men entirely on the earth, they are men of God, that's all. But my work is to see Him and say thank you to Him for all the things he has put on the earth. That is for me to do, that's all.

DB: Yes. True.

O: You look, I see everything. I see the sea—it never ceases to break at its boundary. I see the wind: it changes. I see the sun: it does not cease. I see the night: it's the same. And everything must work in this way. God has put everything for all time, for all years. for all months, for all weeks—for eternity. Me, too, the same. I cannot cease to be. The same, too, all good lives. They do not cease to work among all, around the whole world. They must work. I am not surprised when something comes to me. I say: ach, now, that's all, it comes up to me. It does not have work to do around in all places, and it comes up to me, and I find this thing. And I know it is something from before yet. But its work is to keep going around in its work in all the world.

Organization

Beginning Again: Tutukuvul Isukal Association

Out of the views held in common by the missions, that the cult held energies that could be constructively channeled, an American Catholic priest led cultists to organize a new endeavor: Tutukuvul Isukal Association (T.I.A.).

By October 1966, some people had been jailed for the third year in a row for nonpayment of taxes. Each year the number of defaulters decreased as jail lost its appeal as a symbol, and as people became discouraged about the effects of their protest. Nothing was happening. The cultists had been unable to follow through from consensus to organization; unable to provide structure, and unable to throw up a leader like Paliau of Manus (Mead, 1956; Schwartz, 1962).

Into this vacuum of leadership came Father Bernard Miller, M.S.C., of Toledo, Ohio, who became resident priest at Lavongai Mission in 1965. He had been at Lemakot,[30] but he exchanged places with Father Philip Kelly after the latter, also an American (from Pennsylvania), became an enemy to the cultists for his refusal to help them contact Johnson.

Father Miller spent a great deal of time listening to cultists and trying to think of something he could do to improve the situation for everyone. After more than a year in Lavongai, he sent out word that there would be a meeting at

Pacific Ocean
MUSSAU
MANUS
N
W
E
S
NEW HANOVER
NEW IRELAND
Bismark Sea
NEW BRITAIN
Mount Hagen
BOUGAINVILLE
PAPUA NEW GUINEA
SOLOMON
ISLANDS
TROBRIAND
ISLANDS
Port
Moresby

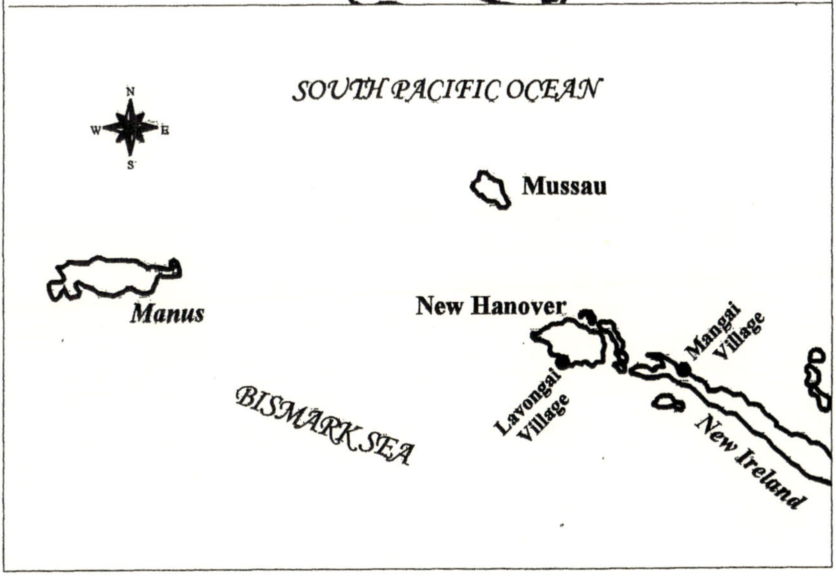
SOUTH PACIFIC OCEAN
N
W
E
S
Mussau
Manus
New Hanover
Mangai
Village
Lavongai
Village
BISMARK SEA
New Ireland

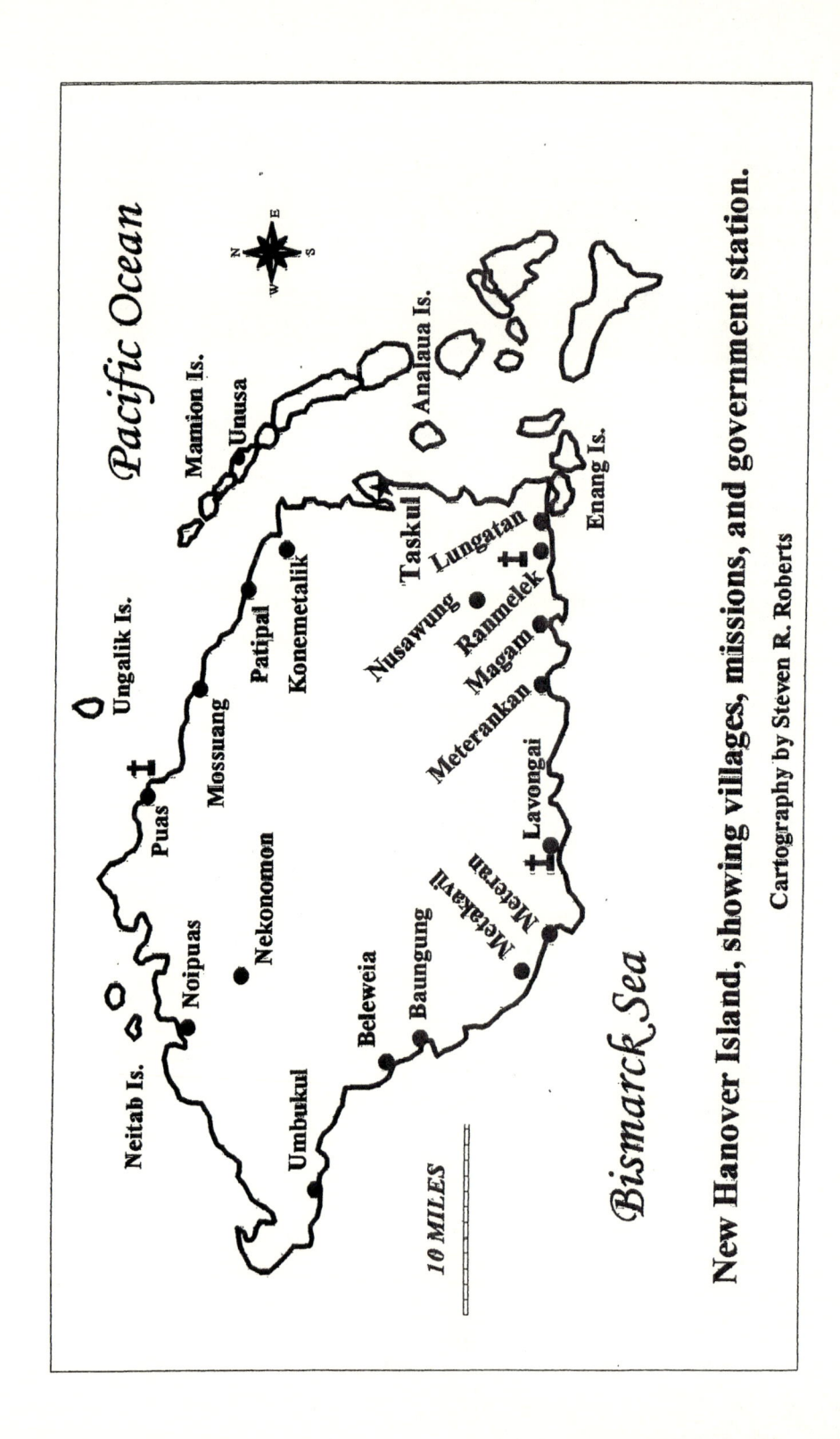

New Hanover Island, showing villages, missions, and government station.

Cartography by Steven R. Roberts

the mission at Lavongai in October 1966. Cultists came by the hundreds, from miles away, many no doubt hoping that at last the American Catholics were going to tell them what to do in order to bring America to New Hanover. Instead, Father Miller initiated discussion of what New Hanover people could do to improve their own place, with their own resources.

It was later difficult to find out what happened at that meeting, and policies remained vague for some time as the people considered what to do. Father Miller had himself thought of collecting money in order to buy the European-owned plantations on New Hanover, but this idea was not mentioned later by the people. Two or three of them claimed, each more or less certainly, that it had been his own idea that everyone plant coconuts. The Agriculture Department had been encouraging the planting of coconuts for years, but with small effect. No one ever mentioned this.

However, the proposed planting of coconuts in October 1966, was to be a project carried out by an organization, and communally. Father Miller tried to return the burden of decision-making to the people, and he succeeded in the sense that the people considered the whole project to have been their own idea. Nevertheless, Father Miller's influence was evident in most aspects of the organization. He thought that people would like to have some signs and symbols, and he suggested first that a name be chosen. Tutukuvul Isukal Association ("stand up together to plant" association) was agreed upon, and shows in its language its dual origins. It was written down as Tutukuvul Isukal Association, and became known as T.I.A. At that first meeting, rules were formulated: People may become members upon payment of dues of ten dollars (two dollars for women alone), and members will elect *bord* (board members) to represent them in the governing body of the new organization. One *bord* will be chosen for each thirty members in a village. There will be officers: president, vice-president, secretary, and treasurer. Most important, all members must pay council tax. The reason advanced (by Father Miller, and then by others) for this last rule was that men who did not pay tax would go to jail, where they would not be available to help with the work of T.I.A. A face-saving device was thus provided and, subsequently, used by all. For example, when I asked T.I.A. members who had been in jail if they would pay next time taxes were collected, typically they responded that while they still felt the same as ever, and still wanted America to come, they would pay taxes because it was a T.I.A. rule. Some referred the rule more personally to Father Miller.

The land on which the coconuts were planted was said to belong to a particular clan, but under the control of a particular man, who donated it to T.I.A. Men were proud to have done this, and unconcerned about future problems. By the time I arrived in New Hanover in February 1967, this new movement was well under way. It had officers: all cultists. It had money: over $8,000. It had enormous native enthusiasm; it had internal problems which people were determined to control; and it had government opposition. Top members of the Australian administration called T.I.A. jokingly, "Father Miller's cult." But administration opposition was serious, and in some instances it became official policy to restrict T.I.A. activities.

Factions Again

The Methodist Mission (Australian) soon joined the administration in opposition to T.I.A. When news of the new organization reached Rev. Allen Taylor, he wrote to Fr. Miller asking questions. He was satisfied with the answer, and sent out a written notice to all Methodist villages, explaining to them that T.I.A. was a new kind of "business," and that it had nothing to do with the election for Johnson. Rev. Taylor felt that this was necessary because he had been informed by some natives that the people who were joining T.I.A. thought that by so doing they would help to bring America to New Hanover. Rev. Taylor saw the same people who had collected money for Johnson now collecting money—large sums, and quickly—for T.I.A. He saw the same enthusiasm for T.I.A. that he had previously seen for Johnson. He saw a new movement over which he had no control, taking leadership from the Catholic mission, getting started in Methodist villages. He objected. Rev. Taylor and the Catholic missionaries agreed, then, that T.I.A. should have a trial period in the Catholic villages before the Methodists were allowed to join.

Native enthusiasm, however, overwhelmed this careful plan. By the time this decision was made, much money had already been collected from Methodists. Since careful records had been kept, the money could be, and was, returned; in some instances by the priests themselves. But it was very difficult to make the Methodists take back their money. They wanted desperately to "be inside." The dues money from Methodist areas went back and forth several times; and, finally, late in 1967, with T.I.A. one year old, people from Methodist villages were allowed to join.

T.I.A. was identified by noncultists in New Hanover with the election for Johnson; and, with what some people viewed as encouragement from the Australian administration and from the Methodist Mission, noncultists hardened into a pro-council, anti-T.I.A. faction. Where there had been fear amongst the opposition that T.I.A. would turn into cult, there came to be jealousy over the ability of T.I.A. to get money, attention, enthusiasm, work, and support out of the cultists. Cultists had said they had no money for council tax, but they had the same money (ten dollars) for T.I.A.! The council, led by administration officers, prepared a letter of opposition to send to T.I.A. Medical Assistant Carroll Gannon, persuaded them against this action when he heard about the letter from some of the councillors, on the grounds that factionalism should be discouraged, not encouraged.

The factions had been defined in terms of the election: the same people (with a few exceptions) who voted in the box now supported the council and its president, Steven; and those who voted on the board supported T.I.A. Some Catholics who had voted in the box, e.g., Silakau and Barol, joined T.I.A. because of Fr. Miller's support for the organization.

Working

T.I.A. members began to clear their grounds. It had been anticipated that there would be many conflicts over ground, but there were few, and they were minor. None prevented large areas of ground near each village on the south coast, and villages on the east coast and in the Tigak Islands, from being selected and marked as T.I.A. ground. At the Lavongai mission, "flags" were produced to stand over T.I.A. plantations. These were signs, painted on wood, showing a green New Hanover map in the center of a blue background, and symbols painted in the corners. There was a coconut tree for New Hanover, along with three Christian symbols for compassion and hope: a cross, a heart, and an anchor. That, in any case, is what the flag meant to Father Miller and to some members of T.I.A. There were several who asked me or each other (reportedly), quietly and intensely, what the meaning of the flag was. Probably some cultists thought, hoped, or felt that somehow the flag meant something more, perhaps that America would come.

Most members were, however, adamant: the work of T.I.A. must go on. Many said that they did not know what the fruit of T.I.A. would be, but they were determined to work hard, to work strong, and not to let the *fasion* of New Hanover spoil their work. The *fasion* to which they referred was their tendency to get angry and go off to work independently or to do nothing at all. And the tendency to steal. In October 1967, $12,000 had been collected, of which only $80 had been spent—all for tools. There were 20,000 new coconuts in the ground.

Dealing With Problems

To meet their traditional problem with money, T.I.A. members insisted, over his protests, that Father Miller keep their money in his house. Whatever problems arose in T.I.A. were discussed at the regular meetings attended by *bords*. Organizing the work force presented many problems which were never solved in a standard policy. For instance, some *bords* tried to organize the work the way it was organized on European plantations. They "lined" everyone in the morning and at noon and again at night. But some did not do this: everyone knew that all members were supposed to work, and each was expected to do so without supervision. Of those who "lined," some wrote down the names and some did not. After the names were noted or written, some went straight to work for T.I.A., while others went to their own gardens first. The most difficult problem was posed by those who were members but not resident in New Hanover, or by those who were sick or too old to work. People were supposed to find substitutes or else pay four shillings to T.I.A. for a workday missed, the amount paid a laborer per day by the mission. Father Miller gave his labor lines the day off, but Mr. Pitts did not.

It was these kinds of problems that usually defeated Lavongais. Their fashion was one of contention, always fearful that someone was taking advantage of them. But they were aware of their *fasion*, and determined (or so they said, and so it seemed) not to let their *fasion* defeat or "boss" (as they said) T.I.A.

Some Early Successes

At the time of the Johnson cult there was no regular transportation for native copra from New Hanover to Kavieng. Some had tried to carry copra in canoes, but as often as not they went down at sea, "we swam along with the coconuts," and the copra was ruined. Getting space on a Chinese or mission ship for native copra presented obstacles: money, timing, know-how, humiliation. Thus, it was a major step forward when, in 1968, T.I.A. acquired three boats to carry coconuts and copra to Kavieng. Father Miller had found them through various channels: one was an old mission boat, which was reconditioned and renamed the "*TiaWalla*." The council had a "ship fund," but even if taxes had been collected on schedule they would not have had funds to buy the expensive new boat budgeted by the council until 1970.

The planting of coconuts continued: by 1970, according to letters President Walla Gukguk wrote to me, there were 70,000 in the ground.

The Election of February 1968

In June and July 1967, when I asked cultists how they would vote in the election for House of Assembly representatives when it came again in 1968, some said that they would have to wait and see. Most said they would stand by their election for Johnson. However, many had not realized that there would be another election. They had not thought about it, as some of them said. Then Steven, council president, announced his candidacy, and T.I.A. members began to worry about defeating him. All things considered, it seemed unlikely that Johnson would be elected again in 1968. But if not Johnson, who?

T.I.A. members were well satisfied with their second president, Walla Gukguk of Meteran village. They thought about nominating him for their member in the House of Assembly. However, Father Miller suggested that Walla was doing a fine job of T.I.A., and that he was needed by T.I.A. Instead of Walla, Father Miller suggested that T.I.A. support Daniel Bokaf as their representative to the House of Assembly. Daniel was from New Ireland, and had taught at the New Hanover Catholic Mission school at Lavongai since 1965, and was generally respected for his work there. He was very much opposed to the Johnson cult, but he had worked hard for T.I.A.; often spending his Saturdays tramping through the bush surveying T.I.A. lands, and his free evenings (i.e., evenings when he did not have school duties in relation to boys who were boarders) making maps. Most important from Father Miller's point of view was the fact that Daniel had spent a year studying in Australia, under Catholic auspices. Father Miller thought that Daniel had gained the understanding of English and of European culture necessary to make his voice effective in the House of Assembly.

T.I.A. members took Father Miller's advice, and nominated Daniel. In February 1968, Daniel Bokaf easily won in the open electorate in the Kavieng

District. His victory reflected the solid confidence of the people in Father Miller's opinion, rather than any particular personal charisma or social position of Daniel Bokaf.

Later that same year, Walla was elected president of the council, while he retained his presidency of T.I.A. At the next meeting of the council, councillors, including President Walla, voted it out of existence. This was seen as the great and final victory of T.I.A. over the enemy, the Lavongais who had voted in the box.

T.I.A. and the Fruit of the Johnson Cult

T.I.A. developed from the cult and successfully directed the actions of those who voted on the board, as well as many who voted in the box. Coming as it did when hope was dwindling and jail seemed pointless, cultists seized upon it with great enthusiasm. Old directions were not completely forgotten: some people, perhaps, maintained a partly mystical view about T.I.A. being a forerunner to the coming of the Americans and the beginning of a new existence.

But T.I.A. had its own rewards. It gave people something to do, and it provided organization and structure. Students of cargo cults have pointed out that cults integrate people who previously lacked unity and overriding structure. Walla, president of T.I.A., saw that T.I.A. had that function, and saw that it was important. On August 31, 1967, he made a speech to members about the importance of acting together. First he drew an outline map of New Hanover on the blackboard. Inside it he drew little circles around the coast and in the center, representing different clans. This, he said, was their old fashion: many clans and many lines. Men did not unite, and they were not together.

Then in the middle of his map he wrote in large letters: T.I.A. Then he put a big "T" in each of the little circles representing clans. He explained his map and finished his talk with a statement of his vision, to which he remains true in the year 2000:

> Now T.I.A. stops all around. It puts its name everywhere. No longer are there five lines in Meteran village: there is one line now, on the ground. You and I all hear the talk of T.I.A. now. All men stop with T.I.A. If we did not have T.I.A. we would not have anything or anyone to unite us. This is the course that will straighten us, that will make us all one. T.I.A. showed us this road, and by and by we will be one.

The Johnson Cult and T.I.A. So Far: 1998

I have been able to follow the course of events in Lavongai and northern New Ireland through correspondence with people who are there and through seven return field trips (1972, 1974, 1983, 1988, 1990, 1994, and 1998). I have also kept up with the news from my Catholic missionary friends, especially Fr. Miller, who remained at Lavongai Catholic Mission until 1980; and Fr. David Deluca, who came to Kavieng after I left in 1967, and was one of the priests who took Fr. Miller's place after he was transferred to Tabar.

Hopes that America would come lingered, but were gradually adapted to concepts less startling to European perspectives than the original vote for Johnson had been. In May 1970, Walla wrote to me that people were pleased that Wally Lussick, a New Ireland planter, then a Member of the House of Assembly, had come to see them and listened to the idea they now had about joining with America: someday they would like to become a state, like Hawaii. In the meantime, in these early years they were still planting coconuts in New Hanover. And the administration was still worried about the "cult" spreading to New Ireland.

The Fruit of T.I.A.: Did the "Cargo Cult" Spread to New Ireland?

In June 1970, Walla sent me a clipping from the *South Pacific Post* containing the headline: "Cargo Cult Spreads to New Ireland." Walla wrote that this was the same kind of ridicule that had been used against cultists and T.I.A. members in New Hanover, and that it was not true. Not long thereafter, anthropologist Anton Ploeg sent me the same article, and suggested that I might want to come back to look into the situation. In a letter to me in 1971, Father Miller said that rumors similar to those that he had heard earlier in New Hanover were being told about Lihir Island and about New Ireland: that the people were building warehouses and waiting for the cargo. In each case where he himself talked to the people accused, they claimed they were merely building houses for meetings of their own T.I.A., called T.K.A. in these areas. Father Miller saw their efforts, as he did those of the Lavongai, as focused on economic development. He added (as he always did) that he could not be sure, however, that the information that reached him was full or true.

It was hard for me to believe that the "cult" had spread to New Ireland; but there was no way for me to be sure except by returning to see for myself, which I did in June-July 1972.

T.K.A. in New Ireland: 1972

I found that T.I.A. had, indeed, "spread" to New Ireland, and to some of the islands to the north and east of it, where it was called T.K.A. (to stand for United Farmers Association in one of the local languages, I was told). My good friends and most reliable informants in Mangai village, Kas and Eron, were reluctant to support it because of its origins in the Johnson cult in New Hanover. However, Matunga, an older man whom I had known well (as he was Sirape's clan brother), was enthusiastic. Kas and Eron had spent a great deal of time in the European world, but Matunga had not. He had lived most of his life in Mangai, but in 1972 was living with his second wife in her village, Ngavallis.

One day he rode his bicycle the fifteen miles from Ngavallis to Mangai to see me, and was pleased and excited when I proposed that I come to Ngavallis to speak to some of the people there who wanted to know, he told me, whether or not America was going to come.

This discovery was something of a disappointment to me. After all, I had predicted (Billings, 1969, 1972) that New Irelanders would not take up the cult. But my most comprehensive work had been in Mangai village, and in 1965-67 I had noticed several incidents in Ngavallis that were uncharacteristic of New Ireland life as I knew it.[31] I was relieved, in any case, to have my old friend from Mangai help me carry out my research into the matter: had the Johnson cult spread, or only T.I.A., or neither, or both?

T.I.A. in New Hanover: 1972

Before I visited Ngavallis with Matunga, however, I returned to Lavongai to find out what was going on there. The journey itself gave evidence of the success of T.I.A.: I rode aboard the big Catholic mission boat, the *Margaret*, which was captained by Brother Tony Freitas, a long-time favorite among local people. He brought with him a tractor and a grader, second-hand equipment which he and Father Miller had found and bought. With it T.I.A. proposed to begin to build a road, at last, around New Hanover.

Walla and Paulos of T.I.A., as well as my old friends in New Hanover, welcomed me back and talked enthusiastically of the work of T.I.A. They had, for instance, begun to plant "pocket plantations," small plantations of 200-300 coconuts from which they kept a portion of the profits, the bulk of which went to T.I.A. T.I.A. members continued to control the local government council, and Walla was still its president. They continued to plant coconuts, and this and other practical work was discussed by the *bord* members representing each village in regular meetings in the T.I.A. thatch house in Lavongai village.

People continued to be concerned, however, about "the enemy," Lavongai nonmembers and their European allies; and they still thought about ways to try to get America to come. At one meeting Paulos suggested that I be charged with the responsibility of telling the United Nations that they wanted America to come, but Father Miller assured the assembled members that I was only a "little mouth" in America. Those who spoke to me about America seemed clear about this, and I wondered if Paulos was mainly just trying to include me in their efforts, or just trying to think of some way to capitalize on my presence. Nevertheless, from the point of view of many of the men, I thought that America's coming remained a possibility. Now, however, adapting to keep realism current, they phrased their hopes in terms of a new concept, part of the pre-independence conversation: they wanted a "Presidential System" when Papua New Guinea became self-governing, not the Westminster system favored by others and finally adopted by the country. Their ideas continued to be founded primarily on concepts that came in from outsiders. They knew that Johnson had died, and they sang a sad song about it, but his death seemed unrelated to their commitment.

Their activities continued also to be founded on what they did not like: the split remained between those who were in and those who were out and had ridiculed. The insiders, those who had voted for Johnson and then developed T.I.A., were still determined that those who had made fun and doubted, along with their progeny, should never join the new organization. Walla was personally open in this regard and sought unity, but he had not tried to push his view on an organization of unwilling members determined to stand fast against the enemy.

Walla and others in New Hanover were, however, happy to welcome New Ireland supporters into their organization, and saw the growth of T.K.A. in New Ireland as a vindication of their own work and leadership.

T.K.A. in Ngavallis Village, New Ireland

When I returned from New Hanover to New Ireland, I went with Matunga to Ngavallis to find out what people there were thinking and doing. I found a group of twenty-five people waiting for me, a circumstance which made me uneasy: I had always been allowed and helped to fade into the group before. Most of them had known me from earlier visits. We greeted each other comfortably and with pleasure. I wondered how I could have been so wrong about these people, and set myself the task of finding out what I had missed: where was the break in the system that allowed these New Irelanders to be actively seeking to join a cult? Or were these New Irelanders really New Hanovarians who had moved their cultural character to this village along with the term "Lavongai" which named one of its large hamlets?

Slowly and shyly, in the manner which I took to be characteristic of New Ireland, they told me of their work in T.K.A., and asked me if it were true that America was going to come. I said that, so far as I knew, this was not true; and told them what I knew of the situation in New Hanover, in Australia, in America, and in the world.

Their response was entirely different from that of the Lavongais, who heard only what they wanted to hear. They sighed with some disappointment, and, in some cases, with a touch of disgust for having allowed themselves to be tempted; and, apparently, they accepted what I had said. These Tikana, who were accustomed to successfully trusting authority and authorized channels of information, trusted me and my information. Then they asked me about T.K.A.: was it a good thing? Should they continue to work with this organization? I said I thought it was a very good way for them to develop their resources, that it meant working together as they always had, but now with cash crops. They seemed quite relieved. They told me that their educated children were embarrassed and made fun of them for joining T.K.A. because of its association with T.I.A. and with the New Hanover Johnson cult. But, they said, *maski* (never mind), "We want to develop something for our children. Later, they will see that what we have done is good, and we will have something of value to give them, and they will join us in this work."

In Ngavallis, then, the split was between the old and the young, and the old were preparing to give the benefits of their labor to the enemy faction, their own children, even though this faction had ridiculed them; and they trusted the young to eventually understand and accept the gift, and their own responsibilities to help with the work. New Ireland, it continued to seem, was, after all, a different place with a culture different from that of New Hanover.

Development Options: 1974

When I returned again to the Kavieng District of Papua New Guinea in July-August 1974, following the declaration of self-government under a Westminster system in 1973, I found T.I.A. apparently still bustling along in New Hanover. There was, however, some discouragement. Many people were giving their attention to improving their own houses, gardens, and pigs, rather than focusing their attention on T.I.A.

The condition of the sawmill told an ambiguous story. Father Miller had got a secondhand sawmill which he installed in Lavongai village, next to the new T.I.A. office. The policy adopted for the use of the sawmill stated that of every three trees which people brought in, two were to be sawed into planks for T.I.A., and one was to be sawed into planks for the person who brought in the trees. There was a tendency for the first tree to go to the bringer, and for the next two trees, meant for T.I.A., to be a long time coming. Finally, the sawmill broke down, and no one moved to fix it.

Still, T.I.A. had built a splendid two-story plank house where members could meet and sleep, as well as a plank office, both in Lavongai village on the land where the government house I lived in had been in 1967. And many men had small outboard motors for their canoes, which seemed to markedly increase local mobility. There was still no road, and no council to blame for its absence: councillors, most of them strong T.I.A. men, had voted their council out of existence. In 1968, T.I.A. was, effectively, the local government in New Hanover.

There was some, but surprisingly slight, interest in the new Japanese fish cannery that had been built on a small island near Kavieng. Laksia, my young New Hanover friend who had lived in Mangai village in 1966-67, drove a boat for them; but otherwise no Lavongais were employed by the Japanese. Still, it was clear that the Japanese had potential; and, a little gently, so as not to hurt my feelings I thought (or was it so that he would not appear inconsistent?), Walla told me that perhaps the Japanese would come first, to prepare the way for America.

The Japanese were very much present in Mangai, where a Japanese timber company had taken over the old Tikana council house in which Nic and I had lived in 1965. Now the Tikana had a difficult decision to make: should they continue to try to develop their own timber, through T.K.A. (now called T.F.A., the "F" being for the English word "Farmer," which fit, or did not fit, equally in all the language groups included in the organization)? Or should they work with Nakmai, a company which belonged to the local people, but which sold its timber to the joint venture company, New Ireland Industries, which belonged to both local people and the Japanese? Kas tended to favor T.F.A.: we should do it ourselves, he thought, and not lose any of our profits to the Japanese. Eron tended to favor Nakmai: if we do it ourselves, he argued, when the equipment breaks down we will not have the money or the know-how to fix it, and nothing will get done. Anyway, the Japanese had agreed to leave their local industry, and trained workers to the New Irelanders in five years.

People asked me what I thought they should do, and I did not know. I thought I should know, or that I should be able to find out, and I made inquiries; but, in the end, I also did not know what they should do. In theory, I was against the entry of exploitative multinational corporations, or Japanese corporations, into Third World countries. In practice, I saw the people of New Hanover explicitly asking for help with development, and the Japanese there offering that help in New Ireland. New Ireland timber was being exported and New Hanover timber still stood. The Japanese timber company officials seemed to be very courteous to the local people, taking them into the Kavieng Club which had been exclusively European until self-government came in 1973. Some Europeans sat in the club with their local friends, too; but they did not have major business prospects to discuss with them.

If the local government was carefully safeguarding local ecology and interests, I thought, the people could learn from the Japanese what the Australians had not taught them. But the local European public servants, now working for the self-governing country of Papua New Guinea as experts, thought there was no hope that local interests would be protected by the inexperienced new government.[32]

Daniel Bokaf, the New Ireland Catholic teacher in Lavongai who had become the cultists' successful candidate for the House of Assembly in 1968, had moved back to New Ireland and continued to be a strong supporter of local development. He was working hard for T.F.A. because, he said, it was working for development, and because it kept all the profits in the new country. Nakmai, by contrast, was working for the immediate benefit of its owners, and let some of the profits go to the Japanese. In a public meeting of T.F.A., however, Bokaf urged his fellow members to concern themselves only with doing good work for T.F.A., not with ridiculing Nakmai. "The good work of Nakmai lies in their hands, and the good work of T.F.A. lies in your hands," he told them. T.F.A. had the help of the Catholic mission in New Ireland as in New Hanover: Fr. Freeh, of Lemakot, was advisor to it.

T.F.A. in New Ireland then, unlike T.I.A. in New Hanover, was an inclusive group working toward economic development. Its members talked not about the coming of America, but about getting a loan from the World Bank. There was a group of "outsiders" to T.F.A., but they were not considered, nor did they consider themselves, "the enemy." There continued to be some conflict between the old and the young in New Ireland, but it was within T.F.A., not between T.F.A. and an outside faction. Thus, Lisom, the young man who was president of T.F.A., heard the strongest opposition to his plans from his own father, a member of the board.

The people of Mangai still seemed, in 1974, more interested in their own local developments than in the large-scale changes that a timber industry of any sort might bring. They had built a new cement brick church in the village; and, less than a mile into the bush above the village, they had helped the Methodists build the new brick buildings for Manggai High School. Mangai also had instituted a brick factory to service all their constructions. The people of Mangai and the Tikana area were still working together, pooling their resources and their labor, focusing on what they could achieve by their own efforts together rather than on what profit they might individually make through some remote business activities.

T.I.A. Wanes, Waxes in New Hanover

The Americans Finally Come: 1979
In 1979 Father Miller was in the United States on leave and he visited me. I besieged him with questions. "Well," he said, "the Americans finally came." What! Where? When? What happened? What are they like? "They're Korean," he replied, straight-faced. The Japanese had sold the fish cannery to an American company, which had sent a Korean delegation to work in it, and the Lavongais continued to take very little interest in it.

T.I.A. continued to be very active, however. The organization had bought a Chinese store in Kavieng. Unfortunately, the old *"wantok* system" had nearly destroyed the store: clerks gave things away, as they had in the cooperative society, to their friends, relatives and other *wantok*, i.e. those who speak "one talk," one language. This is the greatest problem of "development" everywhere in Papua New Guinea, and in many other places: for various reasons, people feel compelled to respond to personal claims in "impersonal" businesses. Finally, the former Chinese owner had been hired to manage his old store again, and things were running smoothly. T.I.A. had also bought several Chinese plantations in New Hanover; and these, too, declined in productivity under inexperienced management. Some people thought there was corruption.

One young, formally educated Lavongai who came home to work for T.I.A. was jailed for trying to organize the physical takeover of a European plantation, which he viewed as still rightfully belonging to the local people. This approach never became T.I.A. policy, however.

The work of T.I.A. had been unaffected by the death of Oliver, who was only about 50 years old when he died. Father Miller knew of no special recognition of his passing in New Hanover. He was not a Big Man, but he was widely known. I had not seen him since 1967; I had gone to his island in 1972 and in 1974 but did not find him either time, and left my greetings. I thought that he had played a special role in bringing about the raised consciousness of the Lavongai and Tigak Island peoples, and in his interviews with me he had certainly shown himself to be a man of power with words. I mourned the passing not of a prophet, a status which he never claimed to me, but of a poet.

148   Chapter Three

A widely known man in New Ireland had also died, but his death was widely noted. The priest at Lemakot had said that the east coast road was blocked with trucks of people coming from all over the island to fulfill their obligations when Francis of Livitua, also a man who had command of words, died. In New Ireland, the work of economic and political development in T.F.A. and other organizations continued to be instrumental not to social change but to the celebration of the changeless events of life and death, which have long dominated and shaped the people and Tikana culture of New Ireland.

1981: T.I.A. Protest

Walla sent me a letter which he had issued specifically to explain a protest march that T.I.A. held on September 18, 1981. The statement was written in pidgin, typed, and reproduced by mimeograph.

The following is a translation of part of it:

Tutukuvul Isukal Association announces a Protest march, or demonstration by T.I.A. in Kavieng on 18 September 1983. T.I.A. has talked clearly to the government about breaking loose from Australia because it is the guardian [*papa lukaut*] along with the law of the Westminster and because it is not very good at running New Guinea.

T.I.A. is a Party of we people of the place that we got up on the ground that belongs straight to us. T.I.A. is a number one Party because it started before Papua New Guinea had Self-government.

Papua New Guinea did not become a country because Australia wanted it to, no. The thinking of Australia was that it would bring Self-Government to our country so that Australia would still boss us and we would just remain underneath their guidance: meaning that we all will just *wok boi* [work as "boys," servants] for them.

All of us in PNG are truly lucky because we ourselves, all the people of New Hanover, are strong and we made the election for President Johnson of U.S.A. of America in the year 1964. It looks as though we ourselves downed this thinking of Australia and it left.

We got back our country so that it came back again to our hands straight, so that we ourselves boss and look after it, and we called it Papua New Guinea. It is true that if we all had voted for Self-Government in 1964, following the thinking of Australia, it looks as though we would not have been able to develop a country like the one we now have.

Now T.I.A. talked out clearly to them themselves that they should break off and stand up clear. . . .

The true reason for T.I.A.'s protest march, our thinking is this: we ourselves have worked hard to get back our country because our country is a truly rich country. Inside, in our ground, in the bush, and in the sea, it is completely full with all kinds of resources,[33] enough truly to develop the place, the people, and the country altogether.

But one thing stops us in this country: we are truly short on savvy about working all these resources that belong straight to us, on our own ground. . . . We have lost seven years since independence that we have got up straight inside on our own ground, in order to show the people of Papua New Guinea that it is true that we stand up independent. . . . Australia hurried with its own thinking, and brought Provincial Government to fasten PNG so that Independence is just nothing in PNG.

Now PNG still does not stand up straight on its own legs. PNG has already turned its back on all the resources that belong straight to them and it looks back to Australia . . . . Australia must show respect to PNG and must stand up clear, and PNG itself must run its independence according to its own savvy.

The worry of T.I.A. about P.N.G. is that it works to follow the thinking of Australia and forgets the thinking of the people who belong straight to PNG. Now T.I.A. will break off and stand up with America.

It is true that T.I.A. has had three elections that went straight to America, starting with 1964, then 1978, and now 1982. This shows that T.I.A. believes truly strongly in America.

In Lavongai village there was a T.I.A. meeting on 27 January 1983. Martin Sopoi moved this motion: T.I.A. will break loose from all government work of PNG together with Australia. And T.I.A. will stand up together with America. Now T.I.A. calls for America, that it must come straight to the island of New Hanover, because that is the place which belongs straight to T.I.A. T.I.A. calls for America to come work along with it to get up development work in order to show T.I.A. how to work something with the hands, the true wish of T.I.A. In New Hanover island there is good water, mountain, ground to make a town, good harbor for all big ships like *Mamirum*, and there is a place to get up a factory. Also there is gold and copper in the ground, timber in the bush, and fish and oil in the sea. Whatever kind of thing there is in the island of New Hanover, it is in a place that voted for America. So T.I.A. itself now calls out for America that it should itself come straight to the island of New Hanover following the invitation of T.I.A. straight to the ground belonging to it in order to come and get up T.I.A. Because the island of New Hanover is a rubbish place from a long time ago, starting with Germany and later with Australia and all the way to PNG now. Now, still, New Hanover has no development getting up. It stays just as it was from time immemorial. Up until now, T.I.A. sings out for America because it is the country belonging to us straight, that it should come work along with T.I.A. following the true wishes of the people of New Hanover and PNG all together. This talk is very true.
That's all. Walla Gukguk, President of T.I.A.

1983: T.I.A. Strong Under Pressure
When I returned to the Kavieng District in 1983, I was again denied

permission to go to New Hanover, as I had been in 1965 and 1966; this time by the government of the Province of New Ireland, whose officers were mainly New Irelanders. I would not have been given a visa even to New Ireland but for the strong efforts made on my behalf by two men of Mangai: Kas and Mesulam Aisoli. Apelis Kasino ("Kas"), my long-time host and colleague in anthropological endeavors, whose leadership in many projects over his lifetime had been recognized in the award of a title, Member of the Order of the British Empire (M.B.E.), in 1982, had written a letter and had been to the main government office in Kavieng to request that I be allowed to visit. Mesulam Aisoli had been away from Mangai studying when I lived in his village and I did not know him well, but I had heard of him often: he is the brother of Konda Aisoli who helped Nic and me in 1965, and of three sisters, all well known in their own rights, and all my old friends. In 1983 Mesulam was away in Australia on leave from his position in the Anthropology Department at the University of Papua New Guinea. He had also been an official of the Education Department in Kavieng, and he saw anthropology as useful to the local endeavor to expand the curriculum to include Papua New Guinea subjects. He wrote to me and to his compatriots and also, in the end, made telephone calls from Australia. Without the help of these two men, I wonder if I would have ever got a visa in 1983.

The reasons given by the New Ireland officers of the provincial government for denying me permission to go to New Hanover were the same as those given by the Australian colonial governors eighteen years earlier in 1965: the Lavongais, led by President Walla of T.I.A., are crazy, irresponsible, and will misunderstand your visit. I was told that just before I arrived in Kavieng, in September 1983, that there had been a kind of pilgrimage of T.I.A. members to the top of Mt. Patibung where Walla said that Jesus would meet them and give them money. The newspaper carried this story, as it had carried similar stories in times past.

During the four months that I spent in New Ireland in 1983, I exchanged several letters with Walla, and I also had long discussions with the few remaining faithful to T.I.A. in New Ireland. Several of them had gone to the Mt. Patibung events, which they said was a celebration of the successes of T.I.A., beginning with the vote for Johnson in 1964 and continuing through their declaration of independence from the New Ireland Province in 1982. Lisom had recorded a tape of the proceedings, which I heard and copied: Jesus was not mentioned except in the Methodist prayers for help and guidance which opened and closed the gathering. Pictures showed Walla wearing a traditional grass costume. In his letters to me, Walla assured me that what I was hearing from the provincial governors and others was the same kind of ridicule the Johnsonites had been subject to when I began my research in New Hanover.

Walla sent me a copy of the statement that T.I.A. had released in which the failure of the provincial government to develop New Hanover was cited and condemned. T.I.A. demanded a Presidential System, and still wanted America to come. My friends in Mangai had heard Walla on the local radio station, angrily denying the rumors that T.I.A. expected to meet Jesus at Mt. Patibung. Kas, who counted Walla a friend and respected him, said that he thought Walla cherished no unfounded hopes about T.I.A., but he thought that some others had false expectations.

I was able to talk with people from New Hanover in Kavieng, and several of them told me that T.I.A. was breaking up because of the many lies it had told. Important founders had withdrawn: Pengai was out, along with all in his village, Nusawung; Bosap was out, and so was Makios, very old but still alive.

Through interviews with the few remaining T.I.A. members in New Ireland (who no longer called their organization T.F.A.), I found out that the T.I.A. "passbook" (that is, the book which recorded the money in the T.I.A. savings account at a bank in Kavieng) had gone to at least nine different places, including to two places along the Sepik River. People did not seem to know where either the money or the multiple passbooks were.

Father Miller had been transferred away from Lavongai in 1981, and it seems likely that the loss of his firm hand on the money box is what led to this dispersal of funds. Walla wrote to me that he was aware of the problem and was going to get all the money back into one account. Privately, I wondered how he would be able to do so.

And yet T.I.A. was still in control in the part of New Hanover which had voted on the board for Johnson in 1964. Two men from a company searching for oil and minerals throughout Papua New Guinea told me that the meeting they set up with the people at Lavongai village in November 1983 was the toughest one they had ever attended. After they arrived, by helicopter, they were sharply questioned and told to stay out of New Hanover until they came back to set up processing factories. The Lavongai people had pointed out that big companies came to the islands; took away what was of value; carried it to factories down in Australia or elsewhere where it was made into things; then these things were brought back to sell to the people in the islands. Both their resources and their money went to Australia, they said. New Hanover registered a resounding "No!" to this system. Just days before, gold had been found by these prospectors in Tabar, a discovery that was sure to bring huge amounts of quick money to that island, as well as to the provincial government, in royalties.[34]

I do not know whether or not T.I.A.'s determination, in this and other cases, to turn away Australian and British companies (still waiting, they said, for an American company which would show them how to process their own valuable resources) was at least partly responsible for the defections among top leaders. In my continuing efforts in 1983 to at least visit New Hanover to see my old friends, I kept in contact with Steven Taung, the man, then young, who had tried to lead a unified council when I was in New Hanover in 1966. Steven was very respectful to me, perhaps partly out of respect for my host, Kas, whom Steven visited to discuss my situation. Finally Steven told me, in answer to my questions, that it was my good friends, Silakau and others, who were among those in Lavongai who did not want me to return. They were afraid my return would give T.I.A. strength. They had not voted for Johnson, but they had been in T.I.A., and were now out. Steven probably did not talk to T.I.A. leaders, who still saw him as the opposition. Steven had started a new local government council for the west and north sides of the island, which had not gone into the cult or T.I.A. A coastal road had been built from Umbukul, Steven's west coast home, to several other nearby villages.

It hurt, and I was disappointed. At that point I wanted mainly a chance to see my old friends and their families. However, after I learned that Silakau, whose judgement I trusted, did not want me to come, I made no further efforts to gain permission.

1983: The Lavongai T.I.A. Connection in New Ireland

Those men who were still in T.I.A. in New Ireland were clustered around Matamakas. He was one of the three men tried for treason in the 1965 trial Nic and I had attended, though I had not realized it until Matamakas told me his stories. The other two men were dead.

Bokaf and others who had changed the name from T.K.A. to T.F.A. and had worked for local control and ownership of economic development had long since abandoned this organization. Kas continued to go to meetings that Matamakas called from time to time, to be polite and to see what was going on. He told me Matamakas and the few others leading T.I.A. in Kableman village, near Kavieng, were unrealistic: for instance, they talked of buying back for T.I.A. all the plantations which Europeans owned in New Ireland, but they only had two hundred *kina* (about two hundred dollars at that time). One of the followers of Matamakas was a man from the Sepik River who had worked for many years in New Ireland. He wanted to start a T.I.A. in the Sepik, and apparently had sent some T.I.A. money to his family there. Limon of Lossuk village was strong for T.I.A., had gone to the 1983 celebration, and gave me a copy of the tape he had made there. His interest was focused on doing the will of God and Jesus, and he thought that working in T.I.A. was a divine obligation. One other man, Tele, had abandoned his attempt to work with T.I.A., as his fellows did not like his ideas. He was extremely bright, a former teacher, wise about the outside world: I learned a lot about international development and trade from him. His views, I think, were tediously complex to the other T.I.A. members in New Ireland, and too much focused on the utilitarian aspects of economic development.

Matamakas himself seemed more nostalgic about T.I.A. than active. He had spent much time during World War II in Lavongai and knew Peter Yangalissmat well. His interest was based partly on the good feelings he had about both Lavongai and Americans at that time, and partly on his anti-authority feelings derived partly from his arrest for treason in 1965. His stance against authority had, however, preceded this event: Kas and Matamakas, both men of sixty or more, had been schoolmates; and Kas remembered that Matamakas did not like to do as he was told as a young boy in school, and was finally put out. Kas remained, as always, respectful.

Matamakas talked a lot about his experiences in jail and in court, giving me a detailed account of this incident. As I already knew, he was not involved directly with the vote for Johnson. In 1964, when the west coast villages were arrested for refusing, with some militance, to pay taxes at about the same time that people in New Hanover were refusing to do so, Matamakas led a group of New Irelanders to the jail to free their compatriots. They were, instead, jailed with them. While the Australians persisted in seeing these events as part of the Johnson cult, New Irelanders did not. However, Matamakas went to New Hanover after his release from jail and gave support to the resistance movement there. He said in 1983 that the provincial government was trying to end T.I.A., but "they cannot do it." Still, in New Ireland it was only a shadow of history, not a force to be reckoned with. While Matamakas was loyal to it, he, and others, had left it to vote for Michael Somare and the Pangu Party in the last election. Somare had taught high school in New Ireland, and he was highly respected in the area. T.I.A., Matamakas said, was like a political party. Clearly, it was not, for him, like a religion.

Those interested in economic development in New Ireland had gone into Nakmai, the people's company which had entered into a joint venture with a Japanese timber company. Kas, who had at first stayed out of Nakmai in favor of T.K.A., became the chairman of Nakmai in 1976-78, and chairman of the parent company, New Ireland Industries, 1979-81. In this capacity he, and other local leaders, went twice to meetings in Osaka, Japan, and saw with their own eyes the work of the factory: sawmills, complex machinery, finished timber. This was, Kas told me, one of the high points of his life.

What had happened was just what Bokaf and others had feared would happen: the Japanese had paid huge sums of money (by local standards) for timber, and village people no longer needed to work in order to eat. They could buy their food at the store. When the Japanese left, however, there was no timber factory or any other kind of major development in New Ireland which might sustain this standard.

Did New Ireland Traditional Culture Continue? 1983 and Beyond

The work of cutting timber had left some good results: there were roads into the bush, and much ground had been cleared. Many people made gardens much larger than any I had seen in 1965-67. Now, however, people often worked alone in their gardens, if they worked at all. People still liked home-grown and home-cooked meals, and the work was falling unequally on older women. Many young people were at school or at work in town or even further away. There were harsh words between men and women, mostly from women about men, which I had never heard before.

I was concerned that there were basic structural changes in New Ireland culture, even though people and houses looked much as they had in 1965. When Kas invited me to the Mangai school one night to attend an awards feast to honor outstanding athletes, I went with a heavy heart. In the old days, I thought, New Ireland would not have selected out the strong for special honors. I well remembered a school athletic event in 1967 where I saw children of all ages running in the same races, the big ones waiting to take the hands of the small ones so that they could cross the finish line together. "Good," said the teacher-umpire, "same time." This major metaphor for me of New Ireland culture, I expected, was about to suffer an assault of modern times.

I was relieved when I saw who got the awards: every single boy and girl who had played any game got exactly the same prize, a gift-wrapped Bible. One prize also went to a faithful mother for "clapping and shouting" for the teams. Education Minister Demas Kavavu, Mesulam's friend from further south, was the guest speaker. He told the children that athletics was a new art form, just like the traditional *malanggan* art form, and that it was important to do both well.[35]

I told Kas that I was happy to see that the awards went to everyone, which seemed to suit Tikana culture. I told him that in our culture only the winners would get an award. "Who are the winners?" he asked. "They stand on the shoulders of all the others."

In 1990 there was a big *malanggan* for Konda Aisoli, who died so young in 1983. And in 1994, just after I left New Ireland, a *malanggan* on a more modern scale for Kas. He had died, his family told me when they met me at the airport that year, when I was already traveling in the plane to come. He had been looking forward to my visit and was getting his house ready for me. I had lost my strongest colleague.

That there were *malanggan* for these two modern men reassured me that *malanggan* was not "doomed to certain and early extinction," as Groves (1933: 351) had predicted in the 1930s. I felt that the undergirding of New Ireland culture would not easily be eroded. There would be no cargo cult among the Tikana in the near future.

The Fruit of T.I.A.: Did the "Johnson Cult" Continue in New Hanover?

Several anthropologists gave me information in 1987, gleaned at a distance, about the continuing activities of the Lavongais and their opposition. Only a few people from New Hanover voted properly in the 1986 provincial election, while several thousand voted for Johnson. The biggest lode of gold ever found has been found in Lihir, and conflict between the people of that island and the Kavieng provincial government is intense. Lavongais are still refusing to pay taxes, and two villages in New Ireland have now joined them. Apparently the breakup of T.I.A. predicted by its detractors in 1983 has not yet come to pass.

Father Miller wrote (1987) that "the colonialists are really in power" in Kavieng. His replacement at Lavongai, Father David DeLuca, was transferred to

Tanga because of his political activity: he led a sit-in with his people against unwanted exploitation of their timber. Fr. DeLuca had told me in 1983 that he did not want to become involved in T.I.A., but apparently he had become involved in at least related activities. And Walla spent three months in jail.

T.I.A. Continues: 1988

Just before my return to the Kavieng area in July 1988, I received a written report from Walla of a meeting of T.I.A. in Lavongai village on 5 May 1988:

> The big thinking of T.I.A. is that New Hanover must lose all government work of Australia and break loose of PNG and stand up together with America. It is time for us in New Hanover to get up a government belonging straight to us. We ourselves stand on top of ground belonging to us and we talk and we are not afraid. Now New Hanover will break and stand up along with America because we will go outside of our prison wall because New Hanover is a place belonging to Christ. New Hanover is restful and Paradise and a place where all men know each other. When the West Minster System came up in the year 1914, it itself came and downed us and bossed us as though we were all SLAVES and they did not know that this place belongs to us straight. Now T.I.A. finds Christ's government belonging to us all black men, because Christ, too, was a black man just like us, and our government is all black men.

Sometime in the mid-80s, letters signed by Walla began to focus on Christ. The format of the letters also changed: instead of being written in pidgin in Walla's strong hand, they were neatly typed and written in English in a distinctly different style, or tone, or voice. When I returned to Mangai in 1988, Kas told me he thought that Walla was trying to keep his organization going by taking views that some of his followers wanted him to take. When I visited Lavongai, I sat with Walla and some of his comrades for a long talk. Walla said little, but confirmed that T.I.A. was now interested in Jesus. However, they were now calling him by his Lavongai name: Kiukiuvat. Two of my old friends were working in the T.I.A. office and seemed to be carrying on as usual.

Otherwise my communications from Walla over the years have remained consistent: the demand for help in understanding how to make use of New Hanover's resources for the benefit of New Hanover people, and the determination to remain separate from all those who want to take for themselves, but either will not or cannot give what New Hanover needs.

The great sadness of this trip was that I had to visit the graves of Silakau and Joseph Pukina, neither very old. Their families were anxious to tell me that they hoped I was not angry about asking me not to come in 1983. I assured them that I was not, and that I relied on their opinions.

Lavongai in 1990: Peace and Prosperity Without Development

My return to Lavongai in 1990 was a happy one for several reasons: people seemed to be optimistic, Tombat had built a big new house, Tamangamiss said he was fine, and I had a reunion with Josephine, Silakau's daughter. Josephine had been a very good companion to me when she was five, and I had always looked for her, but she was away teaching, or working, or in her husband's village in southern New Ireland. In 1990 she and her small son were home for a visit. We were both pleased to see how much the other remembered of our joint projects. I expected her to remember how she beat out a fire in my house with her *laplap*, but she did not. Her mother and siblings were also at home, and we had a good time remembering the old days.

Another highlight of my 1990 return was meeting Walla's daughter, Tukul Walla Kaiku, in Port Moresby. She had majored in anthropology at the University of Papua New Guinea, and was working in the National Archives. From what she had found there, she had written a series of very informative articles for the local newspapers. I wanted her to come back to New Hanover with me, but she had a big family to look after and could not go at that time. She had also been in conflict with her father, who had refused to vote for her in the New Ireland provincial election. I told her that from what I knew I thought Walla could not honorably vote at all, after all his years of boycotting such elections. She has since been home and made peace.

Walla was living in Lavongai in 1990, and I had a good talk with him, too. He was optimistic about T.I.A. Members remained strong. When I asked him about Tukul, he said that of course he could not vote for his own daughter when he had boycotted the elections, though he would very much like to see her in a strong position.

I also saw, as I always do, Barbara Bullock, daughter of Joseph Pukina, major helper of Sister Regine when she was a teenager, and long-time head of the preschool in Kavieng. Barbara has looked after many people's children, not only in the preschool but wherever there is need. Unlike Tukul, she had heard of the culture hero "Kiukiuvat" who is still mentioned as someone for whom T.I.A. is waiting in Lavongai. Tukul thought the name had been imported from the east side of the island for political reasons. Barabara did not know about T.I.A's use of the figure, but she remembered hearing his name and some story about him when she was a child.

Evolution of a "Cargo Cult": Waiting for Greenpeace, 1994

In 1994 I found that some people of all ages, men and women, were working in the Local Environment Foundation. They were led by Marias who, as a nine-year-old boy, had worked every day with Fr. Miller on the development of T.I.A. In 1990 he was head of the NGO (nongovernmental organizations) organization for all of Papua New Guinea, and had been to Malaysia. He had founded the new environmental group.

In August 1990, I attended a week-long seminar that Marias had organized in New Hanover, in Puas, where the Catholic mission has a church, a school, and a house. He had arranged an impressive panel of speakers: it included three forestry officials, including a man who had been national forestry minister, a woman who was the present head of the forestry division for New Ireland, and her counterpart from the Tigak Islands. One of the main presenters of information was John Aini, the head of the Stocks, Fisheries and Agriculture Department in Kavieng. He was one of the much loved little boys born to Fr. Miller's most reliable mission workers in Lavongai. Also on the panel was an Australian who had taken PNG citizenship and decided to stay when independence came, and who was serving in local government. A major impetus for this and other similar seminars came from Barry, one of the NGO organizers in Port Moresby who had been an American Peace Corps worker many years earlier and was still finding ways to help.

The seminar went on for a week, with about thirty-five people sitting on the hard, sometimes wet, concrete floor of a classroom, hot under its typical corrugated iron roof. We were feasted every evening by women who cooked locally and across on the island of Ungalik. On Thursday, in the rain, Marias took the forestry ministers west in a speedboat to see for themselves the conditions of the people and ground at Noipus, where a Malaysian company, with Filipino workers, was cutting timber. At the end of the seminar the people had only one complaint: they wanted more. They wanted it to last longer. They wanted another seminar.

One of the old men who sat through the whole week was a man who had been my former neighbor in Lavongai village and an early member of T.I.A. After the seminar, he went with me in a speedboat back to Lavongai village, several hours away on the south coast. Neither he nor Marias saw themselves as in opposition to T.I.A., but just as moving on beyond it. Marias said it was just the older people who wanted to keep trying to work with T.I.A.

When I talked to Walla in Lavongai village, I asked him if he thought T.I.A. and the organization Marias was working with wanted the same things. At first he said no. Then he modified his views: he realized that many of the goals they had were the same, but he wanted to maintain T.I.A. as a separate organization. He and a few followers who gathered to hear us were still interested in the role of Jesus in their work, now calling him by his New Hanover name: Kiukiuvat.

The News in 1998

I was scarcely off the plane in Kavieng in August 1998, when I met Piskaut, one of my old neighbors and friends from Lavongai village whom I had last seen working in the T.I.A. office. He told me enthusiastically that just the week before they had celebrated the T.I.A. and New Hanover Independence Day, and they had raised the American flag. He was sorry I had missed it, and so was I. I did not get to New Hanover in 1998, but soon after my return to America I received a handwritten letter from Walla affirming their continued determination to achieve independence.

I did not hear anything more about the environmental movement, but it is now widespread and strong all over Papua New Guinea, and I have no doubt that Lavongais, including Marias, are doing their part. They are practiced in protest, and they still have their resources. Someday I believe their grandchildren will be grateful to their ancestors for their efforts.

The Johnson Cult and T.I.A. So Far: May 2000

I received a copy of a proclamation Walla had issued on May 12, 2000. As usual, I also got a copy to send to the United Nations. In his statement, Walla affirms that "I'd like America to take over New Ireland Province to replace Australia for he will step down and stop forever." He also repeats, as he has for nearly two decades, that "I authorized the Presidential System of government to take place." What is new is this:

> T.I.A.'s first priority is to give money in sponsoring Canale 5 a company from Italy to come to New Hanover and make T.I.A.'s name known in New Ireland now in the year 2000. . . . I would like Canale 5 to establish and fix capitalism on New Hanover and New Ireland as the basic source of Human development for the betterment of our children and all the people.

The particular plans, however, are not new: Walla asks Canale 5 to extend the Kavieng Airport to become an international airport; to build a national wharf at Mamirum (North Lavongai); to upgrade schools, aid posts, and hospitals; and "to help establish a better community on New Hanover to become Paradise because it is KIUKIUVAT'S homeland, rather a land of light ready for the coming of KIUKIUVAT."

Whatever you want to call it, the spirit of restless, enthusiastic, optimistic struggle definitely continues in New Hanover.

Notes

1. Boski Tom and his village are Methodist.
2. "Sit down and 'grease' or talk easily at one time or together."
3. Progress Report, March 1964
4. Lincoln Bell was a well-respected European whose history is partly given in Eric's *The Coast Watchers*.
5. *Australian New Guinea Auxiliary Unit*
6. Later Peter Yangalissmat committed suicide by eating fish poison. No one tried to stop him, or anyone else who ever said they were going to kill themselves, because it is considered an individual decision that outsiders cannot change.
7. Joseph Pukina's two-year-old son was named John Kennedy. But people did not remember the name of the man who had replaced President Kennedy in America.
8. This term was used in a government report.
9. Quote from the progress report for this date. It is a major, not a peripheral, point of my interpretation here that government officers, as well as cultists and noncultists, enjoyed the "game" aspects of the cult. The "cops and robbers" tone of the reports is one manifestation of and piece of evidence for this interpretation. In this instance, the government officer was making a bit of fun of himself for arresting a quite harmless man who was just working in his garden.
10. Mr. Grose is a plantation owner; a child of plantation owners who was raised in New Ireland, who raised his own children in New Ireland, and who was well known to the people.

11. Acting District Officer Benhem gave me this justification for his actions after I had pressed him in vain for some time to discuss his views with me. No doubt, he felt, reasonably, that it was not his duty to do so. Finally I told him that I was after all, going to write a book, and that if he wanted the government's view represented he had better tell me what it was. He probably thought that it was obvious, but it was not so to me. Aside from this one brief, serious expression from Mr. Benhem, I have not been able to adequately express the administration's point of view, a deficiency for which I am, of course, ultimately responsible.

12. Patrol Officer Lawrence Menjies, who was among the European officers at Lokono, New Ireland when there was violence associated with refusal to pay taxes, told me that European personnel were carefully protected while policemen were attacked. This circumstance was generally known in New Ireland.

13. This is Carroll Gannon's line. Some people thought that jail labor might have been used more productively than it was, that the men might have built roads rather than beautiful winding steps up the hill to European houses.

14. Four policemen were charged in court with assault in connection with related incidents on the west coast of New Ireland, and another twelve were charged with refusal to obey orders.

15. An apt term, first applied by Carroll Gannon.

16. A.D.O. Ken Williamson used this expression when discussing the Johnson cult with me.

17. Silakau was never attacked over the election, but he had been attacked in the past due to jealousy over women.

18. *Tok Bilas* is pidgin for ridicule, make fun of.

19. Pengai had learned to read while he was a patient in the leper hospital at Analaua. He had read about Aborigines there. But he had also learned a great deal from the pastor of the Seventh-Day Adventist mission at Nusuwung.

20. He refers to the cement pegs the Australian government uses to mark surveyed land for specified and registered ownership, in contrast to the unsurveyed communally owned land common to traditional village people.

21. He spoke this word in English.

22. Carroll Gannon's term for the noncultists.

23. A.D.O Ken Williamson used this expression in discussing cargo cults with me.

24. Oliver himself told me about one of his "prophecies" and how it came about as a satiric response to government ridicule. It was for the enemy, not the cultists, to believe.

25. Fr. Miller and Brother Tony Freitas continue their good work at Milmila Catholic Mission in the Duke of York Islands.

26. I did write it up as a dissertation, and I have now made some efforts toward a musical comedy. I did say to Fr. Miller at the time that I thought the Lavongais needed a theater more than they needed European cargo, and Fr. Miller tried to include their artistic interests in T.I.A. when he helped to design the T.I.A. flag. It took me about fifteen years to finally incorporate these insights into my interpretation.

27. By 1974, two American Peace Corps workers were in New Hanover, starting rice plantations. By the mid-80s, volunteers from Canada, Australia, and other countries were working out of Kavieng.

28. This kind of idle talk is common in Lavongai, but not in New Ireland.

29. Despite feeling silly, I was dogged in my determination to get this into the record.

30. Lemakot is the site and name of the major Catholic hospital and school in New Ireland, as well as of the adjoining village.

31. I knew a Ngavallis woman who had been raised in Lavongai, and there was a hamlet named "Lavongai" in Ngavallis village. I once saw the Ngavallis councillor, also a Big Man (*memai*) and an elder, weaving a roof for a community house by himself, and he told me he was angry about it. This kind of thing never happened in Mangai or anywhere else I visited in New Ireland..

32. That has certainly been the case in many instances. However, so far Papua New Guinea has done much better than many other countries with its pristine resources, and they seem to be regaining control. They have the help of many international organizations, but most of these have limited resources for the struggle

33. He used the English word "resources."

34. So far this site has not been developed, partly due to local opposition. However, a similar site is producing in Lihir, and changes have begun. This will be the next story. I heard few say that it was good, and many express fear and distress over the social changes under way in Lihir.

35. And he told me when I saw him perform as a *memai* in a local *malanggan*, that if you wanted to be a leader in contemporary politics in New Ireland, you had to also lead in traditional roles.

III
Analysis, Interpretation, and Conclusion

4
Analysis and Interpretation

Cults and Movements: Theories

Cults have usually been seen in the context of change: not orderly, progressive change, but disruptive, disoriented change which leaves in its wake confused, alienated actors in fragmented cultural scenes into which cult and cultists rush to the rescue. In Melanesia, cargo cults have classically been seen as a response to European contact. Often cultists seem to seek fundamental structural changes, and many researchers have made this common element basic to their interpretations. My research provides evidence that the Johnson cult was a dramatic expression consistent with the traditional style of Lavongai culture, and not in itself an expression or sign or even a cause of structural change. This perspective gives support to the argument that cults may be conservative, not radical; that they may be attempts to resist, not to achieve, change. In the broad view, it was, of course, a reaction to contact with European actions; and in the long run, the Johnson cult provided an opening in traditional events which allowed influences from neighboring historical circumstances to have an impact on Lavongai culture. Changes of a structural nature did, in fact, result from the Johnson cult, but they need not have; they would not have in a different historical environment; and they seem now to have mostly faded away as traditional culture has reasserted itself. But the impact of the Johnson cult has not disappeared.

The Johnson Cult As Theater

Expressive Aspect Primary

The Johnson cult must first be understood, then, as an expression of traditional, or indigenous, Lavongai culture. The analysis in this chapter attends to that task.

The style of Lavongai culture includes dramatic confrontation and a heavy reliance on verbal interaction; in contrast to Tikana culture, which prefers literal and predictable exchange without comment. There is substantial theoretical support for the hypothesis that cults are related to cultural style or pattern, and it is that aspect of the "Johnson cult" on which I focus attention. Research on cultural style or pattern, along with other prominent and more general theories about cults, is reviewed in the following chapter. Here I want to try to make sense of the Johnson cult in terms of the events and statements that compose it, and in terms of specific theories that I think help to interpret it.

My attempts to understand the Johnson cult in relation to structural-functional dimensions of culture and to historical factors explained a great deal, but left unexplained some of its most visible aspects. I now believe that much of what I know about the Johnson cult can best be understood as improvised political theater; as a drama which used ridicule, mockery, and satire to resist established authority. I have settled on this interpretation partly through a process of elimination and partly through identification of characteristics it has in common with other artistic expressions. It was not only art but good art, judged by its consequences in the effective manipulation of the affairs and outlooks of people both inside and outside New Hanover: a brilliant symbolic action; a drama which fundamentally altered its actors, its audience, and the play in which they all took part together.

Other Factors Considered: What the Johnson Cult Was Not

Anthropological scholars who have written the classic professional literature on cults and movements of this sort emphasize one or more of several major dimensions of cultures as factors leading to cults: political, economic, religious, social, intellectual, psychological, historical, and so forth. Analyses of cargo cults in Melanesia, in particular, always include contact with Europeans as a triggering factor, although there are some cases where contact has been very limited.[1] In the case of New Hanover, local plantation managers, government workers, mission personnel, and local observers, both cultists and noncultists, often mentioned the following as causes of the cult: failures of economic development, lack of education and understanding of the modern world, isolation, inaccessible transport, the stress of uncomprehended change, envy and a longing for material goods, inadequate communication, and the absence of regular patrolling.

I conducted my field research with these local views, as well as the interpretations put forward in the anthropological literature, in mind. While each category of factors contributes to an understanding of the total phenomenon, I found them all, taken together but absent theater, insufficient to interpret what I knew about the cult. Viewed as theater, many of the most powerful, unique, and interesting aspects of what happened make sense.

Some of the major categories proposed by local observers as well as by scholarly theorists are here considered in relation to the evidence.

Intellectual, Educational Deficiencies: The Johnson cult was not built on misinformation about the world, as many people suggested. Cultists and native anticultists shared the same body of information from which ideas for the cult were elaborated. Many of these ideas derived from experiences with Americans which some Lavongais had during World War II; and from more recent experiences in 1963, when a U.S. map-making team spent several weeks in New Hanover. Native anticultists never thought, as most Europeans did at first, that cultists were just misinformed. Noncultists had not voted for Johnson, not because they knew he would not come, but because they thought the vote for him would make the Australians angry—and they were right.

Cultists did not "believe" that Johnson was going to come in the sense that they expected his arrival and thought they had evidence for it. They had merely hoped he would come; but when Australian officials and native anticultists constantly demanded evidence, occasionally a cultist would offer some. For example, Oliver told me that Australians kept badgering him with the question, "What proof do you have?" and he finally told them that he had talked with Americans in the bush, who had told him that Johnson was coming on 25 January 1965. Oliver laughed when he told me this, explaining that "I was just talking."

The Johnson cult was not, then, just an intellectual mistake that could be terminated with explanations and education. Many Europeans who found themselves cornered in a debate with cultists commented on the flawless logic in the arguments they gave in support of their position, which they reinforced with facts which were not in dispute. For example, when Joseph Pukina told me that the Australians had prevented the Americans from coming and I expressed doubt, he explained that he had heard on the radio that morning that 400 American Peace Corps workers had wanted to come to help the people, and the Australians had stopped them. Further investigation revealed that this news had, in fact, been reported on the morning news. The Australian administration explained that they wanted to attend to development in their territory themselves.

Cultists developed not an irrational obsession but a new paradigm within which to define their situation, based on an evolutionary ideology in which they perceived the work of the Germans and of the Australians as finished. The latter had failed to give the people the savvy they needed to develop their place sufficiently so that they could manage alone under self-government. It was time, then, for the Australians to leave and for the Americans to come: "They will give us savvy," the intellectual tools they needed to master their new world.

Religious: The Johnson cult was not fundamentally religious. There was no return to old-time religious or magical devices, of which there were few; nor any reliance on new ones, of which there were none: no unusual psychic states, no secret meetings, no ceremonies relating to the dead or other supernatural agencies, no behaviors that were bizarre from the European point of view except the cult-defining one, the vote for Johnson itself. In the religious sphere, there was only a general hunch that the Lord was on their side and, when they raised their hands in support of the vote for Johnson, a promise to remain strong for America that many, but not all, made to God. Some made this promise just to themselves.

Psychological: The Johnson cult was not based on pathological thinking induced by paranoia, or imaginary complaints in response to the stress of change. All European residents agreed that the Australian administration had neglected New Hanover. Cultist assertions that they had not been given adequate guidance in the running of the cooperatives or in the production of coffee, and that the council just took their money without giving them a way to make that money, were generally viewed as valid by noncultists, European business people, service personnel officers, missionaries, and even by administrators themselves. Some European planters blamed themselves for having unintentionally encouraged the protest with their own anti-administration remarks. No one thought cultists were paranoid, i.e., out of touch with reality, or mentally ill, as one government medical report facetiously suggested.[2]

Nevertheless, Europeans and anticultists often accused the cultists of being "crazy" and often attributed to them "bizarre beliefs" that they denied having. I finally understood that these accusations were ridicule, not evaluations of thought processes.

Economic: The Johnson cult was not a manifestation of crass materialism. Cultists did not simply want free cargo. Evidence for this generalization lies in several areas:

a) They said they did not just want cargo, that they wanted broad social and cultural change. Invoking memories of the Americans some of them had worked with during the war helped them to articulate what they wanted: Makios said of the Americans, "Their ways are not the ways of all men. Their ways are very good." Pengai made certain that I did not misunderstand him when he told me about the good ways of the Americans which the Lavongais had experienced: "It was not the food that [we] liked, just the way."

b) In their daily lives, they manifested a sort of easy contempt for "the things of this world."[3] Lavongais had not capitulated to the forces that define the value of a person in terms of cargo, but the people were afraid that they were losing their right to not have cargo and not have savvy and still "count one," even on their own ground.

c) When they were given chances to acquire some of the cargo that some claimed they wanted, they manifested little interest in it. For instance, when Fr. Miller helped T.I.A. to acquire equipment to start a sawmill, in which the planks for the plank houses they said they wanted could be easily acquired, not one person built a house; though many sawed up some of the necessary planks, and stored them under their thatched houses. Europeans, seeing this kind of apparently inconsistent behavior, sometimes said that the people did not want to solve their problems and that it was, therefore, not possible to help them. In my view, what cultists wanted was the substantial social change of which cargo was a symbol, and they were not going to be bought off with a few planks.

In summary, economic, religious, psychological, and intellectual factors provide only background and context for the Johnson cult. If intellectual confusion had been basic to the cult, explanation and education should have diminished it. If economic interests had been primary, economic activity and success should have altered it. If religious questing was its essence, no one outside the cult ever saw any signs that this was so. And if cultists were crazy, their detractors, who found themselves agreeing to cultists' demands, were hard pressed to give evidence of this craziness beyond the "crazy" vote for Johnson itself.

What the Johnson Cult Was: Improvised Political Theater

I argue that the Johnson cult was, in its primary focus, a politically engaged dramatic presentation; an interpretation that saves some of the most interesting data I have, data that cannot be made relevant to any of the aforementioned categories of factors. It was the comments of sympathetic Europeans, who had known the cultists over a period of time and quite well, that set me on the track of this view. Australian Medical Assistant Carroll Gannon asked me, partly in jest, "Does it ever seem to you that they're just acting?" and he commented, in front of some of his Lavongai friends, "They're all Academy Award winners here!"

When I asked teacher Jim Hancock what he thought of Carroll's observation he said, "Oh yes, they're all great actors here!" And Fr. Miller seemed mysteriously onto something when he said to me, "You should write this up as a musical comedy!"

Nevertheless, I felt that we were looking at the vote for Johnson as outsiders, and that it was not something that anthropologists should laugh about. However, when I began to try to tell the story to my classes without allowing their laughter or mine, I found that the story of the Johnson cult and much of what happened in it disappeared. I then realized that the cultists had relished the telling of what happened, and laughed when they told me about making the Australian officers uncomfortable, I finally saw that they, too, thought their cult was not only serious but also funny. It took me years to piece this all together, but I finally made all these insights central to my own interpretation.[4]

The Johnson cult was a symbolic action that used a dramatic form of communication and authentic Lavongai forms to present an aesthetic truth, and to take on this truth a political stand. The declaration for Johnson at the Ranmelek polling station was a dramatic event, a presentation in which people created a scene, played the roles they wanted to play, ad libbed a script, and in so doing redefined, for themselves and for outsiders, their own situation. But it was also an act that empowered the voters, both personally and in the colonial society of the day. As the cult continued, the Lavongais took control of the description of their own history as well as of their own future. These characteristics identify art in general, and political drama in particular. Evidence for this interpretation lies in the following several arenas in which the Johnson cult took place.

Symbolic Action: The defining feature of the Johnson cult, which distinguishes it from a union protest, a political movement, a new religion, or a nervous breakdown, lies in its expressive aspect. It recognized a crisis in the symbolic universe that it met with symbolic, not instrumental, action; directed at change in the symbolic, not the natural, supernatural, or social world. The crisis lay in the feeling Lavongais had that they did not have the savvy they needed. Pengai said, "Plenty of men have savvy about English, and what have they done? They know English for nothing, that's all." English is not what they needed to know: "Where is one more kind of savvy to be a friend to this one?" Pengai asked. And Oliver said, "Who will show us about everything?" They knew they needed a broad kind of savvy that they found hard to specify; but Samuel did well when he said, in his speech to a meeting with Australian administrators, "We want the Americans to teach us how to live good, happy, and useful lives."

People who had always prided themselves on self-reliance and mastery of the symbolic universe now found themselves intellectual dependents. People who had always sought knowledge within themselves as individuals and had been ashamed to turn to others for help found themselves humiliated when they did by what they saw as Australian deception. Now they would return the insult by belittling Australian savvy and competence and by asking the Americans, instead, to come and give them savvy. The Johnson cult was a savvy cult, not a cargo cult, a symbolic response to a crisis of symbols.[5]

Aesthetic Truth: The vote for Johnson, like any aesthetic expression, began as a matter of taste, of preference. When I was trying to make sure that I understood what Oliver meant when he said he "believed in" America, he said, "Just like, like; it's just like, like, that's all." And when Joseph wrote a speech to be delivered to the United Nations Visiting Commission, he wrote: "In the minds of us the people of New Hanover want to ask the love of this country America if he loved our wish to him he could come and care of us now. But if America doesn't want to love our wish to them then we say okay."

The Johnson cult was an aesthetic truth for the Lavongais, not a scientific one. The scientific truth or falsity of the ideas in the election was of little interest to cultists (who found European attention to this line of questioning puzzling), not because they were held by some religious experience or blinded by traditional cognitive patterns, but because they had discovered an aesthetic truth: they had found an idea they really liked. Kenneth Burke has written of artistic truth:

The distinction between the psychology of information and the psychology of form involves a definition of aesthetic truth. It is here precisely, to combat the deflection which the strength of science has caused to our tastes, that we must examine the essential breach between scientific and artistic truth. Truth in art is not the discovery of facts, not an addition to human knowledge in the scientific sense of the word. It is, rather, the exercise of human propriety, the formulation of symbols which rigidify our sense of poise and rhythm. Artistic truth is the externalization of taste. (Burke, 1968: 100).

The Johnson cult was an externalization of Lavongai taste, which they, but not Tikana or other outsiders, felt, and often said, was true. In the vote for Johnson of America, they were true to themselves.

Authentic Lavongai Forms: The Johnson cult was an expression of their own, based on their own genuine experience and their own truth. What the Australians had offered them was, from the people's point of view, more false promises. The candidates from whom the people could "freely" choose were educated elites and Europeans who had had their chances to help solve the development problems of New Hanover and had failed. In response to the election format that the Australians offered, a few men engaged in their traditional art of greasing[6] and came up with a format which suited them better. They quickly found out that it suited everyone else, too, which surprised them: Lavongais are not accustomed to finding themselves in accord. Pengai said that before the election each man knew in his own way that all was not well with his world, but " . . . in the election, all our knowledge came together."

The Johnson cult was an expression that was peculiarly Lavongai, and obscure to the rest of us, in that it used complex patterns that occur in both institutionalized and noninstitutionalized aspects of New Hanover culture. Some of these may be described as follows.

a) *Liking something*: Public pronouncements concerning one's wishes are often made in New Hanover, and they are considered final. It is expected that what a person wants will be treated as inviolable: "Like is a big thing," they often said.

b) *Shaming someone*: In the vote for Johnson, the people shamed the Australian administration for not having done a better job of developing New Hanover, while pretending that they were just following Australian orders to vote for whomever they wished. This double play is common in New Hanover life and used to be common in a tradition that allowed people to give food in a large public display, ostensibly in a show of respect, to someone who has been somehow stingy, to make him feel ashamed. Everyone knew, of course, that the gesture was one of contempt and mockery, but it was difficult for the recipient to prove the donor's ill will. People laughed when they told me instances of these satiric acts of generosity, just as they laughed when they told me about the look on the faces of the Australian patrol officers when the Lavongais innocently voted for Johnson and then quickly disappeared into the bush.

c) *Dramatic communication*: The use of dramatic forms is common in New Hanover life and speech. In telling me about what had happened, in the Johnson cult or in any other events of their lives, people reenacted scenes in a naturalistic copy of the dialogue, moving around, changing their voices as they repeated what they, or someone else, had said rather than giving an abstract representation.

They often spoke metaphorically: e.g., Silakau, describing the Lavongai fashion of each doing as he likes, said, with a smile, "We are like little streams coming off a river. Each goes in a different direction." Dramatic and other elaborated modes of communication are, then, "traditional art forms" for New Hanover.

In summary, the Johnson cult may be interpreted, then, as an art form in that its action was symbolic, not instrumental; it was a genuine creative expression of the Lavongai people, which suited their own particular version of human culture; and they found it not just comprehensible but aesthetically pleasing. They liked it. The form this artistic expression took may be best designated as political drama, in that the cultists used dramatic action in a political arena to achieve control over their own lives.

The Pervasive Theme: Inequality

There would have been no dramatic action in response to a symbolic crisis had there not been fundamental related crises in the social, political, and economic aspects of Lavongai life. The condition in all these spheres which the Lavongai perceived and found unacceptable was inequality. They had long experienced inequality as a people in relation to representatives of colonial powers, first German and then Australian. While Australia had been with them, they had done all the work and Australians had got the rewards. Joseph said that he "worked coolie" for Europeans. Pengai said, "I work bullshit for you," and "Now all the money remains only with the master." Lapantukan said, "Everything you see, we pulled the paddle."

They had lived, as they said, "like dogs or pigs" under the colonial masters; but these were relatively few in numbers and the people saw little of them. Now things were to be different: they were to be given self-government, and they were to be ruled by those among them who had learned the way of the white man. This was now the way of their children and the way of the future, and, suddenly, total cultural and political domination loomed on the near horizon. They were going to be treated permanently, not just occasionally, as inferior in their own place, on their own ground, by their own people, even by their own children, just for doing their own thing. Oliver made graphically clear his concern about the unequal status that local people would occupy in relation to each other in this new world:

"Some men are well-off; some men are not well-off. And all men of savvy savvy well, and one man, he does not savvy; he is just the same as one man shit-nothing, that's all. Later, when self-government comes, it buggers up again this man who is already buggered up. Before, he was buggered up, then self-government comes, buggers him up again. About money, that's all."

The Lavongai people have never liked inequality. Not only did they have no chiefs, they did not even have Melanesian big men: no feasts, no exchanges of pigs, no exchanges of valuables as part of the marriage system. It was Australia that had created conditions of inequality, wherein only a few were able to gain access to cargo and savvy. Americans had treated them as equals during the war:

Pengai: If America sat down together with us, I think it would be very good. Because their ways are good. For instance, when they prepare food, it's not like the way of Australia. They prepare food, you and I together, we sit down, and I eat now. Now, Australians, they see us, and they tell us to get out.

Thus, at the American table, cultists expected to peck as equals with their hosts.

Oliver made it his job to travel around spreading understanding about Australia's role in their plight, raising consciousness, and urging people to hold fast to their election:

DB: Those who heard you, what did they do?
Oliver: Their minds were clear; that is, they got our thinking, that's all. They must all stand up and be strong in this work and make this trouble, so that it will have a name, or a year, or a time, that, by and by, all places must hear of this trouble and seek out the meaning of it. It has come up from what? It has come up from lies, that's all: making bullshit at this time, for plenty of years.
DB: From the lies of Australia?
O: Yes, about looking after everyone.

Australia, then, was at fault for bringing inequality into Lavongai life; so cultists publicly accused the Australian administration of not living up to its responsibilities in hopes of getting the Americans, or someone, to see the injustice of their situation and to, somehow, bring aid.

Oliver: But who will straighten it, the road? Because you, all whiteskins, you have another kind of road and another kind of law. Now, with us, all black men, another kind. That is, we are down more yet. Now a man who has got savvy, he goes and jumps up a little, and he goes and jumps a little on the step: he goes together with you all. But we, some of us, we "sleep" [remain] truly no good; down below. And what road will you—will they—make so that, by and by, all men who are not well-off, and all men who have savvy, all must be equal ?

Seizing Expressive Power Through Art

Redefining the Situation: "Common Sense"

If people have been misled, unjustly treated, and kept down, but their oppressors blame them and jail them instead of helping them, it may be, as it was in New Hanover, that the greatest power to create change and establish cultural and material hegemony which the people have available to them is expressive power. The Johnson cultists used this power when they took control of the symbolic universe which the European world had previously been imposing against little resistance. The vote for Johnson was not only a public exposé of Australia's failure in New Hanover and a challenge to the authority of the Australian administration, it was also a challenge to the authorized mythology of the world as Europeans had presented it, which in many ways made no sense to the Lavongais.

The election was the beginning of a Lavongai effort to gather their experiences together and formulate a coherent statement that made sense to them, a new "common sense." The general ideological stance expressed by cultists was apparently obvious, or "common sense," to everyone from the beginning: there were no long meetings during which some sought to persuade or explain to others why they had voted as they did. The Johnson cult required no leaders, and acknowledged no mentors or prophets. From the Australian point of view, the vote for Johnson, which seemed so sensible to the cultists, was "crazy." But it is just such an assault on "common sense" as this one that has been identified, by Gramsci and others (Sassoon, 1982), as a crucial first step in social change:

> Like all ideologies, common sense may have "true" elements but it is never a confirmation of truth; its relation to truth is wholly subordinate to its function as the cultural cement smoothing relations between state and civil society. . . . From the point of view of political education, then, common sense is not only its necessary starting point but also its most formidable obstacle. (Adamson, 1980: 151)[7]

It was this obstacle—adherence to someone else's "common sense"—that the Lavongais overcame with their vote for Johnson. Suddenly, their "knowledge came together,"[8] and they realized that they could break loose from Australia's image of them, its lies, and its idea of what was possible, and take control of their own destiny.[9] As they were sitting and talking about the forthcoming election, Pengai, who had been thinking about what could be done, said: "We can vote for America; we can vote for President Johnson." And, without any discussion of the matter, everyone suddenly knew that they could.

In voting for Johnson, the Lavongais rejected the common sense definition of the election offered, vaguely, to them in terms of authorized procedures, authorized candidates, and authorized goals. They devised their own usage of this form and seized power to define the meaning of their vote. They declined to accept the argument of missionary and government personnel that they could not do this. They had, after all, done it. They made clear that they would not obey the logic of the European system, which claimed that they owed tax monies to the Australians and that the Americans would not come. Why should they go on believing what whiteskins said? As Joseph Pukina's brother, cultist Boserong, said to me: "You say America will not come. I say it will come. Now both of us will wait and see."

Symbolic Control and Cultural Dominance

As the definition of the situation proposed by cultists gained ascendancy, they began to gain power over the actions of believers and nonbelievers alike. They clung to their idea, as Fr. Miller put it, "like a dog to a bone" (Miller, 1966: 20); and because they refused to give up, eventually others began to give in. A hospital was built by the administration, high officials came to visit and listen, and white people began to vie with one another, in small ways and then in larger ways, to show good will and egalitarian good manners. Even leading anticultist Edward, an old government worker, told me (turning first away, then toward me): "The government had turned its back on us. Now it has turned around to face us."

When Hamlet was turning over in his mind what to do, he had an idea in the context of an opportunity that suddenly appeared: he would allow the players who happened to come by to perform a play which would expose the King's evil deed and make him feel guilty.[10] The Lavongai apparently also spent some time pondering in soliloquy about their situation, and it was in the context of an opportunity that suddenly appeared that they enacted their dramatic vote for Johnson partly to expose the neglect of New Hanover of which they felt the Australians were guilty. It was "the play," then, that caught "the conscience of the king" in Lavongai, as it did in Elsinore. But just as it was Hamlet's will to act, not the King's guilt, that was at issue in Shakespeare's play; so it was the Lavongais' will to act, not Australia's failures, that was at issue in the vote for Johnson. Having gathered their will in the vote, they went on to more practical actions. The king had said he was going to retire, in any case; and the Lavongais were no longer taking orders from him. By 1968, T.I.A. had elected its own members to the council, and then voted the council (which they saw as the king's council) out of existence. T.I.A., the respectable vehicle of the cult, reigned supreme in New Hanover. Power had indeed come up inside T.I.A., as Walla said they hoped it would.

Attempts by the Australian "kings" to restore their authority in New Hanover without the use of coercion came too late. They had, in Gramsci's terms, lost their hegemony: "The hegemony of a political class meant for Gramsci that the class had succeeded in persuading the other classes of society to accept its own moral, political, and cultural values. If the ruling class is successful, this will involve the minimum use of force" (Joll, 1977: 129).

The power of the vote for Johnson, a mere symbolic action, was not underestimated by the Australian administration. They sensed that they had lost noncoercive control of the situation, and they produced, at great expense, coercive actions "to restore order."[11] All their police, and guns, and jailings did nothing to return their definition of the situation to a position of moral authority, or common sense. They regained only some respect for themselves as individuals through private acts of camaraderie when they stepped out of their roles and off stage.

The Johnson cult may be seen, then, as primarily a dramatic statement demanding respect for the perspective on reality of a particular group (the Lavongais) that felt that it had been unjustly forced into a position of inferiority in relation to other groups (Australians and other Europeans and the local educated elite). Gusfield (1976: 248) has discussed symbolic actions of this sort as "status politics," struggles in which status groups which are separated by divergent styles of life rather than only by economic issues compete for the dominance of their symbols and, hence, of themselves. People in government positions particularly affect the outcome of this kind of competition: "The distribution of prestige is partially regulated by symbolic acts of public and political figures. Such persons "act out" the drama in which one status group is degraded and another is given deference" (Gusfield, 1976: 224).

Applying these generalizations to the Johnson cult, it may be said that Lavongais viewed the Australian administration's version of the election as an alien symbol, one which belonged to the Europeans and educated elites who had learned how to function in the European world. They felt they were not equipped to take part in this symbolic election as equals, and the pretense that they could do so constituted a satiric insult to them, a mockery of their own life-style. They did not wish to play the lowly roles assigned to them in that drama; so they devised their own satiric form, in which the Australians and their local followers were "degraded," while deference was given to the Americans and, by implication, to their Lavongai constituency. With their vote for America, the Lavongais hoped to regain not just political, but also cultural dominance over their land.

Art, Drama, Power, Change

The political power that is created, maintained, and implemented through the arts has not regularly been sought out in the works of anthropologists.[12] Questions about art and power have been stated and considered by philosophers of the Frankfurt school and by students working in what has been called the "underground tradition of Marxism." This group "recognized the importance of the 'subjective' side of the dialectic, the reciprocal action of men and culture upon the economic determinants" (Harrington, 1976: 343). Art has a special position for some: Gramsci, for instance, saw art not as merely reflecting political ideology but also as related to eternal values and, hence, autonomous; capable of visions outside of common sense, capable of visions of change (Salamini, 1981: 202).[13]

Lukacs' description of drama as the "poetry of the will" (Kiralyfalvi, 1975:130) is of special interest here. Through the drama of the Johnson cult, Lavongais expressed their will poetically, and, as is the case with most poetry and with art in general, the message was not easy for outsiders to read: "Poets, their heads being in the clouds, are those who see whales and camels where others see only a chance of rain."[14] The Lavongais were poets who saw a chance to redefine the direction and meaning of their lives, where the Australian *kiaps* saw only a routine election; who saw the whales and camels for which they had been waiting, where outsiders saw only a storm coming up. They saw new hope for their future, where the government saw only the irrational deviation from "common sense" it called a "cargo cult."

The Lavongais, masters of poetry, carried on the struggle only with words and other symbols; while the government, determined to win and lacking more in imagination than in coercive power, relied on jail. In 1986, Walla was imprisoned for three months. Unlike those who went to jail as individuals in 1964, 1965, and 1966, Walla at that time represented his people in prison. In T.I.A., he said in 1966, "by and by, we will be one": and this, in many ways, has come to pass. Lavongai poetry was politically powerful not because of what it said to others, but because, through it, Lavongais communicated among themselves.

"The Election for America:" The Play

Unlike the revolutionary theater of the 1960s in America (Brustein 1971), the Lavongais' intention was originally merely resistance, not social change. They came to the confrontation equipped only with arms from the everyday arsenal of Lavongai life: mockery, dramatic confrontation, words. Surprised by the power they suddenly saw they had, they have continued to move together, although with a reduced cast, in their satiric drama for over thirty years. They won one thing they sought: the ability to prevent others from making all the decisions about their lives. But they never got what they asked for: help in overcoming their isolation and developing their island.

In telling about the Johnson cult drama, I will have to tell how it was done, not how it *is* done: while it has continued its epic course over the years, the Johnson cult, unlike the recurrent New Ireland performances of *malanggan*, had not been played before and will not be played again. It is improvisational political theater, a genre based on daily life wherein repetition is tedious and meaningless, and inclusion of real world events is fundamental.

The history of events in the Johnson cult can be seen as developing dramatically, and analyzed in terms of its script, acts and scenes, scenery, props and costumes, and other categories relevant to a theatrical production. The following summary and description ends with a critique of "the play."

Creating the Play, Setting the Stage: Backstage, Down Front

The Plot of the Play
The central problem of the play was the struggle for "moral equivalence" (Burridge 1960) with everyone else in this world against men whose morals were in question and whose competence had amply been found wanting.

The Script
All drama grows out of people's lives, and it was the Americans present "backstage" on Mt. Patibung, and those remembered from wartime, who significantly defined the social and cultural context within which "The Election for America" was played. Suddenly, what had been a half-hearted obedience to a government order became an opportunity for self-expression.

The script for the Johnson cult had not come down through the generations: it had to be ad-libbed. Since this art comes easily to Lavongais, having no script was no problem: they had a common understanding. The vote for America offered a perspective on reality that pleased them, and their script grew and flourished.

Production Arrangements
The whole show was originally arranged by the government officials: cultists and anticultists merely responded to government cues. But the actors did not like the version of the myth they were asked to reinforce in the show; so they eventually quit trying to influence it, ignored the producers' orders, and took over the entire production themselves.

The Director
No one took responsibility for directing the show once it split off from the official version. There were messengers and spokesmen, but each person took responsibility only for himself and his own actions and beliefs. It was hard for Europeans, used to centralized control, to believe that there was no director: "This was a very well-organized thing," Sister Liboria of the Lavongai Catholic Mission told me one day. Those who are familiar with contemporary European theater or the New York Living Theater, however, are aware that drama may be developed, sometimes in relation to audiences, by actors without interference from directors.[15]

Props, Costumes and Special Effects

There were not many props or costumes in the Johnson cult, but cultists made the most of what they had. It was the blackboard, the guns and nightsticks, and the red jail *laplaps* (wrap-around skirts) that recurred in their accounts and in their reenactments. The red ballot box became a symbol for the enemy, as did the hated badge of the councillor.

A few gunshots rang out and into the story line, and one smoke bomb: a young man, to everyone's horror, was ordered to go stand in it. "The people," the government officer who gave the order told me, "must understand our strength."

The red jail *laplaps* became a symbol of solidarity. When Lapantukan was finally sent to sleep in the jail house, he insisted on being given the red *laplap*: meant to be the shameful mark of a convict, it became, for cultists, the proud mark of the martyr. Rev. Taylor wrote me that when a song and dance to tell the story of the jailing was performed at a Methodist *Wartabar* (the day mission offerings are collected) in 1966, near Bolpua village, it was danced by lines of men in grass skirts dyed red. I saw the story enacted again in the red skirts in 1974, at the festive opening of the new Catholic church in Lavongai.

When the drama shifted to scenes of T.I.A., new props became crucial. Fr. Miller provided planks and paint, and T.I.A. members painted new signs, or "flags," to identify T.I.A. plantations.

Auditoriums, Scenery, and Stages

Stages, scenery and auditoriums were provided by villages, jails, prison boats, and the bush—wherever confrontations occurred. All the world's a stage for the Lavongais, and wherever two were gathered together there were players.[16]

Performing the Johnson Cult: Getting the Show on the Road

In order to see the Johnson cult as political drama it helps to look separately at the dramatic format, the story, and the dynamic motive which carried the action of the play forward.

The Program, in Retrospect: A Summary of the Play In Acts and Scenes

The program for the play could be seen in retrospect as three acts of three scenes each, beginning with the vote itself, proceeding to the confrontations between cultists and the Australian government, and concluding with the evolution of T.I.A. An epilogue notes the ongoing status of efforts in New Hanover. (See Figure 1, Program, The Election for America.)

Act I: The Election

Scene 1: A Fireside Chat: Mulling Over the Upcoming Election
People in the villages heard about the election only second- and third-hand from their councillors: they did not know most of the candidates (Europeans), did not like the rest (some Europeans and some educated Lavongais and New

---

Program

"The Election for America"

Act I: The Election
Scene 1: A Fireside Chat: Mulling Over the Upcoming Election
Scene 2: Gathering at the Mission, the First Polling Station
Scene 3: The Vote for Johnson of America

Act II: Government Versus Cultists: Responses and Initiatives
Scene 1: Meetings to Hear Gentlemanly Explanations
Scene 2: Surprise by Census Patrols, Tax Patrols, "the Spanish Armada," and Mass Arrests
Scene 3: Waiting for Johnson

Act III: The Last Act: New Directions and Old Fashions
Scene 1: "Why Not Develop Our Place?:" The Emergence of T.I.A.
Scene 2: Hard Work, Strong Faith, Vague Hopes, and "The Enemy"
Scene 3: From Political Drama to Dramatic Politics: Seizing Control Without and Within the Power Structure

Epilogue: What Did We Get? What Have We Got? What Did We Want? What Shall We Do? What Is To Be Done?

Figure I: Program, "The Election for America"

Irelanders), and had no developed interest in being represented by anyone. Pengai and others in Nusawung village began to mull over the idea that who they really wanted to have boss them was the Americans, for whose return they had hoped since the end of World War II. In this situation, which was, to them, absurd, they found it easy to make an absurd suggestion: Let's vote for the president of America! The idea immediately caught on and was quickly and enthusiastically carried from one person to another.

Bosmailik went to Mt. Patibung to find out from the visiting American map-making team the name of the new President of America. The night before the election, at a meeting in Magam village, old Savemat was given the important role of writing the vote on the blackboard; to which he, as a local mission worker, had access. His nephew helped him choose what words to write in pidgin English: "We want Johnson of America. That is all."

From there on, people improvised the script from their life experiences and their participation in contemporary events, creating noninstitutionalized roles and improvised scenes. They had found a way to play themselves, all leading roles, instead of the dull, subservient roles assigned by the government.

Scene 2: Gathering at the Mission, the First Polling Station

Word spread quickly, and when people gathered at the Ranmelek Methodist Mission station to vote on 15 February 1964, they found a blackboard set up before them on which had been written: "We want Johnson of America."

Individuals who converged at the mission station on that Saturday had not thought of this day as being special. They did not expect this election to help them solve the problems with the co-ops, coconuts, coffee, and the council about which they had long complained. When, suddenly, the word spread that some people were going to vote for America, people were elated, and they all agreed to the idea: "We like it."

The accounts given of the vote at Ranmelek show the sense of drama and excitement that built toward the events of that great day.

However, one man, Silakau, who had walked all day Friday to get to the polling place the night before the vote, and who had heard about the vote for America when he attended the evening meeting in Magam, remained puzzled. When he got up early the next day to wash his face in the sea, he did not know what he was going to do.

Scene 3: The Vote for Johnson of America

When the government officers came out of the mission house, where they had slept, early on the morning of 15 February 1964, they saw the blackboard and its message next to their red plastic ballot box. They looked at it briefly, and, without comment, they turned the board around. They then proceeded to call the people of the first village on their list, Lavongai, to come forward with their ballots, which they were to mark and drop in the red plastic box.

There was a tense pause after the *kiaps* called for the people of Lavongai to step forward, during which no one knew what to do. Then, suddenly, it was Yaman, a man whose arm swung uselessly at his side, who stepped forward at this decisive moment as others hesitated, and created his historic, and his only, part in this drama: "Our vote is already written on the blackboard," he said. "We want Johnson of America." "True?" he asked, looking back at the crowd pressing forward around him. And then every man, woman, and child shouted out, "Yes!" and ran away, leaving the place clear of people! Nearly everyone shouted with laughter as they retold and reenacted this scene. They loved the joke they had played on the Australians.

Consensus flashed at the mission on that day, and no one who was there will ever forget it. It all happened so fast that no one had time to decide who would do what, but that is a feature of improvised dramas: scripting is not necessary, not possible. People were guided by common understanding and perspective.

But one actor, guided by his own thinking, played a lonely role in this scene. As everyone melted away into the bush, only Councillor Silakau remained behind. He saw that the patrol officers were upset and ashamed; and he, a man who sometimes cried in church over the plight of the helpless, felt a little sorry for them. He and the Australian missionary and his wife voted by dropping their ballots into the red box. No one was left to see them.

Later Silakau said he had not allowed other men to "boss my thinking," and he had played the part that was true to himself. He did not remember for whom he had voted.

Thus began the division between "Those Who Voted in the Box" and "Those Who Voted on the Board," which continued throughout the drama. The government officers were unable to get people to put their ballots in the red plastic ballot boxes prepared for them at this first and then at several other polling stations on the south coast, but on the north coast people voted "properly," i.e., in the box.

Act II: Government Versus Cultists: Responses and Initiatives

Scene 1: Meetings to Hear Gentlemanly Explanations

At first, the government officers of various ranks did not play themselves, but, rather, their own busy roles as professionals. Still, it was hard for them to "act well their parts"[17] because they had to abandon the script with which they had come to New Hanover, and they were not allowed to ad lib a new one. They needed authorization and instructions: cables were sent, cables were received. Back in government headquarters on the mainland, meetings were held, decisions were made. A new script was forwarded, but it was the same old script: business would proceed as usual. The vote for Johnson would not be mentioned, law and order would be restored, patrol officers would patrol the villages, meetings and explanations would clarify everything.

Over the next few months, government officers patrolled the villages to explain that Johnson was not a candidate. Never mind, said the Johnsonites, now identified by the government as "cargo cultists," we want to vote for him anyway. American servicemen were present at some of these meetings, and they denied that America intended to come. Nevertheless, cultists continued to express their right to vote for Johnson, and their determination to continue to do so. Cultists noted that the educated elite of New Hanover sat, in western clothes, with the government officials at these meetings.

Occasionally outsiders were brought in specifically to be "audiences." Most notably, a United Nations Visiting Mission and other outside "experts" came to hear Lavongai grievances. But they were really there, Lavongais sometimes thought, to make them stop acting like this, pay their taxes, and get off stage.

Scene 2: Surprise by Census Patrols, Tax Patrols, "the Spanish Armada," and Mass Arrests

When the administration found that "explanations" were not changing behavior, patrol officers were sent on surprise patrols to gather census data. At hastily assembled meetings on beaches or further inland, *kiaps* threatened jail for any who did not appear to be counted. Finally, tax collectors, accompanied by eighty police in one instance, began to patrol by boat: "I looked out one day," Sister Liboria told me, "and there was the Spanish Armada in the harbor!" Patrol officers tried to line people up, and then began to take people off to jail in handcuffs, to give chase, and in at least one instance to shoot coconuts off a tree as, in A.D.O. Benhem's words, a "demonstration of strength." Mass arrests began, and continued for three years. The charge: tax evasion and default.

Opposition changed the Lavongai expression from an impulsive to a serious demonstration. The cultists were forced to play in earnest because the government did. "You can hang us all from the rafters," Joseph Pukina shouted at *kiaps* at one meeting, "but we will not pay tax!"

Scene 3: Waiting for Johnson

As the drama progressed, the parties to the conflict defined their positions. It was the third year after the vote for Johnson, and cultists were being jailed for the third time for nonpayment of taxes. They were ridiculed, talked to patiently, taxed, jailed, and, still, the Americans did not come. The ideology of colonial history and failure developed for the cult seemed to make their coming inevitable. It not only explained changes in the past and justified cultists' demands, it also seemed to predict further change: the coming of another country, of the last country, America. First Germany, then Australia, and now America. The citing of prior truths seemed to give credence to the final one that fit so consistently with the pattern of their history. But America did not come.

I asked Pengai if he still, in 1967, followed his thinking about America, and he said, "Today, and all the time more that is yet to come. New Hanover, altogether, stays with this—not me alone."

And so they waited. The drama was at a standstill, inspiration thinning, and still no word from the Americans. Their cue had come and gone several times, and they were nowhere in the wings. The show had been very successful in many ways, but it was lagging. It needed Johnson to arrive, deus ex machina, to straighten out all the tangles that had evolved in various directions. The background dynamics for the plot became clear, but its forward direction began to blur. Why did the Americans not appear?

Act III: New Directions and Old Fashions

Scene 1: "Why Not Develop Our Place?:" The Emergence of T.I.A.

It was here that one of the American missionaries, who had been in the background throughout most of the drama as a spectator, decided to move the performance along to its conclusion. His call to a meeting brought the whole cast on stage again for a surprising denouement, where people decided to work together to develop their island.

At that first meeting, Tutukuvul Isukal Association (T.I.A., "Stand Together to Plant") was founded.

Fr. Miller said that he tried not to impose his own views, but he did argue strongly for one rule: all members must pay their taxes, so that they could stay out of jail and be available to work. This gave the cultists an honorable reason to pay taxes if they could, and all of them used it. While they all told me they still did not want to pay taxes to Australia, they said they did it for Fr. Miller, and to be part of T.I.A. Suddenly, everyone paid his taxes and began to go to T.I.A. meetings and to work in the bush.

Most of the cultists, however, were unwilling to say that the play was over: T.I.A. was only an *entre-acte*: the last scene was yet to come. But what would it be?

Scene 2: Hard Work, Strong Faith, Vague Hopes, and "The Enemy"

People were not sure what the truth about T.I.A. was, and what its fruit would be, but they "believed." Whatever they individually thought or felt or hoped, they cut and slashed and burned and hauled away, and great clear patches of ground could be seen on the mountains. These changes in the landscape alone engendered new faith that the pristine natural state in which they felt trapped could be developed into the modern world by following this new road to the new life they all wanted. Just as urban people like to see little parks and reminders of nature deep in their cities, so it lifts the Lavongai heart to see some signs that nature can be overcome by the work of man, even Lavongai man.

The work of T.I.A. began at Lavongai Catholic Mission. The new organization established rules, collected dues, elected officers, claimed communal lands, cleared trees, planted coconuts, and met regularly to make decisions.

They placed the new T.I.A. "flags" on ground donated by various men for the new T.I.A. plantations. Father Miller accompanied T.I.A. officers when the signs were set up to bless the land and the work to be done on it. People often wondered what these flags meant, and did not always fully accept a mundane explanation, but did not dwell on this aspect of the situation.

Those who were the enemy, the anticultists who had voted in the box, carried vicious rumors to the government officers, claiming that the cultists were crazy, that they expected cargo free from the Americans, and that T.I.A. was just a cover: those who voted on the board, they said, were still waiting, as T.I.A. members, for Johnson to come. Cultists said that they did not answer these charges: they just worked hard.

Scene 3: From Political Drama to Dramatic Politics: Seizing Control Without and Within the Power Structure

In a dazzling set of political maneuvers, Johnsonites become *membas* (members of T.I.A.) put themselves far ahead of their adversaries in the pecking order. In 1968, T.I.A. president Walla was elected president of the local government council, to which cultists had refused to pay taxes, and he and his supporters then voted the council out of existence. As they had hoped, "government came up inside of T.I.A." In 1972, Walla was elected to the seat in the House of Assembly that Johnson had failed to claim in 1964, but he found it a do-nothing body, and he came home to pursue T.I.A.'s work in New Hanover.

Epilogue: What Did We Get? What Have We Got? What Did We Want? What Should We Do? What Is To Be Done?

During the 1970s and early 1980s, plantations were purchased, transport acquired, and outside companies seeking to explore and exploit were prevented from gaining access to New Hanover resources. Some of the enemy struggled in vain to join the activities of the new provincial and national governments; both of which had ceased, by 1980, to try to collect taxes, or to jail, or to govern New Hanover. In 1983, T.I.A. members held an independence march and, later, proudly gathered at Mt. Patibung, site of American map-making activities in 1963, for a celebration. On this occasion, Walla declared independence from the Westminster style government of Papua New Guinea, and demanded rule by an American style presidential system. They were, it seemed, on this day, king of the hill.

But was that, after all, what they had wanted? To be powerful and alone?[18] Was that the direction their play meant to take? The actors, gradually realizing that the audience (the Australian administration) had left the theater (but not the backstage area), have begun to wonder themselves what the play was about. The ending so far in view is neither happy nor tragic, but the vague and rather sudden trailing off of improvised drama, where actors just wander off the stage down into the audience, and the rise of general conversation signals that actors and audience alike are weary of the complications of the play and ready to go home.

Critique of the Play

Actors and Audiences: Pivotal Conflicts among the Cast of Characters

The audience for "The Election for Johnson" was composed of participants in general: actors were also audiences and vice versa. Each actor seemed most interested in telling me about his own role in the drama, less interested than I was in the whole play. But that is as it should be: an improvisation is played primarily for the players, not for the world, and each plays primarily for himself, though in relation to each other and to a general theme. Each actor enhanced primarily his own understanding and only incidentally that of other people. In living theater, the individual may express all his feelings: in this case, resentment and longing, sardonic wit, and the inalienable right of each individual to be his own hero.[19] But the power from which each person gained strength was the power of the people together. Pengai clearly understood the power people felt when they found out that they thought as others did.

There were some actors who tried to clarify, for themselves, each other, and the audience, what was happening. Oliver was the most philosophically articulate of these, and he took his own little show on the road. He traveled from village to village after the vote, talking to people. As a result, he said, "their minds were clear."

Seeking deep personal meaning and clarification is one of the goals of a contemporary people-oriented "poor" theater (Grotowski, 1968). Those who heard Oliver did not try to decide whether Oliver was just acting or whether he was sincere in his beliefs: they just listened. The enemy and the government officers, however, said Oliver was a fraud.

Were the cultists just acting? Dramas have steady characters, but in improvised dramas the personae of the cast and characters are mixed and blended, as they were in the Johnson cult, and it is difficult to clearly know, then, when people are acting and when, if ever, they are not.

The conflicts between groups of cultists, noncultists, government officers of various sorts (administrative, police, service), missionaries of various faiths and nationalities, and European residents are all basic to the plot and pivotal to the action of the play, and these were sustained. Sometimes, however, individuals stepped out of character to follow their own individual insights. Disgruntled in their own work, some of the Europeans began to dislike their parts and to like the Lavongais. Downstage, away from the others, government officers and other Europeans slipped some tax money to the cultists and noncultists to show they were really good guys, just acting out the villain role assigned to them. Bosap said, in response to my attempt to find out about different personalities on the European side of the cult, that officers were all alike, just doing their jobs; but some of them found ways to step out of character. And while the missionaries tried to stop the cult, their efforts were educational, not punitive; and they had mixed feelings about playing on the side of the Australian administration. "I wish America would come, too," Father Miller said one day when he had felt some pressure to stop T.I.A., which some *kiaps* called "Father Miller's cult."

Scenes from the Johnson cult were dramatically reenacted several times by the cultists when they performed for various events, usually holidays in the mission calendar. It was the arrest and jailing of the men on which these reenactments focused. The government officials with guns were always played as clowns.

T.I.A.: Entre-Acte, Denouement, Sequel, or New Production?

The Johnson cult turned into T.I.A. and a lot of work. People were determined to prevent their old fashions from spoiling T.I.A. What had been a drama drawn from Lavongai cultural character became a work based on many directly opposite principles. Still, the work was sanctified by the sacrifices and dramatic confrontations that had created it, as well as by a Catholic priest.

Cast and audience alike would have been a little disappointed if Johnson had been entirely forgotten, and he was not. News of Johnson's death was noted sadly and formed the subject of a new song which I heard some men sing to the accompaniment of a guitar in 1972. But the Americans in general were, after all, known giants to only a few of the cast, total myth for most; and the choice of Johnson was poetic license in the drama.[20] But poetry is essential to this expressive movement, and the Americans have not been forgotten: in 1983 and again in 1998 T.I.A. declared its independence and demanded a presidential system, like that of the U.S.A., for New Hanover. The drama, then, still starring many of the original cast, continues.

Ongoing Production: Epilogue 1998

The Johnson cultists, now T.I.A., now few in number and concentrated in Lavongai village, celebrated their ongoing victory in 1998, and no one was jailed. According to the news I received in writing from T.I.A. and in person from informants in Kavieng, an American flag was raised in Lavongai in late July to celebrate "Independence Day." Thus, Walla and others continue to create new scenes of meetings, of independence day celebrations, and of flag-raising occasions which call the name of America.

Some of the actors have moved on over to a meeting of the Local Environment Foundation, an organization led by a man who began to work for T.I.A. when he was only nine years old. This organization has substantial ties to major international organizations, and will not have to suffer from the cheap gibes that tormented those who voted for Johnson, and even those who became members of T.I.A. At least, not yet. The stage has expanded far beyond New Hanover, New Ireland, and Papua New Guinea, and whatever happens with this organization is best seen as a new play. But it will be played by people reared in the Lavongai style and is, even now, proceeding in a Lavongai way. We can expect to see, as we do in all of Shakespeare's plays, the unmistakable touch of the bard: in this case, of the Lavongai bards.

Lavongai Cultural Style: Foundation for the Drama

Forms of Analysis

I am primarily interested here in analyzing the patterns of behavior in the Johnson cult in relation to the structure and style of Lavongai culture: that is, in relation to precult or noncult patterns of behavior that seem to have been traditional, at least for the last several generations. I will show how these dimensions molded the election and its descendent, T.I.A. It is because the Johnson cult expressed important structural and stylistic tendencies in Lavongai culture that are antithetical to the structure and style of Tikana culture that the cult spread easily and quickly in New Hanover and, still today, has found only a few partial and discordant echoes in New Ireland.

Stylistic Analysis: Individualistic, Noninstitutionalized, Peck-Ordered Style
The style of New Hanover culture and of the Johnson cult is

1) *individualistic* in that the rights, freedoms, and expressions of the individual, and the integrity of the person, are valued above whatever need the group might have for him or her.

2) *noninstitutionalized* in that no individual is expected, and certainly not forced, to conform to any set of rules or laws, although some are offered. But none is offered without contradiction, nor is any routinely followed; so patterns are noninstitutionalized, even when they show some regularity.

3) *peck-ordered* in that individuals behave assertively, exploring all possibilities, seeking the main chance, and producing among themselves a system of integration which I have called peck-ordered. Lavongai individuals do not see their places in the system and line up. Rather, each sees himself alone among his fellows, receiving no help in an atomistic whole. The strong must contend with the weak, who beg for mercy and are more severely and frequently trounced than are the strong. It is the outside observer who sees the whole pattern, and who sees that the system is peck-ordered.

New Ireland comparison: Group-Oriented, Institutionalized, Egalitarian
Tikana work, think, and feel in groups, going through life "in shoals" (Lomax, 1968: 287), following known rules without resentment or feeling that they are being coerced, but acting as individuals to give to the weak and withhold further giving from the strong. Thus the style of their culture is group-oriented,

institutionalized, and egalitarian; and not suitable as a vehicle to accept and carry on the Johnson cult.

T.I.A.: A New Style Attempted

The Johnson cult eventually turned into Tutukuvul Isukal Association, T.I.A., which reversed the fundamental style not only of the Johnson cult but of New Hanover culture generally. It institutionalized relationships among its members and between them and their resources. T.I.A. created a corporate group within which individuals were obligated to each other and to the institution. Equality, rather than peck-ordered ranking, was institutionalized among members, not just equality as moral beings, but as contributors to the organization. The productions of T.I.A. were to serve only the group, not any special interest groups nor any individuals within it.

Some rules of T.I.A. carried along, unnoticed, some fundamental structures of Lavongai culture that worked against the new organization's stated goals. Most notably, the rule that required each individual to contribute equally to the organization in some way failed to provide, as Lavongai culture also failed to provide, for the old, the sick, and the weak. Probably partly because of their loose attitude toward institutionalization, however, rules were not enforced in this area and the unequal contribution which individuals made to the work of T.I.A. did not become a major issue. For many years, T.I.A. was able to work productively in a new style, under the leadership of a man from outside: Fr. Miller.

Structural-Functional Analysis

I also view the Johnson cult from the perspectives of seven aspects of culture: communication, history, social structure, political structure, economic organization, psychological characteristics, and expressive functions. Some of these are common categories in structural-functional analysis and some are not. Style is, itself, a structural category, though it has not been so treated in cultural anthropology.

Communication Aspects of the Johnson Cult

Modes and Media of Interaction

The modes and media of communication typical of Lavongai culture were also those that functioned in the Johnson cult, and were somewhat changed in T.I.A. The people of New Hanover are masters of verbal communication: articulate, subtle, loquacious, given to complexity and the use of figures of speech and double meanings. As against mere actions, New Hanover weighs words and finds them heavy, events in themselves: people, it is said, "get up with talk."

Verbal: Most of the events of the cult were talk: informal discussions, stories, confrontations, meetings, and so on. The idea for the vote for Johnson was formed in the local language, Tungak, and carried on in pidgin, the language ordinarily used with Europeans; but also in English, the elite language, when the United Nations came and public addresses in that language were called for.

Other than these speeches to the United Nations, there were no public addresses, no addresses by Big Men at Big Meetings: not the elegant, eloquent, erudite oratory of Polynesia, or even the long exhortatory orations of New Guinea; but unrehearsed, ad libbed, improvised statements full of figures of speech newly created for their dramatic effect. The Johnson cult was in large part a "war of words," a choice of weapons which made the Lavongai second to none.

Nonverbal: There were occasional crowd scenes, where defiance was expressed through solidarity, as at the original vote. Crowd consensus of this sort gave support to Oliver later when the *kiaps* came to arrest him. The *kiaps* did feel the presence of a crowd as a threat, and asked that only six men come to talk to them. They were not obeyed and they could not carry out the arrest. In one incident Oliver's shirt was ripped. There was tension, fear, running away, firm stands, but, so far as I could learn, only one serious attempt to shoot. Violence was rare in exchanges between cultists and others, though always feared by the government.

T.I.A.: New Modes and Media of Interaction

The Johnson cult had about it the sound of a swan song for these traditional patterns, because they would not serve other fundamental interests of the people of New Hanover, who found that their likes could not be satisfied with the old way of life.

In T.I.A., the New Hanover cultists were straining against the most fundamental tendencies of their traditional culture. The spontaneity and individualism of men challenging each other with wit and the enemy with barbs and disdain; the mass meetings with important white men; the elan of consensus in a surprised crowd; the heroism of the lone messenger or preacher hurrying between villages; the long suffering of those who were jailed, made strong by the hope and promise of the sanctity of their endurance: all this was replaced by the tedium of formal meetings, wherein speeches needed to be to the point, interesting rambles voluntarily trimmed off, free flights of fancy squeezed into the standard vocabulary, and the satisfaction of direct confrontation buffered by a seriousness of purpose and a serious President Walla.

In T.I.A. meetings, people sat in rows, met at formally decided upon times, and generally set down and abided by institutionalized structures that allow many people to function together as a group. A new meeting house was built in Lavongai village. The problem of where *bords* were to sleep when they came for two-day meetings was solved, however, not by new institutions but by an old one: by the construction of a traditional *rangama* house, a mens house, which addressed a practical problem but also recognized and nourished a new experience of commonality, like that of the old days, growing among T.I.A. members. A grand new T.I.A. plank office and sleeping house was built on the strength of this new solidarity.

New Ireland Tikana by Contrast

Tikana talk little and act easily. Acts of giving and receiving, or exchange, characterize everyday life and are institutionalized in *malanggan* and many other smaller ceremonies. New Ireland grace in arranging and rearranging themselves in groups makes their actions seem almost choreographed, while the slight raise of the eyebrows (yes) or silence (no) or a few words serve most of their verbal purposes. Accomplishing large tasks, whether building and roofing a traditional house or a modern concrete house, come easily and regularly to the people of Tikana communities. The rules are simple, clear, and continuing: give, help, work together.

Historical Aspects of the Johnson Cult

The Past Reconsidered: Themes in the New Script

Questions about what cultists wanted were often answered by referring to the ways of the ancestors and of the Australians, which Lavongais generally did not like; and the ways of the Americans, which they did like.

The Ways of the Ancestors Rejected: Cultists certainly did not remember a traditional "golden age" to which they wanted to return. Their traditional culture was a "rubbish fashion," not just because they lived "like pigs and dogs" in a material sense, but also because of their traditional character faults, as they saw them. "We lie," Joseph Pukina said to me earnestly one day, in the presence of several of his friends, who agreed. People also recognized their inability or unwillingness to work together. One night after a late-night meeting the men were complaining about how no one "bossed" them well, and then they laughed and said that no one could boss them. Joseph then explained to me the Lavongai fashion of followership: "When I was boss of the co-ops, suppose I talked about something," he began. Joseph spoke dramatically, gesturing first to one and then another of his fellow Lavongais, who smiled in accord, as he spoke. "Him, he goes paddling [his canoe]; and him he has already gone to the bush. Him, he wants to go get leaf [to chew with betel nuts]; him, he is chopping out sago up there. Him, he wants to go sit down in his house; and me, I talk, my mouth fills up with flies!"

The Australian Way Rejected: Cultists felt that they could not go successfully into the modern world with what the Australians had taught them. They were afraid of self-government, partly because Australia would leave behind an unequal distribution of skills and power. They thought the educated elite no more willing and even less able than the Australians to help them gain the savvy they needed to control their lives.

They were also afraid that Australians would push them off their land, as they had the Australian Aborigines, and that Lavongais would be powerless under "self-government" to stop them. Even the old noncultist Edward said, "There are not a lot of things that we have planted for this thing, self-government, to come to us. Just to be boss, with nothing, by and by it will be no good." Pengai, who told me that "power is the foundation of government," might have added that "just to be boss, with nothing," is not power.

The American Way Remembered and Idealized: Many men in New Hanover had, or had heard, memories of the great days of World War II, when Lavongais had worked in Emira or Buka with American soldiers who treated them as equals. Americans also gave them clothes and food and other goods, but Pengai and others made clear that "it is not the food that they liked, just the way." They did not expect to be kings or angels when the trumpet sounded, just men equal to all other men in the developed world.[21] Remembering the Americans helped them to define and describe what they wanted in their new lives.

New Ireland Tikana by Contrast

In New Ireland the Tikana remember the past with reverence. They spend much of their time preparing *malanggan* ceremonies which honor not only the dead, but the traditional virtues and institutions of their culture which they value highly and explicitly: "We are so lucky. No one is poor here."

They generally see the Australians the way they see each other: as people who make mistakes but are trying to help. They did not spend much time with the Americans. They liked some of the Japanese they met in the villages, and they felt appreciated by the wartime Australian officials.

Tikana recognize *malanggan* as the backbone of their culture (pidgin: *fasion*), and some are working hard to maintain it. Others just maintain it by going about meeting their regular obligations as their ancestors did.

Social Aspects of the Johnson Cult

Social Structure

Kinship, Affinity, and Locality: Cultists and noncultists are not distinguished by any particular categories relevant to social structure. Beyond the nuclear family, kinship and affinity impose few obligations on individuals in Lavongai culture generally, and this pattern was reproduced in the Johnson cult. Here lies the core of distinction between Lavongai culture and that of the Tikana, who are in all ways embedded in extended families that have clear obligations to other extended families.

The nuclear family of orientation loses its unitary status as the children grow up. As manifest in the election, for instance, Silakau's younger half-brother, Bonail, was for Johnson; whereas Silakau, a councillor, tried to convince people to abandon their vote for America. There was no ill feeling between the two because of their opposing views: each expected that the other would do as he pleased and respected his right to do so. For a while, Silakau was afraid some cultist would beat him up, but no one ever did.

If any kinship group was reinforced by the cult, it was the nuclear family of procreation. While cultists' wives generally saw the cult as "men's business," they liked the idea of the coming of America and supported rather than condemned their husbands in their efforts and in their resistance. Children supported their fathers, sometimes at some cost: Oliver's sons suffered some harassment in school, and one of them, a teenager, was briefly jailed for interfering with a cement marker which the government placed on Tsoi Island.

When I was trying to find out what kinship relationship a cult messenger had to the recipient of his message, Bosap first tried to tell me and then said, "He is just a man," meaning that the kinship relationship between the two, if any, was irrelevant.

Systems of kinships and affinity overlap with proximity, and proximity did play a role because it allowed for differential access to communications. Thus, south coast villages were in, and north coast villages were out, of the cult. There were no fundamental differences in social structure between the two areas: it was just that in a slightly different communicative environment the leadership of two men, Boski Tom and Barol, who were noncultists, tipped the balance in the north.

Sex and Age: If I asked a man what his wife thought of the election, he would say, "She has no talk. She stands up [waits], that's all." If I asked a woman what she thought of the cult, she said, "It is something that belongs just to all the men." If I asked an old man what side he was on, he would say, "Oh, no, I wasn't in the election; I am already old, I just watch." Neither women nor old men were required to pay taxes; hence, what support they gave could not be put to the test of risking a jail sentence.

The age group that primarily constituted the cultists also constituted the noncultists. It consisted mainly of middle-aged men who, in their own or other people's children, began to see what they had—almost—missed. They wanted something for themselves before it was too late.

Educated Elite: There was a division among Lavongais that was only mentioned in passing: that between the men, mostly middle-aged or older, who had little formal education; and those, mostly the young (but some old) who had gained what Australia had to offer in education. Some of these young men, like Pamais, were in New Hanover and were in the cult. Some were away at school or at work, and some sent letters home opposing the cult. But some sent money home for T.I.A. membership. The most highly educated of all, the one who spoke the best English, was Boski Tom: born in 1911, he had long been a spokesman for New Hanover, and he was among the candidates rejected by the cultists. The cult served primarily the interests of those with little or no Western education, who may have resented being bossed by their own young, or old, elite more than they resented the Australians.

The Divided Group: No Ties Bind or Expand

In the Johnson cult there was a nearly impenetrable boundary marking the division between cultists and their enemy. There was no way, once the election was over, to expand the category or group that voted for America. There were no continuing ties among cultists after the vote except jail, until T.I.A. was created.

Most of the Australian *kiaps* kept the division between themselves and the cultists clear and active, partly by jailing the cultists. Some of the *kiaps* tried to make friends with particular individuals and woo them to their side, but no cultist ever sold out his cause. Thus, when Carroll wanted to pay taxes for Lapantukan, and when the *kiaps* refused to jail him along with his people because he was a councillor, he was angry. These acts set him apart from his people. He told Carroll not to pay his tax, and he gave his councillor's badge back to the *kiaps*, in order to rid himself of this symbol of association with the government side of the cult.

Social Structure of T.I.A.

Women, alone or with their husbands, and old men, could and did join T.I.A. Otherwise, the membership of this new organization, with a few notable exceptions, consisted of the same individuals who had voted for America. The exceptions were mostly Catholics who respected Fr. Miller.

T.I.A followed European custom in singling out the village as the body from which representatives would be elected by members. It was the matrilineal clan, however, which was cited as owner of the land which was donated by a particular man for the communal use proposed by T.I.A. I could see no evidence that there was any clarity in this situation, and the fact that individuals did not want to ossify claims in European documents created by the demarcation committee testified to a flexibility they thought they had. They also had conflict: it was to end this conflict that T.I.A. was able to gain permission for all its members to use large tracts of land; the ownership status of whose many claimants was, no doubt, endlessly disputable. Thus, the clan reemerged briefly, but immediately disappeared into T.I.A. I and many others thought that there would be great problems about this land in the future; but, so far as I know, there has not been.

The rules of T.I.A. intended it to be an inclusive body, but New Hanover culture and circumstances rendered it, for most, exclusive. The enemy were, of course, to stay out forever. Inside T.I.A. the feelings of camaraderie that had been created in the cult continued, and these blossomed into a *rangama* (men's house) where T.I.A. *bord* could sleep when they attended meetings. Those left out of T.I.A were, then, also left out of an important reinterpreted "traditional" men's group as well, one which probably was exclusive in the old days,[22] as it was in 1967 and as it continued to be in 1998.

Caste Divisions

The Johnson cult sought an end to the caste division between Lavongai natives and Europeans, but not until all the natives had had a chance to catch up with some of their successful compatriots. Oliver said clearly that some men were "up a little" and others were "shit nothing." He did not want the Australians to leave behind them a replica of their own system, and, since Australia seemed to be making plans for a hurried departure, Oliver and others sent their urgent message to America.

Why did the cultists never complain about not being equal to the Chinese? Occasionally I heard a Lavongai make fun of the Chinese accent in speaking pidgin, but otherwise they were never mentioned. When people went to Kavieng, most went into some of the fifteen or so Chinese shops, all filled with wondrous things—not just all the clothes, pots and pans, beautiful towels, primus stoves and lanterns that the village people need and buy, but also all the beautiful jewelry, embroidered robes and slippers, and delicate pottery for which Chinese shops are famous everywhere.

The European stores, of which there were only two, were, by contrast, dull, their proprietors often rude. They prided themselves on not selling "*meri* (women's) blouses and *laplaps*" and other things that "natives" need. They said they did not want *kanakas* (people who lived in the villages) in the stores. Usually only the educated, western dressed local people, some from other parts of the territory, shopped in these European stores in 1967.

Villagers bought their clothes in Chinese shops, from rows and rows of beautiful garments laboriously sewn up by Chinese women, for a price they could afford. The relationship the Chinese have with the people is one of service: in their stores, they stocked things that natives wanted to buy, and they even set up little stores in villages, and in trucks that plied the New Ireland road, buying coconuts and selling soap, rice, cigarettes, kerosene, and so on. In Kavieng, local people and Europeans alike bought and continue (in 1998) to buy wonderful, great fresh loaves of bread at the Chinese shops, a fine treat one is always supposed to bring back to the village, or to the plantation, after a trip to town.

Why were not the Chinese—who also managed plantations, some in New Hanover; and who also had the boats that the people could hope to send their copra to Kavieng in, boats that plied the waters irregularly between New Hanover and New Ireland—the object of a cult? Local girls were taken as partners by European men, true, but most old Chinese men had local wives. Why not the Chinese, why not vote for China to come and to bring boatloads of those marvelous little cloisonné jars and jade bracelets and bolts of cloth bearing designer-quality patterns from Hong Kong for five shillings (or fifty cents) a yard?

Though there was far more "cargo" in evidence in Chinese shops than in European stores, the Chinese were not the object of envy. Who could envy them? They worked so hard, and they did not strut the way Europeans do. They did not seem to have things for nothing. They served others, Europeans and natives, from dawn until way past dusk in some cases, while the European stores were open from 9:00 A.M. until 4:00 P.M. with an hour and a half off (and closed) for lunch. Local Europeans seemed to be not good at business, perhaps because they did not seem to like to serve.[23] The Chinese are themselves discriminated against by the white political structure, but they are too rich, too involved with the family, and too much better off than the Europeans to notice. One beaming Chinese woman to whom I often went, who ran to other stores to get what I needed if she happened not to have it, had put seven sons through the University of Sydney with her labors. She endeared herself to me by never failing to ask when I came in, "How is your research?"

But I never heard any villagers say anything that implied that they felt unequal to the Chinese, even though they sometimes felt that Chinese employers were very hard on them. What bothered the cultists was the enormous caste differences between themselves and their European *mastas*,[24] exacerbated by clear hints that under self-government some of their own men would become those "masters," would take the place of the governing class, leaving their compatriots and, literally, their brothers, behind. It was this sociopolitical situation, not cargo and economic power, that was at issue.

Cultists did not seek equality with the Chinese not because they could not hope to achieve so much, but because in the Territory of Papua New Guinea in 1967 the Chinese were in a politically and socially weak position.[25] Cultists sought, instead, identification with those who appeared to them to be strong: the Australians, or, failing them, the Americans.

Lavongais talked a great deal about equality, but they never wanted to lower themselves to make themselves equal to the weak, or to help the weak to become equal to themselves. The only people they were interested in being equal to were those who had already won first place in the pecking order.

New Ireland Tikana by Contrast

While Lavongai quickly created divisions projected as eternal, Tikana have instead a network of crosscutting ties which obliterate isolated individuals or groups across the generations, such as is created and maintained in the New Ireland *malanggan*. Extended family, clan and subclan membership, and hamlet residency are primary but give access to many other groups through marriage, much moving about, participation in communal work activities, and ceremonial giving in different contexts. Elders, men, women, children, even infants are announced as the owners of pigs and the contributors and receivers of currency. Chinese, Europeans, and the young western educated when they return home can and do join in easily: Tikana find ways to include, while Lavongais find ways to exclude.

Political Aspects of the Johnson Cult

Leadership

The Johnson cult did not have a prophet. It hardly had leaders. It had, at most, spokesmen; but there were some of these in each village, and different people spoke on different occasions. There was no attempt to consolidate leadership. The early spokesmen and inventors of the cult, e.g., Oliver and Pengai, never sat down and talked and planned together. None of the spokesmen ever asked me what any of the others had told me.

Yaman, the young man who stepped forward and insisted on the vote for America as it was expressed on the blackboard at Ranmelek, had no office, traditional or modern, nor any special qualities, except that his arm was "dead"—it swung loose at his side. I did not hear much about him, and I did not meet him. If he had not saved the day at a crucial moment at Ranmelek, probably someone else would have. Other people wrote blackboards and stepped forward in other villages.

Pengai singled himself out as a leader by saying that he had offered to take the "name," and, hence, the blame, for the vote for America. No one else, however, put the blame on him as they had on Peter: each insisted that he himself was fully committed and responsible.

Oliver became well known, partly for his daring (or cowardice) in escaping the police attempts to arrest him, and partly for his genuine acts of leadership. His style was in keeping with the style of the old-time Big Men in New Hanover, who became "big" by acquiring, but without subsequent distribution. He thus belonged—though not entirely—to the traditional culture and was not the man to unite these people in the new way of life which they claimed to seek. Cultists wanted new leadership from outside, men who were not like the old New Hanover ones, or the old Australian ones, all far ahead in the pecking order, keeping their distance and not sharing their know-how.

Outsiders found it hard to understand why cultists would think that America would want to come and bother with them. Probably it was mainly wishful thinking; however, it also makes sense by analogy with their experience of colonial situations. Australia seemed to want to boss Papua New Guinea, as Germany had wanted to before; so, presumably, all big countries want to boss small countries, and America, therefore, would want to boss New Hanover. Those of us accustomed to thinking of colonial peoples striving to be free must take careful note: New Hanover cultists did not want to be free from outside rule. They merely wanted more powerful and competent leaders and rulers. When Lavongais talk about being equal, they do not talk about pulling down or destroying the strong. They wish to emulate them.

New Hanover did have one strong, competent outsider who provided leadership, an American who rose to the occasion: Father Bernard Miller, M.S.C. Would a local man have come forward eventually if Father Miller had not? I think not, because Father Miller, unlike local men, had access to resources, money, knowledge, and institutional contacts that the people knew they needed and knew they lacked. While Yaman's role could have been played by someone else, Father Miller's role could only have been played by another dedicated man connected to institutions of power from outside. He was not only a resource person. He was also a man whose known, missionary tradition gave the people something they had never had before: a Big Man who would hold the money on behalf of all and spend it only as they told him to. With his guidance, the Johnson cultists turned their energy into building T.I.A., which grew and prospered under the leadership of President Walla Gukguk of Meteran village.

By 1998, young people had come to think of T.I.A. as an obstacle to what they want now, one that should be encouraged to fade away. While the present status of T.I.A. is, thus, uncertain, the status of Walla in history is, I think, not: he has been a true hero. He has not become a glorious leader, and he has not become corrupt or a "big head." An uncommon man among Lavongai leaders, he has been a servant, not a boss, of his people.

Factions, Ideology, and Belief

The factions which the vote for Johnson defined have been described in chapter 3. There were cultists and noncultists, distinguished mainly by locality, but also by status in the Australian administration at the time of the vote. There were missionaries, government officers, service personnel, and plantation managers. In T.I.A. there were some realignments, but cult factions remained stable, and continued on a diminished scale into the 1990s.

In the Johnson cult, it was the idea, not a prophet, that had charisma, that was viewed by some as coming from God, that formed the core of an ideology; and constituencies formed for, against, and around the idea, not a leader.

Whether cultists did or did not really believe that Johnson or the Americans were going to come was not an issue for them. Their strong assertions of belief were political, meant to alert Australians that the cultists had not given up; not confessional, meant as statements about cosmic perspectives. Whatever their individual differences in belief, they publicly subscribed to an ideology which amounted to a political platform on which they took a political stance.

Noncultists also had an ideology, which they shared with the *kiaps*: that cultists were crazy. Cultists called this accusation *tok bilas*, ridicule. People were aware of the relationship between their beliefs and the faction to which they belonged; thus, when I asked Edward whether or not he had believed that America might come, he answered, "Oh, I was in the council, I didn't believe."

Some government reports indicate that some officers felt that the cultists would not give in and give up because they did not want to lose face, but the government never addressed this possibility. Probably this was because government officials were worried themselves about losing face and were concerned with reestablishing "authority," the most fundamental concept in government ideology. Thus constituencies and ideologies perpetuated each other.

Networks of Relationship

One of the generalizations about millennium movements that many students make is that they occur in areas that lack integration, and New Hanover fits easily into that category. Even by Melanesian standards, New Hanover traditionally lacked integrating mechanisms. The *malanggan* ceremonies that link neighboring New Ireland villages with each other and with Tabar did not include New Hanover, even though they made some of the red shell currency used in the *malanggan* circuit.

What New Hanover had that was akin to the typical Melanesian feast, *maras*, collapsed, apparently, at the first touch of European contact; in contrast to the New Ireland *malanggan*, which continues with adaptive vigor. Boski Tom blamed the missionaries for putting a stop to feasting in New Hanover, but early missionaries insisted in vain in New Ireland that *malanggan* might have to do with false gods, or just be a waste of time, and should be discontinued.

In the Johnson cult and then in T.I.A., large numbers of people from many villages, clans, religious affiliations, educational backgrounds, and so on were organized together in common cause for the first time in the history of New Hanover. Whatever may be the destiny of the Johnson cult or of T.I.A., this evolution of political awareness and networks is not likely to be reversed. By 1998, T.I.A continued to function occasionally on the south coast, and the new growth of an environmental movement was led by some young people and middle-aged people who had grown up in T.I.A.

New Ireland Tikana by Contrast

Leadership and networks of relationship for the Tikana are founded on kinship and marriage, and draw people together who are separated by hundreds of miles and several decades away from common residence. Leaders are situational but secure in any given context. Ideas are heard and accommodated, but tradition shapes the course of actions. Factions are broken up by individual memberships in many groups among which people shift for different occasions.

Economic Aspects of the Johnson Cult

Production

The Johnson cult resulted in a decrease in domestic production, in that during the three years that substantial numbers of men were in jail, or out of jail but thinking about the election for Johnson, there was some lessening of effort with respect to making gardens, and, perhaps, with regard to keeping pigs. Many women seemed embarrassed, when I asked, to say that they did not have gardens; but no one attributed this directly to the cult. Over the years of my return visits, I have seen a clear increase in subsistence production and in the construction of big, beautiful thatch houses. Probably the cult did slow people down in their daily tasks, but I saw no structural changes.

Men were necessary to the clearing of new land, and it was this great task that T.I.A members, men and women together, first accomplished. People planted food first in the cleared areas, and only later did they plant the coconuts for which the ground was cleared.

The fact that people all worked together, went together to the areas to be cleared, cut and carried off brush together for T.I.A. was an important change in New Hanoverian production techniques. Unlike the Tikana, who regularly processed sago and created gardens in groups of a dozen or more, people usually did not work together in large groups, and often worked alone or only with another member of the nuclear family; which was one reason they despaired of clearing large areas for copra production.

Distribution

In the old days, there were no steady trade partners in New Hanover, nor any reciprocal obligations between any two individuals or social groups. There was some exchange carried on impersonally, wherein food was obtained for currency, I was told. In 1967, people brought what they ate from the bush or sea, or bought it at the mission or Chinese store.

Men gave shell currency to other men, fathers or uncles usually, of women to confirm a marriage. There was no subsequent distribution to other family or clan members. People ate food provided by the immediate relatives of the dead at the wag, the funeral of the dead held at the time of death. As one Lavongai young man, Laksia, told me when we attended a *malanggan* together in New Ireland: "We are like you. When they're dead, they're dead;" meaning that there were no later memorial services like *malanggan* in New Hanover.

Boski Tom told me there used to be feasts wherein one group hosted another, and each provided the other with incentives to production, as well as to distribution. These were disrupted, unfortunately, he said, by the missions, which considered them a waste of time and resources. He did not attribute any further deleterious effect on production or distribution to the Johnson cult.

Economic Growth

The collection of money for Johnson showed people that they did have resources which they could accumulate, themselves, without passing the money on to the government or the council, where it seemed to disappear. The money which Oliver collected also seemed to disappear: the collection of resources by a strong man for his own consumption is a traditional pattern in New Hanover, one which people do not like, but which they do not seem to resent. These Big Men sold hope, as Oliver did. When people gave money, they were "gambling." A person may be disappointed, but not outraged, if one loses a gamble.

The only economic development that the cultists ever got from the administration resulted from Carroll Gannon's strong efforts: a hospital was built.

T.I.A. Economic Development

In T.I.A. people confirmed and expanded their potential to pool their own resources. Traditional fashions were strictly outlawed: every penny was brought to the T.I.A. office, to the locked box which Father Miller kept in his house, and then to the bank. A man could come and check the membership book to make sure his money had been recorded. And there were no accusations of money gone astray, until after Father Miller was transferred from the island in 1980.

New Hanover had never done much with cash crops, mainly, perhaps, because there was no stable transportation to the port of Kavieng. It was hoped that T.I.A. would accomplish the communal cash projects the co-ops and the council had failed to produce, e.g., transportation facilities, a road, and a "business." Fr. Miller worked to provide an old work boat for T.I.A., called the *T.I.A. Walla*.

In T.I.A. people became for the first time economically dependent on each other. When the copra was produced and sold from the coconuts T.I.A. planted, all the money was to go into the coffers of T.I.A. There was to be no public, individual distribution, no rebates as promised, but never delivered, by the co-ops. The economic ties created among T.I.A. members was a revolutionary change in their economic system, within which each had previously worked alone.

This communal work in T.I.A. continued at least until 1983, when the money began to go astray and Pengai and other founders began to leave as members. Fr. Miller's participation seemed to be a linchpin in this organization. However, T.I.A. coconut plantations still stand and provide individuals with opportunities for cash.

At present writing the provincial government has ceased its efforts to collect taxes, but it has given no economic aid to the cult area of New Hanover. A road was built, in the late 1980s, to and from Umbukul, the village of Boski Tom and Steven Taung, supporters of the council during the cult, and steady workers for the government.[26] But the road goes nowhere.

Marias, who worked for Fr. Miller and T.I.A. as a child and as a young adult, was building on his T.I.A. experiences when he began the Local Environment Foundation, which shared aims with T.I.A. and which will, perhaps, become increasingly important in New Hanover.

Psychological Aspects of the Johnson Cult

The vote for Johnson and subsequent behavior depended on characteristics typical of Lavongai personalities: individual initiative, spontaneity, and a willingness to explore.

Individualist Personality: Exploratory
The individualistic personality is, as manifested in the Lavongais (and elsewhere), exploratory.[27] Lacking a known path, unwilling to follow each other, Lavongais must strike out on their own, or else just wait in frustration. Oliver told me in explaining why he believed, "I have to believe: otherwise I just sit and do nothing." The Johnson cult represented an exploration, faith in the possible, rather than a naive or fixed belief.

Discontent with Familiar Stimuli and Wanting Change: Cultists wanted change but they did not specify clearly or in detail what change they wanted. Lapantukan spoke metaphorically of wanting a new *laplap* (wrap around skirt), and Oliver used the analogy of food: if you eat only one kind your body will get sick and die, but if you change foods you will have good life. Makios said, "We want to see a good way come up among us inside of Lavongai," and Pengai wanted something to "straighten our way of life." Unlike the Tikana of New Ireland, who continued to cherish the repetition of their institutionalized rituals, Lavongais were restlessly in quest of novelty. America seemed like a good country to, as they said, try.

Spontaneity: The vote for Johnson was a spontaneous synthesis of Lavongai experience. It was a "peak experience" (Maslow 1970): everyone remembered where he or she was, with whom, and what he or she was doing when they first heard of the vote for America.[28] In a synthetic flash that rivaled the vote for Johnson in its spontaneity, T.I.A. emerged from the cult. Impulsive behavior is valued for its power to move, and is required strategically in a culture, like that of New Hanover, that moves according to no general plan. The loss of control that would spoil a *malanggan*, and which Tikana have institutionalized ways to prevent, was the psychological foundation for the Johnson cult.

Source of the New Idea: The idea for the vote for Johnson drew on idealized memories of Americans during the war and during their 1963 presence on Mt. Patibung. Each person felt that the idea was his own in some special way, some attributing to God a role in bringing it into his head. This fits with some traditional theories about getting ideas for songs and dances from the spirits of the dead, sometimes in dreams. Pengai had a dream in which a man in a white suit told him to stand up and speak to an assembled crowd, which he later interpreted as some kind of foreknowledge about his leadership role in the vote. His wife, however, made fun of him, saying that it only meant that he wanted to be a councillor. This was not a cult of dreamers, but of the occasional dream which reinforced a tentative direction already taken by the wide awake.

Self-Reliance: The source of the idea was clear in one respect: it came up from the Lavongai people themselves, and in following it they were asserting their traditionally valued self-reliance and independence of thought. The fact that it was their own expression, not someone else's, in itself gave the idea great appeal. Fr. Miller wrote in 1966 (p. 23): "The Johnson movement became a cult with spokesmen like Oliva (sic), a Castro-like leader. Above all, it was a native-born movement. The Lavongais reason, 'This is our idea. We like it. It came from ourselves. No one else told us about it. It is ours. The *Kiap* did not tell us. The Father did not teach us. It is ours. We are going to stick with it.'"

Idea-Oriented Behavior: Cultists followed an idea which they liked, not one suggested by some particular person, prophet, deity, authority, dream, or tradition—a pattern typical, then, of Lavongai culture. It was activities of the government which provided a plan of action: cultists could refuse to pay taxes and go to jail to "suffer for their idea," as Father Miller wrote (1966, 23).

Detached Analysis and Emotional Commitment: The commitment crucial to the election for America and to T.I.A. was not easy for Lavongais to achieve. It is a kind of psychological institutionalization which terminates exploration, and seems almost deliberate self-deception for people who are stark empiricists, as characterized in their typical remark, "I don't know, I did not see it." Thus, even the intense cultist Alipes wondered if the idea that the ancestors made cargo was true or only a figure of speech.

Traditional religious beliefs also languished under positivist attention among the Lavongai: Lapansinnung, a very old man of the Tsoi Islands who supported the Johnson cult, told me that people went after death to Tingwon Island, where the *tambarans* (ancestor spirits) look after the door. I asked him if these *tambarans* work there, perhaps to produce cargo, and he answered with a smile: "This place here (where they go after death) is down below. We do not know."

Commitment was never taken for granted: men came together to help each other keep the faith in the big house in Bolpua, and Oliver and others went around giving pep talks to help people remain committed. T.I.A. gave people something to believe in for which they could gain some European support, something that fit into the fixtures of world mythology and, thus, an idea to which cultists could more easily sustain commitment as time passed and Johnson did not come.

Individual Similarities and Differences

The clearest line between cultists and noncultists was drawn not by personality but by locality and political interests. Neither cultists nor noncultists were men of particular personality types: leaders and followers, assertive and passive, were found in all factions.

Silakau, the noncultist, and Joseph, the outspoken cultist, were neighbors, old friends, and easy companions. Silakau was gentle and talkative, Joseph Pukina a powerful person who told his stories dramatically and well. Joseph was quick to anger and rather frightening, while Silakau was never angry, but sometimes hurt and asking for sympathy. They teased each other a little in telling me, together on my verandah, stories of the cult. Both told me stories about their courtships of their wives, and adventures with other women, and both were unusually close to their mothers.

Edward, the noncultist, was sober and serious, as was Saripat, the cultist: both were men in their sixties. Cultist Pengai was as gentle as noncultist Silakau, noncultist Bengebenge as angry as cultist Joseph Pukina. I have considered whether or not the cultists, or the noncultists, are insecure "big-heads," or "mama's boys,"[29] those who take responsibility or those who lag behind, those who are handicapped or advantaged—the short or the tall, those with happy marriages or those with broken ones. There are no simple, obvious correlations. At the psychological level, it was the *similarities* of psychological structure, induced by the individualistic social structure and characteristic of both cultists and noncultists, rather than personality or temperamental *differences*, that made the cult, and its opposition, possible.

Traditional Psychological Patterns Continued

Peter Lawrence (1964) has pointed out that the cargo cult he studied was not radical but conservative in that people continued to act on the basis of the cognitive structure, or Total Cosmic Order, built by the traditional culture. In the Johnson cult, the traditional beliefs that continued to function were not about mythological persons or the efficacy of ritual; but, rather, about human nature, Lavongai character, the foundations of epistemology, and the efficacy of particular kinds of psychological manipulation of oneself and of other people. Lavongai cultural character is constructed of the psychological experiences and expectations that allowed people to understand each other and to act in concert even though none of them had ever had a Johnson cult before. The following discussion excerpts some of the patterns which either I, or they, or both, thought were important in the Johnson cult, as well as in New Hanover culture generally.[30]

What One Likes: One authentic Lavongai axiom about human nature that dominated New Hanoverian behavior in the cult, and in general, and that maddened Europeans who were supposed to deal with it was the assumption that what a person wants in incontrovertible: *"Laik e bigpela samting"* [What a person likes is a big thing].

One cultist suggested to the *kiaps* that they quit wasting their time trying to collect taxes and just wait until cultists "finished their liking" for America and then came back to Australia. This concept was commonly used with regard to romantic relationships: when Yama's husband went off to another woman, by whom he fathered two children, she did not worry. "He finished his liking," she told me with a smile, "then came back."

Justification for continuing their vote for America was made in terms of the clarity and intensity of their wishes, rather than in terms of any other evidence. Joseph said at a meeting, "Suppose America does not want to come, *maski* (never mind), me, just me, I want it." People did not try to dissuade each other from courses of action, like love affairs or suicide, which they said they wanted to follow; hence, they saw the Australian attempt to persuade them to withdraw their vote from Johnson as very odd. It seemed to them that they were being asked to not want what they clearly wanted, a request that made no sense.[31]

How One Knows: The introspective mode of knowing was general in New Hanover and in cult thinking. When I asked Oliver if he had believed what the church taught him as a child, he answered, "I believed. But I found it for myself, too." Even those who thought that probably God had put the idea of voting for America into their heads believed in America not because it was God's idea but because it was their own idea.

Relying on different channels of knowing, Europeans initially saw the cult as a problem of communication and tried to alter Lavongai views by repeating their own. Cultists also attributed some of their problems to a failure of communication: if Johnson had received their letters, they thought, surely he would have at least written to them. They wanted to hear only from the man himself.[32] The administration thought that if they could only get it across to the people that Johnson was, of course, not going to come, and make them see how bizarre their request was, they would stop acting like this and pay their taxes.

Only the noncultists in Lavongai never attributed the vote for Johnson to a failure of communication. Epistemologically, they were with the cultists; politically, however, they were with the government. While the Tikana look to authorities, and Europeans look to experts, Lavongais trust only themselves for crucial knowledge.

Provoking Quarrels: Large public quarrels among adults and small spats among children are common in New Hanover, and seem to end with better, rather than worse, relationships—at least, temporarily (Berne, 1964). Children promote jealousy by favoring one and excluding another, who runs crying to a higher power to "tell on" the bad ones. These bad ones eventually show how good they really are by showering attention on the hurt one and excluding someone else. Adults create entertaining confrontations which often end in laughter and self-mockery, but which may end in broken bones. Even in that case, however, the retelling of the story of the fight is performed with mirth.

It is common knowledge among New Hanoverians and others who know them that they are an especially jealous people, anxious for attention. In part the Johnson cult became an attempt to engage the Australian administration in a public quarrel. Just as Lavongai children "tell on" each other in hopes of getting a persecutor into trouble and of gaining redress for wrongs; so cultists "told on" the Australians to the Americans. Similarly, anticultists "reported on" cultists to Government officials in hopes of provoking punishment for cultists and of gaining allies for themselves. In return, cultists kept lists of offending acts and actors in notebooks, some noncultists said to show to the Americans when they finally came.

New Hanover tendencies to provoke competition or hostility among others was summed up this way by Mrs. Pitts: "If they can put two people against each other that makes their day," she told me. Carroll Gannon told me that people often came and asked him to scold other people for what they had done.

Lavongai views about human nature are not likely to have been altered by the cult. Cultists did gain attention, if nothing else, where they had been ignored,[33] and they did provoke jealousy: they pitted the Australians against the Americans, and created rivalry amongst various groups of Europeans who all tried to do the right thing to end the cult. Cultists feigned indifference to some of this attention, e.g., jail: now they were the strong chick who ignores the peck of others who seem, therefore, weak. The analogy between the cultists and their opposition, on the one hand, and the wooed and the wooer on the other, was noted by the cultists themselves. Some men compared Australia's loss of the allegiance of New Hanover explicitly to a man's loss of a woman that he does not provide for well. The cultists provoked a quarrel as a woman provokes a quarrel with her husband, partly to express anger and hurt, and partly to evoke an emotional, loving response. Joseph used the word "love" in describing the hoped-for relationship with America. If Australia would not care for them, perhaps America would.

While this pattern of confrontation was suppressed within T.I.A. in order to achieve a unified front, it continued to be expressed against the enemy outside. No doubt this available outside opposition against whom hostility has been directed has been a factor in the continuing power of T.I.A. over the years.

Blaming Someone: The Fault Lies Where?: Carroll Gannon and others noted in the cultists a tendency to prefer to go on blaming other people for their problems instead of trying to solve them. "The people will fall apart if T.I.A. doesn't work," he told me, "because they'll have no one to blame but themselves." Father H. Fischer noted similarities to other groups with whom he had worked, who, he said, would rather tear the other guy down than build themselves up. Assistant District Officer Mr. Brightwell noted that the Lavongais "can hardly wait to bugger up T.I.A. so they can complain."

Was it true that they did not seek to solve their problems? If so, one reason was that they did not know how to solve them or exactly what they were. Let us firmly note here that, given adequate help with their new tasks in T.I.A., members did not "bugger it up," and it accomplished important development aims. Nevertheless, there were also more profound problems, partly those which characterize the human condition: not just taxes, but also death. Not all societies, however, plunge into a furiously busy and dramatic effort to escape these inescapables. The Lavongais sense, however, and even state that their problems, however general in the external world, are also related to Lavongai cultural character, now in contact with a new set of circumstances; and that it will not be easy to change themselves.[34]

I think the "discontents," as Boski Tom called them, that stirred up the Johnson cult, that will still be there when Johnsonites or *membas* have achieved their stated goals of development, have strong roots in the individualism of Lavongai social structure and concomitant cultural system. No matter how successful they are in creating solutions to their development problems, their culture demands of them that they continue to strive to be self-reliant, achieving, antagonistic, rejecting and rejected, exclusive and alone. But how can they change this old system, which, they think, cannot bring them, with equality and justice, into the modern world?

One reason for the maintenance of angry rather than constructive (from an outsider point of view) action in the cult was that, in this way, cultists and noncultists kept everyone focused on problems that were not the structural ones from which their anger emanated, and from which they saw no escape. If the stated problems had been solved, the real ones, much more complex and difficult to articulate, would have been left without a place to hide. These relate to jealousy, insecurity about being excluded, and fear of each other's status elevation. No one offered a solution on the scale of the problems they saw and felt.

But most cultists, like individualists generally, have quite a bit of insight into themselves, and ultimately agreed with Boski Tom: that they had no one to blame but themselves that their island was underdeveloped. No matter how strong a case they built against others, they did not really blame them, because they believe they can rely only on themselves: the fault, they feel in their bellies, is not in the Australians or in their stars, but in themselves that they are underlings.[35] With the cult and T.I.A., they showed their determination to take responsibility for their lives, to take on the one enemy they could hope to control: themselves.

The Reluctant Individualist

Self-Reliance Reconsidered: Why should grown men of New Hanover be looking for something so remote as "love," in Joseph's terminology, from a country, either Australia or America? I think cultists would not have wanted so much to be accepted by, and acceptable to, the distant unknown Americans (and even the distant, scarcely known Australians) if they had been more securely accepted by each other. The love they really wanted, the acceptance that might have quelled the cult, was love and acceptance and help from family and peers: the love of each other. In a society wherein people feel they have the help they need, the *marmari* ("mercy" in pidgin and in the church) Lavongais talked about so much, they would not have had to fear being left behind by their compatriots. The Tikana do not leave people behind: they take the whole group along with them.

As in other individualistic societies, however, people not only valued self-reliance but also scorned dependence. Still, they felt guilty about the old and the sick who could not take care of themselves, feared that they might also become helpless, and demanded something be done, by somebody, about it. They did not like being rejected by Europeans or by their own elites, and they wanted to become rich and powerful so that they could resist that rejection: "We want to join," Pengai said.

Lavongais know rejection and ridicule well, having experienced it in their own society from childhood on.[36] During the war, the soldiers granted, or seemed to grant, equality and friendly acceptance to them. It was especially the Americans who gave them food cheerfully, a simple pleasure the average Lavongai cannot lightly expect at home, even from his mother—though she is his best hope.

The Johnson cult was an escape from the freedom[37] of individualism: freedom from obligation to and from others, freedom that left everyone alone in the face of tasks that required group efforts and a higher level of coordination than New Hanover had ever achieved. How could such a people survive independence?

What Father Will Save Us?: The individualistic Lavongais often asked for help with a metaphor about fathers: "What Papa will save us?" In searching for parallels to the father image for Australia and America in the cult, I found out that fathers in the old days were primarily responsible for teaching their sons to "save" themselves in battle. Father and son fought side by side until the young man proved himself, perhaps by killing someone. This must have been an important exception to the expectation of self-reliance so widely expressed in Lavongai life. Men treasured instances of their fathers giving them savvy about things, especially *singsings* ("magic") to help with love and conflicts. They called on their dead fathers' powers as threats to others who had wronged them.

On the other hand, sons might have been killed by their fathers in the old days so that the sons would not swell the ranks of an enemy clan, that of their mothers. Still, Joseph Pukina imagined that the Good Papa, America, would be shocked when it finally came and saw that the Bad Papa, Australia, had not been looking after the New Hanover people well. They said that Australia had not been a good papa to them, but in fact no papa, or father figure, had ever been a good papa to them. Singarau had lied to them about the cooperatives, Iguarangai had taken 100 virgins to wife; even Peter Yangalissmat had lured their women and charged them rent for living on their own lands. And Oliver had bought himself a radio and wristwatch with the money they gave him for Johnson's plane fare.

Closer to everyone's experience, children lose the attention of their fathers, to their great distress, when they are about two years old, or when they become second-last children. As infants, they have their fathers' full attention, and may be ever hopeful of finding it again. Children learn very early that it is everyone for himself, but they are constantly in tears as they learn this lesson.

In President Walla, New Hanover may have found a "papa" at last, but he needed the help of another father, Father Miller, in one crucial way: Father Miller kept the money box, locked. Walla was determined that the traditional ways of New Hanover were not going to spoil T.I.A. and that T.I.A. would be the road to the new life, and the new psychological character, they claimed to want. Time has been telling a wobbly story in this regard since Father Miller was transferred out of New Hanover in 1981.

New Ireland Tikana by Contrast

Tikana children were always with someone, often with their fathers. Fathers, like mothers, are revered and loved. There is no need to look beyond one's own place, one's own family, to be saved: people feel lucky and able to help and be helped. People worry much more about whether they have given enough than about what they receive.

It is true that the Australians had not granted even legal, let alone psychic or moral, equality to the Lavongais, but they had not granted equality to the Tikana, either. Some Tikanas knew this, and it annoyed them; but it did not hurt them, and it did not cause a cargo cult. They were more puzzled than angry: it did not touch them deeply the way it touched the Lavongais. Having never experienced the kind of status rivalry that is common in the western individualistic, civilized world and in New Hanover, the Tikana did not really comprehend their rejection by Europeans, and even occasionally pitied Europeans, especially European babies, for their loneliness.

Expressive Aspects of the Johnson Cult

The Johnson Cult: Creating a New Script

Expressive Aspect Directed the Cult: The raison d'etre of the Johnson cult was expressive. The vote for America marked clearly, and dramatically, and irreversibly for all the end of an unjust era of pretense and subservience and the beginning of a time to assert that all people are equal in a moral universe; that each individual, his true wishes and beliefs, his equal worth with all others, is of

Ultimate Concern;[38] and each person is worthy of being saved in this world, in his own lifetime.

In their election, Lavongais restructured their symbolic universe through a satiric drama, the meaning of which was never quite grasped by those who had not shared the Lavongai experience and swift consensus.

The time and place of the outburst were determined by a set of historical accidents. If this conjunction of circumstances had not occurred, the Johnson cult might never have happened. Indeed, on the north coast, where circumstances were only slightly different, it did not happen. It could have happened there, however, but not on the west coast of New Ireland, where political and economic conditions were similar to those in New Hanover, but cultural conditions were not. There, confrontations with armed opponents bent on collecting taxes created violent, but not dramatic, resistance. There was stealth and anger and coordinated fighting, but no vote for Johnson there.

Underlying Themes: Fundamental Crises in New Hanover: The Johnson cult was a response to fundamental crises in New Hanover and in Lavongai culture in relation to change. The imminence of self-government brought about a political crisis, and people demanded not only the right and the power, but also the ability to control their own lives. Without such control, they knew they risked being a socially inferior caste in the future among their own people, as they had been in the past in relation to Europeans. The economic aspect of their crisis was the easiest to get other people to understand: how could they learn to make a living in a world where money was becoming essential for survival?

The psychological crisis—fear of being left behind, left alone, and ridiculed—was met by standing up to those who made fun and thought that they had gone on ahead. Cultists told the bumbling Australians and their own English-muttering compatriots and children that they were incompetent and that their services were no longer needed: cultists had sent for the Americans. But in doing so the cultists had to admit that they, too, were incompetent to carry on alone. People who had always prided themselves on being self-reliant, who valued competence and independence in themselves and others, desperately needed help in an aspect of life where they had always heretofore been masters: the symbolic universe. All knowledge had always come from within the Self, but now the Self, even prodded by wandering Spirits, was not enough: they needed the Americans, or someone, to come to give them savvy.

The Johnson cult was a savvy cult, not a cargo cult, an expressive response to a crisis of "understanding."[39] People were not asking for cargo, they were asking for intellectual clarity, expressive responsibility, symbolic control, a last act structurally consistent with the needs of their drama. Who will save us with savvy? they were asking. We can no longer save ourselves.

Finding the New Script through Telling the Truth: Since the Johnson cult was fundamentally an expressive act, telling the truth was its sine qua non. Without public commitment it would have been, ipso facto, nothing. This is why cultists emphasized that they, themselves, told the truth: Pengai said, "I cannot lie. If I lie, that's no good;" and Lapantukan said, "I cannot hide anything." In T.I.A. they began to be concerned that those who were half-members might be half-hearted as well as half-paid in their dues, but T.I.A. was an organization which involved a group. In the cult, individuals were responsible only to themselves. Lying would diminish, somehow, not only their cause but also their own selves. The only way to find a new script was to tell the truth.

The Meaning of the Johnson Cult: What the Drama was About

The Johnson cult was a drama about the struggle to create a moral order where people felt that one was lacking, a quest for human dignity. Cultists strut and fret their hour upon the stage[40] and then went to work in T.I.A. They let the world know[41] in a powerful and compelling expression that they affirmed the value of their lives, which were of Ultimate Concern however barren of the world's goods and savvy. In 1998 they continued to reject opportunities for material wealth when offered in exchange for their submission to outside domination. T.I.A. housed hopes beyond economic development, and has continued the dramatic demands of its members for genuine power through dramatic confrontations with those who now seem to deny it to them.

The Tikana *malanggan* relates to Ultimate Concerns by remembering the strength and goodness of the dead when they were alive. As one Tikana man said at a *malanggan* for his brother, "He was everywhere with me, helping me; and I was everywhere with him, helping him: we two, together, all the time, all the time." And another said, "We see in this *malanggan* the strength of the two [honored dead] in our work here." Like the medieval morality play *Everyman*, *malanggan* ceremonies are about each person's mortality and about coming to grips with the inevitability of death. The spirits of the dead do not linger near the village, or perhaps anywhere, to hear themselves praised. Like Everyman, the dead who are celebrated and "finished" in *malanggan* "are deserted by Kindred, Goods, and Fellowship. Eventually only Good Deeds goes with Everyman into the grave" (Brockett, 1977: 117).

In contrast to the Tikana, Lavongais who remembered the dead saw in their lives nothing to emulate, and much to abandon. It was the anticipated death of the Self, not the past deaths of others, that figured explicitly in cultists' explanations of their actions. They wanted something for themselves in this world: not mere cargo, as their detractors claimed, but "good, happy and useful lives," as Samuel put it; some Good Deeds to accompany them into the grave.

The Johnson cult seemed to address a less cosmic crisis than did the New Ireland *malanggan*. The play was not directly about our deepest fears that life is meaningless. The Johnson cultists started with the assumption that life can be worth living, and then asked why their own lives were so miserable. This question did not call forth a trivial answer. Some cultists said they would die, if necessary, for the beliefs which responded to this concern.

The meaning of the play was told in many monologues, dialogues, and public shouting matches:

Our skins pain from their way.
If you like whatever country, that's your business.
We talked about it; the thinking came up.
Brother, it would be better if you alone wrote the blackboard.
Everyone left. The *kiap* stayed alone.
Their way is another kind.
I believe strongly. My liking remains.
This talk doesn't belong to us. This talk, these men make fun. The enemy.
They said it would help men that were not married, old women, all who sit down no good.
They just think of standing up with all the whiteskins.
Our hands on top, to God here.
Our promise still stands.
And how they push poor native to jail? Is this good?
We are like rubbish; we sit down like pigs . . . like dogs . . .
I am no donkey. I am a man!
Our lives haven't got changed from our grandfathers.
In the minds of us, the people of New Hanover want to ask the love of this country America; if he loved our wish to him, he could come and take care of us now. But if America doesn't want to love our wish to them, then we say okay.
I want to know how to make this teapot.
A man who does not savvy is one man shit-nothing.
There was plenty of rubbish talk that came up inside it.
And when you'll get nothing out of it, what are you going to do?
New members can come inside like this.
There is one line now, on the ground. T.I.A. stops all around; it puts its name everywhere.
They were not crazy.
At that time, we were not afraid.
We don't know about the work of America, but we believe.
Our ancestors didn't plant coconuts.
They kicked a little: that's what makes a man get up.
All things do not come up from nothing: they come up from strength.
They always say, "work, work, work." Now, I would like to ask you: work what?
You haven't got money? Go to jail!
Suppose I want something, what should I do to get it?
Who will give us savvy? Who will save us? Who will straighten our lives?
We want to join.

The meaning of the Johnson cult was told in many words, but it must be measured, finally, in actions. Men who had always feared the government officials deliberately incurred their anger; and men who had worked for the missions all their lives ignored the advice of the missionaries and risked, and lost, their jobs. Men who seemed to value their freedom above all else went to jail to preserve it. In the cult, many Lavongais found, for a while, something they could believe in and commit themselves to, something worth being honest about, worth going to jail for, and something, at last, for which they could respect themselves and each other. Theirs was a struggle to gain acknowledgment that everyone "counts one" in this world. Joseph Pukina's angry speech to the district commissioner brings to mind Shylock's plea for equality: Joseph said, "I am no donkey. I am a man. I have got legs, arms, eyes, nose, head, just like you."[42]

And so the play goes on without finishing. I do not know, at this writing, how they have all fared; but I know they are still struggling. An improvised drama based on the true lives of the actors does not end, but shifts its focus and rests. The Australians have moved far backstage, but their lines are now spoken by those local men who now sit at their desks and play their roles. As the Lavongai actors wait, "turning things over in our thinking," I suspect that they are wondering, still, what really happened: how the play ended, or if it ever did, or if it ever will. Had they, indeed, won all their confrontations, consolidated their power? And was that what they had wanted? Perhaps when the drama picks up again, it will meander its way toward some clearer answer, or some truer question.

Now, as I think Homer or T. Cosfelder said:
You know, lads, the trouble with even the best story is,
It all too seldom tells what happened to us.[43]

Notes

1. For example, a cult that occurred in the Eastern Highlands: see Berndt, 1952, 1953.
2. Carroll Gannon told me about this report, which he felt was not a serious diagnosis. The medical officer's request for a speedboat in which to visit his "mentally ill" islanders called this bluff: he was turned down.
3. As they expressed this thought in pidgin, "*Samting bilong peles daun tasol*;" something belonging to the "place down," the earth, that's all.
4. See Billings, 1983, 1989a, and 1992a.
5. Father Bernard J. Miller makes this point in his article (1966).
6. Pidgin for the easy talking and laughing about nothing in particular that occurs in groups of friends.
7. "The property-owning class feels secure with informational pluralism when the rest of the cultural apparatus is firmly in its hands. When work sites, the schools, the armed forces, the professional organizations, and the unions are fulfilling their properly assigned

roles of system reinforcement, fairly wide-ranging informational exchanges in selected media are acceptable and even useful to the maintenance of stability and legitimacy. But when the social process and class forces create pressure that interferes with the orderly functioning of a good part of the social machinery . . . in short, when the assumptions and the security of the prevailing system of property and organizational structure are challenged directly across the entire economy—then full debate on the future of the social order becomes intolerable to the privileged classes. And this is understandable. The discussion at this point is no longer just a debate: it is a meaningful process that may very well lead to direct and decisive social and economic change" (Schiller, 1976: 101-2).

8. Pengai said this.

9. "Revolution. We have seen that colonization materially kills the colonized. It must be added that it kills him spiritually . . . In order to free himself from colonization, the colonized must start with his oppression, the deficiencies of his group. . . . Finally, he must cease defining himself through the categories of his colonizers" (Memmi, 1965: 151-52).

"[I]t is clear that *kastom* [custom] and *skul* [school] are notions which . . . have come to have very broad and powerful references to two alternative ways of life. . . . [K]*astom* . . . is resolutely anticolonial, antichristian, anticapitalist, and antigovernment. In opposing the ways of *skul*, they are opposing the reconstruction of their religious, economic and political life to conform to European models" (Jolly, 1982: 340-41).

"Recognizing the problem of categorization as central emerges not only from general analytic interests, but also from problems of radical action" (Barnett and Silverman, 1979: 36).

10. "The play's the thing / Wherein I'll catch the conscience of the king." William Shakespeare, *Hamlet*, 2.2.641.

11. This was always the government's priority.

12. Some students of the arts have looked at its political implications, especially those reviewing the arts of the powerful West African kingdoms. Students of political organization have been less likely to look to art for understanding political processes.

13. Some self-identified materialists mention Marx ceremonially and seem to think, or hope, that they are Marxists. They belong to a long tradition of "vulgar Marxism" (Friedman, 1974) that also has a long tradition of opposition in the work of "underground Marxists" like Gramsci and Lukacs. From a critical point of view, crass materialism is not just bad Marxism; it is good capitalism. See Billings, 1983, for an expanded argument of this point.

14. This line is from an article about poet Robert Lowell by Alwyn Lee ("Poets," *Time* Magazine, June 2, 1967, p. 67).

15. The Living Theater is the prime example of this kind of dramatic performance. See Brockett, 1964 and Berthold, 1972. My own interest in improvisional theater derives from my elementary school experiences with "Creative Dramatics" at Milwaukee State Teachers College Training School. My awareness of the use of dramatics in politics derives from my participation in various progressive movements. I also learned from the perspective offered by Combs and Mansfield (1976). I believe the power of art in life is still only weakly represented in academic programs.

16. "All the world's a stage and all the men and women merely players." William Shakespeare, *As You Like It*, 2.7.139.

17. " Honour and shame from no condition rise; / Act well your part: There all the honor lies." Alexander Pope, *An Essay on Man,* Epis. iv, line 193.

18. In coming to my present understanding of the Johnson cult and the people who created it, I have often thought of Max Weber's work on prophets and pariahs (Weber, 1952), and especially of a poem about Moses by Alfred de Vigny, which contains these lines:

> Je vivrai donc toujours puissant et solitaire?
> Laissez-moi m'endormir du sommeil de la terra.
> [Must I then live always powerful and alone?
> Let me lie down in the sleep of the common man.]

19. Grotowski has written clearly about this point: e.g., "[T]he decisive factor in this process is the actor's technique of psychic penetration. He must learn to use his role as if it were a surgeon's scalpel, to dissect himself. It is not a question of portraying himself under certain given circumstances, or of 'living a part' nor does it entail the distant sort of acting common to epic theater based on cold calculation. The important thing is to use the role as a trampoline, an instrument with which to study what is hidden behind our everyday mask, the innermost core of our personality" (1968: 37).

20. Professor Mischa Penn of the University of Minnesota said, when I told him this story, "Any myth in a storm." This remark points to as aspect of cult ideologies that we rarely make central to our interpretations.

21. The reference is to Worsley (1957).

22. Traditionally a few Lavongai men sponsored *maras*, and initiation of some, but not all, of the young men.

23. I hasten to add that they were always very helpful to me.

24. All white men were referred to as *masta* while I was in Kavieng before independence in 1975. The word is occasionally still used. White women were called *missis*. Like all anthropologists, I think, Nic and I insisted on being called by our first names. Chinese were referred to by their names.

25. Their children are now very much involved in the modern political system.

26. Ironically, Umbukul got some "developers" in 1994, while the south coast was still resisting them. These loggers were destroying the land, and Umbukul residents became alarmed and complained. Their complaint was reported in internet communications and I was able to include this response, which resembled that of the earlier Johnson cultists, in a paper I presented in Moscow in 1994 (Billings, 1994).

27. Some of the literature supporting this generalization is cited in chapter five.

28. In the American experience, this is comparable to Pearl Harbor or the deaths of Roosevelt or Kennedy.

29. Schwartz suggested this to me about cultists when he visited Lavongai in 1967. Ted Schwartz mentioned to me informally when he visited New Hanover that many cultists appear to be "mama's boys," a characteristic which I had noticed in some. However, a broader survey takes in many who were not. Hsu's analysis of patterns within families (1971) can be applied here.

30. See the earlier discussion of authentic Lavongai forms in this chapter. While those discussed largely fit into the psychological category, they are part and parcel of the entire societal structure discussed here.

31. Fr. Miller told me in 1980 that he had named his new boat *I don't want to* in the local language. He was following the local custom of giving children names that repeat something someone has said for which the namer wants to reproach him. Thus, people were

named "no-good woman," "choked with excrement," and the like to shame forever not the namee, but someone who had once taunted the child's parent or other namer. Fr. Miller had caught the custom and was showing the people he wanted to critique a tendency he had noted in their behavior.

32. I sent former President Lyndon B. Johnson my first article (1969) on New Hanover just before he died, and he wrote back that it was nice to know that America had such great support so far away.

33. D.C. Bill Seale told me, not unsympathetically, when I was finally able to go to New Hanover, "They just want attention."

34. I want to quickly note that Lavongai strengths, too, are founded on their cultural character. I think it is clear that I have great admiration for their achievements. I think that, perhaps, I appreciate them more than they do themselves.

35. "The fault, dear Brutus, is not in our stars / But in ourselves that we are underlings." William Shakespeare, *Julius Caesar*, 1.2.134.

36. The rejection and ridicule they experience is certainly no greater, and usually much less, than we experience in American society. We Americans are, of course, individualists, too.

37. I am thinking here, of course, of Eric Fromm's book, *Escape from Freedom* (1942).

38. Paul Tillich uses the term "Ultimate Concerns" to refer to religion in its broadest sense.

39. Pengai used this word in English.

40. William Shakespeare, *Macbeth*, 5.5.19: "Life's but a walking shadow, a poor player / That struts and frets his hour upon the stage / And then is heard no more."

41. Literally, through the United Nations Visiting Mission.

42. Shylock: "I am a Jew. Hath not a Jew eyes? Hath not a Jew hands, organs, dimensions, senses, affections, passion?" William Shakespeare, *The Merchant of Venice*, 3.1.62.

43. Kenneth Patchen, "Because to Really Ponder One Needs Wonder," in *Because It Is*. New Directions: New York, 1968.

5

Theories: Cults, Movements, Ceremonies, and Culture

Cultural Style and the Explanation of Cults

Much has been written about cargo cults and millenarian movements in general in an attempt to define their essential features and to explain their occurrence. Theorists have focused on the aspects of situations where cults or movements occur that seem to be somehow provocative, and that are cited explicitly as reasons for seeking change. There has been little attention given to the differences between cultures where cults occur and those where they do not occur.

Cultural Style

My work in New Ireland and in New Hanover suggests to me that, all other things being equal, cargo cults and other millenarian movements will occur in societies ordered by individualistic, informally and inexplicitly structured cultures and will not occur in societies ordered by group-oriented, integrated, formally and institutionally structured cultures. Furthermore, I suggest that some cults, at least, are perennial, recurring, static expressions of individualistic, informally structured cultures, rather than mechanisms representing or creating change.

Plexus

In drawing attention to the factor of cultural style in relation to cargo cults, I do not mean to suggest that other factors are not important. LaBarre has reviewed the literature on "crisis cults" and supports, on both theoretical and empirical grounds, his position against single-factor theories of explanation. He concludes that

> No particularist explanation—whether political, military, economic, psychological, or anthropological—can exclusively and exhaustively 'save the data' of any single crisis cult; [and that when single-cause theories are applied] the explanation impoverishes the phenomenon. The most that one can concede is that, in some cults, certain components seem relatively more salient; in other cults, other components appear to be; but all components are likely, in some degree, to be implicated in any cult. (LaBarre, 1971: 26-7)

This view makes sense to me not only because cults appear in great variety (Burridge, 1969), but also on theoretical grounds alone.

Is Explanation Possible?

Students have looked to various factors for the causes of cults. Some who have looked most systematically at the problem think that it has no solution. Kopytoff, for example, advocates, along with LaBarre, a multidimensional analytic approach, but thinks that full explanation remains elusive (Kopytoff, 1964). And Inglis concluded that "[i]t is not possible to give a general explanation of their occurrence, on the grounds that nobody has yet isolated the external conditions which are the common and peculiar antecedents of every cult outbreak" (Inglis, 1957: 261). The conditions, she asserts, which exist in societies where there are cults also exist in societies where there are not cults. Inglis thinks that we know enough to know that it will never be possible to explain them.

Inglis classified theories of cults accordingly as they emphasize cult as a traditional religious movement; the response to charismatic leadership; an expression of economic dissatisfaction; an effort toward political change; an expression of moral protest (against low status); or as expression of a particular state of mind. While she argues that none of these factors is sufficient to explain why a cult breaks out in one society rather than another, she does not reject explanation as a goal, as does philosopher Peter Winch.

Winch (1958) has questioned whether or not "explanation" is possible in the social sciences as it is in the natural sciences, because human beings, unlike units of study in the natural sciences, can reason and follow rules. Arguments of this sort against the use of scientific method have become prominent in the last three decades in anthropology, as people with literary or philosophical interests, sometimes called postmodernists (Billings, 1996a), have critiqued traditional anthropology. This argument leans heavily on a mistaken view that Real Science can make perfect predictions, and that Reason is less predictable than the weather. The philosophical tradition, which was heavily felt in some anthropological quarters during the late 1980s and early 1990s (Spiro, 1990), seems hopelessly mired in an ancient deductive mode that does not apprehend, despite the labors of some notable philosophers, that Science is a way of systematizing and finding regularity in experience, not a way of gaining access to Final Truth.

Physicist and philosopher Gerald Holton has written extensively on the cultural shaping of scientific knowledge (Holton, 1973, 1975), in support of a view common among theoretical natural scientists: that there is no value-free science. Social scientists do not have powers of perfect prediction, but neither do our colleagues studying animate and inanimate objects and forces presumed to lack both souls and reason. Philosopher Ernest Nagel has pointed out that while natural scientists control a great deal of information about forces in general, and wind velocity in particular, no one has yet predicted individual events: e.g., when the first leaf of autumn will fall, or which one it will be (Nagel, 1961: 461). Particular events are not predicted in the natural sciences, and yet we do not say that explanation is impossible in these disciplines. By analogy, the failure of anthropologists, so far, to predict, at least in published form, the occurrence of a particular cargo cult does not mean that we cannot explain them. Anthropologists and others have, in fact, agreed on many characteristics common to cults.

Cults and Movements: Characteristic Features

Many recent scholars have argued that cargo cult does not exist as a unitary and recurrent cluster of features; and that, if such things do appear repeatedly, the term "cargo cult" does not designate their core character (Steinbauer, 1979; McDowell, 1988; Lindstrom, 1993; but see Schwartz, 1999). There is a general movement against generalization,[1] for "deconstruction," for particular histories, even for a focus on specific analytical categories or "traits" (e.g., "ritual") as markers for the phenomenon under study (e.g., Kaplan, 1995). I will leave these debates about terminology to others: the term "cargo cult" continues to be used successfully (Trompf, 1990; Burridge, 1993) to point to a collection of events in Melanesia that anthropologists generally recognize; and which, researchers without fail reminded us, were movements that were not just about "cargo," and were not just "cults." Regarding deconstruction, I will merely state my view, without argument, that anthropology has always been about deconstructing points of view (Spiro, 1999); and generalization in cultural anthropology, as in any art or science, is useful and necessary.

A review of some of the primary and secondary literature on cults shows that there are a large number of features which are present to a greater or lesser extent in them, and that generalizations can be made. Cults commonly, but not invariably, have prophets and faithful followers, beliefs and ideology, invocation of the supernatural, moral instruction, high value on riches or poverty, perfection in the past or future, the expectation of change at some designated time, ceremony or ritual, achievement of unusual psychological states, and so on.

True Believers

Deprived, Depraved, Depressed

While cults often seem to have only vague leadership, there can be no cult without believers, true believers. As Eric Hoffer defined them, true believers come from the ranks of the undesirables: the poor, misfits, the bored, sinners, minorities:

> For men to plunge headlong into an undertaking of vast change, they must be intensely discontented yet not destitute, and they must have the feeling that by the possession of some potent doctrine, infallible leader, or some new technique they have access to a source of irresistible power. They must also have an extravagant conception of the prospects and potentialities of the future. Finally, they must be wholly ignorant of the difficulties involved in their vast undertaking. Experience is a handicap. (Hoffer, 1951: 20)

Furthermore,

> People who see their lives as irremediably spoiled cannot find a worth-while purpose in self-advancement. . . . Nothing that has its roots and reasons in the self can be good and noble. Their innermost craving is for a new life—a rebirth—or, failing this, a chance to acquire new elements of pride, confidence, hope, a sense of purpose and worth by an identification with a holy cause. An active mass movement offers them opportunities for both. (Hoffer, 1951: 21)

This self-contempt is not a characteristic noted, however, in the description of an enthusiast given by Taylor in 1834, in which the believer appears to others to be self-centered and self-indulgent:

> The enthusiast, therefore, whose piety is fictitious, has only a choice of immoralities, to be determined by his temperament and circumstances. He may become, perhaps, nothing worse than a recluse—a lazy contemplatist, and intellectual voluptuary, shut up from his fellows in the circle of profitless spiritual delights or conflicts. The times are indeed gone by when persons of this class might, in contempt of their species, and in idolatry of themselves, withdraw to dens, and hold society only with bats, and make the supreme wisdom to consist in the possession of a long beard, a filthy blanket, and a taste for raw herbs: but the same tastes, animated by the same principles, fail not still to find a place of indulgence, even amid the crowds of a city: and the recluse who lives in the world will, probably, be more sour in temper than the anchoret of the wilderness. An ardent temperament converts the enthusiast into a zealot, who, while he is laborious in winning proselytes, discharges common duties very remissly,

and is found to be a more punctilious observer of his creed, than of his work. Or, if his imagination be fertile, he becomes a visionary, who lives on better terms with angels and with seraphs, than with his children, servants and neighbors; or he is one who, while he reverences the "thrones, dominions and powers" of the invisible world, vents his spleen in railing at all "dignities and powers" of earth. (Taylor, 1834: 18-19)[2]

Much more recently, Kaminsky offers a view of the cultist that has some points in common with that of Taylor: the cultist is

> objectively alienated, [the] man whose social and economic position is so precarious that he lacks even the attachment to the existing order that may be presupposed for the ordinary lower classes. [He is the] neurotic [or] the man belonging to a persecuted race or religion. . . . Obviously, then, the typical member is a person radically alienated from the existing order, and, either inherently or temporarily, lacking in qualities of criticism, realism, and intellectual honesty. (Kaminsky, 1970: 216)

And, yet, for all his faults, or discomfort in the world, Hoffer thinks that the true believer plays a necessary role in change:

> The discarded and rejected are often the raw material of a nation's future. The stone the builders reject becomes the cornerstone of a new world. A nation without dregs and malcontents is orderly, decent, peaceful and pleasant, but perhaps without the seed of things to come. It was not the irony of history that the undesired in the countries of Europe should have crossed an ocean to build a new world on this continent. Only they could do it. (Hoffer, 1951: 27)

Creative, Gifted Leaders

Because so many theorists seem to find cultists to be deprived, depraved, or depressed, the work of those who do not is particularly important. Negative images are not prominent in the work of LaBarre, for example, who sees cultists not as "dregs and malcontents" but as specially talented:

> In every age, sensitive, aberrant, creative individuals, in their personal anguish with life, and defrauded somehow of the comforts to be expected from old beliefs, come close to awareness of the dire contingency of all symbols. (LaBarre, 1971: 27)

It is these persons, LaBarre thinks, who have the creative power to initiate cults.

Organization and Recruitment

Once such a creative or alienated person initiates a cult, he or she will not be noticed unless there are followers. Gerlach and Hine (1968) have examined several contemporary movements—Pentacostalism, Black Power, Environmental movements—and have suggested five factors which they have found to be crucial to the growth and spread of all of them. These are also common in cargo cults:

Commitment. There is "a bridge-burning power-generating act" which may be personal but is more generally objectively observable.

Ideology. Characterized by dogmatism, there is rejection of a gap between the ideal and the real (a gap philosophically accepted by established authority), serious involvement, and positive fatalism—i.e., a certainty that they are doing the right thing, which makes it difficult for them to perceive failure as such.

Recruitment. Face-to-face recruitment takes place along lines of preexisting significant social relationships.

Reticulate organization. Organizational structure focuses on linkages between individuals and groups because "the concept of individual access to the spiritual source of authority, when taken seriously, tends to prevent organizational solidarity and centralized control."

Real or Perceived Opposition. The complete lack of opposition inhibits the growth of a movement as successfully as total control and repression of it.

Some of the organizational characteristics proposed in the above analysis are related to an individualistic style of culture: the emphasis on individual commitment, the person-to-person distribution of the movement, the leadership of ideas as ideology and of oppositions as part of this ideology, have all been found to be important in the Johnson cult, and in various guises in individualistic societies generally.

Cults and Movements: Overview of Interpretations

I do not seek here to exhaustively review particular cult theories.[3] I will, however, survey the ideas which have been put forward, noting some prominent anthropological studies as illustrations of general kinds of theories.

The Individual, Personality, and Psychology

Regardless of the perspective on the prior condition of cultists favored, general attributes of personality characteristic of them has not been taken to explain cults; nor is a Great Man theory of history to be found in the anthropological literature. However, some anthropologists emphasize the role of the individual and his personality more than do others. While Mead (1956), for instance, has especially emphasized the role of the individual in all her work, and, along with Schwartz (1962), the role of Paliau in Manus, their work does not claim that Paliau's leadership created a cult or movement. Paliau was an important but not a sufficient condition in the development of change in Manus, in Mead's interpretation, in which it is always necessary to know the total context (Mead, 1964).

There is sometimes an emphasis on unusual psychological states, e.g., excessive excitement, paranoia, or trance. The mass hysteria and trembling which characterized individuals who were committed to the movement is what led Williams to call the phenomena he studied *The Vailala Madness* (Williams, 1923). Williams thought that mental confusion in response to new ideas, and the loss of social excitement provided by old activities, were factors leading to cults. Schwartz wondered if those individuals who become deeply involved in cults may have somewhat paranoid personalities (Schwartz, 1973).

Wallace's concept of "revitalization" designates processes within a system, but it begins with the experiences and initiatives of a single individual, usually a prophet who has had a vision (Wallace, 1956: 273). The relationship between the leader and his followers is well described, Wallace says, with Max Weber's concept of "charismatic leadership." Wallace's descriptive work depends on written accounts by nonspecialists, who know most about the leaders; and this may account for his emphasis on the individual (Wallace, 1966: 30-34).[4]

Worsley has been particularly at pains to reject the view that cults are a response and submission to a charismatic leader, maintaining that charismatic leaders derive their charisma from social factors rather than from individual personality qualities (Worsley, 1957, 1968).

All theorists look beyond individuals to the circumstances of the society in which they live. The problem of explanation, for anthropologists, lies in isolating those factors in society which cause, or prevent, cults.

The Power of Ideas

That humankind's power to reason is not irrelevant to the study of anthropology in general, and of cargo cults in particular, is what philosopher Jarvie (1963, 1964) has tried to show. He does not reject the comparative method, as Winch does, in seeking explanation, but merely exclusive reliance on the structural-functional method; partly because he thinks it cannot deal with change[5] and partly because structural-functional analysis makes ideas dependent variables. He says:

> I feel I should point out that my attempt to explain cargo cults essentially turns on what Stanner calls a "belief in belief;" a belief, that is, that people's theories and beliefs influence their actions and can, to a certain extent, explain their actions. (Jarvie, 1964: 128)

Thus, Jarvie would like to see "belief" restored to a generative role in the study of society.

Lawrence (1964) has also emphasized the power of ideas, but only because, like Jarvie, he is trying to redress the balance against them after three decades of structural-functionalism:

> The Movement must be understood in terms of both its sociopolitical and epistemological aspects. My purpose is to lay equal stress on both. The first has been given close attention by recent scholars, but the treatment of the second has so far been inadequate. [I am] using the term [epistemology] to cover the general questions: From what sources do the people of the southern Madang District believe knowledge to be derived? And what kinds of knowledge do they hold to be available to themselves? (Lawrence, 1964: 5)

In reconstructing events over time, Lawrence is interested in formulating the Total Cosmic Order from which native action springs and takes its meaning:

> It would be naive to expect people, for whom the religious and secular are so inextricably interwoven in the same order of existence that it is impossible to classify any important event as exclusively either one or the other, to switch from a non-rationalist outlook to a rationalist outlook in the matter of a few years. (Lawrence, 1964: 265)

Lawrence (1967) relates the ideas that constitute the Total Cosmic Order to the occurrence and nonoccurrence of cults: thus, highland societies in New Guinea are less religious and more secular than are seaboard peoples, and this difference, rather than the intellectual confusion resulting from contact with European intellectual systems, may partly explain why cults, along with other religious forms, are nearly absent in the highlands and common on the seaboard.

Similarly, it has been suggested by sociologist Neil Smelser (1963: 319-20) that the religious or secular focus of a culture influences not whether or not a cult will occur but, if it does, whether it will be a religious cult or whether it will be a secular cult. Smelser cites a supporting "classic article on religious sects" by the sociologist John L. Gillin, in which Gillin observed that religious sects will arise only when religion is the dominant interest; and when political interest predominates, political parties will spring up (Gillin, 1910-11: 246). In these accounts by Lawrence, Smelser, and Gillin, the terms "religious" and "secular" refer primarily to the content, rather than the social structure, of group expressions; and they are, then, pointing to a cognitive dynamic in the occurrence and shaping of cults.

Both Linton and Wallace use the content of ideas as the basis for typologies of movements. Linton (1943) contrasts "nativistic movements" which use magical means with those which use rational means, and those which seek revival of the past with those which seek to perpetuate elements of the present scene. Wallace suggests a four-part typology for "revitalization movements" based on the attitudes of adherents to their own and other, particularly dominating, cultures: revivalistic, utopian, assimilative, and expropriative. The ideas which people have about their goals, purposes, and intentions and about their culture are the core of Wallace's concept: "A revitalization movement is defined as a deliberate, organized, conscious effort by members of a society to construct a more satisfying culture" (Wallace 1956: 265). Furthermore, like social scientists, revitalization movement organizers must perceive their cultures as a systems and seek changes not in "discrete items," but in the whole cultural system.[6]

Lattas focuses on the attempt by people to understand new situations in terms of ideas which not only make sense to them but which return some power to them.

> I see cargo cults as a struggle to control the conceptual placing power of the space of death, where the struggle to control the conceptual terms of one's existence is dependent upon controlling those borderlands of otherness used to define the boundaries of lived existence. (Lattas, 1998: 102)[7]

The Force of Material Circumstance

While the pursuit of cargo is the best known aspect of the ideas associated with cargo cults, students do not seriously designate this pursuit as the cause of movements of this sort. May writes of "micronationalist movements:"

> If one can distinguish a common primary objective it is that of material improvement through the mobilization of local resources. The demand for material returns, however, cannot be interpreted in simple economic terms. The desire for improvements in subsistence living and for success in modern business is motivated also by considerations of status. (May, 1982: 422)

Worsley has defended himself against charges that his analysis of cults was based on economic determinism, and granted that millenarian movements do not always arise among the "oppressed," as Lanternari (1963) calls such people, although in the context of a different analysis. However, he maintains that all such movements that have been "historically important" have been movements of the oppressed. He sees that this argument is tautological but thinks that the argument is not thereby invalidated (Worsley, 1957).

The Quest for the Good, the True, the Beautiful, the Transcendent

Most theories see the universal quests for a moral order at the core of cargo cults; which, however, take different forms. Lists of rules may be made, or clear new moral imperatives may be set. A positive value may be assigned to suffering and sacrifice as is the case for many religions, whether new or old. Cultists often seem to be searching for ways to access the power of the supernatural to improve their lives; sometimes through rituals which imitate the misunderstood behavior of white men, who seem to achieve power and wealth through strangely indirect actions (e.g., raising a flag, waiting for a plane to bring cargo).

For what cultists are seeking, Burridge (1960) uses the term "moral equivalence." Aberle speaks of feelings of deprivation, and Lanternari and Hoffer see cultists as the oppressed and as outsiders. Many refer to the demand for equality, which is an important value in most of Melanesia, and central to the demand for justice in cargo cults. Lindstrom (1993) states that he is not interested in the historic details of cults, which he sees as an expression of the universal desire for material things and for love.

Epeli Hau'ofa recognizes an interest in moral systems as especially characteristic of the anthropology of cargo cults: "We know little of [peoples'] systems of morality, specifically their ideas of the good and the bad, and their philosophies; though we sometimes get around to these, wearing dark glasses, through our fascination with cargo cults" (Hau'ofa, 1975: 286). Perhaps, as implied here, it is easier for outsiders to see other peoples' moral systems, even through a glass darkly, when much is made of what is wrong with them—as is often the case in cargo cults.

The Pursuit of Power

Guiart emphasizes the political, and specifically nation-building, aspects of cargo cults (Guiart, 1951a, 1951b). In the first edition of his book Worsley (1957) deals with cargo cults in an explicitly Marxian frame of reference, viewing them as stages in an evolution toward nationalism. Religious cults will, he thinks, give way to political movements.

Writing twenty-five years later, May concludes that

> micronationalism in Papua New Guinea cannot be seen simply as a phase of 'nation-building,' but rather reflects the continuing strength of localism, regionalism, and ethnicity in Papua New Guinean society. To the extent that micronationalism in Papua New Guinea has been a revolutionary force . . . the micronationalists have sought their new order not so much in the overthrow or capture of the colonial regime, as Worsley and others seem to have anticipated, as in the withdrawl from it. (May, 1982: 445)

The political component of cults has been noted in particular cases, where cults are seen as organizing local people especially in resistance to the white man's power in one form or another. Keesing (1978), for example, emphasized the anticolonialism of "politico-religious movements" on Malaita, where Maasina Rule has had a long history.

The Significance of Social Structure

Both Lawrence and Worsley see cults as occurring in large-scale societies which are divided into two parts: the haves and the have-nots. It is the have-nots who have the cults, because they do not have access to knowledge, in Lawrence's account; or economic goods and political control, in Worsley's account. This idea is common, but not universal, in theories about the causes of cults; most, but not all, state or presume that cults occur among the have-nots in divided societies. Aberle's well-known "relative deprivation" theory investigates especially the perspective cultists have of their own condition relative to that of others, rather than objective circumstances. "Relative deprivation," Aberle has written,

> is defined as a negative discrepancy between legitimate expectation and actuality. . . . The discovery of what constitutes serious deprivation for particular groups or individuals is a difficult empirical problem. It requires careful attention to the reference points that people employ to judge their legitimate expectations, as well as to their actual circumstances. (Aberle, 1970: 209)

Aberle claims that

> It is not necessary . . . to assume that all deprivation experiences are primarily concerned with (material) goods. He suggests four types: possessions, status, behavior, and worth. . . . I conceive of any of these types of deprivation . . . to be the possible basis for efforts at remedial action to overcome the discrepancy between actuality and legitimate aspiration. (Aberle, 1970: 210-11)

Aberle does not see his theory as providing a basis for total explanation of cults:

> [T]he fact of deprivation is clearly an insufficient basis for predicting whether remedial efforts will occur, and, if they occur, whether they will have as aims changing the world, transcending it, or withdrawing from it, whether the remedy will be sought in direct action or ritual, and whether it will be sought with the aid of supernatural powers or without. (Aberle, 1970: 211)

He thus makes very clear that "relative deprivation" is only a broad general category which points to a common element in cults which differ in many other dimensions.

It is deprivation in the areas of status and worth that afflict the people of Tangu, according to Burridge's diagnosis (Burridge, 1960). He, along with Lawrence and, earlier, Firth (1955), takes care to emphasize that cargo is wanted for its symbolic value in relation to social status, rather than simply for its utilitarian value. He sees the cult in Tangu as a kind of striving for "moral equivalence" in reaction against the loss of self-respect experienced by Melanesians in contact with Europeans.

It is this contact with Europeans that Lanternari emphasizes in his conclusion after having surveyed modern messianic cults in Africa, North and South America, and the Pacific:

> The messianic movements of modern times constitute one of the most interesting and astonishing results of the cultural clash between populations in very different states of development. . . . Although these movements are primarily religious in character, they also demand and strive to secure for their followers certain riches without which life itself is scarcely worth living. These riches are freedom and salvation: freedom from subjection and servitude to foreign powers as well as from adversity, and salvation from the possibility of having the traditional culture destroyed and the native society wiped out as a historic entity. (Lanternari, 1963: 239)

Lanternari thus emphasizes political and cultural oppression as a cause of cults, and the cult as a seeking to rectify what Aberle would call deprivation primarily of status and of worth. He also sees the value of self-expression through traditional culture, the value of each unique historical cultural entity, as part of the millennium for which people in contact with dominant European cultures struggle.

The high value which people place on their own cultures is at the center of the theories of political sociologist Joseph Gusfield. He discussed cults and movements as symbolic actions which are part of "status politics": struggles in which status groups which are separated by divergent styles of life, rather than only by economic issues, compete for the dominance of their symbols and, hence, of themselves (Gusfield, 1976: 248). According to this theoretical perspective, groups that enhance the status of their symbols enhance their own power to control what happens to them. This emphasis on cultural hegemony is prominent in the Marxist tradition in the work especially of Lukacs and Gramsci[8] the latter of whom identified a break away from the common sense of the establishment and the elevation of the common sense of the powerless as a crucial first step in social change (Adamson, 1980: 51).

Political subordination is also a major component in the theory of Smelser, who classes "millenarian" with other "value-oriented beliefs" and sees them as occurring where societies are divided in relation to access to political power:

> When avenues for influencing political authorities are absent, blocked, or atrophied, value-oriented beliefs begin to flourish. . . . [They] arise when alternative means for reconstituting the social situation are perceived as unavailable. (Smelser, 1963: 331)

Groups who are likely to become involved in such movements are those who

> rank . . . low on wealth, power, prestige, or access to means of communica-

tion." [Typical situations in which cults occur are] among politically disinherited peoples . . . among colonially dominated peoples . . . among persecuted minorities . . . [and] in inflexible political structures. (Smelsser, 1963: 325)

Lanternari, Aberle, Worsley, Taylor, Hoffer, Gusfield, Smelser, and others all point to cultists as outsiders, and outsiders who are in various ways disadvantaged. Kaminsky makes this point and suggests that a "fruitful approach" to the interpretation of millennial movements would be "to relate the movement to society by constructing typologies of alienation and withdrawal." He has high hopes for this "analytic" approach: "typologies of withdrawal and of societal crisis could produce valid statements about the development of millennial movements and their origins, respectively. Thus the movement would be explained." (Kaminsky, 1970: 216).

But not all theorists have found cultists outside the mainstream, or in the lower strata of society. Cohn has studied cults in Europe and finds that some of them occur only among the upper echelons or among a cross-section of groups.

> Marxists have sometimes tried to interpret the millenarism of the Spirituals . . . as a protest by poor peasants against a church which was exploiting and oppressing them. This interpretation is certainly mistaken. Research shows that the Spirituals were drawn mainly from the more privileged strata of society, notable from the mixture of noble and merchant families which formed the dominant class in the Italian towns. Far from belonging to the poor peasantry, many of them had renounced great wealth in order to become poorer than any beggar. And when they condemned the wealth and worldliness or papacy and church they were protesting not against economic exploitation but against a defection of [the] spiritual authority . . . traditionally responsible for regulating relations between society and the powers governing the cosmos. (Cohn, 1970: 35, 40)

The abandonment they protested was that of the spiritual authority. It was a struggle for religious, not economic, security, then, that brought about this cult.

Cohn's analysis shows the Spirituals arising in a divided society, and also sees the cultists as in a subordinate position not in relation to wealth, but in relation to spiritual or cultural, authority. In these cases, it is the weakness, rather than the strength, of the dominant segment that is alleged to cause concern among cultists. However, Cohn does not see sociological factors as causes of cults: it is the "psychic prerequisites for these movements" rather than their "contribu[tion] to cultural evolution" that Cohn thinks the data lead one to most consider (Cohn, 1970: 42).

While Cohn emphasizes emotional factors in those who separate themselves from mainstream society to follow a prophet, he does not reduce religious movements to psychic attributes. He sees in various movements not just psychological but cosmic woe, "the workings of mass anxiety concerning the stability and orderly functioning of the cosmos" (Cohn, 1970: 41).

The Dynamic Dimension

The study and comparison of cults in Melanesia over time has shown that they share remarkable similarities, some of which May (1982) has analyzed. Some scholars, like Lawrence, see themselves as writing particular history, while Worsley, for instance, is seeking the compelling force of system among events viewed diachronically. Worsley used a basically unilinear system of evolution and anticipated an increasingly centralized and complex system, while May's work may be said to use a multilinear model: groups diversify and micronationalism "[plays] a continuing role in the expression of regional, communal, and ethnic elements in Papua New Guinea society" (May, 1982: 447).

Many researchers see cargo cults as movements toward change, and some have made this common characteristic central to their interpretation. Maher (1961), like Mead (1956), looks at the economic development aims and consequences of activities that others might see as cult. Steinbauer (1979: 158) writes that "we are dealing with a Melanesian form of a worldwide development which aims at the enhancement of life."

Christiansen has extensively reviewed the literature with regard to the question of whether cults are changes in response to external contact or are generated from within a culture. He points out that it is far from clear that cargo cults are a response to European colonialism:

> To judge from the accounts discussed here, everything seems to indicate that the cargo cult rests upon a purely traditional basis. It is striking that those authors whose knowledge of the cargo cult comes from the former Dutch part of New Guinea are all fairly unanimous about it, while authors who have obtained their knowledge elsewhere, anyhow up to 10–15 years ago, pretty well exclusively considered cargo cults as a contact or acculturation phenomenon. (Christiansen, 1969: 66)

This difference in emphasis could derive from several sources, including both the different kinds of colonial presence visible in the two New Guineas, and also the different backgrounds of the researchers. What concerns us here is that the importance of the colonial presence in causing cults is not unanimously accepted; nor is it unanimously found that cults are new responses to new stimuli, rather than traditional phenomena.

Wallace's model of revitalization movements focuses on their dynamic aspect, specifically on the power of such movements to enhance the lives of individuals through culture change; rather than on change brought about in the direction of economic or other societal goals. The revitalization model is derived from a functionalist model of an organic system which passes through stages: beginning with a steady state and ending with a new steady state. Between these two steady states there is increased individual stress, cultural distortion, and finally revitalization. Wallace makes clear that many different kinds of agencies may "interfere with the efficiency of cultural systems" (Wallace, 1956: 265), and contact with a dominant culture is only one, though a common one, of these. Wallace's model sees disorganization as a condition which eventually requires rectification, but the organization of a system does not necessarily become more complex or change cumulatively. Thus the changes to which he attends may be cyclical rather than lineal.

The Strength of Cultural Tradition

While most theorists see cultists as outsiders in some way in their own societies, some see them as insiders working according to major core values and traditions of their cultures. Ribeiro, who has studied Brazilian cults, takes this view; and, like Cohn, he takes special care to counter reductionist arguments:

> Various authors have sought to explain the Brazilian movements. Most of these explanations have been of a reductionist character, holding that each outburst of religiosity was due to political and social unrest, to chronic deprivation or to acute deprivation caused by some calamity, to the arousal of mass anxiety and tension, or to mass psychopathological disturbance; or they have seen each outburst as essentially a collective form of protest. (Ribeiro, 1970: 64)

One such interpretation which Ribeiro cites

> was however unable to explain why the Negro in Brazil, although relegated to the lower social levels and exposed to the most severe frustration, has never resorted to messianic movements.
>
> No one could in good faith deny the relevance of these sociocultural factors. Yet in my understanding of the matter, due consideration should be given to the aesthetic appeal of the idea of a perfect age, to the need for renewed dramatic experience, and to the appeal of new types of leadership along with the new social relationships that develop among the members of a movement.
>
> It is clear that wherever a long-established tradition of hope exists, one that gives a dramatic explanation of the cosmos and allows of active participation in the drama in such a way as to fulfill people's fantasies and to take them out of the daily toil or routine of their lives, there any change in social, economic or cultural conditions will favor the rise of a messianic movement. (Ribeiro, 1970: 64-5)

This emphasis on the aesthetic qualities and contribution of cult is also underscored by Jones, who writes about the poetic aspects of cult. Thrupp supports the view that

> Poetic appeal must be a factor in millenarianism—defined as anticipation of

the return of a hero or divinity who will establish by fiat or leadership a revolutionary polity for the benefit of a coterie. (Jones, 1970: 207)

The aesthetic factor alone, however, in Thrupp's view falls short of adequate explanation:

> [T]o explain the power [of the millennial tradition] to incite action we have to look beyond the aspect of aesthetic appeal, to circumstances that are not present in the long periods when the tradition is latent or merely talked about. (Thrupp, 1970: 221)

The presence of a tradition carries weight, then, for these analysts, even though other factors must also be considered.

The Press of Pattern: Style

When Christiansen examined the literature on the important general issue of whether the Melanesian cargo cult is internally or externally caused, he pointed out that while it was earlier thought that cults resulted from contact situations, there is evidence of differences between cultures that have cults and those that do not:

> The research workers who have studied the phenomenon in the field at the source have gradually almost reached agreement that the cargo cult is an autonomous phenomenon with its origin in traditional ideas which have existed before the arrival of Europeans. (Christiansen, 1969: 63)

> But this is naturally not tantamount to every single cargo cult being an independent phenomenon without any connection with other movements. It is certain that many of the movements have spread like wildfire. (Christiansen, 1969: 66)

Christiansen here is talking about ideas, not about structures. Contact with the alien European culture is not alone what causes a cargo cult, but contact with neighbors of similar culture may be what at least partly causes, by diffusion, a particular cult. When such cults occur and spread, however, it is important to note that they do not spread everywhere they touch:

> We know in fact nothing at all about why some societies are apparently immune to the cargo cult, while others seize upon it at every opportunity and at the slightest change. If we could explain why we have a cargo cult in one place and not in another, it would also be easier for us to explain what causes the cult. (Christiansen, 1969: 67)

While no systematic and exhaustive review of cult distribution has been undertaken, it is well known to anthropologists that cults are common in Melanesia and uncommon in Polynesia and Micronesia. Some students have gone on to ask why some societies in Melanesia have cults while others do not. Williams has suggested that the *Hevehe* ceremonies in Orokolo village provided people with important activities absent in nearby Vailala, where the "Madness" was acute (Williams, 1940, 1969). In his foreword to the report, Seligman (Williams, 1940, 1969) emphasizes the importance of traditional ceremonies in preventing the cult. Van der Kroef (1959) has come to similar conclusions regarding this question. He has compared societies with and without cargo cults and has thought, as I do, that the presence of an undisrupted cooperative exchange system within a cooperative society may be related to the nonexistence of cult in such a society.[9] In my study the cooperative society is that of the Tikana, and the undisrupted cooperative exchange system, carried out with traditional ceremonies comparable to the *Hevehe*, is *malanggan*.

Cultural pattern or style has not yet been given much attention by students of cargo cults, though some anthropologists have used it in their analyses of contrasting types of North American religions and cultures. It is this total-pattern approach that Benedict used in contrasting Plains Indian religions, which emphasized the individual and his personal experiences and knowledge, with Pueblo religions, which emphasized the group and traditionally sanctioned ritual and knowledge. Her work became widely known in her application of this approach to the Pueblos, the Northwest Coast Indians and Dobu in *Patterns of Culture* (1934). However, Sapir, as Barnouw points out, had already made the fundamental distinctions with which Benedict later worked: between the Pueblos, who repudiated anything orgiastic and relied on ritual, and the Plains Indians. "Protestant revivalism could perhaps be taught to a Blackfoot Indian, but not to a Zuni" (Sapir, 1928; as reported in Barnouw, 1963: 40).[10]

A clear analysis of the two religious types distinguished by Sapir was published in 1930 in an article by Barbara Aitken, in which she contrasted the religion of the Winnebago and others from that of the Pueblo. Winnebago religion is "individualistic, emotional, centered on personal experience," conducive to speculation and dissent, urging individuals to "pitiable dependence" not on each other but on the "spirit who has blessed him" (Aitken, 1930: 369, 372, 387).

Pueblo religion, by contrast, is "socialized, ritualistic," urging individuals to be happy in cooperation, in taking care of each other, and in the "subordination of individual self-assertion." Speculation is discouraged, and individuals in fact do not speculate; nor are they self-conscious or given to exploring their feelings or to autobiography (Aitken, 1930: 372, 378, 379, 381, 387).

Aitken is careful to present her views within a framework of complexity:

> Two religious temperaments, the individualistic and the social, are present in every human society. The economic environment, acting not directly, but

through the forms of human society, gives predominance to one temperament or the other. Whichever temperament prevails, manifestations of the opposite temperament appear as counter-reactions and as protests. (Aitken, 1930: 387)

Aitken makes a contrast that Weber (1952) has made for different purposes between Catholic and Protestant religions:

I am convinced that the two religious temperaments, the "mind naturally Catholic" and the "mind naturally Protestant," have their representatives in every human society. But in Hopi society the Catholic temperament sets the tone, in Winnebago society the Protestant. (Aitken, 1930: 380)

Douglas has more recently undertaken to present a systematic social analysis which explains the regular occurrence of particular types of religion in particular types of society. Cults are found among people who are "low group" and "low grid" on her diagram, i.e., who lack institutionalized clarity of division and classification in both their social and cosmological structures. "Here [in this type of society] we can locate millennial tendencies from our early history to the present day" (Douglas, 1970: 17).[11] By contrast, ritual and clearly defined and institutionalized belief systems are found among people who live in equally well-structured groups.

The contrast between these two types of religion corresponds to the two types of expressive style Lomax has found in studying folk song and dance. The important characteristics of the expressive style of the songs of individualistic cultures are these: wordiness, precise articulation, textual complexity, narrative direction (e.g., long ballads), and other features that help to create a clear and unique message that carries a heavy semantic load (Lomax, 1968: 16, 132). Heterogeneity characterizes this expressive style. The opposite characteristics define the song style of groupy peoples: songs are simple, repetitious in text, and frequently use nonsense syllables and slurred enunciation. This kind of song is one in which "all those present can join in easily" (Lomax, 1968: 16). Homogeneity characterizes this style.

Extending this characteristic to expressive behavior in general, and to religions in particular, it may be said that groupy cultures communicate in nonverbal ways, through doing simple things repetitively together, perhaps singing or saying together words that are familiar, or slurred, and not primarily conveyors of information. In religion, these kinds of communication are called ritual. Individualistic cultures, on the other hand, depend on verbal elaboration of ideas to achieve integration, a mode of communication that may be called in religion "belief."[12]

Cargo cults are, then, among other things, attempts to integrate individualistic societies through new beliefs, or doctrines, or ideologies. New ideologies are verbal, wordy attempts to unify individuals into groups through common beliefs, not unlike, in form and function, the wordy texts of songs of individualistic cultures.

Referring back to the description of Pueblo-style religion given by Aitken, where is there a place in a ritualistic culture which deplores innovation, which does not speculate, and where individuals do not talk of themselves and their feelings, for the kind of innovative ideology, individualistic self-assertion, and cosmic speculation found in cargo cults, or in millenarian movements in general? We would not be surprised, however, to find a cargo cult among a people like the Winnebago, who are given to speculation and dispute, trust their own experiences, and seek "pitiable dependence" on spirits or cargo or Johnson or something far away from their own lives.

Groupy people do not need a new experience or a new ideology or a cult to bring them together. Their simple, repetitious songs, performed with slurred enunciation, reflect the fact that they are already together and no one needs to say anything about it or lead them forward to a new joint effort. Repeating the old joint efforts is pleasing and meaningful, successful and cherished. The semantic load of their songs (perhaps nonsense syllables), and of their rituals, is small, but "these cohesively inclined people," as Lomax has called them, are nonetheless in close communication with each other and may be seen "dancing beautifully together, walking in unison, paddling in incredible synchrony, even splitting conversation into supportive and matching leader-response patterns where the phrases of two speakers mirror and complement each other like the steps of a pair of dancers" (Lomax, 1968: 287).

Bernstein's analysis of the "elaborated code" in conversation style, used by individualistic peoples, in contrast to the "restricted code" used by group-oriented people, reveals the same contrast in patterns expressed in linguistic phenomena that Lomax has found in song and dance, and that the anthropologists discussed in this section have found in religion (Bernstein, 1964, 1971). The restricted code is more formal and repetitive, but supportive of social bonds; while the elaborated code is less predictable, carrying more complex content, and used among people who do not have strong preexisting social bonds. There is considerable evidence, then, from independent sources to support an interpretation of the form of religion as isomorphic with the form of expression in other media in a culture, and thus with the style of the culture as a whole.

Firth has put forward a general interpretation of cargo cults that rests on a distinction between types of societies similar to that under examination here. He has suggested that well-integrated societies are not likely to have cults. Tikopia has had no cults, and Firth at first thought the idea that one might occur there was "absurd. The Tikopia have too well-integrated a society." (Firth, 1955: 130). He found points of looseness, however, that he thought might allow a cult. Still, "while it would be incorrect to say that the Tikopia type of social structure with well-developed unilinear descent groups and chieftainship with strong political authority necessarily prevent the development of a cargo cult, they do seem to some extent to act as inhibiting factors" (Firth, 1955: 132).

At first glance, Firth appears to agree exactly with the view supported here. However, Firth, like Smelser, emphasizes hierarchical authority and lines of command as enforcing agents against cult, whereas I am emphasizing the absence of generative forces for cult in a group-oriented society. Lomax wrote, "One thinks of Africans, Polynesians, and East Europeans [n.b., but not Melanesians] as outstandingly gregarious, social folk who move through life in shoals." (Lomax, 1968: 287) Shoals of people do not need chiefs to prevent cults.

The study of cultural style is closely related to the study of cognitive style in psychology (Witkin et al, 1962; Witkin and Goodenough, 1981), and was part of the foundation for early studies by cross-cultural psychologists (Berry, 1976). Cross-cultural psychology has developed the contrast between individualism and collectivism as characteristic of different cultures, rather than of different individuals or different genders (Gilligan, 1982, 1988) as was the case among earlier psychologists, who did not take culture into account. This dimension of contrast has been documented now in many different ways by many different researchers in cross-cultural psychology (Berry, 1976; Hofstede, 1980, 1991; Hui and Triandis, 1986; Triandis, McCusker, and Hui, 1990; Fiske, 1991; Kim and Berry, 1993; Kim et al, 1994; Triandis, 1995, to name only a few). Isomorphic contrasts suggested by Mead (1937) and explored intensively by Hsu (1953, 1971, 1983) and Kluckhohn and Strodtbeck (1961) were acknowledged and used in the early studies in cross-cultural psychology, but have not been followed up in anthropology (Billings, 1992d).

Plexus Again

In looking for explanations of cargo cults, or for any other phenomena, a multidimensional analysis is necessary. It is best to consider as many factors as one can. Taxonomies are useful, as LaBarre points out, to remind us of "what we may have left out" (LaBarre, 1971: 27). I am concerned to point up a factor which "we may have left out" and which is, while not decisive in itself, an essential part of the total context which creates cults and movements. That factor is the pattern or style or type of culture that characterizes societies that have, and do not have, cults.

It must be stressed that in underscoring the role of cultural style in the emergence of cargo cults I do not mean to give less weight to other factors. When any single-factor theory is doggedly asserted, to cite LaBarre again, "the explanation impoverishes the phenomena." Cults are multifaceted, as are their causes:

> 'Crisis' is a deeply felt frustration or basic problem with which routine methods, secular or sacred, cannot cope. Any massive helplessness at a critical juncture may be a crisis; the recurrent and insoluble problem of death is, in a

sense, a permanent crisis [which may precipitate a cult wherein people] indulge the appetite to believe. (LaBarre, 1971: 27)

Cult, then, is a creative expression about life and death, as are the other arts; expressions which may be about political oppression, or economic deprivation, or may be about the more or less permanent crisis of death. The appetite to believe in, and the ability to create, cult ideas is, I think, stronger in individualistic societies than in group-oriented ones.

Conclusions

One important set of theories that can help to explain why cargo cults occur in some cultures but not in others is that relating to patterns of culture. Looking at patterns does not require that other theories be rejected, but, rather, that they be looked at differently in the context of cultures of different styles.

Some cultures need explicit, verbalized, discussed, and shared beliefs more than do other cultures, because they do not have the togetherness of people who, without shared explicit beliefs, "move through life in shoals" (Lomax, 1968: 287), singing together songs and performing together rituals that have no meaning beyond the critical and crucial meaning of shared performance and participation. People who lack this togetherness in their whole social and culture structure are not likely to create it in a burst of new, speculative ideology, suggested by one individual amongst the many assertive individuals generating their own, equally valid ideas.

In group-oriented societies, channels of legitimate information are perceived as controlled by authorities who know how to achieve access to them. The Tikana elected people to work within the system and to find out, through legitimate channels, what is going on. But in individualistic societies, any individual may have access, through insight, to legitimate information and may, tomorrow, be a new prophet. As LaBarre writes:

In every age, sensitive, aberrant, creative individuals, in their personal anguish with life, and defrauded somehow of the comforts to be expected from old beliefs, come close to awareness of the dire contingency of all symbols. (LaBarre, 1971: 27)

These are the individuals who initiate cults. I suggest that these individuals and the cults they help to start are more common, and more understood, in an individualistic society than in a group-oriented one; and, further, that the appearance of these individuals and of cults in an individualistic society may be a recurrent expression of the structure of that society under certain conditions, rather than a manifestation or cause of lasting change in its cultural style.

Notes

1. Steinbauer (1979) states that "the cargo cult does not exist. [W]e find various movements about which generalizations cannot be made." He proceeds directly to make a long list of generalizations about cargo cults, e.g., "The cargo cults are socio-religious phenomena which sometimes show a trend towards secular-technocratical stages in the end" (p. 158). Similar statements could be found in other publications.

2. Rev. Allen Taylor told me that in the early days after the vote for Johnson, some men wore rope belts around their *laplaps* and let their beards grow.

3. Christiansen (1969) has already ably provided us with a critical review that is most helpful for anyone wishing such an overview.

4. Much of Cochrane's work (1970), which emphasizes Big Men, is also based on reading other people's accounts of what happened. Stories about what happened are perhaps likely to hang on the names of individuals who play prominent roles.

5. Nagel denies that this is so: see Nagel, 1961: 531-32 (note 18).

6. Wallace, 1956. Mead (1956) also makes this point about Paliau.

7. The struggle for power is given in the following terms by Lattas (p. 108): "The struggle to control the world of the dead is a political struggle over space and especially over those spaces of alterity that map out the boundaries of knowledge, power, and identity in the present. The struggle to control the world of the dead is also a struggle over time, for the underground world of the dead is that world of the past that needs to be reclaimed by the living, if the living are to have a future, if they are to situate themselves differently in a time other than the present."

8. Lukacs and Gramsci are part of the tradition of "underground Marxism" which opposed vulgar materialism. This perspective has been interpreted in a contemporary context by Harrington (1976: 343). Kiralyfalvi (1975) discusses Lukacs in relation to drama. Their views are briefly introduced in chapter 4 of this book.

9. Van der Kroef, 1959; as reported in Christiensen, 1969: 68-74. Christiensen notes (p. 68) that "By a comparison and analysis of societies where we find the cargo cult and societies in which cargo cults do not occur, it should be possible to approach this intricate problem [of the reception or rejection of cult] in a new and fruitful way. Van der Kroef is apparently the only one who has risked tackling such an investigation." He also reports, however, an early opinion of Mead's that the contrast in receptivity presumably depends on "structural, functional, ethological, or ideological similarity or non-similarity" (Mead, 1938: 163).

10. Barnouw (1963) discusses competing interpretations of Pueblo culture.

11. The general characteristics I called "institutionalized" and "noninstitutionalized" could be called, in Douglas's terms, "high grid" and "low grid," respectively. There is some difference in emphasis on social relationships, which for me are primary.

12. Elsewhere I have discussed these and other isomorphic analytical systems that support a contrast between individualistic and group-orientated cultures in expressive styles as well as in social structures: see especially Billings, 1972, 1987, 1989a, 1991d, and 1992c. All the research originating in different disciplines is mutually reinforcing in all aspects of culture except one: I have found that group-orientation does not necessarily correlate with hierarchy. As among the Tikana, egalitarianism is enforced by group-orientation. Mead (1937) also finds this correlation, between cooperation and the absence of hierarchy in her terms, for the Zuni.

6

Conclusion: Cargo Cult as Political Theater

Summary

The Johnson cult has been described here in terms of the history behind it; the events, ideologies, and beliefs which constituted it; and the individuals and groups which played parts in it: as cultist, opposition, mediator, observer, bystander, and so on. The descendant organization, T.I.A., which emerged from it has also been described in terms of its goals, structure, history, and personnel.

In the analysis following the description, the Johnson cult was compared to Lavongai culture generally: the forces which drove the Johnson cult were sorted out to show that they are the familiar traditional forces of New Hanover culture, emergent from the structures of Lavongai society. I argued that only after discovering the major structural categories on which Lavongai culture is built was it possible for me to see why the vote for America made sense to the Lavongai, but not to the Tikana. I argued that the Johnson cult was essentially an expressive phenomenon which was performed in the context of a particular history and culture; and which could not, therefore, be directly taken up by people, like the Tikana, of another history and resultant contrasting culture. The expressive genre "improvisational drama" emerged through a continual process of sifting and winnowing as the frame of reference through which the Johnson cult can most fully be described, analyzed, and understood.

Theories were reviewed and found often to see cults and movements as the protests of the oppressed; but sometimes also as recurrent, aesthetic expressions by no particular segment of society, generated within particular cultures which are not necessarily under pressure from outside contacts or forces. The Johnson cult can clearly be seen in the context of both these kinds of theoretical approaches. Applying the first, we see that cultists felt relatively deprived, and outside observers agreed that they were. This is a clear finding of the research. Still, this condition of deprivation is insufficient as the explanation for the occurrence of the cult; because, as several theorists point out, explanation requires that we also account for the absence as well as the presence of cult. The Johnson cult as a response to neglect seems to make sense in the context of New Hanover history, but it does not make sense as a scientific explanation. The scientific method requires comparison within a frame of reference: a Johnson cult could, in some ways, have made sense in New Ireland, too; but to people of New Ireland, even those on the west coast where political and economic conditions were similar to those of New Hanover, it did not: and they did not join the cult.

Both the Lavongais and the Tikana were under pressure from outside forces, presented urgently in the form of the election of 1964; but the Tikana voted for the candidates offered, while many Lavongais voted for America.

Cultural Style: Individualism and Group Orientation

The approach formulated herein invokes the theories that look to factors internal to the culture, as well as those external, to explain cult: when examined closely, a Johnson cult would not make sense in New Ireland. At a very general level of analysis, the societies of New Ireland and New Hanover are similar, but their cultures contrast in crucial ways: a cult is not part of New Ireland's cultural style. Everything in the structure of the culture, which works for unity and avoids confrontation, is against it. Everything in the values of the people who create and are created by Tikana culture is against it. But Lavongai, who build relationships partly through confrontations in their traditional lives, easily generated a Johnson cult, and they enjoyed parts of it immensely. They are proud of it.

When I first interpreted these two cultures in terms of individualism and group-orientation, I found support for this contrast in the work of Alan Lomax (1968) in cantometrics and in the work on conversational style by Basil Bernstein (1964, 1971). Now there is a vast literature available on this contrast, thanks largely to the work of cross-cultural psychologists. Here I will merely summarize this quickly growing literature by stating that researchers have supported a contrast between individualism and collectivism that is comparable across cultures; that systematically shapes values, personalities, and behaviors within cultures; that is consistent with the early anthropological work in culture and personality, and that is isomorphic with the findings of my research in New Ireland and New Hanover.[1]

Political Theater and Cultural Style

I argued that the Johnson cult was an expression in dramatic form, that it was part of the repertoire of Lavongai cultural style, that the drama began as a protest directed at the Australian administration as audience, and that it achieved some of its aims. Actors from the Johnson cult have created new organizations which mesh better with contemporary global visions elsewhere, and which may continue to consolidate some of the power they need to maintain some control over their island.

Some scholars of theater think that all theater is political, while others restrict the use of the term to that which is intended to be political.[2] As an anthropologist, I prefer to see all theater, and all art, as having political aspects. I think it is more difficult for us to see that all political acts also have dramatic aspects, and are led by artistic dimensions.

Art, and specifically theater, no doubt has universal underpinnings; but the forms built on top of these are certainly culture-specific edifices (Hauser, 1952). My Lavongai friends who attended *malanggan* ceremonies with me in New Ireland found them astonishingly boring: "If we had to wait this long to eat in New Hanover," said one, "we would all have gone home a long time ago!" The fullness of symbolic and personal associations swelling the meaning of actions for Tikana in New Ireland, where *malanggan* have for generations generated, arranged, and exercised power, were unknown and unfamiliar to Lavongais. And Tikana who were asked to join the Johnson cult found the very suggestion, made in a church building, rude and disrespectful.

The deliberate marshaling of insult to shame others is unknown, unfamiliar, and profoundly unpleasant to the Tikana. People of cultures like theirs use other forms with which to try to effect change. The *malanggan* ceremony establishes open access to young individuals and new ways of performing, while reinforcing a structure which maintains public morality. It is a kind of religious drama similar to the morality plays of the Middle Ages, which is reliably and reassuringly repeated, like Mass in the Catholic church, which some scholars have viewed as drama (Brockett, 1977: 117). Its personnel and special events vary with the particular deaths honored, and changes in context can be, and are, accepted and legitimated in *malanggan*. Its meaning is primarily acted out, rather than thought out; believed or accepted for its established and directly apprehended impartation, rather than for its argument or utilitarian functions or service to the dead. It is not a supernatural ritual: the dead are not helplessly stranded in some unpleasant place or condition without it. *Malanggan* is performed because, as one leader told me, "it eases the thoughts of the living about the dead."

It also eases thoughts of the living about the living. While all the ceremony is progressing, it is guiding not only the social and emotional transformations of a rite de passage ending mourning, but also guiding exchanges that create or strengthen or rearrange social, political, and economic relationships among the survivors. A major goal of *malanggan* is to resolve any conflicts which might exist in relation to the dead, and major efforts are made to prevent any conflicts from arising during *malanggan*. For Tikana, to deliberately seek out confrontation, as those who voted for Johnson did, is incomprehensible, unthinkable and unnecessary.

The performance of satiric dramas is widely, but not universally, known among oppressed groups in the world, and is institutionalized in the role of the court jester or religious clown. It is important for anthropologists to use theatrical and other art models in the analysis of society, culture, and politics, if we want to understand any of these. Without politics, art has no power; without art, politics has nowhere to go, and no way to get there.

Whole Views and Understanding Symbols: Plexus Again

The interpretation I have proposed for the Johnson cult is one which can fruitfully be made within the concept of culture that operated with some power in the anthropological academy in the 1930s when culture and personality studies were being undertaken; and again in the 1970s when "symbolic anthropology" gained a place. These approaches conceptualize culture as a whole system, and view our statements about culture as composed of generalizations about symbols and patterns of behavior, ideas, and things in systematic relationship. In our work, the anthropologist is not completely dependent on native informants for the articulation of all the connections that create meaning for them in their culture, although "the native point of view" (Malinowski, 1922: 25) is now, as it was for Boas and Malinowski, at the summit of our research.

The role of cultures as symbolic structures in evolution or revolution cannot be assessed in theories that define them out, as reductionist theories and many philosophically-based postmodern theories do. Symbols must be understood, if at all, within the framework of a concept of culture that listens to what people say, in word and deed, but also supplements their views with holistic analysis that includes other factors: social relations, power structures, biology, environment, and so on.[3]

It is not easy to understand other peoples' symbols, but then it is not easy to understand our own, either. The people of New Hanover were struggling, as Pengai said, to find the "meaning" of their vote, as I was. In the words of their sympathetic Australian medical assistant, Carroll, "The people who were in the cult had a wonderful time. Those who were not always wondered what was going on." In trying to figure out what is going on, the efforts of those inside and outside a culture are complementary. Understanding of culture in general is enhanced by an "exchange of competencies" (Crowe, 1981: 181) between the people whose culture is being studied and the anthropologists, working together to achieve a whole view.

Anthropology: The Definition of Our Situation

Like all other intellectual positions, anthropological theories have political correlates, although exactly what they are is not beyond dispute in any particular case. Omitting or trivializing native views of their own culture in our descriptions and theories is, in my view, a fatal blow to anthropology as an intellectual enterprise. The kind of analysis I have been pursuing here puts into focus, I think, the unwelcome political implications of theories that allow such omission.[4]

A people's political and social status is related to whether or not their definition of themselves and of their situation is subordinate to, or dominant over, the views others project of them. When we adhere to theories that claim that people's ideas of themselves are either unknowable or else irrelevant (mere dependent variables trailing universal forces) and that anthropological theories of what really moves people are somehow more objective truth,[5] we are demanding for ourselves dominance over people in the powerful act of defining their situation. Melanesians use the terms "cargo cult" and *kastom*, and it is our job, in my view, to find out what they mean by these terms; rather than to claim, as some anthropologists do, that the terms have no useful meanings in anthropology. Reductionist theories directly or indirectly deny that native definitions of their own situation have any significant power over even their own behavior, let alone ours.

Our definition of their situation is our contribution, for better or for worse, to the status politics in which the people we study are engaged. In the case of the Johnson cultists, shall I define them as confused, irrational, paranoid materialists? Do they understand their own position less well than we do? Or are they brilliant, dramatic activists, far beyond our grasp? Am I able to comprehend what they tell me? As an anthropologist and an outsider, I ought to be able to bring to bear on the understanding of their behavior, and of ours, perspectives gained from experiences different from theirs. And yet I am obliged always to remain humble in my task. As one anthropologist put it, "Anthro-pological writings are themselves interpretations, and second and third order ones to boot. (By definition, only a 'native' makes first order ones: it's his culture.) . . . In finished anthropological writings . . . what we call our data are really our own constructions of other people's constructions of what they and their compatriots tare up to" (Geertz, 1973: 15). The Banabans, a group of Pacific islanders on tour in Europe, defined themselves as no anthropologist ever could when they responded to the question, "Who are the Banaban people anyway?" with the performance of music and dance; stating, operationally, "We . . . are the people who dance like this" (Shennan, 1983: 193).

Our definition of ourselves, as well as of the people we study, is formed by what we do in the field and by our dissemination of information following our return home. We are the people who go to other societies, do research, and then go back to our universities and write up our reports, or otherwise communicate our findings, "like this."

We anthropologists have always been entangled in status politics of our own, vying for the ascendancy of the theories and methods we prefer, arguing for their dominance at the center of the discipline. The theoretical stance which I favor gives, I think, political support to the people we study; but others may dispute this view. Whatever else we do in anthropology, I think that we must continue to listen to what people say about themselves (in all forms of communication) and to try to understand their point of view, as they try to understand ours.

While traveling in the field in the company of teachers and nurses and others engaged in work intended to enhance human welfare, I often felt that the only thing I had to offer to people was attentive listening and genuine appreciation. Perhaps these offerings were not so small as I had feared they were. Throughout the history of our profession, we have been the people who listened. We were the audience when there was no other, and when other outsiders, with other purposes, wanted to be downstage center, feeling that it was more blessed to give than to receive messages. We have tried, at least, to gain an inside view of culture, to understand what people thought they were up to: and we have accepted their definition of their situation respectfully, when others have thought they were heathens or savages or underdeveloped peoples who needed, most of all, to be changed.[6]

Reductionist theories, unsystematic fragmentary narratives, and statements that dwell on our own responses do not demand of us, as more complex theories of culture do, a central commitment to this purpose, which I think is the one that essentially defines us: listening. It is true that the depiction of other people's culture is complicated by rapid change, that people argue about what their culture is or was, and that individuals do not agree. The concept of culture is an overgeneralization, as are all concepts, in science or outside it. We never step twice into the same river or culture. The arts are a particularly fleet-footed part of culture, which is probably the main reason we have neglected them. It seems more necessary and less intrusive to take genealogies and count pigs, to measure gardens and record interviews than it is to achieve a philosophical discussion or to understand a joke or a work of art in any culture. But if we do not achieve these understandings, we are not only leaving our explanations reduced and bare, we are also stripping the people we study of human complexity, of the social status they want and deserve, and of the political position they have claimed in this century. At the very least, we can avoid defining people as unknowable or as units in reductionist theories in which they appear as nothing more than passive dupes of their own repertoire of ideas or of their own genes or appetites. People ask for more:

> Our lives shall not be sweated
> from birth until life closes;
> hearts starve as well as bodies; give
> us bread, but give us roses.[7]

By our works they will know us. If we want respect for our work, it must strive to be as artfully complex as are the cultures, and people, we are privileged to seek to understand.[8] Regardless of what we intend for our words, we can no longer expect them to disappear into academe or to fall without effect. As one who taught me about his culture, and about mine, said to me: 'Talk is just wind, but wind can break a tree.'[9]

The Future

The future for the people of New Hanover is part of the future of the global village. The industrialized parts of the village want the raw resources of the subsistence economy areas, and the people who are providing themselves with food want the manufactured products, including medicines, of the industrialized areas.[10] New Hanover has counterparts in other rainforest areas, and in other areas where resources exist, or may exist, that the industrialized world can use.[11] The exchange between the two kinds of areas has not been, of course, the kind of equal exchange that is valued by all the cultures of Papua New Guinea. The industrialized world has the power to take what it wants, and so far the subsistence areas of the world have not had the power to stop them.[12]

The great task for the people of Papua New Guinea is to go forward together while maintaining the various, even contradictory, strengths of their many and diverse cultures. So far they have made a remarkable beginning, creating occasions for many kinds of celebration and for the celebration of diversity. The accommodation to each other that the peoples of New Hanover and New Ireland work out in the Kavieng District will be one of many local accommodations to differences in culture and in cultural style in their nation, and in the rest of the world. We all have to make some kind of peace with the larger governments and with the universal thorn, or blessing, of tax paying. In the global village, we all now share these tasks.

Notes

1. I have cited some of the literature that supports these generalizations in the introduction to this book.
2. Schechner (1974) holds the former view, Kirby (1975) the latter. Schechner (1985), Schechner and Schuman (1976), and Victor Turner (1957, 1974, 1982) have led the way to the kind of analysis I attempt here. Potential pitfalls of the approach have been probed by Sandall (1978). See also Edith Turner (1989).
3. Hanson (1975) offers a clear and illuminating discussion of the relationship between different approaches.
4. I tried to discuss issues of politics and ethics, in general and in the field where I worked, in Billings, 1992.
5. Harrington (1976: 343-48). For a clear and concise account of the problems encountered by the concept of "objective truth" from the point of view of philosophy of science, see Chalmers, 1976.
6. "Applied anthropology" is based on outsiders' views concerning the need for change, while "action anthropology," as developed by Sol Tax, is based on insiders' perspectives. See Piddington (1960), for a defense of action anthropology in the South Pacific. Assimilation policies, under many names, continue and continue to be "cultural dictatorship" (Geddes, 1961: 219).
7. From the poem "Bread and Roses," by James Oppenheim (Meltzer, 1967). Oppenheim watched the strike of 23,000 workers in Lawrence, Massachusetts, in 1912, and wrote his poem after he saw a group of young mill girls carrying a banner which read: "We want bread... and roses too!" It is reprinted and illustrated in *Images of Labour* (New York: The Pilgrim Press, 1981).
8. This view has been eloquently supported by Hau'ofa (1975).
9. Francis of Livitua, New Ireland, said this during the course of a dispute settlement in 1966.
10. See Bodley (2000) for a review of this situation from an anthropological perspective.
11. Dramatic forms of protest have been used elsewhere in the world by peoples in positions similar to those of the Lavongai: e.g., the Native Americans of the Amazon river basin have presented themselves in their traditional garb at white men's meetings and made demands for local control of their resources.
12. See Bodley (2000), Billings (1994, 1996b, 1998a, 1998b, 1998c, 1998d, 1998e).

Bibliography

Aberle, David F.
1970 A Note on Relative Deprivation Theory as Applied to Millenarian and Other Cult Movements. In *Millennial Dreams in Action,* edited by Sylvia L. Thrupp, 209-14. New York: Schocken.

Adamson, Walter L.
1980 *Hegemony and Revolution: A Study of Antonio Gramsci's Political and Cultural Theory.* Berkeley, Calif.: University of California Press.

Aitken, Barbara
1930 Temperament in Native American Religion. *Journal of the Royal Anthropological Institute* 60: 363-87.

Allen, J.
1984 In search of the Lapita homeland. *Journal of Pacific History* 129: 186-201.

Allen, J., J. Specht, and J. Mangi
1984 Draft Research Proposal: The Lapita Homeland Project. Canberra: Department of Prehistory, Australian National University.

Allen, Jim, Chris Gosden, Rhys Jones, and J. Peter White
1988 Pleistocene Dates for the Human Occupation of New Ireland, Northern Melanesia. *Nature* 331: 707-9.

Allen, J., C. Gosden, and J.P. White
1989 Human Pleistocene Adaptations in the Tropical Island Pacific. *Antiquity* 69: 101-12.

Allen, J. and P. White
1989 The Lapita Homeland: Some New Data and an Interpretation. *Journal of the Polynesian Society* 98: 129-46.

Barnett, Steve, and Martin G. Silverman
1979 *Ideology and Everyday Life: Anthropology, Neomarxist Thought, and the Problem of Ideology and the Social Whole.* Ann Arbor: University of Michigan Press.

Barnouw, Victor
  1963   *Culture and Personality*. Chicago: Dorsey.

Bellwood, P.
  1979   *Man's Conquest of the Pacific*. Auckland: Collins.

Benedict, Ruth
  1928   Psychological Types in the Cultures of the Southwest. In *Proceedings of the Twenty-third International Congress of Americanists*, September: 527-81.

  1934   *Patterns of Culture*. Boston: Houghton Mifflin.

Berndt, Ronald M.
  1952   A Cargo Movement in the Eastern Central Highlands of New Guinea. *Oceania* 23: 40-65, 137-58, 202-34.

  1953   Reaction to Contact in the Eastern Highlands of New Guinea. *Oceania* 24: 190-228, 255-74.

Berne, Erik
  1964   *Games People Play*. New York: Grove.

Bernstein, Basil
  1964   Elaborated and Restricted Codes: Their Social Origins and Some Consequences. *American Anthropologist* [special issue] 66: 6, part 2: 254-69.
  1971   *Class, Codes, and Control*, vol. 1. London: Routledge & Kegan Paul

Berry, J. W.
  1976   *Human Ecology and Cognitive Style: Comparative Studies in Cultural and Psychological Adaptation*. Beverly Hills, Calif.: Sage.

Berthold, Margot
  1972   *A History of World Theater*. New York: Frederick Ungar.

Billings, Dorothy K.
  1969   The Johnson Cult of New Hanover. *Oceania* 40: 13-19.
  1972   *Styles of Culture: New Ireland and New Hanover*. Ph.D. diss., Sydney: University of Sydney.
  1983   The Play's the Thing: The Political Power of Dramatic Presentation. *Journal of the Polynesian Society* 92: 439-62.
  1987   Expressive Style and Culture: Individualism and Group-Orientation Contrasted. *Language in Society* 16: 475-97.
  1989a Is Fieldwork Art or Science? In *The Humbled Anthropologist: Tales from the South Pacific*. Edited by Philip De Vita, 1-7. Belmont, Calif.: Wadsworth Publishing Co.
  1989b Individualism and Group-Orientation: Contrasting Personalities in Contrasting Melanesian Cultures. In *Heterogeneity in Cross-Cultural Psychology, Selected Proceedings of the IXth International Congress of the International Association for Cross-Cultural Psychology*. Edited by

D. M. Keats, D. Munro and L. Man, Part I, 92-103. Amsterdam/Lisse: Lisse, Swets and Zeitlinger.

1991a Cultural Style and Solutions to Conflict. *Journal of Peace Research* 28: 249-62.

1991b Social Organization and Knowledge. *The Australian Journal of Anthropology* (formerly *Mankind*) 2: 109-25.

1991c Little Collaborations in Papua New Guinea. *High Plains Applied Anthropologist* II: 1.

1991d Genus Individualism/Collectivism: Perennial Sightings of an Untamed Beast. Paper presented to the *Society for Cross-Cultural Research*, Puerto Rico, February, 1991.

1992a The Theater of Politics: Contrasting Types of Performance in Melanesia. *Pacific Studies* 15: 211-33.

1992b Cultural Hegemony and Applied Anthropology. *Canberra Anthropology*, 15(1): 35-57.

1992c Cultural style and solutions to conflict. In *The Anthropology of Peace: Essays in Honor of E. Adamson Hoebel*, Edited by V. H. Sutlive, M. D. Zamora, and T. Hamada. Studies in Third World Societies Number 47.

1992d Individualism/Collectivism in Relation to Hierarchy and Egalitarianism. Paper presented at the XIth Annual Congress of the *International Association for Cross-Cultural Psychology*, July 11-19, 1992, Liege, Belgium.

1994 Contrasting Shapes of Things to Come: Cultures and Natural Environments. *Proceedings of the International Conference on Ethnic Traditional Culture and Folk Knowledge*. Institute of Ethnology and Anthropology, Russian Academy of Sciences, March 21-24, 1994. Published in Russian. Vaitcheslav Roudnev editor, translator, and conference organizer.

1996a But Is It Anthropology? *Occasional Papers, American Anthropological Association,* Association of Senior Anthropologists 1:1:1-18.

1996b Contrasting Shapes of Things to Come: "Development" and the Individualist/Collectivist Paradigm. Paper presented to the XIII Congress of the International Association of Cross-Cultural Psychology, August 12-16, 1996: Montreal, Quebec.

1997 Evolution of a Cargo Cult: Waiting for Greenpeace. Paper presented at the 74th Annual Meeting of the Central States Anthropological Society, April 1-4, 1997: Milwaukee, Wisconsin.

1998a "Can I Help?" Slingshot Anthropology Faces the Development Giant. Paper presented at the 75th Annual Meeting of the Central States Anthropological Society, April 2-5, 1998: Kansas City, Missouri.

1998b New Guinea at Corporate Headquarters: Amungme Versus the Freeport Mining Company. In *Ecology and Folklore III*. Edited by Stanislav Broucek and Violetta Krawczyk-Wasilewska, Institute of Ethnology of the Academy of Sciences of the Czech Republic, Prague. Selected papers from the conference "Ecology and Folklore III," (September 23-25, 1996), Department of Folklore, University of Lodz, Poland.

1998c Taking Control of Development in New Hanover: Cargo Cults, Seminars, and Standing Your Ground. Paper presented in the Symposium "Cultures and Sustainable Development for Humankind in the 21st Century," 14th International Congress of Anthropological and Ethnological Sciences July 26-August, 1998: The College of William and Mary, Williamsburg, Virginia.

1998d   Whose Ground Is This? Adam with Arrows (Again), Lawsuits, and the Internet. Paper presented at the 14th International Congress of Anthropological and Ethnological Sciences July 26-August 1, 1998: The College of William and Mary, Williamsburg, Virginia.

1998e   Forests and People in Papua New Guinea. Paper presented at the 14th International Congress of Anthropological and Ethnological Sciences July 26-August 1, 1998: The College of William and Mary, Williamsburg, Virginia.

2000   Through Culture-Colored Glasses: Is There a Native Point of View? Paper presented at the 14th Congress of the International Association for Cross-Cultural Psychology, July 16-21, 2000: Pultusk, Poland.

Billings, D. K., and Nicholas Peterson
1967   *Malanggan* and *Memai* in New Ireland. *Oceania* 38: 24-32.

Birdwhistell, Ray L.
1970   *Kinesics and Context*. Philadelphia: University of Pennsylvania Press.

Bodley, John H
2000   *Anthropology and Contemporary Human Problems*. Mountain View, Calif.: Mayfield Publishing Co.

Bowen, Eleanore Smith
1954   *Return to Laughter*. London: Gollanz

Brockett, Oscar G.
1977   *The Theatre: An Introduction*. Boston: Allyn & Bacon.

Brustein, Robert
1971   *Revolution as Theater: Notes on the New Radical Style*. New York: Liveright.

Burke, Kenneth
1968   Psychology and Form. In *Perspectives on Drama*. Edited by James L. Calderwood and Harold E. Toliver. New York: Oxford University Press.

Burridge, Kenelm
1960   *Mambu*. London: Methuen.
1969   *New Heaven New Earth: A Study of Millenarian Activities*. New York: Schocken Books.
1993   Melanesian Cargo Cults. In *Contemporary Pacific Societies: Studies in Development and Change*. Edited by Victoria S. Lockwood, Thomas G. Harding, and Ben J. Wallace, 275-88. Englewood Cliffs, NJ: Prentice-Hall.

Chalmers, A. F.
1976   *What Is This Thing Called Science?* St. Lucia, Queensland: University of Queensland Press.

Chinnery, E. W. P.
1929   *Anthropological Report*, no. 6. Territory of New Guinea.

Christiansen, Palle
1969 *The Melanesian Cargo Cult: Millenarianism as a Factor in Cultural Change.* Copenhagen: Akademisk Forlag.

Cochrane, G.
1970 *Big Men and Cargo Cults.* Oxford: Clarendon Press.

Cohn, Norman
1970 Medieval Millenarism: Its Bearing on the Comparative Study of Millenarian Movements. In *Millennial Dreams in Action.* Edited by Sylvia L. Thrupp, 31-43. New York: Schocken.

Combs, James E., and Michael W. Mansfield, eds
1976 *Drama in Life.* New York: Hastings House Publishers.

Crowe, Peter
1981 After the Ethnomusicological Salvage Operation—What? *Journal of the Polynesian Society,* 90:171-82.

Douglas, Mary
1970 *Natural Symbols.* New York: Pantheon Books.

Feldt, Eric
1967 *The Coast Watchers.* 1946. Reprint, London: Angus and Robertson.

Firth, Raymond
1955 A Note on the Theory of "Cargo Cults." *Man* 142:130-32.

Fiske, Alan
1991 *Structure of Social Life: The Four Elementary Forms of Human Relations.* New York: Free Press.

Friedman, Jonathan
1974 Marxism, Structuralism and Vulgar Materialism. *Man* 9: 444-69.

Fromm, Eric
1942 *Escape From Freedom.* New York: Farrar and Rinehart, Inc.

Geddes, W. R.
1961 Maori and Aborigine: A Comparison of Attitudes and Policies. *Australian Journal of Science 24*: 217-25.

Geertz, Clifford
1972 *The Interpretation of Cultures: Selected Essays.* New York: Basic Books.

George, A. C.
1966 We Want President Johnson. *The Missionary Review,* May: 15-17.

Gerlach Luther P., and Virginia H. Hine
1968 Five Factors Crucial to the Growth and Spread of a Modern Religious Movement. *Journal for the Scientific Study of Religion* 7: 1.

Gillin, J. L.
1910/ A Contribution to the Sociology of Sects. *American Journal of*
1911   *Sociology* Vol. 16.

Gilligan, Carol, ed
1982 *In a Different Voice: Psychological Theory and Women's Development.* Cambridge, Mass: Harvard University Press.

Gilligan, Carol, and Jane Attanucci
1988 Two Moral Orientations. In *Mapping the Moral Domain: A Contribution of Women's Thinking to Psychological Theory and Education.* Edited by Carol Gilligan, Janie Victoria Ward, and Jill McLean Taylor, 73-86. Cambridge, Mass.: Center for the Study of Gender, Education, and Human Development, Harvard University Graduate School of Education.

Golson, J.
1971 Lapita Ware and Its Transformations. *Pacific Anthropological Records* 12: 67-76.

Gosden, C., and N. Robertson
1991 Models for Matenkupkim: Interpreting a Late Pleistocene Site from Southern New Ireland, Papua New Guinea. In *Report of the Lapita Homeland Project.* Edited by J. Allen and C. Gosden, 20-45. *Occasional Papers in Prehistory,* No. 20. Canberra: Department of Prehistory, Australian National University.

Green, R. C
1979 Lapita. In *The Prehistory of Polynesia.* Edited by J. Jennings, 27-60. Cambridge, Mass: Harvard University Press.

Grotowski, Jerzy
1968 *Towards a Poor Theater.* New York: Simon and Schuster.

Groves, W. C.
1933 Report on Field Work in New Ireland. *Oceania* 3: 325-61.
1935 Tabar Today. *Oceania* 6: 147-58.
1936 Secret Beliefs and Practices in New Ireland. *Oceania* 7: 220-46.

Guiart, Jean
1951a "Cargo Cults" and Political Evolution in Melanesia. Mankind 4: 227-29.
1951b Forerunners of Melanesian Nationalism. *Oceania* 22: 81-90.

Gusfield, Joseph R.
1976 A Dramatic Theory of Status Politics. In *Drama in Life.* Edited by James E. Combs and Michael W. Mansfield, 244-57. New York: Hasting House Publishers.

Hanson, F. Allen
1975 *Meaning in Culture.* London: Routledge and Kegan Paul.

Harrington, Michael

1976 *The Twilight of Capitalism*. New York, Simon and Schuster.

Hau'ofa, Epeli
1975 Anthropology and Pacific Islanders. *Oceania* 45: 283-289.

Hauser, Arnold
1952 *The Social History of Art*. New York: Alfred A. Knopf.

Hoffer, Eric
1966 *The True Believer*. New York: Perennial Library; first published 1951, New York: Harper and Brothers.

Hofstede, Geert H.
1980 *Culture's Consequence: International Differences in Work-Related Values*. Beverly Hills, Calif.: Sage.
1991 *Cultures and Organizations: Software of the Mind*. London: McGraw-Hill.

Holton, Gerald
1973 *Thematic Origins of Scientific Thought*. Cambridge, Mass.: Harvard University Press
1975 Mainsprings of Scientific Discovery. In *The Nature of Scientific Discovery*. Edited by Owen Gingerich. Smithsonian International Symposia Series, 5. Washington, D.C.: Smithsonian Institution Press.

Hsu, Francis L. K.
1953 *Americans and Chinese: Two Ways of Life*. New York: H. Schuman
1983 *Rugged Individualism: Essays in Psychological Anthropology*. Knoxville: University of Tennessee Press.

Hsu, Francis L. K., ed
1971 *Kinship and Culture*. Chicago: Aldine Publishing Co.

Hui, C. H., and H. C. Triandis
1986 Individualism-Collectivism: A Study of Cross-Cultural Researchers. *Journal of Cross-Cultural Psychology* 17: 225-48.

Inglis, Judy
1957 Cargo Cults: The Problem of Explanation. *Oceania* 2: 249-63.

Jarvie, I. C.
1963 Theories of Cargo Cults: A Critical Analysis. *Oceania* 34: 108-36.
1964 *The Revolution in Anthropology*. London: Routledge and Kegan Paul.

Joll, James
1977 *Antonio Gramsci*. Hammondsworth, U.K.: Penguin Books.

Jolly, Margaret
1982 Birds and Banyans of South Pentecost: Kastom in Anti-Colonial Struggle. *Mankind* 13, special issue: *Reinventing Traditional Culture: The Politics of Kastom in Melanesia*. Edited by Roger Keesing and Robert Tonkinson, 339-56.

Jones, Howard
1970   The Millenial Dream as Poetry. In Millennial Dreams in Action. Edited by Sylvia L. Thrupp. New York: Schocken.

Kaminsky, Howard
1970   The Problem of Explanation. In *Millennial Dreams in Action*. Edited by Sylvia L. Thrupp, 166-86. New York: Schocken.

Kaplan, Martha
1995   *Neither Cargo Nor Cult: Ritual Politics and the Colonial Imagination in Fiji*. Durham, N.C.: Duke University Press.

Keesing, Roger
1978   Politico-Religious Movements and Anti-Colonialism on Malaita: Maasina Rule in Historical Perspective. *Oceania* 48: 241-61; 49: 46-75.

Kim, Uichol, and John W. Berry, eds
1993   *Indigenous Psychologies: Research and Experience in Cultural Context*. Newbury Park, Calif.: Sage.

Kim, Uichol, Harry C. Triandis, Cigdem Kagitcibasi, Sang-Chin Choi, and Gene Yoon, eds
1994   *Individualism and Collectivism: Theory, Method, and Applications*. Cross-Cultural Research and Methodologies Series, Vol. 18. Thousand Oaks, Calif.: Sage.

Kiralyfalvi, Bela
1975   *The Aesthetics of Gyorgy Lukacs*. Princeton, N.J.: Princeton University Press.

Kirch, Patrick Vinton
1997   *The Lapita Peoples: Ancestors of the Oceania World*. Cambridge, Mass.: Blackwell Publishers Inc.

Kluckhohn, Florence, and Fred Strodtbeck
1961   *Variations in Value Orientations*. Evanston, Ill.: Row, Peterson.

Kopytoff, Igor
1964   Classifications of Religious Movements: Analytical and Synthetic. In *Symposium on New Approaches to the Study of Religion*. Proceedings of the 1964 Annual Spring Meeting, American Ethnological Society. Edited by June Helm. Seattle: University of Washington Press.

Kramer, Augustin
1925   *Die Malanggane Von Tombara*. Munich: George Muller.

Kroeber, A. L.
1923   *Anthropology*. New York: Harcourt Brace.
1948   *Anthropology: Race, Language, Culture, Psychology, Pre-history*. New York: Harcourt Brace.

Kroeber, A .L. ed

1953   *Anthropology Today: An Encyclopedic Inventory.* Chicago: The University of Chicago Press.

van der Kroef, Justus M.
1959   Culture Contact and Culture Conflict in Western New Guinea. *Anthropological Quarterly* 32: 134-60.

LaBarre, Weston
1971   Materials for a History of Studies of Crisis Cults: A Bibliographic Essay. *Current Anthropology* 12: 1, 3-37.

Lanternari, Vittorio
1963   *The Religions of the Oppressed.* New York: Knopf.

Lattas, Andrew
1998   *Cultures of Secrecy: Reinventing Race in Bush Kaliai Cargo Cult.* Madison: University of Wisconsin Press.

Lawrence, Peter
1967   Politics and 'True Knowledge.' *New Guinea* 2: 1, 34-49.
1964   *Road Belong Cargo.* Melbourne University Press and Manchester University Press: Victoria and Manchester.

Lewis, Phillip H.
1961   The Artist in New Ireland Society. In *The Artist in Tribal Society.* Edited by Marian W. Smith. New York: Free Press of Glencoe.
1969   The Social Context of Art in Northern New Ireland. *Fieldiana*: vol. 58, Anthropology. Chicago: Field Museum.

Lindstrom, Lamont
1993   *Cargo Cult. Strange Stories of Desire from Melanesia and Beyond.* Honolulu: University of Hawaii Press.

Linton, Ralph
1943   Nativistic Movements. *American Anthropologist* 45: 230-40.

Lithgow, David, and Oren Claassen
1968   *Languages of the New Ireland District.* Port Moresby, T.P.N.G.: Dept. of Information and Extension Service.

Lomax, Alan
1968   *Folk Song Style and Culture.* Publication no. 88. Washington, D.C.: American Association for the Advancement of Science.

McCarthy, J. K.
1963   *Patrol into Yesterday: My New Guinea Years.* Melbourne: F. W. Cheshire.

McDowell, Nancy
1985   Past and Future: The Nature of Episodic Time in Bun. In *History and Ethnohistory in Papua New Guinea.* Edited by D. Gewertz and E. Schieffelin, 26-39. Oceania Monograph no. 28. Sydney: University of

Sydney.

Maher, R. F.
  1961   *New Men of Papua: A Study in Culture Change*. Madison: University of Wisconsin Press.

Malinowski, Bronislaw
  1922   *Argonauts of the Western Pacific*. London: Routledge and Kegan Paul
  1944   *A Scientific Theory of Culture*. Chapel Hill, N.C.: University of North Carolina Press.
  1967   *A Diary in the Strict Sense of the Term*. Stanford, Calif.: Stanford University Press.

Maslow, Abraham H.
  1970   *Religions, Values, and Peak Experiences*. New York: The Viking Press.

May, R. J., ed
  1982   *Micro nationalist Movements in Papua New Guinea*. Canberra: Australian National University.

Mead, Margaret
  1937   *Cooperation and Competition among Primitive Peoples*. McGraw-Hill: New York. Republished 1961, Boston: Beacon Press.
  1938   *The Mountain Arapesh*. Vol. 1, *An Importing Culture*. Anthropological Papers of the American Museum of Natural History, vol. 36, pt. 3
  1956   *New Lives for Old*. New York: William Morrow.
  1964   *Continuities in Cultural Evolution*. New Haven, Conn.: Yale University Press.

Meltzer, Milton
  1967   *Bread and Roses: The Struggle of American Labor*. New York: Alfred A. Knopf.

Memmi, Albert
  1965   *The Colonizer and the Colonized*. Boston: Beacon Press.

Mihalic, Rev. Francis
  1957   *Grammar and Dictionary of Neo-Melanesian*. Westmead, N.S.U.: Mission.

Miller, Rev. Bernard J.
  1966   The Lavongais. *MSC Dimensions*. Aurora, Ill.: Society of the Missionaries of the Sacred Heart.

Murphy, John J.
  1962   *The Book of Pidgen English*. Brisbane: W.R. Smith & Patterson.

Murray, Mary
  1965   *Escape: A Thousand Miles to Freedom*. Adelaide: Rigby.

Nagel, Ernst
  1961   *The Structure of Science: Problems in the Logic of Scientific*

Explanation. New York: Harcourt, Brace, and World.

Nash, Ogden
1952 England Expects. In *The Penguin Book of Comic and Curious Verse*, selected by J. M. Cohen. Harmandsworth, U.K.: Penguin.

O'Neill, Tim
1961 *And We, the People: Ten Years with the Primitive Tribes of New Guinea*. New York: Kennedy.

Patchen, Kenneth
1968 *Because It Is*. New York: New Directions.

Peterson, J. Nicholas, and Dorothy K. Billings
1965 A Note on Two Archaeological Sites in New Ireland. *Mankind* 6 (6): 254-57.

Piddington, R. O.
1960 Action Anthropology. *Journal of the Polynesian Society* 69: 199-214.

Powdermaker, Hortence
1933 *Life in Lesu*. London: Williams and Norgate.
1961 The Artist in New Ireland Society: A Comment. In *The Artist in Tribal Society*. Edited by Marian W. Smith. New York: Free Press of Glencoe.
1966 *Stranger and Friend: The Way of an Anthropologist*. New York: W. W. Norton.

Ryan, Peter, ed
1972 *Encyclopaedia of Papua and New Guinea*. Melbourne: Melbourne University Press in association with the University of Papua and New Guinea.

Ribeiro, Rene
1970 Brazilian Messianic Movements. In *Millennial Dreams in Action*. Edited by Sylvia L. Thrupp, 55-69. New York: Schocken.

Salamini, Leonardo
1981 *The Sociology of Political Praxis: An Introduction to Gramsci's Theory*. London: Routledge and Kegan Paul.

Sandall, Roger
1978 On the Way to the Pig Festival. *Encounter* 51 (2): 63-70.

Sapir, Edward
1928 The Meaning of Religion. *The American Mercury* 15: 72-79.

Sassoon, Ann Showstack, ed
1982 *Approaches to Gramsci*. London: Writers and Readers Publishing Cooperative Society.

Schapiro, Meyer
1953 Style. In Anthropology Today. Edited by A.L. Kroeber, 287-312.

Chicago: University of Chicago Press.

Schechner, Richard
1974   A Critical Evaluation of Kirby's Criticism of Criticism. *Drama Review* 18 (4): 116-18.

Schechner, Richard, and Mary Schuman, eds
1976   *Ritual, Play and Performance: Readings in the Social Sciences/Theatre.* New York: Seabury.

Schiller, Herbert I.
1976   *Communication and Cultural Domination.* New York: International Arts and Sciences Press.

Schwartz, Theodore
1962   The Paliau Movement in the Admiralty Islands, 1954-56. *American Museum of Natural History Anthropological Papers* 49: ii.
1973   Cult and Context: The Paranoid Ethos in Melanesia. *Ethos* 1: 153-74.
1999   Residues of a Career: Reflections on Anthropological Knowledge. *Ethos* 27 (1): 54-61.

Shennan, Jennifer
1981   Approaches to the Study of Dance in Oceania: Is the Dancer Carrying an Umbrella or Not? *Journal of the Polynesian Society* 90: 193-208.

Smelser, Neil J.
1963   *Theory of Collective Behavior.* New York: Free Press of Glencoe.

Sorokin, Dmitri
1957   Forward. *Community and Society (Gemeinschaft und Gesellschaft).* By Ferdinand Tonnies. Translated and edited by Charles Loomis. East Lansing: Michigan State University Press.

Specht, J.
1968   Preliminary Report of Excavations on Watom Island. *Journal of the Polynesian Society* 77 (2): 117-34.

Spiro, Melford E.
1990   On the Strange and the Familiar in Recent Anthropological Thought. In *Cultural Psychology: Essays on Comparative Human Development.* Edited by James W. Stigler, Richard A. Shweder, and Gilbert Herdt, 47-61. Cambridge: Cambridge University Press.
1999   Anthropology and Human Nature. *Ethos* 27 (1): 7-14.

Spriggs, M.
1989   The Dating of the Island Southeast Asian Neolithic: An Attempt at Chronometric Hygiene and Linguistic Correlations. *Antiquity* 63: 587-613.

Stamm, Father J.
1958   A Grammar of the Lavangai Language. Typescript. Lavangai, P.N.G.: Lavangai Catholic Mission.

Steinbauer, Friedric
1979   Melanesian Cargo Cults: New Salvation Movements in the South Pacific. Translated by Max Wohlwill. St. Lucia: University of Queensland Press.

Swaddling, Pamela
1998   Review of *The Lapita Peoples: Ancestors of the Oceania World*. By Patrick Vinton Kirch. Cambridge, Mass.: Blackwell Publishers Inc., 1997. In *Archaeology in Oceania* 33: 44-5.

Taylor, Alan L.
1967   We Don't Want the Council! Their Tax! Australia! *The Missionary Review*, March-April, 26.

Taylor, Isaac
1834   *Natural History of Enthusiasm*. 4th ed. New York: Leavitt; Boston: Crocker and Brewster.

Terrell, John
1986   *Prehistory in the Pacific Islands: A Study of Variation in Language, Customs, and Human Biology. Cambridge:* Cambridge University Press.

Thrupp, Sylvia L., ed
1970   *Millennial Dreams in Action*. New York: Schocken.

Tonnies, Ferdinand
1957   *Community and Society (Gemeinschaft und Gesellschaft)*. Translated and edited by Charles P. Loomis. East Lansing: Michigan State University Press.

Triandis, Harry C.
1990   Cross-Cultural Studies of Individualism and Collectivism. In *Nebraska Symposium on Motivation: Cross-Cultural Perspectives* (vol. 37: 41-133). Lincoln: University of Nebraska Press.
1995   *Individualism and Collectivism*. Boulder: Westview Press.

Triandis, Harry C., Christopher McCusker, and C. Harry Hui
1990   Multimethod Probes of Individualism and Collectivism. *Journal of Personal and Social Psychology* 59 (5): 1006-20.

Trompf, Garry W.
1990   *Cargo Cults and Millenarian Movements: Transoceanic Comparisons of New Religious Movements*. Berlin: Mouton de Gruyter.

Turner, Edith
1989   Zambia's Kankanga Dances: The Changing Life of Ritual. *Performing Arts Journal* 30(10):57-71.

Turner, Victor
1957   *Schism and Continuity in an African Society: A Study of Ndembu Village Life*. Manchester, U.K.: Manchester University Press.
1974   *Drama, Fields, and Metaphors: Symbolic Action in Human Society*.

Ithaca, N.Y.: Cornell University Press.
1982   *From Ritual to Theater: The Human Seriousness of Play*. New York: Performing Arts Journal Press, 1982.

Wallace, Anthony F. C.
1956   Revitalization Movements. *American Anthropologist* 58: 264-68.
1961   *Culture and Personality*. New York: Random House.
1966   *Religion: An Anthropological View*. New York: Random House.

Weber, Max
1952   *Ancient Judaism*. Translated by Hans H. Gerth and Don Martindale. Glencoe, Ill.: Free Press.

Wheeler, Tony and Jon Murray
1983   *Papua New Guinea*. Hawthorn, Vic: Lonely Planet Publications.

White, J. Peter, J. E. Downie, and W. R. Ambrose
1978   Mid-Recent Human Occupation and Resource Exploitation in the Bismarck Archipelago. *Science* 199: 877-79.

White, J. Peter, and James O'Connell
1982   *A Prehistory of Australia, New Guinea, and Sahul*. Sydney: Academic Press.

White, J. P., Allen, J., and Specht, J.
1988   Peopling of the Pacific: The Lapita Homeland Project. *Australian Natural History* 22: 410-16.

White, J. Peter and Mary-Noel Harris
1997   Changing Sources: Early Lapita Period Obsidian in the Bismarck Archipelago. *Archaeology in Oceania* 32: 97-107.

Williams, F. E.
1923   *The Vailala Madness and the Destruction of Native Ceremonies in the Gulf Division*. Anthropology Report no. 4. Port Moresby: Territory of Papua.
1940   *Drama of Orokolo. The Social and Ceremonial Life of the Elema*. Anthropology Report no. 18. Port Moresby: Territory of Papua. Reprinted by arrangement with the Administration of the Territory of Papua and New Guinea, 1969. Oxford: Oxford University Press.

Winch, Peter
1958   *The Idea of a Social Science and Its Relation to Philosophy*. London: Routledge and Kegan Paul.

Witkin, H. A., R. B. Dyk, H. F. Faterson, D. R. Goodenough, and S. A. Karp
1962   *Psychological Differentiation*. New York: John Wiley.

Witkin, H. A. and D. R. Goodenough
1981   *Cognitive Styles: Essence and Origins: Field Dependence and Field Independence*. Psychological Issues: Monograph 51. New York: International Universities Press.

Worsley, Peter
1957 *The Trumpet Shall Sound: a Study of "Cargo" Cults in Melanesia.* London: MacGibbon and Kee.
1968 *The Trumpet Shall Sound.: a Study of "Cargo" Cults in Melanesia.* 2d aug. ed. New York: Schocken.

Index

Aberle, D., 224, 225, 226, 227
Abo, 112
aborigines, Australian, 110, 159n19, 190
Adam, K., 34
Adamson, W., 172, 226
Aitken, B., 231-32, 233
Alipes, 65-66, 134, 201
Allen, J., 11, 25n14
America, Election for America as a play, 175-86; T.I.A. to bring, 42, 68; vote for, 27, 45, 70, 73, 74, 75, 76, 77, 86, 87-88, 96, 100, 110, 128-29, 166, 237, 238; wanted earlier, 47, 55, 78, 79
Americans, beliefs about, 127-28; experiences with American Catholics and other Americans, 36, 37, 38, 39, 40, 41, 42, 43, 44, 50, 62, 63-64, 65, 66, 160n27, 165; like because, 58, 61, 87, 90, 93, 108, 109, 110, 111, 112, 113, 114-15, 125-26, 168, 190, 200, 206, 207, 210; meetings with, 60, 96, 98; on Mt. Patibung making maps, 28, 33, 51-52, 53, 54, 55, 87, 117; in New Hanover during World War II, 13, 73, 94, 114, 115, 165, 200; rumors about, 107, 115-16, 118-19, 130, 131. *See also* Catholic missionaries; election; equality; Johnson cult; T.I.A.; *tok bilas*
Anderson, N., 38, 115
Anthropologists, 14, 32-33, 64-65, 241-43, 244n6
art, 172-75. *See also* Johnson cult, expressive aspects; Hauser; Lomax; style
assistant district officer (A.D.O). *See* Brightwell
Australian Administration, 9-11, 27, 28, 29, 30, 33-37, 71, 39-43, 74, 102, 118-19, 154; failure to develop New Hanover, 58, 86-87, 108-12. *See also* Benhem; Brightwell; Busch; coffee; cooperatives; council; Healy; Hoad; *kiaps*; McDonald; Seale; Spencer; Toughy; Williamson
Australians, friends during wartime, 73, 90, 91, 94

Barnett, S., 212n9
Barnouw, V., 231, 236n10
Barol, 72, 76, 89, 112, 131, 138, 191
Bate, 58, 112-13, 133
Beckett, V., 38, 66, 67, 73, 77, 115
beliefs, about America, 126-28; about cargo, 131-36; about ritual, 128-29; about the supernatural, 129-31. *See also* cargo; religion

261

Bellwood, P., 11
Benedict, R., 25n19, 231
Benhem, B., 77, 98-99, 100, 159n11, 181
Berndt, R., 211n1
Berne, E., 203
Bernstein, B., 233, 238
Berry, J., 234
Berthold, M., 212n15
Betheras, J., 123, 165
Birdwhistell, R., 26n31
Bodley, J., 244n10, 244n12
Bonail, 191
bord, 42, 55, 57, 58, 66, 137, 139, 143, 188, 193
Bosap, 39, 54, 56-57, 66, 67, 68, 73-74, 76-77, 78, 79-80, 90-93, 98, 151, 185, 191
Boski Tom, 24n4, 72, 75, 88-89, 101, 102-3, 104, 111, 116, 117, 158n1, 191, 192, 198, 199, 205
Bosmailik, 28, 87, 94, 96, 98, 179
Bowen, E., 82n3
Brightwell, M., 40-41, 42-43, 46, 52, 63, 77, 204
Brockett, O., 209, 212n15, 239
Brustein, R., 175
Burke, K., 168-69
Burridge, K., 176, 224, 225
Busch, B., 48-49, 50, 51-52

cargo, 55, 56, 58, 60, 68, 74, 75, 113, 134, 166-67; cargo cult, 27, 28, 29, 30, 31-33, 53-54, 142-54, 215-18
Carroll (Karol). *See* Gannon
Catholic mission, 10, 12, 13, 64, 80, 94, 116; Lavongai, 5-6, 16, 41-42, 43-44; local workers, 24n6, 105, 112, 157. *See also* DeLuca; Fischer; Freitas; Jacubco; Kelly; Liboria; Miller; Regine; Stemper
cement markers, 67, 68, 79, 89, 110, 128, 159n20, 191
Chalmers, A., 244n5
Chinese residents, 9, 73, 193-94
Chinnery, E., 14, 18, 24n2

Christiansen, P., 228, 230, 236n3
Claassen, O., 16, 26n22
Cochrane, G., 236n4
coffee, 39, 46, 55, 68, 70, 108, 109, 120, 122, 166, 179
Cohn, N., 227, 229
Combs, J., 212n15
cooperative society, 46, 55, 68, 72, 108, 109, 117, 147, 166, 206
Council, Local Government, Lavonai, created, 100; as faction, 62, 64, 68, 70, 74, 75, 77, 88, 89, 98, 105, 106, 124, 138, 140, 141, 143, 145, 173, 177, 183, 191, 192, 201; failure of, 46, 55, 68, 69, 70, 108, 109-10, 111, 140, 166, 179, 199; meetings, 45, 47, 96; minutes and reports, 40, 49; projects, 53, 77; taxes, 31, 43, 77, 96, 137, 138; Tikana, 4, 5, 14, 15, 31, 35, 145, 160n30; west coast, New Hanover, 152, 199
Councilors, 66, 70-71, 73, 77-78, 85, 101, 102, 104, 178. *See also* Barol; Boski Tom; Council; Edward; Saripat; Silakau; Steven Taung
Crowe, P., 241
cultists, crazy, 66, 70, 72, 74, 80-81, 87, 92, 93, 99, 106, 107, 115, 116-17, 118, 121, 124, 150, 166, 167, 172, 183, 196, 210; collecting money, 96; and government, 95-108; ideologies of, 108-15; leadership, 94-95; meetings, 97-99; and T.I.A., 137-39. *See also* Bate; Bosap; Bosmailik; factions; jail; Joseph Pukina; Lapantukan; Logo; Makios; Oliver; Pamais; Pengai; Robin; Samuel; Saripat; Savemat; Silikan
cults, characteristic features, 217-18; and cultural tradition, 229-30; dynamics of, 228-29; ideas in, 221-23; individual personality and psychology, 220-21; material

forces, 223; organization and recruitment, 219-20; and power, 224; social structure of, 225-27; style or pattern, 230-34; transcendent quest, 223-24; true believers, 218-19. *See also* explanation; Johnson cult

DeLuca, D., 142, 154-55
Department of District Administration (D.D.A.), 10, 36, 81, 100, 119
Department of Native Affairs (D.N.A.), 30, 31, 97, 102, 119. *See also* Healy, McCarthy
District Advisory Council, 78, 96-97, 100, 116, 119, 122
district commissioner (D.C.), 10, 28, 34, 42, 80, 211; assistant district commissioner, 42. *See also* Healy, Seale
district officer (D.O.), 98, 101. *See also* Williamson, K.
Douglas, M., 232, 236n11

Edward, 53, 59, 61, 62, 98, 105, 113, 116, 117-18, 119, 173, 190, 197, 202
Ekonie, 76
election, 3, 45-47; background, 89-94; events, 85-89; and Lavongai cultural style, 169, 172-73, 174, 186, 191-92, 208; leadership, 94-95; Meteran polling area, 66-69; as a play, 175-186; Ranmelek polling area, 54-59; Taskul polling area, 59-62, 76-78; Umbukul polling area, 69-70, 71- 73, 74, 75-76
environmental movement, 156-57, 200
equality, 93-94, 109, 111, 113-15, 127-28, 170-71
Eron, 142, 146
Europeans (white people), subculture, 36-37. *See also* Australian administration; *kiaps*; planters
explanation, 71-2, 76, 78, 215-17, 234-35, 240-41

factions, 104-8, 138
Feldt, E., 25n17, 158n4
field research, 4-7, 9-11, 43-44; in New Ireland, 34-37; permission, 33-35, 39-42
Firth, R., 225, 233-34
Fischer, H., 65, 204
Fiske, A., 234
Francis, 148, 244n9
Freitas, T., 143, 159n25
Friedman, J., 212n13
Fromm, E., 214n37

Gannon, C., 39-40, 49-51, 53, 59, 60, 61, 62, 63, 64, 65, 79, 101, 118, 121-22, 126, 132, 138, 159n13, 159n15, 159n22, 167, 192, 199, 204, 211n2.
Geddes, W., 244n6
Geertz., C. 241-42
George, A., 38
Gerlach, L., 81n2, 129, 219-20
Gilligan, C., 234
Gillin, J., 222
Golson, J., 11
Gosden, C., 11
government. *See* Australian administration
Gramsci, 172, 173, 175, 212n13, 236n8
Green, R., 11
Grose, J. and D., 78, 98, 100, 117, 122-23, 158n10
Grotowski, J., 184, 213n19
group-orientation. *See* styles, of culture
Groves, W., 5, 14, 18, 24n2, 24n4, 72, 154
Guiart, J., 224
Gusfield, J., 174, 226, 227

Hancock, J., 122, 126, 167
Hanson, F., 244n3
Harrington, M., 174, 236n8, 244n5
Hau'ofa, E., 224, 244n8
Hauser, A., 239
Healy, M., 34-36, 96-98, 100, 105,

117, 122-23
hegemony, 172, 173, 226
Hill, K., 39-40, 52-53, 64, 120-21
Hine, V., 129, 219-20
history, 11-14, 189-90
Hoad, B., 41, 49-51, 60, 118, 121
Hoffer, E., 218, 219, 224, 227
Hofstede, G., 234
Holton, G., 227
homosexuality, 60-61
Hsu, F., 213n29, 234
Hui, C., 234

ideologies, administrators, 118-19; cultists, 108-15; missionaries, 124-26; noncultists, 115-18; planters, 122-23; service personnel, 119-22
Iguarangai, 71, 207
individualism. *See* styles, of culture
Inglis, J., 216

Jacubco, 44, 126
jail, 60, 101-4, 177, 181
Jarvie, I., 221-22
Johnson, President of America, 3, 14, 27-29, 30, 31, 41, 42, 43, 45, 54, 56, 67, 68, 69, 70, 71, 73, 74, 75, 76; beliefs about, 33, 47, 53. *See also* election; Johnson cult
Johnson cult, 3, 4, 6, 7, 20, 27-30, 31-33, 34, 35, 36, 37, 38, 39, 43, 44, 46, 59, 60, 63, 72; after 1988, 154-58; communication aspects, 187-89; economic aspects, 166-67, 198-200; expressive aspects, 163-64, 207-11; historical perspectives, 189-90; and Lavongai culture, 186-87; as a play, 175-87; political aspects, 195-97; psychological aspects, 166, 200-207; social aspects of, 190-95; as theater, 163-71. *See also* art; equality; Johnson, President of America; Native Thought; T. I. A.
Joll, J., 174

Jolly, M., 212n9
Jones, H., 229-30
Joseph Pukina. 46, 47, 53, 96, 98-99, 110, 127, 156, 158n7, 165, 168, 170, 173, 181, 189, 202, 204, 206, 207, 211
Josephine, 6, 155

Kaminsky, H., 219, 227
Kaplan, M., 217
Karol (Carroll). *See* Gannon
Kasino (Kas), 5, 24n5, 25n14, 35, 142, 146, 150, 151, 152
Keesing, R., 224
Kelly, P., 88, 96, 136
kiaps (government officers), 37, 40, 43, 48-52, 60, 62-64, 120. *See also* Australian Administration
Kim, U., 234
Kiralyfalvi, B., 175, 236n8
Kirch, P., 11
Kluckhohn, F., 234
Kopytoff, I., 216
Kramer, A., 14, 18
Kroeber, A., 25n19
Kroef, J. van der, 231, 236n9

Lanternari, V., 223, 224, 226, 227
Lapantukan, 60, 112, 130–31, 133-34, 170, 177, 192, 200, 209
Lattas, A., 223, 236n7
Lawrence, P., 222, 225, 228
Lavongai culture, 14-23, 55, 76, 169-70, 186-211. *See also* Johnson cult; styles
Lewis, P., 5, 14, 18, 26n22
Liboria, M., 44, 54, 66, 100, 101, 126, 176, 181
Lindstrom, L., 224
Linton, R., 222
Lithgow, D., 16, 26n22
Logo, Cornelio, 67-68, 73, 79-80, 82n13, 116
Lomax, A., 186, 232, 233, 234, 235, 238
Lucaks, 175, 212n13, 226, 236n8

MacDonald, 49-51, 62-64
Maher, R., 228
Makios, 39, 55-56, 58, 93, 106-7, 112, 115, 132, 151, 166, 200
malanggan, 14, 15, 16, 17, 18, 19, 21, 26n27, 38, 52, 59, 65, 154, 160n34, 175, 231, 239, 240; comparison to Lavongai, 189, 190, 194, 197, 198, 200, 209; Malanggan Lodge, 10
Malinowski, 33, 82n3, 240
Marias, 156, 200
Mansfield, M., 212n15
Maslow, A., 200
Matunga, 142-43, 144
May, R., 223, 224, 228
McCarthy, J., 25n13, 34, 81, 82n14, 97
McDowell, N., 217
Mead, M., 33, 82n3, 136, 220-21, 228, 234, 236n6, 236n9, 236n12
Meltzer, M., 244n7
Memmi, A., 212n9
Mesulam Aisoli, 4, 150, 154
Methodist mission, 12, 30-31, 37, 39, 48, 55, 57, 66, 69; as polling station, 45, 86, 178, 179, 180. *See also* Anderson; Beckett; Logo; Savemat; Silikan; Taylor
Mihalaic, F., 26n21
Milika, 5, 24n5
Miller, B., article by, 125; and field work, 41, 44, 52, 59; and Johnson cult, 46, 53, 67, 73, 82n11, 125-26, 167, 173, 182, 185, 201, 211n5; and Lavongai culture, 211n5; and T.I.A., 42, 45, 55, 67, 136-42, 143, 145, 147, 151, 154, 156, 157, 159n25, 159n26, 166, 177, 187, 192, 196, 199-200
missions, and administration, 124; and cult, 27, 29, 36, 37, 53, 56, 104, 105, 124-26, 138-39, 164, 166, 173, 184, 196, 211; calendar, 185; and cultist view of God, 94, 129; and Carroll Gannon, 121; and Jim White, 58, 78; store, 198; and traditional customs, 18-19, 197, 198; linguists, 26n22. *See also* Catholic mission; Methodist mission; Seventh-Day Adventist mission
Murray, J., 25n12
Murray, M., 25n17
Murray, P. and P., 25n10, 40, 48, 65
Murphy, J., 26n21

Nagel, E., 217
Nash, O., 50, 82n9
"Native Thought" files, 34, 36, 80
New Hanover. *See* Lavongai
New Ireland, culture compared to New Hanover, 186-87, 189, 190, 194-95, 197; and island culture, 58, 76; West Coast and election, 30-32, 159n12. *See also* Tikana
New Zealand, 94
Ngurvarilam, 6, 46, 66
Nolis, 55, 57, 59
noncultists, ideologies of 115-18. *See also* Abo; Barol; Boski Tom; Edward; Silakau; Steven Taung; Tombat

Oliver, 42, 43, 58, 74, 94-95, 97, 118-19, 126, 147, 159n24, 165, 168, 184, 188, 191, 195, 199, 201, 203, 207; interviews, 52-3, 61-62, 101-3, 113-14, 115-16, 128, 134-36, 171, 193, 200
O'Neill, T., 12

Pamais, 98, 109-10, 191
Patchen, K., 214n43
Pengai, 46-47, 55, 108, 159n19, 166, 168, 169, 170, 172, 178, 181, 184, 190, 195, 200, 201, 202, 206, 209, 212n8, 214n39; interviews, 86-88, 94-95, 110-11, 171
Peter Yangalissmat, 47, 54-55, 57, 89, 90-93, 94, 152, 158n6, 207
Peterson, N., 4, 14, 24n1, 25n14, 26n21, 26n30, 30, 34, 80, 82n4
Piddington, R., 244n6
Pitts, Mr. and Mrs., 67, 123, 139, 204

planters, 97-98, 122-24, 142. *See also* Betheras, J.; Grose, J. and D.; Murray, P. and P.; Pitts, Mr. and Mrs.; White, J.
Powdermaker, H., 5, 14, 18, 24n2, 25n7, 26n26, 82n3
progress reports, 81, 101-2, 116, 118-19, 158n3, 158n9

Regine, M., 44, 156
religion, 18-19, 128-30, 134-36, 165-66, 167, 201
Ribeiro, R., 229
ritual, 128-29
Robertson, N., 11
Robin, 43, 52, 62, 94, 103, 119
Ryan, P., 25n10

Salamini, L., 175
Samuel, 52, 63, 109, 168, 209
Sandall, R., 244n2
Sapir, E., 231
Saripat, 56, 58, 106, 111, 113-14, 131-33, 202
Sassoon, A., 172
Savemat, 56, 58, 86, 114-15, 130, 179
savvy, 58, 77, 91, 98, 103, 108-9, 110-11, 113, 114, 116, 121, 149, 165, 166, 168, 171, 190, 206, 208, 209, 210
Schapiro, M., 25n19
Schechner, R., 244n2
Schiller, H., 211-12n7
Schwartz, T., 121, 136, 213n29, 217, 220
Seale, B., 34, 40-41, 43, 48, 63, 80-81, 98-99, 105, 121, 214n33
service personnel, 74-75, 117, 119-22. *See also* Gannon; Hancock; Hill; Shepard
Seventh-Day Adventist (S.D.A.) Mission, 47, 57, 159n19
Shakespeare, 186, 212n10, 212n16, 214n35, 214n40, 212n42; Hamlet, 173
Shennan, J., 242
Shepard, D., 61, 62-63

Silikan, 58, 114
Silakau, 6, 44, 45, 72, 80, 105-6, 138, 151, 159n17, 170, 179, 180, 191, 202
Silverman, M., 212n9
Singarau, 72, 117, 207
Sirapi, 42, 44, 52
Smelser, N., 222, 226-27, 234
Sorokin, D., 26n20
Specht, J., 25n14
Spencer, 28, 77, 97, 101-3
Spiro, M, 217
Spriggs, M., 11
Stamm, J., 23
Steinbauer, F., 217, 228, 236n1
Stemper, A., 41-42
Steven Taung, 49, 151-52, 199
Strodtbeck, F., 234
styles, of culture, 14, 25n19, 215, 230-34, 235, 238, 239; and Johnson cult, 163-64, 168-70; Tikana group-orientation and Lavongai individualism, 15, 19-23, 186-87. *See also* Johnson cult: communication aspects, expressive aspects, historical perspectives, political aspects, psychological aspects, social aspects of
Swaddling, P., 11

Taylor, A., 37-38, 50, 54, 59, 115, 124, 138, 177
Taylor, I., 218-19, 227
Terrell, J., 11
T.I.A. (Tutukuvul Isukal Association), 3, 237; interviews, 54, 55, 57, 58, 66, 70, 73, 74, 75, 76, 77, 78, 80; and economic development, 166, 198, 199-200, 201; factions, 43, 68, 69, 70, 73, 74, 75, 105, 107, 113, 196-97, 209; history to 2000, 136-58; and Lavongai cultural style, 186, 187, 188-89, 204, 205, 207, in New Ireland, 142-43, 144, 145, 152-53; and opposition, 42, 45, 67; and political power, 173,

175, 210; and social structure, 191-93; and theater, 177, 178, 182-83, 185, 159n26
T.F.A. *See* T.I.A., in New Ireland theater, Johnson cult as, 163-70, 175, 186, 207-11, 237, 239-40. *See also* Johnson cult
Thrupp, S., 230
Tikana culture, 14-21, 48, 153-54, 197, 186-67, 207, 209. *See also* New Ireland, styles
T.K.A. *See* T.I.A., in New Ireland
tok bilas (ridicule), 55-56, 68, 73, 116, 118, 130, 196
Tombat, 113, 155
Tonnies, F., 26n20
Toughy, 43, 102, 103, 104, 120
transport, canoe, 58, 59, 62, 73, 78; Catholics, 43-44, 54, 55, 65, 80, 140, 142; government, 35, 47-52, 61, 79, 157; Methodists, 37-39, 55-62, 66-78; planter, 58
Triandis, H., 26n29, 234
Trompt, G., 217
Turner, E., 244n2
Turner, V., 244n7

United Nations (U.N.), 13, 27, 36, 60, 63, 64, 98, 109, 113, 120, 128, 143, 158, 168, 181, 188, 214n41

violence, 30-32, 34-35, 100, 101-2, 158n9
vote, "in the box" or "on the board," 45. *See also* election

Walla, 67, 68, 140, 141, 142, 143, 144, 145, 148-49, 150-51, 155, 156, 157, 158, 196, 199, 207
Wallace, A., 221, 222-23, 229, 236n6
Weber, M., 221, 232
Wheeler, 25n12
White, J. P., 11
White, Jim., 51, 57-58, 62, 78-79, 91, 96-97, 100, 122, 133
Williams, F., 221, 231
Williamson, K., 31, 32, 34, 35, 89, 97, 159n16, 159n23
Winch, P., 216, 221
Witkin, H., 234
World War II. *See* history
Worsley, P., 221, 223, 224, 225, 227, 228

Yaman, 86, 179, 195, 196
Yangalissmat. *See* Peter Yangalissmat

About the Author

Dorothy K. Billings is an Associate Professor of Anthropology at Wichita State University, Wichita. She has carried out field work in two islands, New Ireland and New Hanover, in the Kavieng area of Papua New Guinea since 1965. She has published in several anthropological journals, including *Oceania, Journal of the Polynesia Society, Mankind, The Australian Journal of Anthropology, Language in Society, Pacific Studies,* and *Canberra Anthropology.* Since 1994 she has worked with Viatcheslav Roudnev at conferences in Russia, Poland, and the United States that bring together researchers interested in culture and sustainable development. She studied anthropology at the University of Wisconsin-Madison, the University of Auckland, and Columbia University before receiving her Ph.D. in Social Anthropology from the University of Sydney.